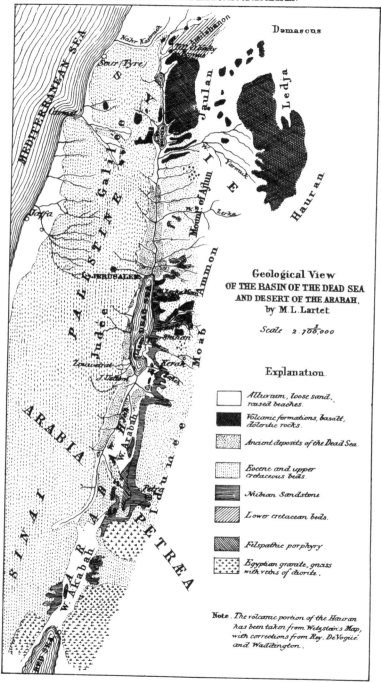

Geological View
OF THE BASIN OF THE DEAD SEA
AND DESERT OF THE ARABAH,
by M.L. Lartet

Scale 2.$\frac{1}{700,000}$

Explanation.

Alluvium, loose sand, raised beaches.

Volcanic formations, basalt, doleritic rocks.

Ancient deposits of the Dead Sea.

Eocene and upper cretaceous beds.

Nubian Sandstone

Lower cretacean beds.

Felspathic porphyry

Egyptian granite, gneiss with veins of diorite.

Note. The volcanic portion of the Hauran has been taken from Wetzstein's Map, with corrections from Rey. DeVogüé and Waddington.

THE COMPARATIVE GEOGRAPHY

OF

PALESTINE

AND THE

SINAITIC PENINSULA.

BY CARL RITTER.

Translated and Adapted to the Use of Biblical Students

BY

WILLIAM L. GAGE.

VOL. III.

HASKELL HOUSE PUBLISHERS LTD.

Publishers of Scarce Scholarly Books

NEW YORK. N. Y. 10012

1969

First Published 1865

HASKELL HOUSE PUBLISHERS Ltd.
Publishers of Scarce Scholarly Books
280 LAFAYETTE STREET
NEW YORK. N. Y. 10012

Library of Congress Catalog Card Number: 68-26367

Standard Book Number 8383-0180-0

Printed in the United States of America

CONTENTS OF VOL. III.

———◆———

CHAPTER IV.

CHAPTER V.

PART II.

CHAPTER I.

CHAPTER II.

PART III.

CHAPTER I.

CHAPTER II.

CHAPTER III.

THE ROUTE FROM THE DESERT OF ET-TIH TO HEBRON : BY THE WAY, ON THE EAST, OF WADI ARARA (AROER) ; AND ON THE WEST, OF WADI EL KHALIL, ... 282

APPENDIX.

GEOGRAPHY OF PALESTINE.

CHAPTER IV.

SEC. 7. THE MOUTH OF THE JORDAN.

THE OASIS OF JERICHO—APPROACHES ON THE WEST AND
NORTH—THE VILLAGE OF RIHA AND ITS SURROUNDINGS
—WADI KELT AND AIN ES SULTAN—THE SOUTHERN
ENTRANCE AND EXIT TO THE JORDAN BATHING-PLACE—
THE EMBOUCHURE OF THE RIVER AT THE DEAD SEA.

THE oasis of Jericho constitutes the southern extremity
of the Jordan valley, but not of the great depression
known as the Ghor,[1] the Aulon of the Greeks; for
Ghor, like Aulon, *i.e.* plain, is a general name given
to the whole sunken valley from the Lebanon or the Sea of
Gennesareth, not only to the Dead Sea, but to the Gulf of
Akaba; and in all periods this entire tract has been regarded
as a limit.

Jericho, which received the name City of Palms as early as
in Deut. xxxiv. 3, lying in the plain of Jericho, comes out
prominently for the first time in the narrative of the spies
(Josh. ii.), who entered the place, and were secreted in the house
of Rahab, which stood upon the city wall. The spies, as the
reader will remember, fled from the city, and first took refuge
from their pursuers in the mountains close by, but afterwards
crossed the Jordan, and entered the camp of their countrymen at
Sittim, or Shittim, *i.e.* the Plain of Acacias, on the east side of
the Jordan. Their camp probably lay at the mouth of Wadi

---

[1] Al-Gaurum, in Schultens' Index Geogr. ad *Vit. Saladini;* and Abulfedæ *Syriæ,* in Koehler, p. 147, Note 1.

Heshbon, opposite the city of Jericho, and at the foot of the Abarim ridge and Mount Nebo. This Arboth Moab,[1] or Araba, *i.e.* the western side of the mountain land, on the plains east of the Jordan, where the acacia grew in former times,[2] was called Shittim, and lay opposite the plains of Jericho, alluded to in Josh. iv. 13, v. 10, and elsewhere. The plain with which it was connected extended northward as far as to the sea of Chinnereth (Josh. xii. 3). Abel Shittim, *i.e.* the district of acacias, sometimes called merely Shittim or Sittim (Num. xxxiii. 49, xxv. 1), was for a considerable time the camping ground of the Israelites. Jericho, which lay opposite, was the first strongly fortified place which they would have to encounter, and must have been a place of great antiquity. It had its walls, its closed gates, its king: as it was known for its palms, it may have had fragrant gardens of balm, and the name of the city itself may be derived from the sweet-smelling odours[3] which delighted those who lived there or passed through. With the capture of Jericho, the conquest of Canaan began. The city was destroyed; but despite the curse recorded in Josh. vi. 26 upon him who should rebuild it, we find that it could not have wholly perished: for in Judg. iii. 13 the same city of palms is mentioned as having been sacked by the Moabites. In the time of David, his subordinate officers, who had been scornfully treated by the king of Ammon, were ordered to tarry in Jericho till their half-shaven beards should grow (2 Sam. x. 5). Under king Ahab the city was rebuilt by Hiel (1 Kings xvi. 34). The prophets Elisha and Elijah lived for a long time in Jericho; the "school of the prophets" rose here; and the place came again into note, and remained so till the time of the Romans. It was during all these centuries considered the key of Judæa, and was the great means of security against invasion from the region east of the Jordan. Under the Christian-Byzantine rule civilisation gradually left Jericho, and the place fell into that decadence in which it has since remained, all continuous attempts to hold back the wild Beduins on the east having long since ceased.

[1] Hengstenberg, *Wichstigste und schwierigste Abschnitte des Pentateuchs*, Pt. i. pp. 229–233 ; comp. Keil, *Comm. on Joshua*, cap. ii. p. 19; and Winer, *Bibl. Realw.* i. pp. 543, 544.

[2] Wilson, *Lands of the Bible*, ii. p. 17.

[3] Rosenmüller, *Bibl. Alterth.* ii. p. 153, Note 8 ; Winer, *i.a.l.* i. p. 543.

From this brief sketch, the value of this oasis to the history of the Promised Land at all times will be clearly seen,—a place which, by its relation to the baptism which took place in the Jordan near by, has gained in a religious sense a very wide interest.

Notwithstanding the many different opinions regarding the ancient and modern ruins, the situation of the Canaanite Jericho, that of David and the school of the prophets, that of Herod, and that of the Byzantine epoch still later, in their relation to the Arab Riha, there is no doubt that all the accounts which we have relate to the narrow oasis of Jericho, to which many ways lead, of which I shall have occasion hereafter to speak.

Formerly there was only the road taken by the pilgrims, the one which all the caravans followed, that in Easter week visited the Jordan to obtain remission for sin, and then withdrew as hastily as they came. Of course the people who accompanied these expeditions could not think of making observations; it was enough for them to care for the attacks of the Beduins. In more recent times other ways have been opened to Jericho, to which we are indebted for many interesting details regarding Jericho, the oasis, and its historical monuments.

Von Schubert[1] and Russegger[2] pursued the ordinary route of the pilgrims in 1837 and 1838, both coming back to Jerusalem by way of St Saba Convent. Irby and Mangles[3] pursued the same track in 1818, Gadow[4] and Wilson[5] in 1847. Robinson came along the west shore of the Dead Sea from Engaddi to Jericho, and thence over a new way, which no traveller had taken before him, to Bethel and Ai. Dr Barth's course was, as we have already seen, over a more northern path through Wadi Nawaimeh and Auje to Jebel Guddus and Nablus. Wolcott's[6] route in 1842 was from the Convent of St Saba to Jericho.

[1] Von Schubert, *Reise*, iii. pp. 71-103.
[2] Russegger, *Reise*, iii. pp. 102-115.
[3] Irby and Mangles, *Trav.* pp. 330-333.
[4] H. Gadow, *Ausflug, etc.,* in *Zeitschrift der Deutsch. Morgenl. Gesell.* vol. ii. pp. 52-65.
[5] J. Wilson, *Lands of the Bible,* vol. ii. pp. 2-33.
[6] S. Wolcott, *Excur. to Mar Saba, Jericho, etc.,* in *Bibl. Sacra,* 1843, pp. 38-41.

Seetzen,[1] who remained in January 1807 for nine days in Jericho, is the only traveller of whom we have a record that he crossed the Jordan at the ford directly east of Jericho (the same ford which is mentioned in Josh. ii. 7), as he set out on his perilous foot journey east of the Jordan. The ford lay about a half-hour's distance north of the entrance of Wadi Heshban into the Jordan valley, and it may be situated near the bathing-place of the pilgrims, and the ford el-Helu of Robinson. Seetzen's account of Jericho is among the most valuable which we possess. Burckhardt appears never to have been there: on his journey from Beisan he crossed the Jordan at Succoth. The course of the Jordan from Jericho has been followed by many travellers on the shore, and by Molyneux[2] and Lynch in boats.

DISCURSION I.

THE ROUTE OF THE PILGRIM CARAVANS FROM JERUSALEM TO JERICHO IN EASTER WEEK, AND OTHER WAYS THITHER; THOSE BY AZARIYYE (BETHANY), KHAN HUDHRUR (CHATRUL), KALAAT EL DEM (ADUMMIM), WADI KELT (THE BROOK CHERITH), AND FORT KAKON, SPECIFIED IN DETAIL. THE GEOLOGICAL CHARACTERISTICS OF THE COUNTRY BETWEEN HEBRON, BETHLEHEM, JERUSALEM, JERICHO, AND THE NORTHERN EXTREMITY OF THE DEAD SEA, ACCORDING TO RUSSEGGER

From Jerusalem, Jericho lies a moderate day's ride, measured according to the distance, but a very fatiguing one. The direction is about north-east: to the plains the distance is about five hours, to the Jordan seven hours, according to Robinson.[3] Every spring, at Easter, thousands of pilgrims go over the road under the protection of a Turkish escort, to secure them against the frequent attacks of Arab robbers. This route, although one of the most travelled, is, notwithstanding, one of the most dangerous[4] in all Palestine, because of the cunning which is displayed in the efforts to inveigle the trains, and also because the escort which accompanies them is strong rather in appearance than in reality, and hence produces a sense of security

[1] Seetzen, *Zweite Reise nach dem Todten Meere*, MS.
[2] Molyneux, *Expedition, l.c.* xviii. pp. 123–129.
[3] Robinson, *Bibl. Research.* i. 559.
[4] Wilson, *Lands of the Bible*, ii. p. 2.

among the wild ruffians of the desert. Europeans who wish to accompany the caravans of pilgrims, are therefore advised by some travellers to take an escort of their own, in order that, in case of an attack upon the main body, they may be independent, and able to control their own movements. Russegger, who went over the road at a different season of the year from that taken by the pilgrims (November), had an escort of only two men; Wilson, who took the same route ten years later (1847), and who accompanied the Easter caravan, had sixteen Arab companions for protection. They were of the tribe living in the village Beit-Tamar, and their sheikh claimed to have the monopoly of the right to convoy travellers from Jerusalem to Jericho. Gadow also accompanied the Easter caravan, to which a Mohammedan train joined itself, whose goal was not the bathing-place in the Jordan, but Nebi Musa, the reputed grave of Moses according to the Arabian legend.

The ordinary pilgrim route leads `eastward from Jerusalem through the Kedron valley, over the southern prominence of the Mount of Olives to Bethany, and thence to Wadi Azariyye, where there is a well[1] at which the caravans and escort are accustomed to rendezvous. From that point the train winds on its serpentine way through vales, up and down hills, and over a rocky wilderness, in which the same perils threaten which were encountered at the time when the man who went from Jerusalem to Jericho fell among thieves (Luke x. 30).

El Aziriyeh or Azariyye is the present[2] Arab name of the place which is called by Christians Bethany, but which is itself derived from el-Azir, *i.e.* Lazarus. In Luke xix. 1, 29, we are told that as Jesus was on the way from Jericho, he drew near to Bethany and Bethphage, which were not far from the Mount of Olives. Here it was that Russegger first encountered the forces of the wild Arabs from the east side of the Jordan. Twenty minutes farther on, and towards the southeast, there lies upon an eminence on the right the ruined village of Abu Dis, which von Schubert conjectured to be the site of Bahurim,[3] the place where David was cursed while flee-

---

[1] H. Gadow, *Ausflug, i.a.l.* p. 52.
[2] Robinson, *Bibl. Research.* i. p. 432.
[3] Von Schubert, *Reise,* iii. p. 71; Russegger, iii. p. 102.

ing from Absalom (2 Sam. xvi. 5), although that place seems
to me to have lain farther north.

After passing onward through Wadi Azariyye for three
hours, the road bends sharply to the south-east,[1] and runs along
the north side of a moderately high hill, from whose top the
way soon leads down to a basin-shaped valley of moderate
breadth, running from north to south; after that is crossed, it
is necessary to climb the high eastern wall, nearly three-quarters
up which there is the not unimportant ruin of Karyat el Kurd.
An old road runs past the ground walls, which form an oblong,
of which the west wall, which adjoins a great pile of hewn
stones, is from ten to fifteen feet in height. At the northern
extremity there are two arches still standing, in a good state of
preservation, and leading to a long and narrow enclosure. Of
the eastern wall a small portion still remains. Probably the
whole was only a building adjoining the Karyat el Chan Hudrur,
an ancient castle which commanded the road to Jericho from
the time of the Crusades. This is a great square, every side a
hundred and fifty feet in length, surrounded by a fosse twenty
feet wide, and excavated to a depth of thirty to forty feet into
the rock. At the north-east corner there are the remains of a
stately square tower, in which a staircase leads to deep vaults,
now full of rubbish, and offering a convenient home to owls
and falcons. The prospect towards the west is limited by the
high line of watershed running from Jerusalem northward, but
eastward the eye ranges across the Jordan valley to the heights
of Moab and Ammon. At this eminence the road divides and
turns to the left along the steep banks of a cavernous path,
filled with picturesque masses of limestone. Upon the more
moderate heights there may be seen here and there traces of
an ancient road, perhaps a *via militaris* which Pompey built
from Jerusalem to Jericho, and which must have been guarded
by the crusaders to prevent being attacked by predatory hordes
from the other side of the Jordan.

An hour farther down towards the Jordan valley, Gadow
saw the well-preserved remains of an ancient aqueduct, with a
canal two feet broad and a half foot in depth. This was accompanied by a second one on the left side of the road, which he
first thought might have been used to convey water to Jericho

[1] Gadow, *i.a.l.* pp. 52–54.

at a former period ; but at a subsequent visit he discovered
that it led to a very large cistern, consisting of three compartments, and arched over. At the side of this were the dwelling-
places of ancient anchorites, similar to those at Barada, near
Damascus. At present no water at all could be found there,
and an unpeopled solitude had succeeded to the abundance of
life which had once animated these hills. From this place there
is an abrupt descent towards the plains of Jericho, which are
reached in a quarter of an hour.

Wilson, who went at the time of the Easter caravan, and
in connection with them, though not in their direct company,
but under the escort of a company of Englishmen, seems to
have followed a course a little north of the last; for, instead of
taking the Azariyye valley, he pursued from Bethany the Wadi
Kedum, which he designates as an important depression running to the Jordan : he passed by the beginning of a similar
wadi, el-Hamd, and came at the end of two hours to a water-
ing-place, in which there was a fountain of clear, sweet water,
which was called the Apostles' Spring;[1] the legend asserting
that the apostles once tarried here and rested themselves while
on the way from Jericho to Bethany. In the neighbourhood
are the ruins of a small khan, which serves as a mere halting-
place by day, as no one dares tarry there over night. The next
important wadis which Wilson encountered, were Wadi Sidr,
which runs south-east in a very irregular course, and Wadi
Khan Hachurah, the last of which he held to be the same as
Robinson's Khan Hudhrur.[2] From the Apostles' Spring Wilson
could behold a great part of the territory of Benjamin, which
extended from Bethel to Jericho, measuring from west to east,
and from Bethlehem northward past Adummim to Ophra (Josh.
xviii. 11-28). From this point on he encountered a great number
of naked chalk hills, broken up into the most fantastic forms,
and very difficult to traverse. On the left there was a great
number of natural and artificial caves, the retreat in ancient
times of the men described in Heb. xi. 38, " They wandered in
deserts, and in mountains, and in dens and caves of the earth."
Besides the wilderness of roughnesses, which made the way
extremely laborious, there was very little to be seen, excepting

[1] Wilson, *Lands of the Bible*, ii. pp. 3-5.
[2] Robinson, *Bib. Research.* i. 437.

at the end of a mountain ridge a cone-like peak called Nebi Musa, and held by the Moslems to be the burial-place of Moses. On the left, and lying toward the north, Wilson saw the reputed mountain of temptation, the "very high mountain" of Matt. iv. 8, for whose localization there, however, there is no authentic testimony. Between these two lay the steep descent to the Jordan, and called by the Arabs Akab Jabar. This runs into Wadi Kelt, in whose Arabic name Robinson believed that he recognised the form of the Hebrew word Cherith. In opposition to the views of former times, held by Sanutus, Brocardus, and others, who held that the brook Cherith of Elijah lay on the west side of the Jordan,[1] it has been lately remarked by von Raumer that this cannot be correct, since Jerome speaks of its flowing from the east side of the Jordan : torrens trans Jordanem in quo absconditus est Elias. But Reland has anticipated this objection, by remarking that the expression "before Jordan," employed in 1 Kings xvii. 3, 5, corresponding to the German "gegen" and the English "towards," indicates merely, "ante Jordanem et orientem versus a Samaria." This has, however, been made by Jerome to mean "trans Jordanem." Wilson follows Robinson[2] in holding that the expression "ante Jordanem," which has generally been interpreted "east of the Jordan," in many places means just the reverse; as, for instance, Gen. xviii. 16, where the preposition must mean toward, "The men rose up and looked toward Sodom." So, again, in Gen. xix. 28, "And he looked toward Sodom and Gomorrah." The argument drawn from this is, that the brook Cherith may be searched for on the west side of the Jordan. Sanutus writes very definitely : Fasælis vel Fasæl tribus leucis distat a Jordane, in campetribus ubi torrens Carith descendit de monte, in quo loco mansit Helias.

At his time, therefore, the legend, on grounds unknown to us, placed this celebrated brook where Elijah hid himself, and was fed by ravens, in the same locality which is now known to us as the Wadi Fassail. Winer[3] doubts the correctness of this connection, in spite of the great authority of Robinson ; yet the

---

[1] Von Raumer, *Palæstina*, p. 63

[2] Robinson, *Bib. Research.* i. 558, 559 ; Wilson, *Lands of the Bible*, ii. p. 5, and note. (On the other side, see Tristram, *Land of Israel*, p. 199.)

[3] Winer, *Bibl. Realw.* i. p. 229, art. *Chrith.*

latter, in propounding this hypothesis, does not maintain that the Arabic word Kelt is not identical with the Hebrew Cherith. He adds a fact, which we do not find in other accounts, that at a little distance from the ravine known as Wadi Kelt, there is in the mountain ridge a desolate tower-like castle known as Kakon.

Von Schubert,[1] who took the same route to Jericho, has given us nothing new regarding it. Russegger,[2] who passed over the same route in autumn, found the road from Bethany rocky, bare, and steep. Between upright walls of limestone, full of caverns and fantastic peaks, he says that the road runs along in some places between gorges from eight hundred to a thousand feet in depth, and only forty to fifty wide. Even in the lowest parts vegetation is very scanty. On the crest of a very steep mountain he reached the Khan Hudrur, to which he heard the name Chatrul given. It is three hours from Jerusalem, and the same distance from Jericho. One and a half hours eastward from that point he descried the plains of Jericho, extending to the Jordan valley and to the Dead Sea,—a most interesting scene to the eye of a geologist. The descent Russegger found excessively steep and difficult, and came to the conclusion that only Syrian horses could go safely down with riders on their backs.

Seetzen, who set out from Bethlehem on his adventurous foot journey around the Dead Sea, took a new route thither, passing by the Khan el Hout. Nebi Musa he left on one side (probably at his right), and then came through a district of wild mountain land to the fallen Khan el Hatrum,[3] with its immense grottos. Thence he passed into Wadi el Kild, evidently Robinson's Wadi Kelt, in which he found a spring at the time of his visit, but which is said to be dry in the summer time.

From Wolcott's route from Jericho[4] to Jerusalem, who entered Wadi el Kelt in February 1842, and left its water-course on the right, we learn that he saw that the Wadi Dabus el Abed has a southerly direction, and that its main arm runs

[1] Von Schubert, *Reise*, iii. pp. 71–74.
[2] Russegger, *Reise*, iii. pp. 102, 103.
[3] Seetzen, *Zweite Reise*, manuscript.
[4] Samuel Wolcott, *Excursion*, in *Bib. Sacra*, 1843, p. 40.

eastward towards Jericho.   After a short hour he reached the
Wadi el Chân, at whose upper extremity the Khan Hudhrur
lies, while another khan called es-Sahil was seen on the west
side of the ridge.   Its course then led him through the Wadi
Sidr and Wadi Hodh, and then into the usual route by way of
Bethany and Jerusalem.

Still another road was taken by Banks and Buckingham,
namely, from Jerusalem, on the north side of the Mount of
Olives.   They left Bethany and Bethphage at the right, and
after a march of three hours over stony country, reached the
encampment of the Zaliane Arabs, consisting of six small tents.
A half-hour farther they passed through a defile between solid
rocks, which a fort, now in ruins, once guarded.   According to
the estimate of the travellers, it was twelve or fourteen miles
from Jerusalem, and therefore certainly not to be identified
with Anathoth,[1] the modern Anata, the birth-place of the
prophet Jeremiah.   This, however, Buckingham has done,
though Robinson, with far more reason, has placed Anathoth
farther west, and on the way to Bethel.   D'Anville's conjecture
that this is the site of Ephraim is not much more probable,
since Taiyibeh, much farther north, is more likely Ephraim or
Ephron.[2]   A third place which Buckingham mentions is most
probably the correct identification ; but in this case it must be
considered rather the result of a happy guess than of well-
considered reasoning.   Schultz, however, confirms this conjecture, and writes to me on the occasion of his fifth excursion,
when going to the help of the unfortunate Molyneux : "On
this ride[3] I found, half-way to my destination, and near the
Khan Hathur, the ruined fortification Kalaat el Dem, without doubt the lofty Adummim of the Bible."   The seemingly
contracted name, as well as the locality, make it very probable, from Josh. xv. 7 and xviii. 17, that this eminence designated the border of the territories of Judah and Benjamin.[4]
Of this height Jerome said, *s.v.* Adommim, that in his time
there was a place there which bore the name Maledomini ; he

[1] Robinson, *Bib. Research.* i. pp. 269–437.
[2] *Bib. Sacra*, vol. ii. New York 1845, p. 398 ; comp. *Athenæum* of June
7, 1845, No. 919, p. 566.
[3] E. G. Schultz, manuscript account.
[4] Keil, *Comment. zu Jos.* pp. 281, 282 ; Winer, *Bibl. Realw.* i. p. 24.

adds: Græce dicitur ἀνάβασις πύῤῥων, latine autem appellari potest ascensus ruforum seu rubentium propter sanguinem, qui illic crebro a latronibus funditur. Est autem confinium tribus Judæ et Benjamini descendentibus ab Ælia, *i.e.* Jerusalem, sibi et Castellus, militum situm est, ob auxilia viatorum. The castle, which was noticed by Buckingham, would seem to be the Kalaat el Dem of Schultz, which, according to Keil, must lie south of the brook of Jericho, to make good the words of Josh. xv. 7, "which is on the south side of the river."

From this narrow pass and the ancient ruined fort,—the desolate place where in 1820 the English traveller Henderson was attacked by robbers, and almost killed, finding a kind Samaritan in a compassionate woman of Jericho,—Buckingham and Banks[1] continued their journey over a fearful wilderness, its horrors yet increased by the yelling and aimless discharge of guns on the part of the Arab escort. Three hours farther on they reached the ruins of the upper aqueducts, near the remains of an ancient[2] *via strata*, on which one stone was noticed still erect,—perhaps a former milestone on the highway, it may be,[2] which once led from Jerusalem to Jericho. On the way down they discovered the ruins of two aqueducts, one of which was still covered with cement. At the extremity were large reservoirs, probably excavated for the uses of the city of Jericho. Not a drop of water was found in them.

All the different routes which have been specified lead from Jerusalem, Bethlehem, or the great watershed ridge running north, through the wild and savage desert of Jericho, well deserving the name, and to the depths of the Ghor. On these roads, therefore, there has been the amplest opportunity to study the geological structure of the soil, since the surface is hid by scarcely the thinnest veil of vegetation. The whole undisguised formation of this singular depressed region is therefore a remarkably accessible field of study, and both Hasselquist[3] and my honoured friend Russegger have made it the subject of special inquiry.

The latter connects his observations on this region with

---

[1] Buckingham, *Trav. in Palestine*, ii. p. 58.

[2] See David Roberts, *Holy Land*, vol. vi. No. 16 : *Descent into the Valley of the Jordan.*

[3] Hasselquist, *Reise*, p. 148.

those upon the more southern mountains of Judæa, in the neighbourhood of Hebron, and states that the chalk formation of the Sinai Peninsula, as the leading geological feature, ends with the mountains of Chalil, *i.e.* of Hebron, where commence the immense strata of Jura limestone which characterize southern and middle Syria.

The mountain ridges south of Hebron, a short day's journey from Jerusalem, rise only[1] a few hundred feet above the vales at their feet; yet they show to the traveller approaching from the south that he has already entered a different country. Rolling, dome-shaped mountain tops, and short and rounded valleys, gentle ascents, an increase of verdure, long ridges, and small plateaus, are the chief characteristics of the southern mountains of Syria.

The limestone of this region is of the same quality as that which Russegger had already examined in the Lebanon and Anti-Lebanon; poor in fossils, full of caverns, solid, firm, friable, inclining to a crystalline structure, white, yellow, and reddish-brown. It is stratified, although the lines of stratification are not very marked. The caverns which are found in this Jura are grotto-like, *i.e.* they have large mouths, and decrease as they recede from the surface, probably owing to the former emission of pent-up gases.

The formation of valleys at Hebron never advanced to any considerable stage; and one entering Palestine from the south, and standing on the outlying hills, sees distinctly beyond the Dead Sea the mighty rock wall which runs from north to south, and which probably also belongs to the Jura formation. This chain rises till it attains its maximum elevation in Jebel Belka, three thousand feet high, whence the descent is abrupt to the deep basin of the Dead Sea.

On the west side of the Dead Sea, the same Jura limestone pervades with great uniformity the whole extent of country from south to north. There are no very marked elevations, excepting the bluff on which Bethlehem stands, the high rock on which Jerusalem is built, and the Mount of Olives; the most of the hills are knob-like in form, and are rich in flinty chalk. The height of the last-mentioned mountain is 2509 feet, and that of Jerusalem 2349 feet above the sea, although

[1] Russegger, *Reise*, iii. p. 246 et sq.

above the Dead Sea they are 3860 feet and 3700 feet respectively. With the Jura limestone of Jerusalem and its neighbourhood there are mingled large masses of dolomite, which seem here, as in the Tyrolese alpine region, to have exerted a mighty influence in the great upheaval to which the whole district was apparently once subjected. This dolomite contains iron pyrites, and manifests a striking inclination to a crystalline structure; it is reddish-white and reddish-brown in colour, is full of small grains of oxide of iron, but lacks fossils almost entirely. Russegger was unable to discover whether it is found in dykes or in great stratified masses, diffused throughout all Palestine. Some parts of the Jura formation seemed to him to have a marl-like appearance, and in their character to be similar to the upper white chalk.

The geological structure of the district between Jerusalem and Jericho is, according to Russegger, the following. For the first two hours there is a light-coloured limestone, containing great masses of dolomite;[1] an arrangement which is prevalent rather in the northern than in the southern part of Palestine. The summits of the mountains, and the loftiest crests, are composed mainly of white chalk full of flint. Two hours farther towards the north-east and east, the strata show traces of iron pyrites, and the stone takes a dark colour; the stratification, too, becomes exceedingly irregular.[2] The traveller has evidently entered a district where great disturbance has been experienced.

White chalk lies at the surface, and increases as one approaches the Dead Sea, gradually creeping down into the valleys, and covering the Jura formations even in the very deepest places. The form of the mountains of the lower Jura district is strikingly different from that of the upper one. They do not have that softly rounded and uniform appearance, but are wilder, more sharply drawn, cloven perpendicularly in some places, full of deep gorges and ravines, evidently hinting at times of powerful convulsions and shatterings. The nearer one approaches the Jordan, the more the height of the mountains declines, considered relatively to the level of the sea, though they tower up in crags to a height of 1500 and 2000 feet above the waters of the sacred river.

[1] Russegger, *Reise,* iii. p. 2   [2] *Ibid.* p. 249.

At Khan Hudhrur (Chetrul) a gorge eight hundred feet in depth affords a passage through the formations of the low Jura system. The wave-like folds in the strata are here so numerous and so singular, that they give a very picturesque appearance to the place; but, at the same time, they make the study of the geology of the place very difficult. The limestone there, as in the higher system, is full of great caverns, and the same is strongly marked with traces of iron. About an hour's distance north-east of the same khan, Russegger discovered[1] a very interesting geological district. Above the road, and shut in by jurassic mountains, he found a little plain filled with chalk hills: they all reminded him in their appearance of a sea tossed by a storm. The compactly set together waves of stone formed a spectacle so strange that the Arabs, although not very sensitive to natural wonders, shared in his amazement.

From this point forward the lower Jura rocks are partly covered with strata of white chalk, which then becomes the leading formation as far as to the valley of the Jordan. In the chalk he discovered a great number of large dirk-shaped masses, some of them three feet in diameter, and six to eight inches thick, regular in form, and exhibiting spiral lines, which made him think them colossal ammonites.

The nearer he advanced to the edge of the Jordan valley, the wilder became the mountain forms. Perpendicular walls of rock sometimes rise to a height of a thousand feet, and leave a passage scarcely fifty feet wide. Here too are seen the traces of the convulsions which once rent the whole district. In the mountains east of the Jordan valley and the Dead Sea, the same limestone which is met on the western side is found; but not only on the summits, but in the valleys, it is covered with white chalk, forming in some places little ridges and hills. Wherever in the plain of the Jordan, which at the mouth of the river is three hours in width, the underlying stone comes to the surface, it is always the white chalk; but the greatest part of the valley is covered with alluvia, and with the accumulations which have been swept down from the adjacent mountains.

The effects of volcanic activity are to be seen abundantly in the immediate neighbourhood of the Dead Sea, manifested, however, by rents and fissures which show the workings of

[1] Russegger, *Reise*, iii. p. 251.

internal forces, and the emission of gases and steam, and not by traces of the eruption of fire. The strand along the north coast of the sea is perfectly level, and consists of a sandy soil intermingled with a salt loam. In Russegger's examination along the margin of the sea from the mouth of the Jordan to Mar Saba in the wild Kedron valley, he saw no other rubble stone than those of the limestone already mentioned, the flints which are found in the chalk, and bituminous marl.

That the present condition of the Dead Sea, and a great part of the lower Jordan valley, at least from the mouth as far north as Riha, was once the bottom of the lake, is beyond question : the proof is conclusive, that the Dead Sea once stood at a higher level than it does now. The fact seems equally clear, that the subsidence in the level is to be explained by the diminution in the tributaries of the Jordan. The diminution in the amount of water which the Jordan receives is the result of the decrease in rain, brought about by suffering the vegetation of the adjacent country to disappear, but most of all by robbing the hills of the forests which once covered them.[1]

The geological observations of Russegger deserve to be followed up with all the more care, since it now does not seem probable that the world is to enjoy in full the results of Brocchi's[2] explorations around Jericho and the Dead Sea.

DISCURSION II.

As one leaves the mouth of the Jordan, there is a distance of two hours' extent to be passed before he leaves the desert waste, and reaches the more abundantly watered region, still tilled, which was once so noted for its groves of balsam and

---

[1] See an article by Dr Coleman in the *Bib. Sac.* for 1864, in which this subject is treated exhaustively.—ED.

[2] Brocchi in *Bibl. Ital.* xxiv. p. 73 ; in the *Nuovo Giorn. d. Litterati*, and in *Asiat. Journ.* 1826, vol. xxii. p. 322.

palm trees, as well as for the magnificence of its palaces and the strength of its fortresses. Desolate and waste as it is now, it still bears the name the Oasis of Jericho,[1] because it yet shows that the old capacities are there, and that, under a system of tillage like the ancient one, the place might put on anew that paradisaical beauty for which Josephus praises it, and which made it, according to him, fit to be the seat of the gods.

Descending from Akab Jahor, which von Wildenbruch[2] estimates to lie three hundred feet above the plains of Jericho, the traveller passes some brooks which come from Ain es Sultan and from Wadi Kelt at the north-west, and the west of the village of Riha. He then meets some remains of aqueducts,[3] almost the only traces of an earlier culture which remain to the few idle and neglectful Beduins who now live in the region. Just so far as their waters extend, there is a flourishing growth of verdure, which is doubly delightful and refreshing when seen in such an arid region as that around. The surprise at finding this little patch of green in the sterile desert, has probably occasioned that praise which has been given to the place by tourists. Robinson, Wilson, and Gadow saw only a single palm, a dry trunk without a crown rising above the hedgerow which, with its bushes, surrounds the nest of little stone huts, the miserable relic and representative of ancient Jericho. The name of the place is Eriha, Riha, or Richa, evidently the corruption of the ancient name. It is sometimes known among the Arabs, however, as Sidr. In the neighbourhood of these huts, which lie a little lower than the very interesting remains of an aqueduct with eleven arches still existing, and near the junction of Wadi Kelt and the watercourse from Ain es Sultan, the pilgrim caravans are accustomed to encamp for the night, and then the next morning go on to their bathing-place, an hour and a half's distance towards the north-east.

In the neighbourhood of this village of Riha, and on the north side of Wadi Kelt, there is a ruined tower, in which a

---

[1] See David Roberts, *The Holy Land*, vol. vi. plate xvii. Jericho : *Encampment of Pilgrims at Jericho.*

[2] Von Wildenbruch's *Profil.* tab. iii. in *Monatsber. i.a.l.* iii. p. 270.

[3] Wilson, *Lands of the Bible*, ii. p. 5 ; Gadow, *i.a.l.* ii. p. 55 ; Robinson, *Bib. Research.* i. p. 559.

Turkish governor resides, with a small garrison. This is called the Castle of Jericho, and, according to the legend of the pilgrims, is the house of Zaccheus. In its neighbourhood there are traces of tillage; and maize, millet, indigo, figs, nabk (*Lotus napeca*), myrobalanas (*Eleagnus angustifol.*), and zaccum or balsam, grow with more or less productiveness. It is at this neighbourhood, where Robinson put up his tent,[1] and remained for several days, that the examinations of this region are wont to begin. Here, on the 12th of May, Robinson heard the croaking of frogs, there being moisture enough there to give those little creatures a home. Their name among the Arabs is Dhafdah', in which word Wilson thought he detected some trace of the Hebrew name for frog.[2] In the bushes he detected the note of the nightingale, in the crevices of the walls the chirping of the crickets, while swarms of mosquitoes swarmed round the tent. Russegger[3] took up his abode in the old tower itself, in an apartment which was thirty-six feet above the ground. Here he made his barometrical observations. The armed force there consisted of an effendi with twenty-three armed hedjalis, whose duty it is to guard the district against the attacks of the Beduins.

The most remarkable relics of antiquity are found in the aqueduct of eleven lofty arches,[4] supplied from the Ain es Sultan, at the north-west, a half-mile away. It crosses Wadi Kelt, and west of the village of Riha and its castle it turns its course, passing over the outlying eastern spur of the mountains. It is considered by some to have been built by Herod, although the appearance of the arches indicates a more modern origin. Gadow remarks that the path from the western mountain range runs along the south border of the Wadi Kelt, the supposed brook of Cherith, and is crossed by two artificial water conduits, the first of which seems to be the most modern of the two. Along the southern border of the same wadi there are left only a few remnants of walls, yet their former course can be traced for yet a hundred paces farther in the plain. They could not possibly have extended so far as to the present Riha,

---

[1] Robinson, *Bib. Research.* i. p. 547.
[2] Wilson, *Lands of the Bible*, ii. p. 11.
[3] Russegger, *Reise*, iii. p. 103.
[4] Von Wildenbruch, *Profil. i.a.l.* iii. p. 270.

which lies fifteen hundred paces farther to the north-east, and on the north side of the dry Wadi Kelt. In the north-western course of this aqueduct there were remains of walls at the foot of Mount Quarantania, west of the so-called sugar-mills. These are the supports of the water conduit, and may be traced as far as to Ain Duk, or the Waters of Dosh, whose waters were conducted to the southern part of the plain for purposes of irrigation. Wilson[1] thought that it also supplied the sugar-mills with water.

The second aqueduct is the one already mentioned, lying a hundred steps east of the first one. It still displays eleven arches, which succeed each other across Wadi Kelt in a direction from N.N.W. to S.S.E. The water is derived from Ain es Sultan, but is soon lost in the sand, giving nourishment to a plentiful crop of thorn-bushes, in which the red partridges and other feathery game find an asylum.

With these aqueducts others seem to have been connected, for Gadow met traces of such on his ride southward between Wadi Kelt and Wadi Santa, west of Ain Hajla: there were five or six walled canals all running in a south and south-easterly direction, traversing the district, sloping gently to the Jordan, and only broken by the moderate row of hills bearing the name Kafr Hajla. These canals must unquestionably have received their water through the two aqueducts just mentioned, and then have distributed it throughout the whole plain. This gave it the appearance of a beautiful oasis in the midst of a desert, and must have produced that profuse vegetation which delighted the Israelites at the time of their entrance into the Promised Land, and which at the time of Pompey and Herod gave sustenance to a large population. This oasis extended for a long distance measured from north to south; within its limits there are many piles of rubbish, making it very difficult to determine the precise locality of the ancient Jericho. Josephus tells us that the spring of Jericho watered a tract seventy stadia long and twenty broad, which, covered as it was with gardens, orchards, and palms, was one of the most fruitful in the world. His praises do not seem to have been exaggerated.

The restoration of the extensive system of irrigation which once prevailed here would restore the former fertility, and

[1] Wilson, *Lands of the Bible*, ii. p. 14.

make this place a very attractive spot, were it not for the inse-
curity of life and property. Wilson remarks, that wherever
water goes there, it is followed at once by an amazing luxuriance
of vegetation. The Herodian aqueduct[1] is surrounded by the
finest of creepers: the nabk or sidr trees are overgrown with
them, while the ground is covered with a profusion of low
shrubs. Swarms of singing birds animate the thick bushes,
prominent among them being a kind very like the humming-
bird in the splendour of its plumage. Von Schubert speaks of
hearing the notes of the lark there, while Robinson was no less
delighted to recognise those of the nightingale. The tropical
Egyptian climate exercises an unmistakeable influence upon
the vegetation of this locality, and causes even dates to ripen
and palm trees to flourish. Wilson,[2] who came to Palestine
from Bombay, was not a little surprised to find many plants
here with which he had become acquainted in India.

When von Schubert[3] reached this place on the 12th of
April, the pomegranate trees were in full bloom, although just
putting forth their buds in Jerusalem; the figs were already
ripe, the nebek trees were laden with their delicious burden,
the vines were doing well without being cared for at all. Of the
palm tree of the ancients, however, he could not gain a trace
more than of the dates which were once so abundant here.
The zakkum tree now supplies pilgrims with the reputed balm,
and the fragrant evening breezes seemed to him to explain the
etymology of the name Riha, *i.e.* the sweet-smelling.

Of the Indian plants noticed by Wilson,[4] the most remarkable is the *Asclepias gigantea*, the osher of the Arabs, which,
according to Dr Roxburgh, belongs to the most common, large,
and branching bushes of that country. During the whole year
it bears blossoms and fruit at the same time. The branches
were just as strong here as Wilson had seen them in India.
The use of the bark in manufacturing a kind of silky flax, as
well as a drug, is unknown among the Arabs. The yellow
fruit resembles the orange in appearance. The Abbot Daniel of
St Saba as early as 1674 thought it to be the *Poma Sodomitica*,

---

[1] H. Gadow, *passim.*
[2] Wilson, *Lands of the Bible*, ii. pp. 7–12.
[3] Von Schubert, *Reise*, iii. pp. 75–80.
[4] Wilson, *Lands of the Bible*, ii. p. 8.

with which Robinson coincides. Wilson does not believe it
to be such, because the interior seems to him to be more
substantial than Robinson's description grants.[1] The same
tree is found also in Upper Egypt, Nubia, and Arabia Felix,
but in Palestine it is only met in the sultry region round the
Dead Sea. Irby and Mangles had seen this plant in Nubia before
meeting it in the Holy Land. In the former place it had the
name oshar, and bore fruit of the size of plums, which hung
down like grapes, and had, together with the leaves, a strong
smell of mustard,[2] even bringing water to the eyes. Between
Beisan and the mountains of Ajlun they also met it, but only
as a shrub; in the deep and hot Ghor, on the contrary, they
found it a tree fifteen feet in height, and with branches two
feet in length. The place where it flourished was at the southern
end of the Dead Sea, where the fruit has the most attractive
appearance, and yet is crushed between the thumb and finger,
yielding only a light down, which envelopes the seeds, and
which could be used as the wadding of guns and the stuffing
of cushions. They, too, considered this to be the apples of
Sodom.

Seetzen became acquainted with this fruit in Kerak, where
the thin down was used as tinder. It was said to be produced
by a tree of the name of Aeoshar, in the Ghor. He did not
see the plant itself, whose juice he was told was used to make
unfruitful women bear children. He, too, thought the fruit
was the *Poma Sodomitica*.[3] Burckhardt speaks of the same
plant, calling it the Asheyr tree : he regrets that the silky
down of the beautiful fruit, some of which was three inches in
diameter, could not be turned to some practical account; but
he left twenty camel loads at least to perish on the trees.
Robinson, quoting Josephus' description of this production,
"De terra Sodomitica et in fructibus cineres nascentes, qui
specie quidem et colore edulibus similes sunt, manibus autem
decerptæ in favillam et cinerem resolvuntur," confirms its
literal truthfulness, stating, that fair as it is to the eye, when
taken into the hand it breaks with the slightest pressure, leaving

---

[1] Robinson, *Bib. Research.* ii. pp. 441, 472–474.
[2] Irby and Mangles, *Travels*, pp. 355, 450.
[3] Seetzen, *Mon. Corresp.* xviii. p. 442. (Tristram, *Land of Israel*, p. 283.)

a thin shell in the hand, and displaying within a mass of seeds, surrounded with a dry, light, silky substance, which only mocks the taste. It must be plucked very carefully, or it will break in the hand; nor could it at all be preserved for inspection. Dr Wilson, however, does not admit this, and thinks that specimens could be brought to Europe with perfect safety. The Bible nowhere speaks of the fruit of Sodom, only of vines and the fields of the region (Deut. xxxii. 32); but the account of its character must have been well known at the time of Josephus, since Tacitus and many other writers allude to it. Von Schubert[1] is inclined to think that a kind of acacia, the *Lagonychium Stephanianum*, is the *Poma Sodomitica*.

The *Leimun Lût* of the Arabs (Lot's lemon) is another shrub growing in profusion in the neighbourhood of Jericho. It attains a height of three to five feet, and bears berries from an inch to an inch and a half in diameter, regarding which there is a tradition among the Arabs that they were once the finest lemons, but that they were cursed by Lot in consequence of the impiety of the people, since which they have been this bitter fruit. Hasselquist, who thought that this is the *Poma Sodomitica* or the *Mala insana* of the legend, recognised the plant as a *Solanum melongœna*, which, however, according to Brochi,[2] is not found at Jericho; only the *Solanum sanctum*. Wilson was inclined to consider this fruit as the *Mala insana*, or mad apples, as well as the grapes of gall mentioned in the song of Moses (Deut. xxxii. 32). A shrub very similar to this, a *Solanum incanum*, which Wilson says is abundant around Jericho, is called by the Arabs Wolf's grapes. Wilson lays no great worth on the description of Josephus, in consequence of his frequent inaccuracies.

Among the most numerous of the thorny bushes in the neighbourhood of Jericho is the nebek,[3] a plant which is very common in Egypt, all over Palestine, and in the Arabian Peninsula. This is the nebk of Robinson (*Rhamnus napeca*), and the sidr (*Zizyphus lotus*) of the Arabs; perhaps giving its name to the Wadi Sidr, north of the Khan Hudhrur. Another name given to this plant is dôm, although it is an entirely dif-

---

[1] Von Schubert, *Reise*, iii. p. 84.
[2] *Asiatic Journ.* 1826, vol. xxii. p. 322. (See, however, Tristram, p. 202.)
[3] Robinson, *Bib. Research.* ii. 539; Wilson, *Lands of the Bible*, ii. p. 10.

ferent thing from the dum palm (*Crucifera Thebaica*). The local legend asserts that the crown of thorns was made from this.

A distinctive characteristic of the plain of Jericho would be seen in the balsam or balm tree[1] (*Opobalsamum declaratum*), if the genuine tree now grew there, as it did in the time of Alexander the Great, when a shell of the balm was carried to him every day. It existed also in Pompey's time, for he bore one of the balsam trees in his triumphal procession; and subsequently both Vespasian and Titus transferred it to Italy. The tree was thought to grow exclusively in Judæa, and there in only two gardens, one containing only twenty acres, the other still smaller. That the place where these gardens were found was Jericho, is clear from a passage in Strabo, who speaks of them in connection with the royal palace there. He says that the cunning Jews cultivated the balm only there, in order to maintain the high price which it bore. Josephus, in his laudatory description of Jericho, speaks of the "opobalsamum" and the palms as the most valuable production of the place. Dioscorides used the same name in speaking of the exudation of the tree, and not of the tree itself, quoting the *Itinerarium Bernàrdi Sapientis*[2] as his authority.

Josephus distinguishes between two kinds of balsam produced at Jericho. Pliny goes further, and specifies several kinds of varied qualities, among which is the sap of the myrobalanus, which he calls an ointment, and not a true balm. This grew not in Jericho alone, but in Æthiopia, Egypt, and Arabia. This manner of discriminating between the different varieties substantiates the theory that the culture of the balm was introduced into Jericho from Arabia, and the name Beshem or Balesan is still current in the latter country. It was possible for the culture of it to die out there, even after it had been transferred to Egypt, where we find it at the time of Cleopatra, and where it is reported as existing as late as 1549.[3] In 1625, however, the balsam garden at Cairo had become extinct.

The myrobalanos or zukkum tree (the *Myro-Balsamum* of

---

[1] Rosenmüller, *Bibl. Alterth.* iv. pp. 146–151.

[2] *Itinerarium Bernardi Sapientis*, ed. Fr. Michel, in *Mem. de la Soc. Géogr. de Paris*, iv. p. 806.

[3] P. Belon, *Observat.* Paris, ed. 1554, liv. ii. ch. 39, fol. 110–112.

Wilson[1]) is still found growing wild at Jericho. Hasselquist terms it *Eleagnus angustifolius*, and it seems to be closely allied in character with the wild olive tree of southern Europe. Von Schubert has designated[2] it as Hasselquist did before him, but has made no detailed comments upon it. It is not a large tree, is thorny, and has a greener and smoother bark than the nebek; its fruit is as green as that of the olive, with a small kernel, and a thick fleshy rind, which yields an oil that, in respect to flavour and colour, resembles the fresh oil of sweet almonds. Maundrell, Pococke, Mariti, and more recently Gadow,[3] saw the Arabs, who shun all field labour, collecting this oil and making it into balm to sell to credulous pilgrims as the genuine balsam of Jericho, and the exudation of the tree on which Zaccheus sat, in spite of the fact that that tree was a mulberry (Luke xix. 4). The *Itinerar. Burdig.*, however, speaks of the tree of Zaccheus as a sycamore, and says that even then the house in which he lived was said to be standing.

The celebrated Rose of Jericho (*Anastatica hierochundica*[4]) —the branching, woody plant, six or eight inches in height, indigenous to the sand plains of southern Palestine and Arabia Petræa—is now as little found in the soil which once nourished it as the mulberry is. It is no true rose, but belongs to the family of *siliquosæ*. Belon, who found it at the foot of Sinai, sought it in vain on the plain of Jericho, and did not hesitate to say, that the statement that it is abundant there is a subterfuge of the monks: "petite herbette, que quelques moines trompeurs ont apellé Rose de Jericho—et n'en croist aucunement en Jericho, etc."[5] These ecclesiastics seem to want to find something corresponding to the rose in Jes. Sirach xxiv. 14 or 18, where the palm tree and the rose bush are brought together; but to this the humble shrub can lay no claim. Seetzen[6] states also, that, in spite of all his efforts, he could find nothing which

---

[1] Robinson, *Bib. Research.* ii. 538, 539 ; Wilson, *Lands of the Bible*, ii. p. 10. (Tristram, *Land of Israel*, p. 202.)

[2] Von Schubert, *Reise*, iii. p. 114.

[3] H. Gadow, *i.a.l.* ii. p. 57.

[4] Robinson, *Bib. Research.* ii. p. 539.

[5] P. Belon, *Observat.* liv. ii. ch. 86, p. 144. (Found, however, "in some abundance" by Tristram, p. 217.)

[6] Seetzen, *Zweite Reise zum Todten Meere.* Manuscript account.

corresponded to the Jericho rose; and Sheikh Achmed confirmed him in this result, by asserting that it is not known there. The true roses, the centifolia, of Jericho are praised very highly by Fabri.[1]

In addition to the palm-groves, which since the time of Arculfus have shrunk from extensive plantations, extending from Jericho to the Jordan, to the pitiful representatives which are now found, there were also the sugar-cane plantations,[2] which have utterly disappeared, although at the time of the crusaders they were very profitable, and the support of many people. The amount of sugar made is specifically mentioned by Jac. de Vitriatico.[3] The bishop of Acco was of the opinion that even John the Baptist, who lived on locusts and wild honey, drew the latter indirectly from the sugar-cane : this is a false conclusion, however, for it was subsequent to his time that it was introduced into Palestine from Susiana. Yet the ruins of the Sugar Mills[4]—called by that name even to this day, and evidently of Saracenic origin—show that the sugar-cane has been cultivated there since the land first came under Saracenic sway. The soil and climate must certainly be adapted to the growth of the sugar-cane, as well as for raising rice, which also, according to Seetzen, has wholly ceased upon the plains of Jericho.

With regard to the culture of the indigo plant at Jericho, to which ancient writers make no allusion, Edrisi, in the twelfth century, asserts[5] distinctly that it was then raised; and the fact is confirmed by Abulfeda.[6] Seetzen[7] remarks, during his long stay in Jericho, that on the southern side of Wadi Kelt, and in some open places, the indigo plant is cultivated; and Robinson heard that it bears for seven or eight successive years. Cotton, too, is sometimes cultivated. The blue stuffs which are made from it are indispensable to the Arabs there,

[1] F. Fabri, *Evagatorium*, vol. ii. pp. 60, 61.

[2] Adamnanus ex Arculfo, *de Loc. Sanctis*, ed. Mabill. T. ii. fol. 514.

[3] C. Ritter, *Über die geographische Verbreitung des Zuckerrohrs*, in *Abh. der Berliner Akad. histor. phil. Klasse*, 1839; printed separately, 1840, p. 86.

[4] Robinson, *Bib. Research*. ii. pp. 530, 541.

[5] Edrisi, in *Jomard*. i. p. 339.

[6] Abulfeda, *Tab. Syr*. ed. Koehler, fol. 35.

[7] Seetzen, *Zweite Reise nach dem Todten Meere*. Manuscript account.

for daily clothing. Everything which is planted there, as well as everything which is wild, grows with wonderful rapidity.

Whether the Kypros—the fragrant tree of Cyprus, the *Lawsonia inermis* of Linnæus, and the schminke[1] of the Arabs, which, according to Sonnini,[2] is mentioned in Solomon's Song i. 14 and iv. 13—is found now in the plains of Jericho,[3] as it was in the time of Josephus, is not known: it is in no way improbable that that is the case, however, since the plant is very common in southern Palestine, Arabia, and Egypt,[4] and extends from Morocco to India and Java.[5]

The abundance of nuts once found in this district, as well as of other fruits, such as the sidr or nebek, the most of which have now disappeared, or have been reduced to insignificance, is understood by simply glancing at the profusion of vegetation which follows immediately wherever water goes over the plain ; and it is easy to understand how, at the time of the Crusades, this spot was declared to be one of the most fertile spots in the whole country. It was at that time made over to the Church of the Holy Sepulchre at Jerusalem.[6] The charge was brought against the third Latin patriarch in Jerusalem, Arculphus, that in the year 1111 he wanted this tract from the Church, and made it over to his niece as a dowry. The Archbishop of Tyre states that the income from the plains of Jericho was five thousand gold pieces, each five Spanish dollars. In 1138 the tract again fell back into the possession of the Church. Queen Melisinda presented it to the nuns' convent at Bethany, to which it brought in important revenues.

There is still lacking, to complete our knowledge of this site of Jericho, a thorough botanical investigation, in continuation of that which Seetzen and Wilson began.[7] I subjoin the names of

[1] Burckhardt, *Trav. in Arabia*, p. 242.

[2] J. Kitto, *Palestine*, London 1841, ii. p. cclxxxii.

[3] Winer, *Bib. Realw.* i. p. 237 ; Robinson, *Bib. Research.* ii. 441, note, and 536.

[4] Hasselquist, *Reise*, p. 503 ; Shaw, *Travels*, p. 103 ; Sonnini, *Reise in Ægypt.* i. p. 16 et seq.

[5] Edrisi in *Jaubert*, T. i. p. 208 ; and Wm. Ainslie, *Materia Indica*, vol. ii. p. 189.

[6] Robinson, *Bib. Research.* ii. p. 542.

[7] For such an investigation, see Tristram's very thorough work, *The Land of Israel*, London 1865.—ED.

a few plants which the former traveller learned[1] from his Arab
guides: gitta, growing to the height of a man, a kind of orach;
mellueh, very sappy leaves; hammt, a shrub growing three or
four feet high, the *Zygophyllum proliferum;* erket or oerk; addeb,
perhaps a variety of salsola; alesszitsh, a kind of Lycium; phurss,
with small juicy leaves, thickly set together as in the grape;
tagma, a plant used in dyeing red, with dill-like leaves; teijera;
ajeram, from which soda, here called al-kally, is made; hush-
ma, like some of the foregoing, employed in the manufacture
of soap; ennib, a parasite that grows on the sidr, and used
in tanning barley.   To these may be added the szammueh,
idsehr, el-garab, szus, and shubbrik.

Wilson mentions, in addition to the foregoing, the azba, a kind
of sisymbrium or water-cress, found along the brooks; ghores,
a nettle, *Urtica pulcherima,* growing in great profusion among
the ruins; nadnah, a kind of mint; harfeish, a variety of thistle;
and bismas, a flower resembling the marigold (*Calendula*).

Seetzen found wheat growing on the brook el-Nawaimeh at
the eastern base of Mount Quarantania, where an aqueduct
sustained by three arches conveys the water from a fine spring
over the fields.   This water conduit was repaired by a local
sheikh about the close of the last century.   The tillage is
carried on by the Arabs, who raise in addition to wheat, barley,
melons, gerkins, and badinjan.

Robinson and Smith were at Jericho at the time of the
grain harvest,[2] the middle of May, and saw many things in the
process of reaping and threshing which reminded them of the
scenes described in the second and third chapters of the book
of Ruth.   The people who had charge of the harvesting were
not from Jericho, but from Taiyibeh, six or seven hours away
towards the north-west, and at the source of the Nawaimeh.
Women, children, and priests had accompanied the working men
to the wheat harvest.   Half of the crop fell to the harvesters, a
quarter to the people of Jericho, and a quarter to the garrison.
The wheat had thriven exceedingly wherever water came: the
greater part had been-cut as early as the middle of March,
bound in small bundles, and then carried to the threshing-floors.
These were round places, fifty feet in diameter, with the earth

---

[1] Seetzen, *Zweite Reise nach dem Todten Meere.*   Manuscript account.
[2] Robinson, *Bibl. Research.* ii. p. 519.

trodden very firmly down so as to give a solid floor. Five oxen were driven around to tread out the wheat, the drags which are in use in northern Palestine not being employed here. Nor is that machine alluded to in Isa. xxviii. 27, the noraj of Niebuhr,[1] known in the neighbourhood of Jericho. The straw, after being threshed, is tossed up with a two-pronged pitchfork, and winnowed, in which rude process much grain is lost. The threshers as a body were members of the Greek Church, and did not heed the Mosaic command recorded in Deut. xxv. 4, regarding the muzzling the mouth of the ox that treadeth out the corn,—a proof that in the most primitive days neat cattle were used for this purpose, just as they are now.

How much the low warm situation of Jericho hastens the growths there, is clear enough from the testimony of Robinson,[2] who found the wheat at Hebron on the 6th of June not so far advanced as it had been at Jericho a month before. The barley harvest in the lower Ghor is gathered about the last of April. Sometimes, however, it cannot be gathered at all; for the Beduin hordes from the east side of the Jordan at times sweep over the river in numbers like the locusts, and prematurely carry it all away. The few inhabitants of Riha are unable to offer any resistance; and, in fact, they are too lazy to gather their own wheat, or even to sow it: all this they leave to the more spirited fellahin of Taiyibeh. In 1847, when Gadow[3] was at Jericho, he found the two sheikhs Abu Dis and Silwan dividing the corn with the sheikh of the Ihtem Beduins: the yield had been twenty-fold that season, and Mohammed Pasha's tract is said to have given a return of thirty-six-fold.

Besides wheat and barley, Robinson found maize (*Zea Mais*), a plant which springs from the root a second year, and then perishes;[4] he did not see millet, however. There are large quantities of gerkins growing there. The *Palma Christi* is also found there; it grows to a great height,[5] and yields an excellent oil. No olive trees are mentioned as found there; but, in compensation, there are fig trees in the most flourishing state.

[1] Niebuhr, *Reise*, i. p. 181, Tab. 17 E.
[2] Robinson, *Bibl. Research.* ii. p. 521.
[3] Gadow, *i.a.l.* ii. p. 57.
[4] Robinson, *Bib. Research.* ii. pp. 539, 524.
[5] Hasselquist, *Reise*, p. 555.

The climate[1] is declared by most travellers to be uncommonly sultry and hot even in spring, but in summer to be almost unbearable. Robinson, who was there in the middle of May, found the heat to be 31° Reaum. in his tent, and 26° Reaum. in the shade outside at two o'clock in the afternoon; it was extremely oppressive. In summer the region is very unhealthy, and fever is exceedingly common, particularly among strangers, who exchange the much cooler air of Jerusalem for it. Judging from the appearance of the people who habitually live there, the climate does not appear to produce the most vigorous constitutions.

Yet it appears from Seetzen's[2] narrative that there is a cold and rough season of the year there as well as elsewhere. On the 8th of January he found it rainy at Jericho; strong chilling winds were blowing; and in the tent of Sheikh Achmed, where there was no fire, it was impossible to prevent shivering. His host was clad in a sheep-skin mantle, and an old camel perished with the cold. At this time the first snow fell, certainly not over the plains of the Jordan, but upon all the neighbouring mountains. All the heights of Ajlun, Belka, as far as Karrak, were white to their base, and snow lay upon the mountains of Jerusalem for a few days. The allusion in 2 Sam. xxiii. 20 to the slaying of a lion by Benaiah in Moab during the " time of snow," may, it seems probable, refer to the month of January. During this period the ground becomes so soft in the Jordan valley as to be almost impassable, according to Seetzen; the wadis were full of rushing brooks; and the Jordan itself was so swollen, that the traveller had to wait a week before being able to cross. When Russegger[3] was there in November, the rains had already begun in Syria; and the Jordan was transformed into such a fiercely-rushing stream, as to render the passage across very difficult.

The little district of Riha was, in the year 1847, when Gadow visited it, hired out by the Turkish Government to a private person for the sum of 20,000 piastres yearly, and who, in order to secure this large amount, was obliged to enforce the taxes by means of a body of irregulars, whom he himself sustained. The village was only a heap of wretched huts, lying

---

[1] Robinson, *Bib. Research.* ii. p. 526.
[2] Seetzen, *Zweite Reise zum Todten Meere.*
[3] Russegger, *Reise,* iii. p. 104.

near the confluence of Wadi Kelt and the brook flowing from
Ain es Sultan : towards the south-west it was bordered by a few
gardens, and by dry thorny hedges.   These also bound the south
side of the so-called castle; and some heaps of rubbish and ruins,
which Wilson found more extensive than they had generally
been supposed, but which, according to Gadow,[1] would not
make it clear that the great city of Jericho once stood there.
All that he saw which spoke distinctly of antiquity was a cistern
and a piece of cornice, which may have been brought thither
from some other place ; though it is possible that an examination of the piles of rubbish might bring other objects of interest
to light.   But to discover the character and extent of the
former city, after all the devastations of time, is not possible,
except by a thorough investigation into the character of the
shapeless heaps of the plain.   Even the present village of Riha
hardly remains the same for any successive ten years ; for,
when Wolcott[2] visited the place in 1842, there were scarcely
any traces of it : two years before, Ibrahim Pasha, in withdrawing from Damascus, and being attacked on the Jordan by Arabs,
sent a detachment of his troops to Riha, and caused the village
to be razed to the ground.

The ruined tower or so-called castle, which towers above
the village, revealed in the interior only the deserted lodging-
places of men and cattle, with a little court in front, which
Wilson likened to an Augean stable.   Yet here an aga or
effendi has taken up his abode, and at the time of Robinson's[3]
visit received his guests with a great deal of ceremony, having
put up a temporary roof and spread carpets for his guests.
The reception given to the American was a very singular one.
Near the aga, who seemed to be of Turkish or Albanian origin,
and who was dressed in the most fantastic manner, sat two
Christian captives, who had been arrested in the mountains of
Ajlun for some misdemeanour ; one of them had been sen-
tenced to cut tobacco, the other to pound coffee in a mortar.   The
wild features of the aga promised a rough reception, but the
letter of introduction from the pasha produced a very soothing
effect upon him.   The region in the neighbourhood of Szalt,

[1] Gadow, *i.a.l.* p. 57 ; Wilson, *Lands of the Bible*, ii. p. 7.

[2] S. Wolcott, in *Bibl. Sacra*, 1843, p. 40.

[3] Robinson, *Bib. Research.* ii. pp. 517–520.

Ajlun, and Jerash was quiet, he said, and could be travelled through, though Kerak was in a disturbed state. Around this lord of a few dozen Albanians there stood as silent spectators some chiefs of the Adwan in the Beduin attire, ready to take the field with their followers, and under the aga, against the insurgents of Kerak. The fellahin of the Jericho district, who lived in villages and tilled the land, were so shamefully treated by the aga, that they had deserted their homes and fled to Kerak, where they found protection. The aga had tried to persuade them to return, but had been unable; he was then on the point of resorting to force, and compelling them back, in order that they might be of service in gathering the ripened harvest.

Notwithstanding the truly oriental scene, the coming and going of slaves and women filling their jars at the spring, and the prancing of the horses of the Arabs, the impression made was far from favourable; everything had a dirty and shabby appearance; nothing but the horses were respectable in their looks. It was to this garrison that Molyneux applied for help after the loss of his boat in 1847, but in vain. The sixteen men who could be spared were too indifferent and too inefficient to be of any considerable service.[1]

The castle itself, which is the subject of common admiration among pilgrims as the house of Zaccheus, is a partially ruined tower, some thirty feet square and forty feet high, to whose roof a stone staircase leads, where is a breastwork with three portholes. According to Roberts, the structure was erected by the Saracens; at any rate, it is of modern origin. It lies three-quarters of an hour's distance from the point where Wadi Kelt issues from the mountains, and on its northern side: in the middle of May there is no water in the wadi. From the top of the tower the eye could easily range up the Akaba pass to the heights of Jerusalem, and could discern the fortress between the mountains which Robinson heard called by the name of Kakon. From the same point, too, the whole wadi can be commanded.

The view northward from the top of the old castle takes in the large section in which lies the bare mountain ridge, north of the Wadi Kelt, having its two symmetrical peaks at the extremities, and descending steeply on the eastern side to the plain from which the Ain es Sultan springs. At the northern

[1] Molyneux, *Exped. l.c.* xviii. p. 126.

end of the ridge is the Karantal or Mount Quarantania, with an old chapel on the summit, its steep sides full of caverns, in which hermits and anchorites once lived, but now the lurking-place of countless wild beasts.[1] Here the Jordan valley attains its greatest breadth, it being from three to three and a half hours' distance from the mountains where they recede the farthest from the river, across to the chain known as Jebel Belka. Opposite the ruins of Kakon, which Robinson discovered on the north side of the Akaba road, Gadow discovered similar ones on the south side : commanding the approaches to Jericho as they do, he thought that they were the ancient fortresses of Thrax and Tauros, unless these be identified in the masses of rubbish between Ain es Sultan and the Sugar Mills. Both ruins lie an hour and a half south-west of Ain es Sultan.

The view towards the south-west from the castle extends past the ridge of mountains along the west side of the Dead Sea as far as to Ras el Feshchah, from which a very difficult path may be seen leading up to the Convent of Mar Saba, and another passing by the Weli Neby Musa, the reputed burial-place of Moses among the Mohammedans.

The castle tower which overlooks this instructive panorama, but which is ascended by few travellers, the most contenting themselves with accepting the legend that Zaccheus lived there, is probably indebted for its erection to the age of the crusaders, to serve as a protection for the valuable gardens of queen Melisinda at Jericho. It is first mentioned by Willibrand of Oldenburg[2] in the year 1211; but even then it had been destroyed, and was occupied by the Saracens. A little village was around it, however, and Brocardus, at the time of his visit, found eight houses there, which he thought occupied the site of ancient Jericho. It was only in the fourteenth century that the legend sprang into being that Zaccheus once lived in the castle : Maundeville did not hear it at the time of his visit. Tucher[3] is the first to allude to it, 1479 ; in 1483 Fabri speaks of it again, and states that it was not permitted to pilgrims to enter it. Later travellers have called it the house of Rahab.

---

[1] For an interesting and novel account of explorations in these caves, see Tristram's *Land of Israel*, p. 209, etc.

[2] Robinson, *Bib. Research.* ii. p. 543.

[3] Fabri, *Evagatorium Terr. Sctæ.* ed. Hassler, vol. ii. p. 58.

The recollection of the hospitable reception which the Saviour had at the house of Zaccheus, the chief of the publicans, of the teaching which He imparted there, of the healing of the blind man who sat by the wayside in Jericho, is, in spite of the perishable historical monuments of the place, an imperishable token of His love, and is cherished in every Christian heart (Matt. xx. 29 ; Luke xix. 1–28).

Robinson tells us, that all the search which he instituted near the village and castle in quest of the once splendid city of Jericho, with its circumference of twenty stadia, its arena and amphitheatre, was in vain,[1] though there were some walls and cisterns at the west, near Wadi Kelt. The *Itiner. Burdig.*, written in 333, says that the Jericho of that day lay at the foot of mountains a mile and a half from the spring, but at the same time it transfers the ancient city of Jericho to the spring of Elisha. Robinson discovered a single massive block of syenite or red granite in the neighbourhood of the castle, probably the same object which von Schubert mentions as seen by him. Is it not possible that, in the remains found around the opening of Wadi Kelt, there are the traces of the Jericho of Herod and of the New Testament? And may not the heaps of rubbish found to the south-east have belonged to scattered houses built in the suburbs? It would seem not unlikely that the ancient city lay very near the spring of Gilgal, but that the city, when rebuilt, was placed farther northward, to avoid the curse mentioned in Josh. vi. 26,—perhaps in the neighbourhood of Ain es Sultan. Both sites, remarks Robinson, would coincide with the statement of Josephus, that Jericho was sixty stadia (three hours) from the Jordan.

Gadow,[2] who visited Jericho a second time in company with Dr Wolff, took the greatest pains to discover the topography of Jericho. He says that twenty minutes west of the castle he discovered the remains of an ancient paved road—a *via militaris*—extending from E.S.E. to W.S.W., and running between ancient walls till it approached the Ain es Sultan. The whole space, covered with the foundations of former walls, he estimated to be three-quarters of an hour in circumference. The nearness of the brook along which these remains extend, together

[1] Robinson, *Bib. Research.* ii. p. 526.
[2] Gadow, *i.a.l.* ii. p. 58.

with a large basin which he discovered near the spring at the
N.N.W., twenty-five feet broad and forty long, left no doubt in
his mind that here was the site of the Jericho of Herod, which
could thus be supplied with water both from Ain el Duk and
the Spring of Elisha. On the eastern slope of the neighbouring
mountain he discovered the extensive ruins of a castellated
structure, which may have been the Kypros of Herod, although
some have put that stronghold farther north.

The copious spring Ain es Sultan flows into a basin nine
feet broad, in which many fish may be seen playing. Josephus
says that near Jericho there is a spring which yields water
very abundantly, and which is much used for purposes of
irrigation: this, he says, was near the ancient Jericho which
Joshua took,—an expression which goes far towards enabling
us to determine with some degree of certainty the site of the
ancient city,[1] of which nothing is likely to be known in minute
detail, so great have been the changes wrought by time,
and so many have been the rebuildings and the subsequent de-
stroyings of Jericho from the time of the Israelitish conquest
down.

The detailed history of the changes which have befallen
Jericho during all the stages of its history; its condition at the
time of the Israelitish invasion and after the captivity; its destruction under Pompey and Herod; its rebuilding as a magnificent city of palaces, castles, theatres, and arenas at the time
of Herod, Cleopatra, and Archelaus; its state at the time when
John the Baptist was living near by, and often within its walls;
the destruction effected by Vespasian, and its subsequent rebuilding as a garrison city for the tenth legion, and as the capital of
a toparchy; the establishment of this place as a residence for
Byzantine bishops, and as the seat of *xenodochia*, churches,
and convents, under the reign of the Emperor Justinian; the
visit of Antoninus Martyr thither shortly before the overthrow
of the place by the caliphs; the changes effected under Mohammedans and the Christian crusaders, when the gardens
bloomed anew, churches rose, anchorites swarmed in the neighbourhood, and the oasis gave food to a large population; the
sinking at last into solitude and desert wildness under the
Saracens, Turks, and Beduins;—all this has been fully given

[1] Wilson, *Lands of the Bible*, ii. p. 14.

in the works of Reland, Rosenmüller, Robinson, von Raumer, Winer,[1] and others.

It yet remains to speak of the Ain es Sultan and Mount Quarantania, which lie north of the village of Riha, and which have celebrity among all pilgrims as the Fountain of Elisha and the Mount of Temptation.

A pleasant walk through the foliage and along the brook brings one, says von Schubert,[2] in a little more than half an hour to the mill-stream, which grows broader and stronger every moment. A quarter of an hour's distance from the village are seen the remains of a paved *via Romana,* which can be traced some thirty paces westward to the mountain-pass leading up to Jerusalem : only a fragment, says Robinson,[3] yet constructed exactly like those which are so often met in Italy. It is probably connected with the *via* discovered by Gadow, and already alluded to. The foundations of walls next come into sight, which lead to the fine spring itself among the nebek trees and the wheat-fields. It springs from the earth directly at the eastern base of a little knoll : the water is sweet, clear, and agreeable, neither cold nor warm, but like that found at Engedi and Ras Fesh-chah. The spring was once surrounded by a walled basin, now neglected, from which various channels led the water to various parts of the plain : at the present time the main one of these is the one which runs to the village of Riha. The masses of stone lying in the neighbourhood, Robinson thought, once belonged to a Saracen fortress. When Wilson was there he ascertained the dimensions of the basin to be five paces long, ten paces broad, and a foot deep : the water was like that of other springs which issue from a chalky soil. He saw fishes in the spring from two to six inches in length. The place was overshadowed by a fig tree called Tin es Sultan, taking its name from that of the spring, which in its turn is called the Sultan's, because of its size and importance : it is the same mentioned in connection with Elisha in 2 Kings ii. 19-22. It is the only one which carries fertility over the whole oasis; for although the Dûk spring is larger, yet it is much farther north. Behind the Ain

---

[1] Reland, *Pal.* pp. 829-832 ; Robinson, *Bib. Research.* ii. 548-551 ; von Raumer, *Pal.* pp. 204, 205 ; Rosenmüller, *Bibl. Alterth.* ii. pp. 153-159.

[2] Von Schubert, *Reise,* iii. p. 74.

[3] Robinson, *Bib. Research.* ii. 528 ; Wilson, *Lands of the Bible,* ii. p. 12.

es Sultan rears the steep wall of the Karantal or Quarantania mountain, from whose base springs a new ridge, which runs off towards the north-north-east, and forms a transition between the higher ranges and the low plains. It is in this ridge that the great Dûk spring rises,[1] whose water runs along the base of the Karantal, behind the Ain es Sultan. It formerly supplied the power for the sugar-mills already alluded to, and which still remain.

Still farther north-east than even the Dûk spring, are the remains of the aqueducts already mentioned leading to Nawaimeh. All these relics concur in showing this at least, that, under wise management, and with a security of the whole district from the ravages of predatory savages, the oasis of Jericho could unquestionably resume the paradisaical aspect which it once bore. What is wanted to secure this result is an efficient government, and with the application of labour this result is almost certain.

The present inhabitants of Jericho belong to a race so lazy and feeble, so depressed and abandoned, that no bright future is to be expected for them. Robinson reckons them among the inhabitants of the Ghor, whom I have spoken of on another page as in circumstances equally humiliating. Their village of Riha resembles in its situation some of those to be seen on the most fruitful and arable tracts on the Nile, but it was the most miserable and the most filthy that Robinson saw in all Palestine. The number of men was forty, of the whole population about two hundred. They appeared to him to be a mixed race,[2] a cross between Beduins and Hudhri or Arabs, who have settled there, lazy, too weak to work, vicious in their way of living, the women given to dissolute conduct with strangers and with the garrison; on the whole, a curse-laden people, perpetuating the life and manners of Sodom and Gomorrah to the present time. Gadow says that the inhabitants of Riha are very swarthy,[3] have woolly hair, are weak in their bodies, have effeminate features, and are strongly inclined to melancholy and to weariness of life. They exhibit the greatest contrast to the restless Beduins. In the time of Fabri the inhabitants of

---

[1] Robinson, *Bib. Research.* ii. p. 530.

[2] *Ibid.* pp. 523–525.

[3] Gadow, *i.a.l.* ii. p. 57.

Jericho used to occasion great trouble to the caravans by their attacks upon them. They were of a dark-brown colour, ho says, powerful and wild, the women as well as the men, so that by their appearance it was difficult to distinguish between the sexes. The mixed garrisons of the castle, composed of Mogrebi, Turks, Albanians, Egyptians, and Arabs of various tribes, have probably contributed somewhat to bring the population of Jericho into its present state.

At Jericho Robinson[1] became acquainted with the three roads which lead thence north-westward to Beitin, the ancient Bethel, Taiyibeh, the ancient Ophra, Deir Dibwan, and to Ai, where the road running northward from Jerusalem attains its greatest elevation. The shortest of these runs along the edge of the crags between Quarantania and Wadi Kelt, and takes a direct course through high though shelving land. The second runs to Dûk, and then by way of Nawaimeh directly to Taiyibeh: near to Rummon it branches, and sends a by-road through a valley to Deir Dibwan. The third route leaves the last directly above Dûk, and runs across into the first. Of these three, the first one is the most direct and the easiest, and according to Robinson, without any question that ancient road so often taken by kings and prophets; for example, by Samuel on his way to Gibeah of Benjamin (1 Sam. xiii. 15), and by Elijah and Elisha when they went to Bethel, and met the fifty sons of prophets who went back with them to the Jordan and witnessed the ascension of Elijah. In order to trace the Old Testament roads, Robinson not only passed through this most direct of the three roads, but also passed up as far as the Dûk spring, and took the cross path of which I have just spoken.

About a quarter of an hour north of the Ain es Sultan, and close by the sloping side of Mount Quarantania,[2] lie the massive ruins through which the water of the Dûk spring runs, and which have been repeatedly mentioned in these pages under the name of the Sugar Mill. Behind these remains tower the almost perpendicular wall of the Karantal or Quarantania, twelve to fifteen hundred feet above the plain. This is the

---

[1] Robinson, *Bib. Research.* ii. p. 557 ; comp. Olshausen's *Rec.* in *Wien Jahrb. i.a.l.* p. 151.

[2] Robinson, *Bib. Research.* i. p. 567 ; Wilson, *Lands, etc.,* ii. p. 12 ; Gadow, *i.a.l.* p. 58.

Mons tentationis of the pilgrims. Its eastern face is full of
caves once inhabited by anchorites; and still it is said that
every year three or four Ethiopian Christians come hither in
order to spend the time of fasting upon these mountains, and
live only upon what grows wild there. Seldom, says Wilson,
is the chapel which stands upon this summit visited; and so
little disturbed by man is it, that Gadow was surprised at seeing
the jackals running around in the open daylight, whereas they
usually issue from their holes only in the night. North of the
Karantal the mountains withdraw from the river in a circle,
and come in direct proximity with the plain lying a little higher
than that of Jericho, and abundantly watered from the Dûk
spring and those of Nawaimeh. The legend of the *Mons tentationis* and the name Quarantania (or forty days) seemed to
Robinson to be not more ancient than the time of the Crusades.
The first mention of this as the place of the Saviour's temptation
is in Saewulf in the year 1103: " Inde ascenditur ad montem
excelsum, ad locum ubi Dominus jejunavit quadriginta dies, et
ubi postea tentabitur a Sathana,"[1] etc. The name Quarantania
first occurs in 1211, in Willebrand of Oldenburg, then in
Brocardus. J. de Vitrico speaks of many hermits who had
followed Christ's example, and after baptizing in the Jordan
fasted forty days in the wilderness called the Quarantania,
living in holes and cells; but regarding Jesus himself being
tempted there, not a word is said.[2]

Seetzen, who was a long time a guest of the Ehteim Arabs
and the Sheikh Achmed, has given us many interesting details
regarding their mode of life. They were encamped just at the
foot of the Karantal, and numbered ten tents in all.[3] Seetzen
engaged the chief to convoy him along the eastern shore of the
Dead Sea as soon as the waters of the Jordan should subside
so far as to allow the ford to be used. In company with
Achmed, Seetzen crossed the oasis of Jericho in many different
directions, visiting in the course of his walks places as remote
from the encampment as the Dûk Spring. His observations
were amply corroborated by Robinson, who went over the same

---

[1] *Voy. de Saewulf*, ed. d'Avezac.

[2] These caves were visited by Tristram. See his interesting description
in *Land of Israel*, p. 211.

[3] Seetzen, *Zweite Reise zum Todten Meere*, 1807.

ground. Near the spring just mentioned Seetzen found some tents, which were inhabited by negroes. These knew nothing of their origin, and could neither read nor write. There were more sick than well in the whole encampment: eye complaints were very common; so, too, were running sores and a kind of leprosy.

The place of this Arab encampment changed every year; the spot that was in use one year being sown with corn the next. In the encampment there lived a Kurd, a tailor by occupation, and not reckoned as one of the Ehteim; neither could his children be considered true Arabs, but were bought and sold as slaves. This fact seemed to throw some light upon the marked negro physiognomy of the people of Jericho, which had been noticed by many travellers.

The whole of the second week of January Seetzen remained in the camp of Sheikh Achmed, who left all the management of affairs to his wife. His children were running around almost naked, with little more than a sheep-skin thrown over their shoulders. As I just said, the wife had everything to do: she brought the wood, kindled the fire, ground the corn, kneaded the dough, baked the bread, prepared every dish, brought water in a goat-skin from the spring, led the horse to pasture and back again, etc. The only valuable possession of the sheikh, for which he pretended he had paid a thousand piastres, was his horse. His people went almost naked, clothed at most in a blue shirt, and wearing trousers only when they rode on horseback; for the feet they had simply sandals. No trace of religion was to be seen in them: though they had the name of the prophet in their mouth, yet they had no prayer, and no holidays. Though abounding in talk, and in interest in their guests, they had no work to do of any moment. Of Seetzen they expected that he would discover hidden treasure, and heal all their sick. They even believed that he could make himself invisible at pleasure. His little Arabic dictionary was thought at first to be a book of charms, since neither Achmed nor any other of his tribe could read it; but on Seetzen's giving it to a fellah to take care of, the latter discovered it possessed no magic properties, and scornfully spit upon it. The poor tents of these Arabs offer but a very slight protection against the weather, and they last at the longest but five years. These poor people had some skill in dyeing, and out of the materials at their command they secured red, yellow, blue, and green for colours. The mortars in which they pounded their coffee, they made of the wood of the carob tree; while for pestles they used the very hard wood of the thorny suat, which grows on the hills around Jerusalem.

Seetzen took occasion to climb the Karantal, and to visit the chapel high up the side,—a place now not much visited, but once the favourite resort of monks and hermits. His course was up a slight depression beginning at the ruined sugar-mills. In his ascent he discovered a tree, which seemed to him to be the only one of its kind, and called by the Arabs el-Dibbke. It has a short, strong trunk, a very leafy crown, composed of large, round, dark-green, coarse leaves, whose berries were used for making a red dye. The tree is considered sacred. Seetzen broke off a handful of leaves ; but the negro who accompanied him was so incensed at this act, which was sacrilege in his eyes, that he threatened to take his head off for it. The path leading to the convent was narrow and often dangerous, running as it did along the brink of steep precipices, in the sides of which huge caverns could be seen. These were inaccessible to Seetzen, and some of these were said by the Arabs to be the storehouses of immense masses of wealth. At the summit of the mountain stood the convent, made in part of stones fitted together, and in part hewn out of the solid rock. A little chapel, a kitchen, and an empty water cistern, are all that can be seen there at the present time. On the wall of the chapel Seetzen discovered some fresco paintings, the pictures of saints. The legend which places the scene of the forty days of our Lord's temptation here, seems to be the main reason why this place, now surrendered to pigeons and jackals, should have been the resort of anchorites.

The view from this height over the Jordan valley, as seen by Seetzen in the month of January, embraced several places where there was a carpet of beautiful green, and even whole acres of wheat one or two inches high; but the most of the prospect comprised a barren, dreary desert. The village of Riha with its leafy environs occupied but a very little spot compared to the whole plain, and the old ruined tower just by could not be made out at all.

Seetzen did not dare to tarry long upon the narrow but dangerous platform just in front of the little chapel. To ascend higher from that point was impossible, although Sheikh Achmed assured him that from Ain Dûk a pathway led to the top. The Karantal, though certainly a naked, sharply pointed, and steep mountain, is by no means one of the highest of the system to which it belongs, and the line of watershed lies much higher. The animals chiefly found upon it are steinbocks, foxes, jackals, and lizards.

DISCURSION III.

THE ROAD FROM JERICHO TO THE PILGRIMS' BATHING-PLACE—THE FORD OF THE JORDAN, AND THE ENTRANCE OF THE RIVER INTO THE DEAD SEA.

The distance of the village of Riha in a south-east direction to the bathing-place of the Jordan and the Helu ford, is estimated at one and a half to two hours. Upon the road there are some ruins which are thought to indicate the site of the ancient Gilgal; at Ain Hajla and Kasr Hajla, a little farther west, the green disappears, and there follows a bare clay soil covered with saline encrustations, and sloping towards the narrow bed of the Jordan. This is bounded by a dense, indeed almost impenetrable, thicket of bushes, opening only here and there to afford a place for the traveller to get a near view of the water. One of the places where there is a clearing is at the bathing-place of the pilgrims, just below which is the ford Helu.

This road it is which is taken every year by the crowds of pilgrims, once numbering hundreds of thousands, but now so reduced, that in 1847 Gadow reckoned only three thousand five hundred. The journey from the camp at Riha to the bathing-place is usually made in the early hours of the morning by torch-light. The most of the company hurry on together, with faces lit up in eager curiosity and expectation, anxious to reach the place where they may wash away their sins. Those who linger behind often become the prey of the Beduins, who in uncounted numbers lurk all along the way, ready to attack any unwary traveller.[1] The river too, as well as the road, demands its victims, and hardly a year passes but some are carried away by the rapid stream, and perish. The bright fresh green of the

---

[1] Fel. Fabri, *Evagatorium*, ed. Hassler, vol. ii. : *De balneatione peregrinorum in Jordane, et de tribus prohibitionis eis datis, etc.*, fol. 36-54.

luxuriant bushes which follow the river in all its windings, and remind the spectator of a colossal snake; the waving and rustling sedge which also accompanies the whole course of the river; the curious path of the stream itself, between banks which have only the sparse vegetation to show as an exception to the desert alongside;—all this, taken in connection with the recollection of the eternal truths once proclaimed upon the shore of the Jordan, exercise an irresistible charm upon the representatives of the most diverse nationalities whom the sacred river brings together—Russians, Servians, Bulgarians, Greeks, Armenians, Georgians, and Circassians.[1]

This miscellaneous multitude of people, many of them half-naked, plunges into the river amid songs and cries so discordant and wild, as to make upon the thoughtful observer rather the impression of a bacchanalian revel[2] than of an act of Christian worship. I refer the reader to the works of several tourists for a picturesque account[3] of this scene. The ford is just below the bathing-place, if I may use a rather indefinite way of describing it; for the division of the church into sects is seen even here, and each has its own place, regarding which it stubbornly asserts that it was the spot where John baptized the Saviour.

As early as the time of Jerome, many were accustomed to expect the spiritual new birth in the waters of the Jordan, ascribing special efficacy to this stream. Even Josephus speaks of the great advantage of a purification in this river, and traces it to the long pause of the priests in the bed of the Jordan while the people passed over, as recounted in Josh. iii. 17. We see the same thing in the time of Elisha, when the leprous Naaman was directed to bathe seven times in the Jordan,—an injunction involving two elements—improved personal cleanliness, and the peculiar efficacy of this stream. This same impression received a higher and spiritual significance when John used the waters of the Jordan as a type of the washing of regeneration, and set it in contrast with the fire baptism of the Holy Ghost (Matt. iii. 11).

[1] Legh, *Narrative by MacMichael, i.a.l.* p. 191.
[2] Gadow, *i.a.l.* p. 60.
[3] Turner, *Journal, etc.,* vol. ii. pp. 214-226 ; Vere Monro, *A Summer Ramble in Syria,* vol. i. pp. 129-144 ; Roberts, vol. vi. Plate 17.

Antoninus Martyr, who visited this spot about the end of the sixth century, before the Moslem invasion, says, in concurrence with Beda Venerabilis and Willibald, that both shores of the Jordan, being regarded as consecrated ground, were paved with marble. In the middle of the stream, where a great wooden cross was erected (mentioned also by Arculfus about the year 700), there used to stand a priest to bless the water. The Alexandrian Christians, remarks Antoninus, used to throw balsam and spices into it, and sprinkled their ships on their return with Jordan water. All the pilgrims went into the water, each clad in a linen garment, which was carefully preserved ever after to serve as a shroud. Thus it seems that the old ceremony known in Egypt as the " paying of homage to the Nile" was transferred from that country and its great river to Palestine and the Jordan. Antoninus Martyr discovered here several cells, and the extensive Convent of John the Baptist, built by the Empress Helena near the ford of the Jordan. Quaresmius says that in his time traces of these were still to be seen. The accounts of the pilgrims have given full particulars of the many changes which have occurred at the bathing-place of the Jordan during the lapse of time ; but it is equally clear from the same records, that the pilgrimages which were taken in the name of religion were of no spiritual advantage to those who made them, and that the effect was always unhappy. Jacob. de Vitriaco, bishop of Acre, says in 1220 : " turba et tumultus hominum plerumque sunt religioni impedimenta." Although the number of the pilgrims has fallen off extremely since the sway of the Saracens and the Turks began, yet it remains considerable up to the present day. Seldom does a year pass when some are not found in the company from the distant heights of Abyssinia.

The fourth Gospel (i. 28) terms the place where John baptized " Bethabara beyond Jordan," consequently on the east side ; the site of the Convent of John the Baptist, on the other hand, was on the west side. In the narratives of Matthew (iii. 1), Mark (i. 4), and of Luke, the expression is general, " the wilderness of Jordan." In the older manuscripts, in the place of this expression occurs the word Bethany, which, in consequence of such a place being unknown there, Origen took the liberty to change to Bethabara. As the name Bethany, according to Lücke, indicates a navigable place (*locus navis, locus ubi navi trajicitur*), and Bethabara also indicates a place where a passage can be effected, the tradition of the Convent of John is probably not without a foundation, since we know from many passages that the Baptist preached on both sides of the river.[1] Bethabara seems to be identical with the Bethbarah of Judg. vii. 24. The place is mentioned by Eusebius and Jerome, but under the name of Libias or Livias. Ptolemy gives its position with exactness, and thereby enables us to judge better than we could otherwise do of the location of Peor and Nebo. This Livias is only mentioned once in Josephus, as a city on the eastern side of the Jordan, sometimes bearing the name Medaba.

Among the many early convents in the plain of Jericho and on the Jordan which Bernard discovered here in the ninth century, the one above mentioned, named in honour of John the Baptist, was the most prominent. It must have been standing even before the time of the Emperor Justinian ; for Procopius says that this monarch had a fountain placed in it, and that he also erected another convent, that of *St Panteleemon in eremo Jordanis*, a church in honour of Mary, and a *Xenodochium Jerichuntium*,—all unquestionably in the neighbourhood of that bathing-place. Phocas says in the twelfth century of that Convent of St John, that it had been destroyed by an earthquake, but had been rebuilt by the emperor ; that two others, those of Calamon and Chrysostemus, were standing ; while a fourth, that of St Gerasimus, had been undermined by the waters of the Jordan, and been converted into a ruin. In the fourteenth century, when De Suchem visited the Convent of St John, it was inhabited by Greek monks ; at the end of the fifteenth century, Tucher and von Breydenbach found it in ruins, in which state it has since remained. Felix Fabri[2] says that at the time of the Abbe Zozima it was inhabited by several monks, and that imposing solemnities were celebrated there at the time of Epiphanius. The Patriarch of Jerusalem and the Abbot of Bethlehem used to go down hither with many monks, with clergy, and with a deputation of

[1] Rosenmüller, *Bib. Alterthk.* ii. pp. 35–37.

[2] Fel. Fabri *Evagatorium*, ed. Hassler, vol. ii. pp. 52–54 : *De Ecclesia St Johannis et loci illius sanctitate.*

the laity, and amid songs went to the Jordan: then the Abbot of the Convent of St John entered the stream and dipped the cross in the water, the sick were baptized and made well, and many miracles were performed for the edification of the believing. Fabri says, however, that in his own time the convent was partially destroyed, and the remainder profaned by the presence of Arabs, who occupied it as a kind of stronghold.

From the ford of Helu, Robinson went a few miles up the river, on whose western shore, near the bathing-place of the Latin pilgrims, he discovered the ruins of the Convent of St John, called by the Arabs at the present day el-Yehud,[1] *i.e.* the Jews' Castle. On Robinson's map it is placed on the side of the hypothetical termination of the Wadi Kelt, and identified with the Deir Mâr Yohanna. North of it the sharply-defined outline of the dome-shaped Karn el Sartabeh towers like a bastion. The bathing-place of the Greek pilgrims, at which Legh[2] compares the breadth of the Jordan to the Thames below Oxford, is about an hour's distance below that of the Latins, and consequently lies nearer the ford Helu. As most travellers follow the Greek caravan, which is usually the largest, the position of the more northern bathing-place has not yet been carefully examined by travellers. Seetzen,[3] however, visited it in 1807, and heard the ruins called the Burdj el Yehud, or Jews' Tower, and traced the remnants of a conduit which seemed to have once brought water from Ain es Sultan. The ruins, which seemed to be those of a convent, were entirely untenanted. Little could be seen in a whole state except arches of the foundation walls. The marl hills in the neighbourhood were wholly naked, but strewed with nodular bits of sulphur encrusted with lime, and varying in size from that of a hazelnut to that of a goose egg. He collected some of these, and sent them with other specimens to the museum at Gotha.[4] It is a little uncertain whether this is the place of which Scholtz

---

[1] Robinson, *Bib. Research.* i. p. 536 ; Wilson, *Lands, etc.*, ii. p. 15.

[2] Legh, *Narrative by MacMichael, i.a.l.* p. 191.

[3] Seetzen, *Zweite Reise*, 1807, MS.

[4] These, as well as the large collection of manuscripts made by Seetzen in the East, may still be seen among the treasures, too little known to the world, stored in the old Ducal Palace at Gotha.—ED.

speaks when he says that, long disturbed by the Beduins, it was at last deserted by the monks, who removed to the Convent of St Saba,[1] taking a portion of their library with them. If one leaves the regular pilgrim route running from Riha southward, he encounters here and there remains of former buildings, and traces of aqueducts—tokens, both of them, that a large population was once scattered over the plain, although it is very difficult now to localize their chief settlements. The ruins which lie nearest to Riha display foundation walls made of well-hewn stones. These are a half-hour's distance away. Ten or fifteen minutes farther, on a hill or knoll, there are similar ruins, perhaps of convents which formerly stood on or near the site of the ancient Gilgal.[2] At any rate, this place corresponds with Eusebius' and Jerome's account of the situation of Gilgal, which lay, according to the *Onomasticon*, two Roman miles east of Jericho, and five Roman miles from the Jordan. According to the subsequent statements of Arculfus and Willibald, there stood at Gilgal in the sixth century a great and imposing church, in which pilgrims used to have pointed out to them the twelve stones which were taken out of the Jordan (Josh. iv. 20), six of which leaned against the wall, while the other six lay upon the floor. Brocardus places Gilgal decisively upon the west side of the Jordan, and says that the spring of Elisha flowed by its south side, and that a half-leuca farther south lay the valley of Achor (Josh. vii. 26, xv. 7). Two leucæ east of Jericho lay the Sacellum, built in honour of John the Baptist; two leucæ southward towards the Dead Sea was Beth-hogla, whence to the Jordan was a leuca. The identity of the locality does not appear to be doubtful, when taken in a general way, although it may be a little difficult to determine the special points with entire accuracy, unless the great foundation stones mark the site of that great church which in Arculfus'[3] time was supposed to stand where Gilgal once lay. This church was probably destroyed before the time of the Crusades; and it is probable that the stones contained in it were used in the construction of the aqueducts hard by. According to Josephus, the city Galgala, or rather the camp of Israel

---

[1] Scholtz, *Bibl. Krit. Reise*, Leipsig, p. 144.
[2] Robinson, *Bib. Research.* i. pp. 546–556.
[3] Adamnanus ad Arculf. ed. Mabill. T. ii. fol. 514.

at the time of Joshua (iv. 19), where the city of Galgala was afterwards built, was fifty stadia, or a little more than two hours' distance from Jordan, and ten stadia from Jericho.

This place, lying on the eastern frontier of the territory of Jericho, was the first spot at which, after the passage through the Jordan, Joshua and the Israelites encamped. This took place four days after the celebration of the passover (Josh. iv. 19).

According to the custom of the East, of erecting great stones as historical memorials, as in 1 Sam. vii. 12 and elsewhere, Joshua caused twelve stones which had been taken out of the bed of the Jordan, where the people passed through, to be set up at Gilgal. At the time when this was done, he gave the injunction that this should be a perpetual memorial, to be sacredly preserved through successive generations (Josh. iv. 20-24). The high religious significance of this locality gained new force by the celebration of the first passover, and the rite of circumcision which had taken place since leaving Egypt; for here in Gilgal, all who had been born in the wilderness were circumcised (Josh. v. 1-12),[1] and the people brought anew under covenant relations with Jehovah. At Gilgal, too, they ceased to be fed with manna, and from that time ate of the corn of Canaan (Josh. v. 12). They had entered the most fruitful tract of the land, and soon became masters of the stronghold of Jericho itself, the key to the whole country.

The recollection of such scenes hallowed the ground for Israel; and there it was that the school of the prophets arose who trained the people to more loyalty to God, their kings and prophets, and inspired them with a greater affection for their native land. All this conspired to make the place one of the greatest interest in the eyes of the Israelites of all times; and Ramah, the home of Samuel (1 Sam. xix. 18-24),[2] Mispeh, Bethel, Gilgal, and the road of the prophets already alluded to, became hallowed places, where now only desolation, robbery, murder, and superstition hold their sway. See 1 Sam. vii. 16, x. 10; 2 Kings iv. 38.

Gilgal seems to have become a city subsequently to the time of Joshua. In his day it appears to have only been the

---

[1] Keil, *Comment. zu Josua*, pp. 54-78.
[2] Shwebel Mieg, *Über Prophetenschulen*, MS.

camping ground of Israel (Josh. ix. 6, x. 6, 15). Here the
tabernacle remained till it was transferred to Shiloh (Josh.
xviii. 1); here Samuel judged and sacrificed; and here the
ground remained hallowed till the time when John the Baptist
began those labours which never extended beyond the valley of
the Jordan.[1]

Leaving the probable site of the ancient Gilgal, and advancing southward along the pilgrims' route to the Jordan, an
hour and a quarter brings us to the spring Ain Hajla,[2] in a
small and well-watered grove. The spring is five feet in circumference, is walled up, and pours forth a profusion of water.
Robinson was surprised that no one had mentioned this spring
before himself, since it is considered by the Arabs the finest
in the whole Ghor. There were no ruins in the immediate
vicinity; but twenty minutes towards the south-west he saw
the tower of Kasr Hajla, which Gadow subsequently visited,
and declared to be the ruins of a convent. He found massive
arches still standing, and walls covered with pictures of saints.
A row of dune-like hills extends from this point southward to
the Dead Sea, and is termed very characteristically by the
Beduins Katar Hhadije, *i.e.* a row of camels tied together.
A deep wadi bounds this, through which a part of the plain
on the north coast of the Dead Sea can be perceived. It was
here that Gadow and Wolf discovered six walled canals, which
give unmistakeable evidence of the fertility of the plain.[3]

Robinson and Wilson both recognised in the name Hajla
the ancient Canaanitish city Beth-hogla, which is alluded to in
Josh. xv. 6, 7 : " And the border went up to Beth-hogla, and
passed along by the north of Beth-arabah ; and the border
went up to the stone of Bohan, the son of Reuben. And the
border went up to Debir, from the valley of Achor, and so
northward, looking toward Gilgal, that is before the going up
to Adummim, which is on the south side of the river : and the
border passed toward the waters of En-shemesh, and the goings
out thereof were at En-rogel." The place itself lay within the
territory of Benjamin, and took the first place after Jericho in

---

[1] Gross, Notes to Schultz, in *Zeitsch. d. deutsch. Morgenl. Gesell.* iii.
p. 56.

[2] Robinson, *Bib. Research.* i. pp. 544, 545 ; Tristram, p. 221.

[3] *Ibid.* p. 545 ; Wilson, *Lands, etc.*, ii. p. 15.

the list of the cities of that tribe (Josh. xviii. 21). The springs retain in the East their ancient names the longest, and we have an instance of this tenacity in the case before us. Jerome mentions the thrashing-floor of Atad as the place where Joseph and his brothers, according to Gen. l. 7–13, accompanied by the whole court of Pharaoh with chariots and horsemen, mourned seven days after crossing the Jordan on their way to the family burial-place in Mamre. The locality of this interesting spot Jerome declares to be identical with the place which in his day was called Beth-hagla, three miles from Jericho and two from the Jordan; the name signifies the place of weeping. But when he adds that it is a *locus trans Jordanem*, this contradicts his own statement regarding the distance, and an error which arises from neglecting the account in Genesis just quoted, particularly ver. 11, where the place where the Egyptians mourned for so long a time is expressly said to be at the farther side, *i.e.* on the west bank, of the Jordan. The meagre account of this place in Eusebius makes it probable that the error was not originally made by Jerome, but by a corrupted gloss. The name Beth-hagla, according to Jerome, is one not so entirely unknown, although it is but seldom met, since Eugesippus and Brocardus speak of it as two leucæ south-west of Jericho. Breydenbach names the place, although Fabri does not; since then, however, it has been looked for with care. Robinson leaves undecided to what convent Kasr Hajla belonged, and simply remarks that in the year 1522 it was occupied for a season, according to B. de Salignac, by monks of the order of St Basilius, and yet that it was known among the Latins as the Convent of St Jerome, probably in vague commemoration of the anchoritic life of that ecclesiastic in the adjacent desert. Quaresmius, who did not personally visit this spot, but followed the accounts of Adrichomius and Bonifacius, calls it Vasta Divi Hieronymi Solitudo, and alludes to the existence of a monastery of great extent there. Von Tuchern calls it the Convent of St Jerome, perhaps because the walls may have been covered with paintings commemorative of his long sojourn in this neighbourhood. Even in Seetzen's time the variegated colours of these walls were in a good state of preservation. The position of these ruins Robinson was able to see as far off as Usdum, at the southern extremity of the Dead Sea. From Kasr Hajla the view ranges up through the Kuneiterah[1] pass to the Convent of St Saba, a route which was taken by von Schubert. The whole neighbourhood of Ain Hajla was rooted up by countless droves of wild swine ; the ground, too, displayed great numbers of jerboa holes. Everything gave token of the greatest fertility, if only human hands could be induced to apply their skill and energy to the soil.[2]

From the sedgy and wooded neighbourhood of Ain Hajla, three-quarters of an hour brings one over a sterile tract encrusted with salt to the Helu ford of the Jordan, below the bathing-place of the pilgrims. According to Gadow, the direct distance along the Jordan's banks, from the pilgrims' bathing-place to the mouth of the river, is an hour and a half, and Seetzen[3] estimated that it was equally far from Kasr Hajla to the Dead Sea. At the time of his visit the waters of the Jordan were very much swollen, so much so that it was impossible for him to cross for days. He saw logs borne down the stream, and concluded that those which are seen on the shores of the Dead Sea are the result of these spring freshets. Seetzen also visited the sulphur hills which lay a half hour's distance southward, finding them destitute of vegetation, and abounding in nodules of sulphur encrusted with lime: they are administered by the Arabs to their sheep and camels, and are also used in the preparation of their gunpowder. Abulfeda speaks of the "sulphur mines" near Jericho, and says that they are the only ones of their kind in all Palestine.

In the middle of January 1807, Seetzen ventured, after several days of waiting, to cross the Jordan at the ford which he calls el-Möcktaa, in his judgment the same by which Joshua and the Israelites crossed. It appears to be the same which Robinson calls the Helu ford. About a half-hour's distance north of the place where the Jordan enters the Dead Sea, Seetzen discovered the Nahr Husbân, the river of Heshbon. On the shore of the Jordan he found a large amount of sedge growing, of a variety unknown to him, but resembling the *Arundo donax* which he had seen on the west side, though

---

[1] Von Schubert, *Reise*, iii. p. 94 ; Robinson, *Bib. Research.* i. 549.

[2] Robinson, *Bib. Research.* i. 544 ; Gadow, *i.a.l.* ii. p. 60.

[3] Seetzen, *Zweite Reise zum Todten Meere.*

with a stem not quite so stout. It was not hollow, but filled
with a porous marrow; the leaves were narrow, yellowish-
brown, inclining towards red. It is probably the same kind
which Wilson[1] saw on the west side, and which so strongly
reminded him of a plant very familiarly known to him when in
India. Seetzen also saw wild sugar-cane growing, and the
Agnus castus. Here he began his pilgrimage along the east
course of the Dead Sea, to which I shall allude further in
subsequent pages. We now turn back to the western shore of
the Jordan. Here, in a district where Wilson saw many plants
and heard the notes of many birds which reminded him of
India, von Schubert[2] was struck with the same resemblance
to what he had known in central Europe.[3] He saw the poplar
and the willow, and heard the familiar notes of the nightingale.
Of the Jordan, Schubert says that it is no Nile, whatever the
poets may say of it; its glory and honour are of a very different
sort. Its inundations, and the natural fertility of its borders,
have induced a comparison between it and the great Egyptian
river, and yet according to the German traveller there is no
analogy between them. The Jordan was at this point, when
he was here, but a hundred feet broad, or only about a thirteenth
part of the width of the Nile at Ghizeh, its depth only about
ten feet; its waters were dark, rapid, and foaming like a Swiss
stream in the spring.

In proportion to the difficulty in crossing the Jordan in
the winter time, when it is almost impossible for any but the
Beduins to pass from bank to bank, is the ease of crossing
in the summer time, when it may be passed in countless
places. Above Beisan these are very numerous; below they
are less frequent, and yet the Arabs appear to cross[4] with
their flocks and herds, judging from the fact that they are

---

[1] Wilson, *Lands of the Bible,* ii. p. 15.

[2] Von Schubert, *Reise,* iii. p. 80.

[3] Does not this coincidence strikingly confirm that remarkable peculiarity
of Palestine, alluded to more than once by Stanley, that that country was
adapted, as almost no other is, to be the scene of a divine revelation, by the
extraordinary manner in which it unites the productions of various climates
and the characteristics of all the zones, and thus becomes fitted to be an
intelligible medium of conveying spiritual imagery to all the people of the
earth?—ED.

[4] Burckhardt, *Trav.* p. 345.

found as often on the west as on the east bank of the river. In July, when Burckhardt passed over the Jordan at Sukkat,[1] where it was eighty paces wide, it was only three feet deep. When Irby and Mangles[2] crossed at the same ford, on the 13th of March, it was about a hundred and forty feet wide; the water ran with much force, and reached up to the girth of the horses. When, twelve days later, they crossed by a ford yet more to the south, which they erroneously considered to be that of Gilgal, the Jordan was to their amazement so swollen, that the horses only reached the other side by swimming, and all the goods were wet through. Buckingham[3] and Banks found a ford two hours north of Jericho, and near the Wadi Fasail, where the breadth of the stream on the 29th of January was twenty-five yards.

Uniform as the character of the Jordan valley is, yet the stages of water in the river are extremely fluctuating and irregular. The comparison which has been made by Reland[4] between the swellings of the Jordan and the periodic floods of the Nile and the Euphrates, are not at all warranted by the facts of the case, and arise from an incorrect interpretation of certain passages of Scripture. These passages, however, such as Josh. iii. 15, referring to the state of the river before the Israelites crossed, 1 Chron. xii. 15 (since the Jordan in the first moon was full to the top of its banks), and Ecclus. xxiv. 36, "like the Euphrates when it is great, and like the Jordan in the time of harvest," allude to the river merely at the time when the wheat and barley are ripe, occurring in former days as now, in April and the opening of May. This spring inundation is not at all to be compared to the annual inundation of the Nile, which indeed could hardly be possible in the Jordan, with its banks ranging from fifty to sixty feet high. Besides, there are not the same sources which could supply the vast amount of water that sweeps down from the Abyssinian snowy mountain land, when the tropical rains of summer unite their own abundance with that of the melted ice masses. The rains which fall in Palestine in November and December are not continuous,

---

[1] Burckhardt, *Trav.* p. 345.
[2] Irby and Mangles, *Trav.* pp. 304, 326.
[3] Buckingham, *Trav. in Pal.* ii. pp. 85-92.
[4] Robinson, *Bib. Research.* i. p. 540 ; Wilson, *Lands, etc.,* ii. p. 18.

but intermittent, and the snow waters of Hermon are soon lost, distributing their waters with all the less tumultuous and destructive violence in consequence of the equalizing influence of Lakes el Huleh and Tiberias. The western tributaries of the Jordan, and in still larger measure the eastern ones, are left nearly if not entirely dry.

There are no allusions to bridges, ferries, or boats as having been used for crossing the Jordan in ancient times,[1] although the transit by fording must have often been effected under great difficulties, and yet must have been a thing of frequent occurrence. How important these passages were in their connection with the history of Israel, may be seen by referring to many passages in the Bible, where, although fords are not referred to so specifically as to be recognised at the present day, yet they are mentioned as involving the fact that the Jordan was repeatedly crossed. Instances of this may be found in Josh. ii. 7, Judg. iii. 28, 2 Sam. ii. 29, x. 17, xvii. 22, 24, not to speak of the allusions in chap. xix.

Aside from the miraculous piling up of the waters of this river at the time of Joshua's crossing, the bed of the Jordan is sometimes filled even now to the top of its banks. That this has been the case at all times, is manifest from Jer. xlix. 19. The rapid risings of this river are alluded to also in Jer. xii. 5, " If in the land of peace, wherein thou trustedst, they wearied thee, then how wilt thou do in the swelling of Jordan ? " We have a proof, too, that the same thick growth of wood which now accompanies the course of the stream, was there at the time of Elisha ; for in 2 Kings vi. 2–5 we have the account of the axe which fell into the water while one was chopping there. The same dark disagreeable colour which is marked now was seen then, and is hinted at in the preference given by Naaman to the clear water of Abana and Pharpar to that of Jordan, as recounted in 2 Kings v. 12. The lower course of the river is muddy, and deposits, when allowed to stand still, a palpable sediment, while its upper course is clear.

At the ford of Helu,[2] south of the bathing-place, and the last in the river before it enters the Dead Sea, Robinson found the current quiet but rapid on the 12th of May, the

---

[1] Excepting one in 2 Sam. xix. 18.—ED.
[2] Robinson, *Bib. Researches,* i. pp. 535–537.

time of his visit. It was easily accessible, the water clayey,
sweet, pleasant, and refreshing, in comparison with those of
Engadi on the west coast of the Dead Sea. The breadth of the
river he estimated at from eighty to a hundred feet, the depth
from ten to twelve. He waded out into the water about twelve
feet, finding a muddy bottom and a depth of about three feet;
then the bottom ceased at once, and he was obliged to swim,
as were all the beasts of burden. Away at the right he could
see a mountain chain extending towards the territory of Moab,
and forming the farther boundary of the plain, which was
about an hour in width, and which was covered with bushes
as far as to the base of the ridge. North-eastward, Robinson
could see Wadi esh Shaib, opposite Jericho, and the heights
of Szalt. At the north towered the conspicuous cone of Karn
Sartabeh.

The upper banks of the Jordan were here not more than
five hundred feet apart : from them there was a descent of
fifty or sixty feet to the bed of the river. The vegetation was
found to be much less abundant than it had been higher up the
stream, and it was observed to diminish as it approached the
Dead Sea, until at length every trace disappeared, except some
saline and alkaline plants (the *Hubeibeh* of the Arabs, and the
Salicornia of von Schubert) : the former waving surface gave
place to one perfectly horizontal, the soil being permeated with
salts. Russegger[1] ascribes this to former extension of the sea
over a much larger tract than it now embraces. So deceptive
is the soil here, that the footstep often settles into it up to the
ankles. Russegger found that the difference of elevation
between Riha and the pilgrims' bathing-place was not much
less than six hundred feet, and the general accuracy of his
barometrical observations gives his estimate a high degree of
value.

Russegger, von Schubert, and Gadow[2] found the distance
from the bathing-place to the Dead Sea an hour and a
half, though Wilson,[3] who followed the line of the river as
closely as possible, found it only an hour and a quarter. The

---

[1] Russegger, *Reise*, iii. pp. 105, 253.

[2] Russegger, *Reise*, iii. p. 106 ; von Schubert, *Reise*, iii. p. 84 ; Gadow,
ii. p. 60.

[3] Wilson, *Lands of the Bible*, ii. p. 20.

breadth of the stream does not change much up to the place where it divides into two arms before entering the sea. The low ranges of hills follow both banks as above, nearer the left one than the right one, however. The Jordan must receive large accessions of water in the winter at this point, for there are abundant traces of brooks there. Gadow, at the time of his visit at the end of March, found many tracks of wild beasts which had come down from the hills to drink. On the east side of the river was to be distinctly seen the opening through which the waters of Wadi Heshbon pour into the Jordan.

We have now come to the place where the eye first rests upon the broad expanse[1] of the Dead Sea, but the sight is often dazzled by the glare reflected from the sand. Sometimes there is a thick haze resting over the scene, the result of the exhalations which arise from the waters; but sometimes the atmosphere is so clear, that the view ranges from the pillar of Usdum northward to Kasr Hajla.

Gadow asserts, that where the Jordan enters the Dead Sea it divides into two arms, enclosing a small delta; its course becomes more sluggish, and finally ceases to have any perceptible motion at all. Pliny noticed this peculiarity, and ascribed it to an unwillingness to pour its sweet waters into the acrid, pestilential sea. The phenomenon is one which illustrates a truth first enforced by Franklin, that rivers always run slowly before entering the ocean, in consequence of the greater specific gravity of sea-water.[2] Herons have been seen wandering around the mouth in search of the fish from the Jordan, who have been strangled at once when carried into the brine of the Dead Sea; and Gadow and Schubert[3] both observed several struggling with death. Russegger, as he approached the shore of the salt lake, saw bits of asphaltum,[4] but no conchylia; the ground, however, was scattered with drift-wood. Hasselquist, too, noticed pieces of asphaltum, which seemed to be thrown up particularly at harvest time; but Wilson[5] found

---

[1] Roberts, *The Holy Land*, vol. vii. Plate 18, Vign. *The Dead Sea*.

[2] Fleming, *Observat.* in *Trans. of the Roy. Soc. of Edin.* vol. viii. 1818, p. 508; Jameson, in *N. Edin. Phil. Journ.* Sept. 1828, p. 341.

[3] Von Schubert, *Reise*, iii. p. 86.

[4] Russegger, *Reise*, iii. p. 106.

[5] Wilson, *The Lands of the Bible*, ii. pp. 21-23.

none, although he saw many sticks impregnated with bitumen, and as black as if they had been burned. They strikingly resembled petrified wood, but kindled quickly. He also found some fresh-water mussels. What struck him most prominently, was an island which he estimated to be about an eighth of an English mile in length, but which he supposed to be no true island, covered with ruins, as Warburton[1] had thought it to be, but a floating mass of bituminous substances. There is no mention of it in Molyneux's account, nor in the unsatisfactory report of the American expedition, published not by the leader Lynch, but by a subordinate member.[2]

As we have now come to the southern extremity of the course of the Jordan, a summary view of the different Beduin tribes inhabiting the Ghor will not be ill-timed. For the materials, allowing such an attempt to be made, I am indebted to the missionary Eli Smith,[3] whose name has often been mentioned in these pages, and who knew this whole country well. There are Arabs who live only a part of the time in the Ghor, encamping there whenever it suits their convenience. The Beduins of the west side are thought to number only about five hundred men; one of their tribes has so thoroughly gone over to the fellah mode of life, that they are scarcely recognised as Beduins, but as mere agricultural labourers. All the Arabs pay tribute to the Syrian government, and are held in subjection; being more easily reached from Hebron, Jerusalem, and Tiberias, than the tribes on the eastern side of the river, who

[1] Warburton, *Crescent and the Cross*, ii. p. 230; cited in Wilson, ii. p. 21.

[2] *Narrative of the late Expedition to the Dead Sea*, from a Diary by E. P. Montague, chap. xxx.-xxxvii. pp. 178-236. Lynch, in his report, however, Am. ed. p. 270, speaks of the place as a gravelly point, with many large stones upon it. He states that it is a peninsula, connected with the main by a low narrow isthmus. When the latter is overflowed, Lynch thinks it unquestionable that the peninsula assumes the appearance of an island. This may perhaps explain the statement that the Jordan enters the Dead Sea by two channels. Tristram states that this island, which, when Lynch was there, divided the channel, is now joined to the plain on the left bank, p. 246.—Ed.

[3] Eli Smith, *On the Tribes of Badawin*, in *Miss. Herald*, 1839, vol. xxxv. p. 87.

are more wild and uncontrollable than even the sons of Edom. They seem to be now, just what the ancient people of Moab were. Some years ago, some of the Arabs on the west side of the river, who were then at peace with those on the east side, were obliged for some offence to the Syrian government to fly and find an asylum in Moab. They were received in a friendly manner; but in the night they were fallen upon by their hosts, in whose tents they were then sleeping, and stripped of all their goods, even of the clothing of their women. This, the robbery of his guests, is the most outrageous offence which a Beduin can commit; and the result was, an irreconcilable animosity between the tribes of the east side and those of the west: one evil result of which has been, that travellers have not been able to pass through the territory of the former.

Smith gives a list of seventeen different tribes which are accustomed to pitch their tents in the Ghor, between Lake Tiberias and the Dead Sea. No one of these lives continually there; they remain on the high land in the summer, and in the winter go down into the valley, on account of the greater warmth there. Nine of those tribes are found on the west side, eight on the east. Some of them are of holy men called Fakirs, who used to be treated with great reverence by all the tribes, and whose acquaintance was of great service in enabling travellers to make their way through the country. This, however, has very much changed within late years. The western tribes do not now seem inclined to commit robberies; some of them are held in subjection, or at least overawed, by those on the east side of the river. Farther north, from the Sea of Gennesaret to Lake Huleh, there are fifteen small tribes, living in black tents, and having small droves of cattle. No one of all these Arabs can read or write, excepting a few sheikhs on the west side of the Dead Sea; they know almost nothing of the Koran; they do not know the prayers enjoined upon Mohammedans; and only an eighth part of them know how to pray at all. Proud of their pure blood and their independence, they consider their ignorance of the arts of reading and writing no reproach, and haughtily answer any one who tries to awaken them to a sense of it, " I am a Bedawy." They never make the pilgrimage to Mecca; they observe only circumcision and fasts ; they divide themselves into sects; and because they know nothing of the Koran, they attach themselves all the more closely to the Wehabi. They are more fanatically disposed towards Christians than towards Mohammedans; they scorn the thought of intermarrying with the latter, believing themselves of royal descent; their etiquette among themselves is like that at the courts of princes, despite the fact that they are clothed in rags. They have four different ways of affirming a thing; but an affirmation must be accompanied with a curse if it is to be accepted as conclusive.

CHAPTER V.

Sec. 8. THE DEPRESSION OF THE DEAD SEA, OR THE ASPHALTIC LAKE:

THE 'Aσφαλτῖτις OF JOSEPHUS ; THE ASPHALTITIS LACUS OF PLINY ; THE BIRKET LUT, LOT'S SEA, AND BAHHERET LUT, OF SEETZEN ; THE BIRKET ZOAR OF EDRISI, ABULFEDA, AND OTHERS.

DISCURSION I.

FLAT NORTHERN SHORE OF THE DEAD SEA, FROM THE MOUTH OF THE JORDAN TO THE FIRST PROMONTORY RAS EL FESHCHAH AND THE MOUTH OF THE KEDRON, AS PORTRAYED BY SEETZEN, RUSSEGGER, VON SCHUBERT, ROBINSON, GADOW, AND WILSON.

HE impression which the first view of the Dead Sea made upon von Schubert[1] was not disagreeable. He was struck with the contour of the shore, which he thought one of the finest in its outline of any that he had ever seen, and not more barren than the coasts of the Red Sea. In some places, particularly on the eastern side, he saw verdure extending down the gorges as far as to the water side. The surface at the time of his visit (the middle of April) was so peaceful and attractive, that some mules rushed into the sea to drink; but no sooner had they tasted the bitter brine, than they hastened out and shook themselves as if in disgust. The heat was oppressive, and seemed to be increased by the weight of the atmosphere in a region so depressed; for if D'Aubuisson's estimate is correct, that three hundred Paris feet elevation or depression are equivalent to a degree north and south on the surface, the heat there must be about that of Cairo or Akaba. At such a place palms ought to flourish, other things being equal, as we know that they once did at Jericho. Directly on the shore von Schubert saw flints of various

[1] Von Schubert, *Reise*, iii. p. 85.

colours, evidently thrown out of the chalk formation of the
adjacent mountain ridge : he also discovered limestone permeated and blackened with bitumen, and masses of asphaltum
thrown up from the sea, but no volcanic rock. The whole
ridge, being of a limestone which was familiar to him at home,
reminded him of the neighbourhood of Lake Como. Some
of the crags on the west shore had an abrupt descent of five
or six hundred feet, and seemed as sharply cut as if they had
been hewn by human hands.

Russegger[1] coincides with von Schubert so far as to admit
that the country around the Dead Sea is not that most oppressive of wildnesses which it has often been represented. He
says that the tract between Suez and Alexandria made a more
disagreeable impression upon him than the neighbourhood of
the Dead Sea. But it must be that the impression made is
one which bears some relation to the country from which the
traveller comes : if he is from Europe, it will be more painful
than if he comes, as Russegger did, from the sands of Libya
and Arabia. To him, many of the stories told about the Dead
Sea seemed like tales which are repeated to amuse children.
Russegger discovered only jurassic, chalk, and alluvial formations in the neighbourhood, no volcanic stone, and asphaltum
in only small quantities. The observations which have been
made, and the generalizations which have been drawn, have
been generally recorded in the works of travellers who have
seen only the northern end of the lake. But this is but a small
fraction of a lake which Russegger estimated to be twenty hours
in length, and whose southernmost point Wilson[2] confesses
that he was unable to discern from the northern shore. The
greatest breadth found at the parallel of Hebron, Russegger
thought to be from four to five hours. The strong south winds
drive the waves vehemently northward, affording, he says, an
imposing spectacle, while the mountains on the eastern side
tower up to a height of about three thousand feet. The waters
of the lake he found to be clear, very salt, and bitter; so strongly
impregnated, indeed, that they produced a very painful sensation when applied to a sore, and an uncomfortable prickling
when brought in contact with the unbroken skin. The spe-

[1] Russegger, *Reise*, iii. pp. 106-109.
[2] Wilson, *Lands of the Bible*, ii. p. 24.

cific gravity of the water he found to be but 1·12, that of the Mediterranean being 1·02, and of the Red Sea 1·03 ; a fact which explains the ease with which bodies float upon the surface, as well as the fact that men bathing in the Dead Sea can hardly dip themselves under. He found among the constituents of the water, nitron, chlorine, sulphurous acid, and bromine.

On the road leading from the mouth of the Jordan along the west coast, and then to the Convent of St Saba, Gadow[1] discovered a large mass of thick trunks of trees lying, all permeated with the brine, and made incombustible. They seemed to him to have lain there for centuries, and to indicate a much greater growth of wood in the neighbourhood of the Dead Sea than now exists. Along the northern shore he did not find an absolute lack of vegetation, but saw a kind of heath, and a variety of thorny, thick-leaved shrubs. Passing a deep wadi, which at the time of his visit (March) was dry, he came to a tract extending far away to the south, and exhibiting not a trace of any green thing—not even of moss. He left this, however, and turned aside to visit the Convent of St Saba, passing near the minaret-like Nebi Musa, which the Mohammedan tradition asserts to have been the burial-place of Moses.

Robinson's[2] course along the Dead Sea was different from that of most travellers, extending from Engaddi northward to the mouth of the Kedron and the promontory of Ras el Feshchah. The lower part of the Kedron valley bears the name of the Wadi en Nar, or "Fire Vale ; " while that portion which is west of the Convent of St Saba is called the Wadi er Rahib, or "Monk's Vale." The channel is a narrow one, between upright chalk cliffs, which seem to be much undermined by the dashing stream ; though at the time of his visit the bed was entirely dry. The Kedron enters the Dead Sea at a cove formed by the Ras el Feshchah, a promontory eight hundred to a thousand feet in height, and not only narrowing the sea at this point, but reducing the limits of the coast to a very narrow strip. The shore line bears away to the east of north, while the mountain range pursues a direction almost due north, withdrawing from the sea. Between the mountains and the coast there is consequently formed a triangular plain, which, though narrow at the southern extremity, gradually

---

[1] Gadow, ii. p. 62. [2] Robinson, *Bib. Research.* i. 532.

enlarges as it advances north. The road leading to it from Ain el Feshchah is less steep than that from Ain Jedi to the coast, though still steep enough to be both disagreeable and perilous. Here is one of the paths which lead from the Convent of Mar Saba to the Jordan. In these wild heights steinbocks are seen, and on the sea-shore wild swine and rabbits. In the cliffs Robinson discovered traces of a stone which seemed to be rich in minerals: it appeared to be a crust, conglomerate in its character, and containing stones of many different kinds. The lower part of the mountain was entirely composed of conglomerate.

An hour and a half brought him to the profuse spring known as Ain el Feshchah, grateful to the eye, but not refreshing to the taste, the waters being strongly brackish and warm. The ground for half an hour was wet and marshy, and overgrown with reeds. The temperature was 23° Reaum., the cliffs from 1000 to 1200 feet in height, and the heat intolerable. Near the spring he saw the ruins of a tower, and a building adjoining it, but was unable to assign any date to them.

Riding on through the reeds, he examined the masses of stone at his feet which had fallen from the cliffs, and found them all to be conglomerate in their composition. He saw the tamarisk and the gharkad, shrubs whose acquaintance he had already made in Arabia. All the bushes which he saw were of great size. In one of them his guides killed a lizard three feet and eight inches in length: the Arabs did not know it, but the Egyptian servants recognised it as an inhabitant of their own country, the *lacerta nilotica* of Hasselquist and Forskal.

As he advanced he found the coast plain constantly increasing in breadth; while the road northward led him past the foot of hills thrown into the most fantastic shapes, and fully confirming a remark of Maundrell, that they looked " as if they had ages ago been lime-kilns."

Three and a half hours after leaving Wadi er Rahib,[1] Robinson reached the place where the north-western coast turns due east. He followed in the latter direction for about half an hour, till it again turns south-eastward, and runs along to the very foot of the mountains on the eastern side of the sea. North of the promontory of Ras el Feshchah, the sea was

[1] Robinson, *Bib. Research.* i. 534.

evidently much narrower than it was south of that point. The northern extremity of the lake did not seem to Wilson[1] to reach a higher parallel than Mount Nebi Musa at the west. The shore was white in many places, and covered with a layer of saltpetre, with here and there bits of sulphur as large as walnuts ; the ground was dry like ashes, and the feet of the horses settled deep in it. Robinson preferred going eastward to the Jordan rather than to go directly north to Jericho. He passed a long succession of thickets, and found the same thick encrustation of salt which he had noticed elsewhere.

DISCURSION II.

EASTERN SHORE OF THE DEAD SEA—SEETZEN'S JOURNEY ALONG THE COAST, PAST WADI SERKA MAEIN (KALLERRHOE), WADI MOJEB (ARNON), AND WADI KERAK TO WADI EL AHSA (ZARED), UP THE GHOR ES SAFIEH, AND AGAIN BACK TO THE JORDAN, IN JAN. 1806 AND JAN. 1807.

It is to Seetzen's bold exploration in the early part of the present century that we owe our first knowledge of the country east of the Dead Sea. What we had regarding that region before his day, was derived from the extremely meagre reports of the Mecca caravans, who, though passing from Damascus through Belka and Kerak, did not come within sight of the sea itself. There was therefore nothing definite known regarding the bitter lake, so interesting in its biblical relations ; and very little respecting the valleys extending eastward from it, covered with villages and ruins, and once the home of the Amorites, the Ammonites, and the Moabites. There was therefore no opportunity of comparing the account in the Scriptures with what is known to have been the character of the country at the time of the Crusades, or with its present condition.

The scanty accounts of Josephus, of Abulfeda, and of a few other writers, all very carefully gathered together by Busching, led to no very satisfactory results in themselves ; and yet they were set, as Gesenius[2] remarks, in an entirely new light when Seetzen had completed his exploration of the east side of the sea. From this time the book of Isaiah received new meaning ;

---

[1] Wilson, *Lands of the Bible*, ii. p. 24.
[2] Gesenius, *Philolol. critischer und histor. Commentar. zum Jesaias*, Pt. i. p. 505.

for although Rau[1] asserts, in 1674, of a certain Daniel, abbot of the Convent St Saba, that he had passed entirely round the Dead Sea, the report which he gives of this tour is so incoherent, and so manifestly fabulous in parts, that it cannot be safely accepted as a guide. The first statements made regarding Seetzen's journey were communicated in letters to von Zach of Gotha,[2] and published in the scientific journal of which he was the editor. His entire route extended from es-Szalt and the Ajlun mountains at the north, along the range east of the Dead Sea, past Wadi Husban, Husban, the upper Arnon, Rabba (Rabbath Moab), and Kerak (Petra Deserti), to Wadi Hössa and the southern extremity of the sea.

This journey hardly touched the district with which we have now more especially to do, and Seetzen was desirous, therefore, of examining without delay the immediate coast of the Dead Sea. Sickness, however, prevented him from undertaking the exploration that year; but we find him in January 1807 making several days' stay at Jericho, waiting for the Jordan to subside so far as to make it prudent for him to cross it, and take advantage of a season of the year which he thought most favourable for investigations in that vicinity. It was an undertaking requiring the greatest boldness and perseverance, the possession of all truly heroic qualities, but it was safely accomplished. In the course of eleven days Seetzen passed along the entire eastern shore of the sea,[3] and retraced his steps in five, examining all the objects of interest, and giving us the first existing map of the region. Among those who followed him in later years were Burckhardt in 1812,[4] Irby and Mangles in 1818,[5] and Legh in the same year.[6] These writers were ignorant to a great extent of what had been accomplished by Seetzen, and their contributions have done much to fill up the gaps which he left open. Mr Banks' work, which would have been a classic on the subject, has never appeared.

---

[1] Robinson, *Bib. Research.* ii. p. 109.

[2] Von Zach, *Mon. Corresp.* vol. xviii. pp. 417–443.

[3] *Ibid.* xxii. pp. 532–551; Bries, *Account of the Countries adjoining Lake Tiberias, the Jordan, and the Dead Sea.*

[4] Burckhardt, *Trav.* pp. 363–378.

[5] Irby and Mangles, *Trav.* pp. 444–478.

[6] Legh, *Route in Syria*, pp. 234–248.

1. *Seetzen's Journey from the Jordan to the southern extremity of the Dead Sea, close to the crags of the eastern shore, made between Jan. 15 and 26, 1806.*[1]

First day. From the Jordan ford past the Szuema, a brook, to the encampment of the Aduan.

The plain extending from the ford to the Szuema brook bears the name of the Ghor el Belka. It forms the southern end of the level eastern margin of the Jordan, and though much less fertile than the northern end, and producing herbage which only camels can eat, is not destitute of game, gazelles and partridges being found there. Half an hour before reaching the brook Seetzen passed the ravine coming in from the east, and bearing the name of the Nahr Husban. At the brook some Beduins who were there demanded money of Seetzen as toll for crossing; and on his refusal to yield to their importunity, they stripped his mantle from him.

Beyond that point he encountered hilly and mountainous country, the stone having an iron colour, being a dark-brown or black sandstone, leading Seetzen to think that it might be the iron mountains mentioned by Josephus. He heard of some ruins which lay, according to the Arabs, two and a half hours south-east of Jericho; but on examining the spot, he could only find heaps of dark, unhewn basaltic rocks, which had no appearance of ever being placed there by man. The first peak, lying close by the sea-shore, and directly in the path of a traveller coming from the north, was called Tur el Hammera, *i.e.* Rock of Asphaltum. Seetzen discovered sandstone at its southern base, and on the northern side a tufa crust, which he thought owed its existence to hot springs once there, many of which he found subsequently as he advanced southward. Notwithstanding what he had heard at Bethlehem of the abundance of asphaltum in the region of the Dead Sea, he found that it was very rare : instances of its being discovered were almost unknown; and in spite of the constant search which he made for it, he saw none in the course of his whole wanderings, and was able to secure a bit only at an apothecary's at Jerusalem.

---

[1] Seetzen, *Zweite Reise zum Todten Meere*, MS.

On the first day of his journey he discovered, in the neighbourhood of the Szuema brook, some wild unfruitful date palms, the sad relics of the ancient culture of the region. Here he turned away to the east, and passing through several valleys and gorges, late in the evening he reached the encampment of Sheikh Nimmer, the father-in-law of his guide Sheikh Achmed. Here upon the high land he passed a very cold night, and was only kept from suffering by surrounding himself with the sheep of the sheikh.

Second day. Resting-day in the camp of the Aduan.

Unfortunately the head of the tribe was absent, a man of forty or fifty years, and of great renown as a poet, having written not far from a hundred odes on love and war. His five wives were there, however, and gave Seetzen a hospitable reception. The custom seems to be general among the rich Beduins of this region, to have several wives. His tribe could put into the field about fifteen hundred men, including horsemen, and had to pay fifteen hundred sheep yearly to the Aga of Damascus. The tribe next south, the Hajaja, numbered a thousand warriors. These Beduins practise agriculture to a certain extent, and live on neighbourly terms with the Greek Christians of Szalt at the north of them, and at Kerak at the south. Indeed, so kindly was the feeling at the time of Seetzen's visit, that Sheikh Achmed advised him to adopt the dress of a Greek monk of Jerusalem, and to travel in that garb, which he did.

(2.) *The second day of actual progress. From the encampment of the Aduan to the upper part of Wadi Serka Maein. Discovery of Mkaur (Machaerus).*

Seetzen inquired carefully of his Arab guides if they knew the location of Machaerus, a place mentioned by Josephus. They spoke, in reply, of several ruins in the neighbourhood, giving their names, among which he noticed that of Mkaur, which he at once conjectured to be the one which he sought. Further inquiry confirmed his suspicion. The ruins are important ; they have but a single approach leading over a bridge. He had the year before suspected that the ancient Machaerus[1]

[1] Seetzen, *Mon. Corresp.* xviii. p. 431.

lay where he now found it to be, but had been unable to confirm his conjecture. The ruins lie on the highest peak of a long ridge, the lower extremity of which towers above the deep rocky valley of Serka Maein. Large hewn stones were still to be seen. The mountain was inaccessible on three sides. It is not at all improbable that the place is the square ruin seen by Irby and Mangles[1] while on their way from Maein, but which it was beyond their power to reach. In descending westward from Mkaur, Seetzen encountered a large tract of lava, red, brown, and black in colour, but very porous and light. Still farther down he saw black masses of basalt, resting on a foundation of limestone, visible only in the bed of the stream which ran through the valley. From this place Seetzen went an hour farther along the southern side of the mountains, to spend the night at a little village of the Beni Hameide, a small tribe, which gave him a hospitable reception.

(3.) *Third day of actual progress. Seetzen's discovery of the hot springs in the lower valley of Wadi Serka Maein. Later discovery of the coast from the mouth of the Arnon past Callirrhoe to the mouth of Wadi Maein. Irby and Mangles' visit to the hot springs and the steam baths in Serka Maein, Jan.* 10, 1818.

After a very cold night, Seetzen hastened, under the protection of two guides of the village, down to the lower course of the Serka Maein valley. A path scarcely discernible, but called in all seriousness the Emperor's Road, led down ; below it became broader, but remained very difficult, and at last so steep that it was necessary to leave the horses behind. Seetzen found that he was leaving the pure limestone region, and coming to one which showed clear traces of volcanic action— lava of various colours, porous and light, through which ran a brook of such dimensions that he could scarcely wade through it. Its bed was thickly overgrown with sedge, and overshadowed with willows and poplars. Here he discovered some hot springs breaking forth from the rocks, and flowing into the waters of the Serka. The stone which bounded the brook on the north side was a brownish red and very soft sandstone. A little farther down the valley he encountered two larger

[1] Irby and Mangles, *Trav.* p. 405 ; Legh, *Route, etc.*, p. 243.

springs, having a very strong smell of sulphur. The heat of the water was not up to the boiling point, yet it was unendurable to the hand: Seetzen thought it hot enough to cook eggs. Besides the scirpus which grew around it, and which was carried to Jerusalem to make carpets of, the variegated sedge which was found in great profusion, and some wild date palms, there were a few large trees known as the Phistuk el ban (perhaps the pistachio) growing in the deep narrow ravine, whose sides rose steeply, displaying basalt at the top. Here the ground seemed to Seetzen to have smoked and steamed since the time when Sodom and Gomorrah perished; and he quotes in support of this position the book of Wisdom x. 7. Two hours north of these hot springs he heard of the existence of important alum pits ; but though he was told that they would well recompense the labour of working them, yet the way up was so difficult, that Seetzen did not examine the place.

Here, then, or at a place subsequently visited, and a half-hour's distance farther south, Seetzen concluded that he had discovered the site of the baths of Callirrhoe, celebrated among the Greeks and Romans, and mentioned by Josephus in connection with Herod the Great, who went thither from Jericho, and spent a few days, hoping to avert the hand of death. It was in vain, however; and he returned to Jericho to die. Josephus says of the waters of these springs, that they were drinkable, and that they flowed into the Asphaltite Sea. Pliny, alluding to them also, mentions that they as well as Machaerus lay on the east side of the Dead Sea : " eodem latere (ubi Machaerus) est calidus fons medicæ salubritatis Callirrhoe, aquaram gloriam ipso nomine præferense." Ptolemy also speaks of these spings as lying at 31° 10′ lat. and 67° 6′ long., but discriminates between them and those of Libias, lying more towards the north-east, and which were often confounded with those of Callirrhoe. We are told distinctly by Jerome in his note on Gen. x. 19, that this Callirrhoe was the ancient Mosaic city of Lasha (a different place from Laish, the subsequent Dan on the Sidonian frontier, already alluded to) : " Lisa quæ nunc Callirrhoe dicitur,[1] ubi aquæ calidæ prorumpentes in mare mortuum defluunt."

It was not till his return from the southern part of the

---

[1] H. Reland, *Pal.* p. 871, *s.v. Lascha.*

Dead Sea that Seetzen explored the southern part of Serka Maein, and discovered other springs which seemed to him to indicate the site of Callirrhoe with more probability than those just described. Here he found a place where there was a better opportunity for such a city to have lain, such as the bathing-place alluded to by Josephus must have been, than could have been offered by the narrow defile where the other baths lay. For convenience sake, I will quote his description in this place.

Passing from his encampment at the mouth of the Arnon on the morning of the 28th of January 1807, he found his way with great difficulty to the shore of the Dead Sea, and then followed a very rough path, beset with precipices, and passing scarcely a single trace of verdure till he came to the traces of springy land. The land then began to be covered with sedge and stringy plants, some of them growing to the height of thirty to forty feet, and testifying to the extraordinary influence of the tropical heat acting on a moist soil. In the wild deep gorges he also espied trunkless palms, willows, and tamarisks growing. Thicker and thicker these became as he advanced northward, until he came to a spring of clear, cold, and excellent water, which slaked the thirst caused by his simple breakfast of bread and salt. Half an hour farther on he encountered a small brook, and still a quarter of an hour farther on a larger one, which murmured delightfully as it ran onward, shadowed over by mimosæ, to the sęa. His course led him on past brook after brook, till he came to a place where the mountains, which had thus far followed the shore closely, receded, and left an amphitheatrical opening—a small, fertile plain, an hour long, a half-hour broad, sown by the Aduan Beduins with wheat, barley, and durra. Here he discovered a large brook, the water of ' which was hot. This spring forms the outlet, his guides told him, of three springs a half-hour's distance farther from the sea, two of which are so hot as to be unbearable to the hand. The Arabs said, besides, that there were ruins also there, bearing the name Sara. Seetzen was inclined to think that these indicate the site of the "Zareth-shahar in the mount of the valley," mentioned in Josh. xiii. 19, and connected with Aroer on the Arnon, Medeba, Heshbon, Jahaza, Kedemoth, Mephaath, Kirjathaim,

Sibmah, and other places, followed (ver. 20) by Beth-peor, the brooks of Pisgah (probably alluding to the many which Seetzen saw), and Beth-jeshimoth. These warm springs Rosenmüller[1] thought were alluded to in Gen. xxxvi. 24, where there is an allusion to Anah, of the tribes of Seir, before Esau took possession of Idumæa, and his discovery of warm springs while he was tending his father's asses. The word meaning warm springs is incorrectly rendered in Luther's translation [and in the English as well] mules,—a reading which has been adopted by the Abyssinian church, to the great confusion of its biblical interpreters.[2]

In spite of the distance from the spring, the water at the mouth of the brook was so hot that it was disagreeable to wade through it. Some thirty date palms were standing there ; and in the wild luxuriance of the spot, traces could apparently be seen of the site of the former Callirrhoe and its gardens. Here was abundant room for the city, offering no comparison with the contracted ravine which Seetzen had explored a few days before, and where he discovered the first hot springs. No traces could be discovered of any architectural use of the place during the middle ages. The path led up over masses of basalt to the dark sandstone through which Serka Maein passes down to the Dead Sea. Apparently the violence of the winter floods has formed at the lower end of the wadi a promontory extending into the sea, and similar in character to that seen at the mouth of the Arnon. The water of the wadi, though not more than a third as broad as that of the Arnon, was swifter, more torrent-like in its flow, and sweet to the taste.

Seetzen found no traces in all this of the pestilential vapours which are said to be exhaled from the lake, and which, according to old stories, caused birds which were flying over it to fall dead. He saw vultures, pigeons, and flocks of quails pass from the west to the east side. He also found that Beduins sometimes drown in the sea on this side, indicating that the access of fresh water there materially changes the specific gravity of the water, which elsewhere in the lake does not permit a man's body to sink.

---

[1] Rosenmüller, *Bib. Alterthk.* ii. p. 217.
[2] J. L. Krapf, *Journal from July* 22 *to Feb.* 8, 1840, MS.

On the following day Seetzen continued his journey southward; but as, not long after his visit, the British travellers
Irby and Mangles explored the same spot, and fully confirmed the account of Seetzen, I will speak here of some of
the results of their researches, which began at a point reached
by Seetzen in 1806—namely, Baal Meon—and which he in
1807 espied north-east from Mkauer, and at a considerable
distance.

The position of Mkauer corresponds with that of Machaerus,
a city closely connected with the history of Herod, and with
the war of Vespasian, and often mentioned by Josephus, Strabo,
and Stephen of Byzantium as a strong military position.[1] It is
said to have first been fortified by Alexander Jannæus: originally it was a lofty rock, approached with difficulty on every
side, and surrounded by valleys which it was impossible to fill
up with earth. The distance of one of these valleys from the
Dead Sea is a three hours' march, which corresponds well with
the sixty stadia which Josephus mentions as the distance of
Mkauer from the Asphaltite Lake. In other particulars the
ancient account harmonized with the discoveries of Seetzen.
The place was destroyed by Gabinius at the time of the irruption
of Pompey into Syria; but it was afterwards fully restored by
Herod, for it lay in Peræa, which extended from Pella to
Machaerus. It touched at the south on the territory of the
Arab king Aretas, from whom in fact it had once been seized;
and it had consequently to be thoroughly fortified against his
attacks.

Herod encompassed the place with walls, strengthened it
with towers, and built a magnificent palace, providing it with
numerous cisterns to hold rain-water in, and adding an arsenal
for arrows and weapons of all kinds, which would enable him
to resist the attacks of enemies.

As a border city of Peræa, Machaerus belonged to the territory of Herod Antipas, tetrarch of Galilee and Peræa, the
same prince who had put away his first wife, the daughter of
the Arabian king Aretas, and had espoused Herodias, the wife of
his half-brother. John the Baptist having boldly charged this
sin upon him, he caused the preacher to be imprisoned in the
fortress of Machaerus, according to Josephus. Herod did not

[1] H. Relandus, *Pal.* 880-882; v. Raumer, *Pal.* p. 255.

dare to put him to death, however, for the people held John to be a prophet; but the revengeful nature of Herodias, a true grandchild of the cruel Herod the Great, prompted her to take such measures as would lead to his being beheaded in his prison at Machaerus.

Later, at the time of Vespasian's fearful persecution of the Jews, the few who escaped the slaughter on the Jordan and the Dead Sea fled to Machaerus. It was to no purpose, however; the city was taken, and all the refugees put to death.

On the tenth of January 1818, Irby and Mangles,[1] accompanied by Legh, left their encampment at the ruins of Maein, and went towards the south-west, meeting in the course of half an hour a large stone, evidently set there to serve as a boundary.[2] It resembled in character many which they had seen in the more southern valley of the Arnon. Thence they passed on to several rude but very ancient tombs or monuments,[3] each consisting of two long, unhewn, and massive side stones, running north and south, and covered with an immense stone projecting on both sides. They had no narrower stones to close the entrance, such as those which the travellers had seen in the neighbourhood of Szalt; and on this account they conjectured them to be much older. A great stone slab formed the floor of each monument. In no instance were these removed from their place. Legh counted[4] fifty of these in one place, in a single group. With more leisure they would have dug down under one of them, and perhaps been able to discover weapons and remains of the ancient Ammonites and Amorites, whose king Sihon used to reside in the neighbouring city of Heshbon. The dimensions of the tombs varied, but none was large enough to correspond to the gigantic size of Og, the ancient king of Bashan. Not only was the height of rock covered with these memorials, but they extended for some distance down into the valley. Soon they came to a road which was not paved in the manner of the *viæ stratæ* of the Romans, but which was laid with edged stones, and was apparently more ancient than the Roman military roads. A gentle winding course led from the height down into the lowest part of the valley, which a variety of green plants beautified: there was a

---

[1] Irby and Mangles, *Trav.* p. 465.
[2] *Ibid.* p. 462.
[3] *Ibid.* p. 325.
[4] Legh, *Route*, p. 243.

dense growth of sedge, overshadowed by poplars and aspens; and here and there groups of palms could be seen.

Through the valley ran a stream of hot water, into which little rivulets were flowing on both sides. One spring was examined after another, till at last the central group was reached about an hour and a half's distance from the Dead Sea. No city could have been built in the narrow gorge, yet there seem to have been some houses there, for there were terra cotta sherds lying here and there upon the ground : the travellers also discovered four Roman coins, whose impression was wholly illegible, however. The Beduins still use the baths in cases of sickness ; and Irby and Mangles found the water so hot, that the hand could not be held in it for any length of time. The water, though tasteless, yet showed considerable deposits of sulphur. The British travellers allude to a very striking plant, mentioned by Josephus as equally foreign to his experience : "A very singular plant grows near the hot sources, of the bulk and stature of a tree; its foliage does not seem to differ from that of the common broom. It bears a pod[1] hanging down from it, about a foot or fourteen inches in length, fluted with convex ribs from the end to the point; we never met with this before." After taking a bath, perhaps in the very spring in which Herod sought the means of his recovery, the travellers left the narrow pass and came back to the heights of Maein, and to the neighbourhood of the ancient Madeba, where they spent the night in an encampment of the Beni Sakkers.

(4.) *Seetzen's fourth day of progress. He passes Attarus and the ruins of el-Korriat, and comes to el-Wal, the northern tributary of the Arnon.*

Passing from the lofty encampment of the friendly Beni Hamide, Seetzen continued his course towards the south-east, passing the high ridge of basalt and porous lava, whose covering is formed of naked limestone. Here Seetzen discovered some ruins bearing the name el-Korriat, which he conjectured (though, as I think, without good grounds) to be the site of the ancient Kiriathaim, where Chedorlaomer achieved his victory over the Emim, but which subsequently, together with many

[1] Irby and Mangles, p. 469.

other cities of Moab, fell into a state of decay, as we learn from Jer. xlviii. 1. They were, however, restored by Reuben, within whose inheritance they lay.

Eusebius and Jerome both make mention of an important place inhabited by Christians, and called Carajatha; it lay a half-hour (ten *mille passuum*) west of the Arabian city of Medeba. Kiriath must therefóre have lain nearer the ruins of the present Madeba, north of Serka Ma'in, than Seetzen supposed, who seems to have been misled by the sound of the word el-Korriat. Burckhardt,[1] who subsequently discovered the ruins of et-Teym, a half-hour's distance west of Madeba, appears to have more reason for conjecturing that the place was the Kirjathaim of the Scriptures, the last syllable being retained.

Between el-Korriat and Mkauer, and upon the Jebel Attarus, there are to be seen well-preserved ruins of a city bearing the name of the mountain, and supposed by Seetzen to be the Ataroth of the ancient kingdom of Sihon, which is mentioned in connection with Dibon and Aroer as within the inheritance of Gad. From this neighbourhood Seetzen took his course along the banks of a stream which proved to be a northern tributary of the Arnon, encamping at night with a party of Beni Hameide Arabs.

(5.) *Seetzen's fifth day.   The passage through el-Kura to the valley of the Arnon.*

With his approach to the Arnon, Seetzen was compelled to lose the services of his guide, whose relations were not amicable with the tribes on the south side of that stream. He engaged a new guide, Mighbil by name, and was obliged to continue his journey on foot through a tract bearing the name el-Kura, in which word Seetzen thought that he perceived another trace of the ancient Kirjath. The name being in the plural—Kirjathaim—he conjectured that one of the cities bearing the name was north, and another south of the Attarus mountain. Heller,[2] however, thinks el-Korriat to be Kirjathaim; while Hengstenberg supposes that a third Keriath existed, the

[1] Burckhardt, *Trav.* Gesenius' ed. ii. p. 626.
[2] Keil, *Comment. zu Joshua*, pp. 253, 334; Winer, *Bib. Realw.* i.—*Kerioth, Kirjath, Kirjathaim*, pp. 655, 659; H. Reland, *Pal.* 724; von Raumer, *Pal.* p. 255, Note 360.

Καριωθ or Carioth of the *Onomasticon,* and the one referred
to by Jer. xlviii. 24, 41, and by Amos ii. 2. From these con-
flicting opinions, it would seem as if no decisive steps had been
taken towards settling the location of the place.

Seetzen found ruins in the eastern part of el-Kura bearing the name of Diban;[1] and a half-day's journey farther
towards the south-east, those of Umm el Orszas; and was led
to believe that they might be the ancient Kirjathaim : he evidently did not look, as Eusebius' statement would seem to
make necessary, in the neighbourhood of Madeba.

(6.) *Seetzen's sixth day. Route to the Mujeb or Arnon, and
down its wadi to the brook Shder and Ain Bedija. The
mouth of the Arnon.*

The rocky tract which Seetzen passed before he descended
into the valley of the Arnon abounded in wild game, embracing even panthers, hyænas, and wolves : the Arabs had many
stories also of jerboas being found there. A brother of Migbil,
named Majjub, was Seetzen's companion down the valley of
the Arnon, which was confined by steep masses of limestone,
and which, though narrow, ran noisily along. In the same
place Seetzen had been waylaid and plundered by the Beni
Hamide Arabs; now he was safely escorted by them. He
followed the course of the Arnon for some hours, till he came
to the brook el-Shder, which flows in from the south. The
Wadi Jerra, which runs down to the Dead Sea south of the
Arnon, as portrayed on many of the best maps, seems to have
no existence, but to have been first laid down in consequence
of misunderstanding the course of the brook mentioned by
Seetzen. This brook was overgrown with sedge and oleander ;
its sides were limestone, while farther southward basalt and
flint were seen. After crossing a second brook called Ain
Bedija, also coming into the Arnon on the south side, Seetzen
reached what, in the largest sense of the word, could be called
the land of Freedom. Here the last traces of the Turkish
power ceased, although in Szalt and el-Belka they have been
so slight as scarcely to be worthy of mention.

As Seetzen paid more especial attention to the mouth of the
Arnon on his return, when he took his way along the shore of the

[1] Is not this the Dibon of Num. xxxii. 34 ?—ED.

Dead Sea, I will anticipate here the result of his observations. He found in front of the mouth of the river a semicircular or half-moon-shaped peninsula. The mouth itself is romantic in appearance, being about sixty feet in width, and hemmed in by gigantic perpendicular walls, into which the sun rarely shines. At the foot of the one on the north side is a natural cave overshadowed by bushes. The little island is low, and has been formed by successive deposits, and would make a lovely hermitage, with the magnificent rocks overhanging it on the east, and the placid water on the west. Game, such as gazelles, steinbocks, and hares, would find support in the mountains along the shore; the river teems with fishes; while the very fertile soil of the peninsula might become, with some help from artificial irrigation, one of the finest of fruit gardens, yielding dates, bananas, lemons, sugar-cane, wheat, and all kinds of garden vegetables. It is now surrendered to a few varieties of wild plants alone.

The Mujeb or Arnon has a very slow current at its mouth: the stream was forty feet wide at the time of Seetzen's visit, and had a depth of about a foot. Here he spent the night in company with his Arab guides, going to sleep amid the account of the plundering expeditions and their attacks on the Mecca caravans. They did not dare keep up the fire, lest it should disclose their encampment to hostile tribes in the neighbourhood, and expose them to danger.

(7.) *Seetzen's seventh day's march. From the Arnon southward through the territory of the wildest Arabs.*

The course led from the brook Ain Bedija to the spring Ain Sgek, past limestone mountains overgrown with wild almond and turpentine trees, then past a high hill called el-Ras, into a deep defile, where there were ten tents pitched. In this encampment he spent the night.

(8.) *Seetzen's eighth day's march to the Wadi Kerak (Dara, Zoar, Segor), and the peninsular Ghor el Mesraa el Karak, to the village of the Ghawarineh.*

After some hours' travel between naked rocks, animated with numerous steinbocks, Seetzen, now on foot, advanced in a w.s.w. direction towards the mouth of Wadi Karak, which takes its name from the city of Kerak, from which it comes. It enters the sea on the north side of the great peninsula Ghor el Mesraa el Kerak, which the year before Seetzen had incorrectly considered to be an island. This Wadi Kerak the English travellers Irby and Mangles[1] subsequently learned to know under the name of Dara or Deraah : it enters the plain at the ruins of a city, which is with the greatest probability the ancient Zoar, the Segor of Jerome, and the Zoghar of the crusaders. The wadi pours only a part of its waters into the gulf, which separates the northern end·of the peninsula from the mainland ; another part is conducted by artificial channels to the village of el-Mesraa,[2] which lies upon the peninsula. So far as the irrigation of the latter is concerned, the soil displays the results of extreme fertility ; but the greater portion of the peninsula, extending as it does a long way into the sea, is a waste of little hills and patches of sand. The peasants sow here wheat, barley, durrha, melons, and a poor kind of tobacco : they collect considerable quantities of sulphur, as at Jericho ; this they use in the preparation of gunpowder, and as a medicament for their sheep. Salt is largely gathered along the seaboard, where it is found in encrustations, and is then sent to Kerak for sale.

(9.) *Seetzen's ninth day's march from the Ghor el Mesraa el Kerak to the southern extremity of the Dead Sea.*

Sheikh Hamade was willingly persuaded to accompany his guest still farther south, to the Ghor es Safieh,[3] at the southern part of the Dead Sea. Their course was between fields of durra, then over a stony tract, through which flow the waters of a spring known as Mojet Nimri. The territory was one much frequented by gazelles. Soon Seetzen discovered boulders of particoloured sandstone, and blocks of white limestone, with breccia conglomerate, containing gneiss, jasper, greenstone, and felspar of various hues. There were no connected masses of these various kinds of stone, however, nor have any been observed by travellers subsequent to Seetzen. The fragments which exist around the Dead Sea appear to have been transported

[1] Irby and Mangles, *Trav.* p. 448.
[2] Burckhardt, Gesen. ed. ii. p. 661.
[3] *Ibid.* p. 660 ; Robinson, *Bib. Research.* ii. p. 112.

from a great distance, but the source whence they were derived will remain an interesting question to geologists who may in future examine that region. Seetzen describes the mountains which run along the shore as mainly composed of limestone, while of basalt he saw no trace. Proceeding farther south towards Petra, the first breccia and basalt blocks appear in Wadi Ghoeyr; then in the upper course of Wadi el Ahsa there appear numerous volcanic rocks conjoined with lava; then in Wadi Jeib the first traces of porphyry; at the pass of Neimelah, north-east of Petra, lofty masses of porphyry become visible, and continued with their steep sides down the Araba valley and in Mount Hor, while only in the immediate neighbourhood of Akaba Æla do granite and other primitive formations appear.

Under the protection of his guide, Seetzen[1] advanced southward as far as the southern portion of the sea, whose low, naked, salty plain is covered at the time of the yearly floods. He crossed some small tributaries of the Kurahy, which cross the bushy plain of the Ghor es Safieh on their way towards the sea, finding there a party of Beni Sakker Arabs. After an hour and a half four miserable huts were reached, which bear the name Mesraa es Safieh. The stream which passes through this place bears the name Kurahy. The Arabs of the place gave Seetzen a hospitable reception, and he spent the night in one of their huts. In spite of the fires which were kept up, it was almost impossible for him to sleep warmly : nor was the cold the only destroyer of rest; next to it was the fearful howling of the jackals.[2]

2. *Return from the southern extremity of the Dead Sea to the mouth of Wadi Mujeb (Arnon).*

First day of the return. The Aduan Bards.

Seetzen had learned, on the occasion of his first visit to this vicinity, that there is a hot spring in Wadi el Ahsa, though less marked in character than those which he had seen farther north. They were said to lie seven hours south of Kerak, and nine hours distant from the Dead Sea. He would have been glad to visit them now, but he was unable to prevail upon his

---

[1] Seetzen, in *Mon. Corresp.* 1818, pp. 435-438.   [2] *Ibid.* pp. 435, 438.

Arab guides to accompany him thither. Burckhardt confirms the account of the existence of a warm stream flowing through this wadi. This seems to be the same which in the ancient scriptural time served as the boundary between Edom and Moab :[1] it is the Zered of Deut. ii. 13, 18, the brook of the willows mentioned in Isa. xv. 7, and the stream of the wilderness alluded to in Amos vi. 14.

Accompanied by a couple of Aduan Arabs as guides, Seetzen began his return march on the morning of the twenty-sixth of January. One of the guides, who possessed a very pleasant voice, sung to him on the way some of the songs indigenous to the district, particularly the odes of one of the favourite poets known as Sheikh Nimr. These Arabs were very much at home in the productions of their own bards ; above all, of one which they called *Beni Helal,* which had a striking resemblance in character to the *Iliad* and the *Odyssey.* The lines were very musical, and were particularly marked by the purity of the rhymes. A certain Sheikh Hassan el Cheddry was mentioned as the author of the *Beni Helal.* A tribe bearing that name is known to exist in the Haj. The poem alluded to above is so well known, that there is not a peasant in Egypt, Syria, or Palestine who cannot recite some passages from it, or who has not heard something about the hero, Abu Sed. The chief charm of the production is, however, the close portraiture which it gives of Beduin life ; and its popularity is so great with the wild Arabs, that they gladly listen to it until the latest hours of the night.

Second day of the return march. From the spring Ain Sgek to the mouth of the Arnon.

It was a truly lovely spring morning when Seetzen left the spring Ain Sgek, which he had previously visited, and attempted to find his way along the very edge of the sea. His guides assured him that it was useless to make the attempt—that it must be unsuccessful. He determined, however, to proceed, and at length prevailed upon one of the Arabs to accompany him. They were unable to use any beast of burden, and had to leave everything behind excepting a skin of water, and meal enough for two days' provision. From the limestone mountains they

[1] Ewald, *Gesch. des Jud. Volks,* ii. p. 205, Note 2.

had already been able to see the Dead Sea ; but it took two hours to enable them to reach it. The horns of steinbocks and the tusks of wild boars were often found on the rocks, and testified in part to the kind of life inhabiting those wild abodes. The path grew worse and worse; and it was only with the greatest difficulty that they could proceed, it being necessary to climb from rock to rock, and oftentimes to retrace their steps for a considerable distance, in order to evade some cliff which could not be surmounted. For horned cattle the way was utterly impracticable ; and only the peasants of el-Mesraa are able to drive their flocks over it, in order to avail themselves of the nearest road to Jerusalem, where they sell them. So far as safety is concerned, this way is very safe ; for the Beduins seldom find their way to the barren rocks of the sea-coast, there being no good pasturage there for their herds. After a hard day's progress over this rough route, Seetzen arrived in the evening at the romantic rock-gate which forms the mouth of the Arnon. His course thence to Jericho was that over which we have already followed his steps.

Seetzen thus accomplished his pilgrimage through the barren and savage district which is alluded to in Ps. civ. 18, " The high hills are a refuge for the wild goats, and the rocks for the conies." Both of these creatures he found there in great numbers; and had he been able to track them to their hiding-places and their homes, he would have been very glad to study their habits. The little creatures inhabiting the rocky places, which he so often heard called by the name webbr, the *Hyrax Syriacus,* are unquestionably the *Shaphan* of the Hebrews, to which, among other places, we have an allusion in the book of Proverbs, xxx. 24–29, where four things are spoken of, which, though feebler than man, are exceedingly wise. In ver. 26 it is stated, " The conies are but a feeble folk, yet make they their houses in the rocks." Wilson, in the course of his explorations on the east coast of the Dead Sea, fully confirmed the fact that the " wabr " of the Arabs is the cony, and has given a detailed account of the animal in his work.[1]

[1] Wilson, *Lands of the Bible,* ii. pp. 28-31. Comp. Rosenmüller, *Bib. Alterthk.* vol. iv. pp. 213-222.

DISCUSSION III.

WESTERN SHORE OF THE DEAD SEA, FROM THE RAS EL FESHCHAH AND THE
MOUTH OF THE KIDRON, PAST AIN JIDDY, SEBBEH, AND THE ES-ZUWEIRAH
PASS, TO THE SALT PILLAR OF USDUM AT THE SOUTHERN EXTREMITY OF
THE SEA.

I pass now back to the western shore of the sea, and shall
speak of the tract indicated in the above heading,—a region
which was a *terra incognita* till within the past few years, but
which has become well known. This we owe to the labours
of Robinson[1] and Smith, Wolcott,[2] von Schubert,[3] Russegger,[4]
Wilson,[5] Tischendorf,[6] and Gadow,[7] in the course of their
direct explorations of the western shore of the sea, and more
particularly of the country in the immediate vicinity of the
Convent of Mar Saba.

I will open this subject by speaking first of

*The Kedron from its source near Jerusalem to the Convent of St
Saba on the Wadi er Rahib, or the Monks' Valley, and
thence to its mouth, the Wadi en Nar, i.e. the Valley of
Fire.*

South of Ras el Feshchah, the deep and almost inaccessible
gorge of Wadi er Rahib, or the Monks' Valley, opens, descending from the celebrated Convent of St Saba at the north-west.
It is from this institution that it derives its name, although it
is sometimes called Wadi en Nar,[8] or the Valley of Fire. Two
and a half hours farther southward lies the promontory Ras el
Ghuweir, with a little spring called Ain Ghuweir, near which
is another wadi which comes down from the neighbourhood
of Bethlehem. This wadi, which is just as steep and inaccessible as the one first named, is so forbidding that no instance

[1] Robinson, *Bib. Research.* i. pp. 450–535.
[2] Wolcott, *Excursion to Masada*, in *Bib. Sacra*, 1843, pp. 60–70;
Appendix to *Bib. Sac.* vol. iii. pp. 399, 400.
[3] Von Schubert, *Reise*, iii. pp. 94–103.
[4] Russegger, *Reise*, iii. pp. 110–113.
[5] Wilson, *Lands of the Bible*, ii. pp. 24–33.
[6] Tischendorf, *Reise*, ii. pp. 118–133.
[7] Gadow, in *Zeitsch. d. deutsch. Morgen. Ges.* ii. pp. 63–65.
[8] Robinson, *Bib. Research.* i. 531.

is recorded of any one's[1] attempting to pass through it from the Dead Sea to Jerusalem, where it becomes known as the Valley of Jehoshaphat, and its watercourse takes the world-renowned name of Kedron. One hour's distance south of Ain Ghuweir, there rises above the spring Ain Terabeh a romantic crag, on which Robinson pitched his tent. From this spot the sight ranges widely over the Dead Sea, takes in the broad table-land at the north, and penetrates to the recesses of a third coast wadi, en-Taamirah, which comes down from the neighbourhood of Bethlehem, taking its name from the mountain of Beit Taamar,[2] east of that place. At its source Gadow saw on a declivity the ruins of a convent[3] which must have been important in its day, and discovered in its neighbourhood two great cisterns very deep, and made of terra cotta. The convent, probably the next one west of St Saba, bore the name Deir Dosi, probably an abbreviation of Mar Theodosius. The greater of the cisterns was found to be sixty feet long, forty feet deep, and to be crossed by a singular wall, which apparently once served to support an aqueduct. The Beduins living in this neighbourhood were called Taamirah Arabs.[4]

The Kedron takes its rise, if the use of that word be permitted in this case, on the north side of Jerusalem, at an elevation of nearly 2500 feet above the Mediterranean, near the graves of the kings, on the great watershed between the last-mentioned sea and the Dead Sea. Its course in the immediate neighbourhood of Jerusalem is accompanied by graves[5] hewn in the rock, the most important of which are those of the kings, and the so-called tombs of Zacharias, Absalom, and Jehoshaphat. South of these the valley passes by the fountain of Siloah, the King's Gardens, the valley known as Ben Hinnom, which comes in from the west, and the spring called

---

[1] This remark, though *literally* true, must be accepted with a certain degree of qualification; for it will appear in a subsequent page that both Wolcott and Wilson have passed through the gorge, the former going down and the latter going up.—ED.

[2] Robinson, *Bib. Research.* i. p. 471.

[3] H. Gadow, in *Z. d. deutsch. Morgen. Ges.* Pt. ii. p. 65, and Pt. i. p. 151.

[4] Wilson, *Lands of the Bible*, ii. p. 25.

[5] Robinson, *Bib. Research.* i. pp. 385–399.

indifferently by the names of Nehemiah and Job. This valley is regarded by the Jews as the Valley of Jehoshaphat referred to by the prophet Joel (iii. 12) ;[1] and they desire to be buried there, because they think that the final judgment of the dead is to be held there,—a belief which is shared by the Mohammedans and by some Christians, although there exists no proof that this valley is identical with the one mentioned by Joel. It is called the King's Valley neither in the Scriptures nor in Josephus.[2] It is only in the *Itiner. Burdig. ad Annum* 333 that the name Vallis Josafat comes into use, but since the fourth century that has been the most common designation of it.

This valley, which lies between the high rock on which Jerusalem is built and the Mount of Olives, forms a narrow rock-bed, and was called by Eusebius, in consequence of its resemblance to Cœle-Syria, Κοιλὰς ʼΙωσαφὰτ, or the hollow Jehoshaphat. It is traversed by no regular stream ; the only waters which always flow into it come from a few springs. It is only at the time of the winter rains[3] that it is the outlet of a strong current. The people who live in the neighbourhood often see years go by without seeing any water in it, and the name which it bears in the New Testament and in the Septuagint is simply Χειμάῤῥους, a winter or storm brook. Josephus terms it Φάραγξ Κεδρών, the deep gorge of Kedron,—a name which was also familiar at the time of David and Solomon, and which has in Hebrew almost the same meaning as the word wadi.

Just at the point where the Kedron turns from its southward course below the well of Nehemiah and the so-called King's Gardens, the site of the ancient Tophet where children were sacrificed to Moloch, and takes an eastward direction towards the Dead Sea, all former knowledge of it ceased ; and indeed it is not long since it was really a matter of doubt whether the wild and almost inaccessible, ravine leading eastward from Jerusalem was the same which passes by the Convent of St Saba. The routes of travellers had not embraced it ; and it was not till 1840 that it was explored. Then Wolcott[4]

---

[1] Von Raumer, *Pal.* pp. 302, 327, etc.
[2] Robinson, *Bib. Research.* i. 269.　　　　[3] *Ibid.* i. p. 232.
[4] Wolcott, *Excursion to Mar Saba, etc.*, in *Bib. Sacra*, 1843, pp. 38-40.

passed down from Jerusalem to the convent, the journey taking
but two and a half hours. The result of his exploration made
it no longer doubtful whether the ravine which opens for the
waters of the Kedron south-east of Jerusalem is the same
which had been often noticed near the convent. Soon after he
entered the gorge he passed the Wadi el Wezy coming in from
the west. Ten minutes farther on was another wadi, called
Kaddum, from a north-north-east direction, passing on the
eastern side of the Mountain of Offence, and communicating
with Bethany. Five minutes later Wolcott passed the village
of Sahur, whose wadi runs from Bethlehem. Barth[1] passed
this place as he crossed the Kaddum gorge on his way from
Bethlehem to Saba. There then sets in a wadi from the north-
west, in which Wolcott saw sepulchral excavations, cisterns,
fragments of pillars and hewn stones,—a proof to his mind
that the region has not always been the solitary waste which it
is to-day.

Here he left the gorge proper, and passed over the side of
a hill, seeing after the lapse of twenty-five minutes the Wadi
Sur Bahil coming in from a village of that name. Only
five minutes after he entered the opening of Wadi el Leban,
through which the way ran again south-eastward to Wadi en
Nar, passing through a wild and picturesque defile before
reaching the Convent of Mar Saba. The rocks showed that
they had once been used as the dwelling-place of hermits, and
explain the origin of the name Valley of Monks, which has
been applied to the ravine.

Wilson does not enter into any details regarding his wandering up this wild defile ; he says briefly that his course was
mainly in the ravine itself, or on the overhanging cliffs, and
thinks that it once[2] must have been possible to look from the
temple of Jerusalem down the gorge to the Dead Sea. He
refers, in corroboration of this view, to the vision of Ezekiel
relating to the reanimation of the shores of the latter.

After traversing half the distance, Wilson tells us that he
found the ravine divided by a kind of rocky island into two
channels, which united about a quarter of an hour's distance
higher up. At the southern base of the Mount of Offence he

---

[1] Dr Barth, MS. 1847.
[2] Wilson, *Lands of the Bible*, ii. p. 22.

was surprised by the sudden vision of the city of Jerusalem which broke upon him there, like a high citadel towering above the King's Gardens at its base. This was the same surprising prospect which von Schubert[1] enjoyed on his return from Mar Saba. He left the convent in the cool of the morning, passing over chalk hills displaying plentiful traces of flint, and over a soil which he thought contained more intrinsic elements of fertility than the district lying north of Jericho. He found here plants in full bloom—*Phlomis nissolii, Dolichos nilotikus, Solanum coagulans :* he also saw corn fields 'in which the *Chrysanthemum coronarium* plays the same destructive part that it does here in Europe. The whole way to Jerusalem was a gradually rising one, though alternating with depressions. The ascent became decidedly visible only in the neighbourhood of Jerusalem, where the city had an imposing aspect as it sat enthroned upon its lofty seat. It can be seen even from the heights in the vicinity of Mar Saba.

Gadow,[2] who in his journey from the Convent of Saba to Bethlehem kept on the high land, was able to view the Mount of Olives and the Armenian convent at a distance of two hours. He passed over the Burj el Humma, a ruin in a very much dilapidated state, and passed then to Wadi et Taamira, and the remnant of the former Theodosius convent, Deir Dossi. These localities, as well as those which were traversed by Dr Barth in his more southerly route from Bethlehem to Saba, are not recorded on the maps ; and only Beit Sahur, Sur Bahil, and Deir Ibu Obeid are given on Robinson's[3] map.

So far as is known to me, no traveller has ever passed through the lower defile to the Mar Saba Convent. Travellers have uniformly taken the route by way of the Kuneiterah Pass.

Von Schubert left the sea-shore, preferring to take the less steep and inaccessible but terribly barren desert path, passing through a tract of gypsum and marl, and penetrated with sulphur and bitumen, fragments of which he had also found strewed around on the sea-coast. He saw many hollows stained

[1] Von Schubert, *Reise*, p. 102.
[2] H. Gadow, ii. p. 65.
[3] Robinson, *Bib. Research.* i. p. 471.

with the colour of asphaltum, but he detected nothing of a volcanic character; and instead of attributing the aspect of the district to the action of internal forces, it looked as if it had been the seat of a terrific conflagration of substances which had exuded from the soil. If so, this would afford an explanation of the allusion in Gen. xix. 28.

Farther on, von Schubert's[1] course took him through deep winding valleys, with green patches here and there, till he reached the high plain on which he saw the lofty castellated Nebi Musa, on which stands a mosque to commemorate the spot reputed among the Mohammedans to be the burial-place of Moses. I need hardly say that his tomb cannot be there, as might be distinctly inferred from Deut. xxxiv. In this connection, it may be remarked that the Beduins on the east side of the Jordan pay their pilgrimage to a spot four or five hours east of Szalt, according to Seetzen,[2] which they regard as the grave of Shoaib. The Shoaib of the Midianites they confound with the priest Jethro, and him with Hobab; but as Shoaib did not accompany the Israelites, his grave is of course not to be looked for in the mountains of Gilead. Von Schubert found the caverns very numerous on the road by way of the pass of Kaneiterah. In the side valleys they were even more numerous, in some places seeming to make a city of caves, in which flocks of doves find their home. Not a trace of man was to be seen; and indeed, in those barren wilds, it would have been difficult for even sheep to find subsistence. Yet in the spring it is not difficult to find pasturage there; and Russegger[3] states, that when he was there at the end of November even, he found countless herds and a Beduin encampment of three tents, where he was hospitably entertained and spent the night.

When Seetzen was in Jericho, he found half of the Ehteim tribe with their camels on the heights around Mar Saba[4] and Mird. Their sheikh had the right of conveying travellers through the wilderness, and the members of the tribe enjoyed the privilege of claiming a certain amount of bread of the monks every day,—a relation between them and the Beduins

---

[1] Von Schubert, *Reise*, iii. p. 94.
[2] Seetzen, *Zweite Reise*, 1807, MS.
[3] Russegger, *Reise*, iii. p. 110.
[4] Robinson, *Bib. Research.* i. p. 545.

which recalls that of the Towara tribe to the Convent of Sinai. When Wilson[1] passed through this district near the end of March, he found members of the Taamarah tribe there with their sheep and goats; they were very hospitable, and offered him plenty of milk. Dr Barth discovered in the same region a company of the same tribe, numbering from two to three hundred; but he did not enjoy the same hospitality which Wilson mentions, and barely escaped from their savage rapacity.

Wolcott,[2] who passed through the Kuneiterah Pass on his way from Saba to Jericho, has given some details regarding the route. It took him three hours to reach the pass, and an hour more to enter the plain lying on the Dead Sea. Leaving the convent, he passed soon through Wadi Ber el Kulah, then crossed the heads of several wadis which run into el-Bukeia, a great depression lying at the south-east, between these hills and the Dead Sea. Ten minutes farther he encountered the Wadi el Gurabeh, and not long afterwards entered the Wadi Kuneiterah, which soon narrows and becomes the pass of the same name. Its normal direction is east-north-east. In forty-five minutes he came to the end of it, and emerged upon the plain north of the Dead Sea.

The Convent[3] of Mar Saba lies on the western slope of a gorge twelve hundred feet deep, shut in in part by lofty precipitous walls, which at the bottom of the gorge recede from each other only a distance of six or eight fathoms. The building is literally clamped to the rock, the whole under-pinning being joined to the underlying foundation with the greatest care. The whole is surrounded by a high wall, on which a couple of towers rest. The convent itself, which is massive and fine, is well preserved, and evidently built with the greatest care. From the great balcony the sight penetrates to the deep abyss at the base of the cliff, where there is not a trace of vegetation. The wall confronting the convent is crowned by another tower. The precipice is full of caverns, once the hermitage of monks, and approached by rude and now wholly useless staircases

[1] Wilson, *Lands of the Bible*, ii. p. 25; Gadow, p. 63; Dr Barth, MS.

[2] Wolcott, *Excursion*, *l.c.* p. 40.

[3] Russegger, *Reise*, iii. pp. 111–113. See Roberts, *The Holy Land*, Book vii. Plate xviii.

cut in the rock. These hiding-places can now only be looked into from the opposite side ; they are wholly inaccessible. Wilson compared the face of the rock to the amphitheatre at Petra, and Count Pückler has in as p^ .uliar a manner sketched the scéne, as have Lamartine and Chateaubriand. I leave the accounts of these to carry their own weight, without adding any comments of my own.

The chief entrance[1] into the convent—closed, however, to all strangers who are not furnished with a letter of recommendation from the Greek Patriarch in Jerusalem—is on the west side. There is first a very steep path, ten or twelve feet wide, leading up to the thoroughly protected door. This leads to the court, from which a staircase of fifty or sixty steps leads down to the servants' apartments. Fifty steps still farther down bring one to the paved square, in whose centre stands the Chapel of Hieromonachos Saba or Mar Saba, built in an octagonal form, and furnished with a cupola. In the north-west corner of this square stands the Chapel of St Nicolaus ; on the eastern side is the entrance into the Church of St Saba. The other buildings surrounding the court are appointed for the reception of the pilgrims.

About twenty steps farther down lie two garden beds, containing some vegetables : here some sugar-cane may be seen growing, and a few trees, including a palm. About thirty or forty steps above these garden beds—to which the earth must have been brought from a considerable distance—is the southern and oldest part of the convent, close by the cavern in which St Saba is said to have found a retreat in company with the lions. It seems scarcely large enough for both. In the northern rock-wall is the cell of John of Damascus, in which he is said to have written many of his learned works.

The main church is built in the form of a basilica, is tolerably large, and is decorated in the modern tasteless manner, with a profusion of gold and silver, pictures, candelabra, and the like, mostly the gifts of the Greek Convent or of the Russian Church. A portrait of St Saba, for example, is finished with a layer of silver foil. Among these poor pictures, however, mostly in the Greek style, there are some which are of interest to the antiquarian. A very ancient picture, to

[1] Dr Barth, MS. 1847 ; H. Gadow, i. p. 63.

which Basedow called attention, hangs at the entrance, and represents the hallowed founder of the convent on a gold ground, with many scenes from his life. The cells of the monks are excavated from the natural rock, and are not rudely wrought. The rooms for the reception of strangers are neat, and are well furnished; the fare is good. The monks pay little or no regard to the guests; and instead of a free-will offering being made, as is customary in other institutions of a similar character, Gadow was presented with a bill which he thought out of proportion to the entertainment which he had received.

The solitude of the great balcony reminded Russegger, as he looked down into the abyss at his feet, of the solitary Spanish Montserrat. The monk who accompanied him tossed a handful of raisins out into the air, and at once the birds began to issue from the neighbouring holes in the rock, calling others continually by their loud cry, and all flew towards the convent. Russegger drew back, but the monk stook still, and allowed them to come and settle on his shoulder, and eat out of his hand, and be freely caressed by him,—a striking picture of the power of man over the brute creation, and of the irresistible might of love. It might almost recall the days of paradise. Scholtz[1] and Tischendorf[2] were both told that Saba, the founder of the convent, was on such good terms with the wild creatures of the desert, that they came regularly every evening into the gorge of the Kedron to take crumbs from his hand. The tameness of all the birds in the neighbourhood now was ascribed by Scholtz to the workings of nature, but by the monks to the abiding influence of the founder of the convent. Lusignan,[3] who spent several days at St Saba, speaks of the familiarity of the monks with the foxes as being so great, that it is one of their chief amusements to catch them and play with them on moonlight nights. The howling of lions, which the same writer alleges to be so common in the neighbourhood of the convent, must be attributed to nothing more rapacious than the jackals. Yet the formidable jerboa is sometimes found in these sterile wilds.

---

[1] Scholtz, *Bibl. Kritische Reise in Palästina*, p. 144.
[2] Tischendorf, *Reise in das Orient*, Pt. ii. p. 124.
[3] S. Lusignan, *Briefe an S. W. Fordyce*, pp. 138, 139.

Fallen as is the Monastery of St Saba at the present time, it was at one time an institution of great eminence, and its founder was called by Cyril of Scythopolis the Star of the Desert.[1] His Life was discover.d by Tischendorf in the library, written upon parchment. He is described as a Greek monk who lived in the sixth century in the laura or monastery founded a hundred years earlier by St Euthymius. The convent which he founded was a great centre of theological strifes subsequently to the meeting of the Synod of Chalcedon. The founder of this monastery established that at Tekoa also. These were at one time in deadly opposition to each other, but they became friendly in 545, and the Convent of St Saba became the stronghold of orthodoxy. When the Samaritans took a position in opposition to the Christians of Palestine, it was St Saba who stepped boldly forward, appealed at once to the powers of Constantinople, and prevented further inroads upon the liberties of the much-vexed Christians.[2]

At the time of the invasion of the Persians under Chosres II. in 614, when so many people in Palestine perished, a large number of, monks, numbering from four hundred to a thousand, met the fate of martyrs. Their bones are said to have been collected in one of the caverns adjoining the St Nicolaus Chapel. In the year 796 the place was attacked by the Saracens; and in 812, after the death of Haroun el Raschid, the friend and ally of Charlemagne, the same tragedy was enacted on a more extensive scale, and attended with great cruelty. These circumstances made it necessary to convert the convent into a fortress, and the Emperor Justinian[3] caused the church and the watch-tower to be erected. Other buildings have followed up till the latest time, but their combined strength has not been able to ward off the occasional attacks of the Beduins. Chateaubriand was plundered[4] at the very door of the convent. Early in the present century a party of Arabs, who were at enmity with the Taamirah tribe, came from the east side of the Dead Sea; and as the door of the convent was made of wood

---

[1] L. Fleischer on the *Codex Rescriptus*, in *Z. d. Deutsch. Morgen. Ges.* vol. i. pp. 148–160.

[2] Robinson, *Bib. Research.* ii. pp. 109, 327, *i.a.l.*

[3] Von Schubert, *Reise*, iii. p. 96 ; Wilson, *Lands of the Bible*, ii. p. 27.

[4] Robinson, *Bib. Research.* i. p. 530.

covered with tin-plate, they threw oil into the cracks, and contrived to set it on fire. In the last few years, however, the place, together with the convents of Bethlehem and other sacred places in the neighbourhood, have stood under the immediate protection of the Greek Patriarch of Jerusalem. The place is, however, never considered as out of danger, the doors are habitually closed, and a watchman is stationed on the walls to watch every Beduin who approaches. The provisions which are consumed, and the bread which is given to the Arabs, are all brought with difficulty from Bethlehem; for the neighbourhood is wholly unproductive, and well merits the appellation which Quaresmius gave it, "sterilissimus et solitarius valde." Yet the convent still cherishes within its walls its valuable collection of manuscripts, which has been examined by Scholtz,[1] and in the present day by Tischendorf. Another critic, Lusignan, is mentioned by Wilson.[2] His work I have not seen, except in the translation. He seems to have tarried for a considerable time in the convent on the occasion of two different visits made in the last century. He had the most unrestrained access to the manuscripts; but his account of their contents is not valuable. Scholtz[3] spent a day in the library in 1822. He found that the monks had little love of letters, and the manuscripts were in a very much neglected state. Scholtz concluded that there might be some valuable parchments there, but that in the repeated attacks which have been made upon the monastery much must have perished. There were traces enough, however, to prove that between the thirteenth and the seventeenth centuries the Aristotelian philosophy, history, mathematics, and church music were much cultivated here. The library, with its two hundred manuscripts, he found to be partly in the main church and partly in the Chapel of St Nicolaus. They were in a state of great confusion. A small part of them once belonged to the St John's Convent, on the Jordan, whose inmates had been compelled to withdraw to St Saba; and it is probable that contributions have been made to the collection from other sources. Among

---

[1] Scholtz, *Biblisch. Kritische Reise in Palästina*, pp. 143–148; Tischendorf, *Reise*, ii. pp. 121–124.

[2] *Series of Letters from Lusignan to Fordyce*, vol. ii. pp. 164–166.

[3] Scholtz, *Biblisch. Kritische Reise in Palästina*, pp. 143–148.

the manuscripts were Greek, Arabic, and Syriac. Among them Scholtz found of the New Testament three of the thirteenth century, seven Gospels of the twelfth and thirteenth, one of the ninth, fourteen *evangelistaria* and *lectionaria*, two containing the Acts and the Epistles. The most were evidently written in Palestine for the use of the churches. There seemed to be also many manuscripts of great interest to the classical scholar. The monks were very distrustful, and Scholtz could not pursue his investigations as he wished. A single day and a part of the night did not suffice to make that careful examination which he wished. He found that the reason why he was constantly watched was, that some wealthy Englishmen had come to the convent, backed by firmans from the Sultan in Constantinople and the Patriarch in Jerusalem, and borrowed some of the manuscripts, but had failed to return them. The books, most of which were edited in Venice, had no great literary worth. A letter of the distinguished Professor Carlyle[1] to the Bishop of Lincoln may have had some connection with these borrowed manuscripts. He seems to have subjected the whole Saba collection to a careful investigation, discovering twenty-nine copies of the Gospels and one of the Epistles, besides three hundred and eighty of the Fathers, Homilies, Legends, and Rituals. The superior of the convent had allowed him to take away six of the most ancient manuscripts, it is stated in the letter, and he hoped to gain the consent of the patriarch to take them to England.

Tischendorf[2] also examined the collection in 1844, and has given a detailed description of it. He found the whole collection not very dissimilar in character to that which he had examined not long before at the Sinai Convent.[3] Among valuable manuscripts of the tenth and eleventh centuries, some of them very neatly written, there was one containing the works of Hippocrates. In addition to those in the Greek language, there were Russian, Wallachian, Arabic, and Syriac manuscripts, as well as ten Abyssinian ones.

[1] Letter III. of Prof. Carlyle, in *Rob. Walpole's Mem.* 1818, pp. 162, 163.

[2] Tischendorf, *Reise*, ii. pp. 121–124.

[3] See fuller account in *Wien. Jahrb. f. Literatur*, 1846, vol. cxiv. pp. 45–58.

DISCURSION IV.

WEST SHORE OF THE DEAD SEA—THE JUDÆAN WATERSHED, AND THE WADIS
RUNNING DOWN TO THIS SHORE—WADI URTAS, THE POOLS OF SOLOMON,
AND THE GARDENS OF ETAM—JEBEL EL FUREIDIS, OR LITTLE PARADISE—
THE FRANK MOUNTAIN OF THE LEGENDS—THE HERODION—THE LABYRINTH
OF KHUREITUN—THE CAVES OF ADULLAM—THE RUINS OF TEKUA, THE
REMAINS OF THE TOKOA OF AMOS—THE DESERT OF TEKOA—THE HALF
BEDUIN TRIBES OF TAAMIRAH, RESHAIDEH, KA'ABIREH, AND JELLAHIN.

As the Convent of St Saba and Bethlehem are the most
important places near the northern end of the Dead Sea, and
on its western side, so the Engeddi and Masada of the days of
Solomon and Herod are the principal points east of Hebron.
The first of these lies on the shore of the Dead Sea, but has
been seldom visited in modern times. Indeed, no valuable
records exist of travels extending to this point, with the exception of those of Robinson, Wolcott, and Lynch.[1] The latter
approached the place by water, and spent a considerable time
there and in the neighbourhood. Wolcott approached the place
from the south, following the road from Masada to Engeddi,
and then passing to Bethlehem through the intervening wadis,
passing Tekua (Tekoa) and the Frank Mountain. Robinson
passed from Bethlehem over the same route to Engeddi, and
thence northward to the Ras el Feshchah and Jericho.

By means of the accounts of these last-mentioned admirable
observers, the high line of watershed lying between Bethlehem
and Hebron, in its relation to the incipient wadis which run
to the Dead Sea, became well known, and many valuable antiquarian discoveries were made. These wadis have generally a
parallel direction, and run eastwardly or south-eastwardly from
the watershed to the rough shores of the bitter lake just mentioned; in the rainy season they form a convenient passage to
convey the tempestuous streams thither.

As Jerusalem, Bethlehem, and Hebron all lie not only very
high,[2] but much nearer the Dead Sea basin than to the Mediterranean, the slope to the latter must be much the more gentle,
and afford better opportunities of cultivating the soil than that

[1] See also Tristram, *Land of Israel*, p. 281.
[2] Wildenbruch, Plate iii. in *Monatsb.* p. 270; Russegger, *Reise*, iii. p.
211; von Schubert, in Steinheil, p. 382.

to the former. Yet, despite the steep and comparatively barren
character of the wadis on the eastern slope, it must not be supposed that there are not there traces of former life and culture;
far otherwise : there may be seen not only the camps of the
Beduin Taamirah and the Jehalin, but the sites of places well
known in history—Urtas, Jebel Fureidis (the Frank Mountain)
with the Herodion, Tekua (Tekoa), Beni Naim east of Hebron,
Kurmul (Carmel), Tell Tawareh, and others. These are all
found on the routes leading to Engeddi and Masada, and they
must all be considered as strictly belonging to the valley of the
Jordan and the basin of the Dead Sea. The regularly travelled
road, so often taken and so often described, leading from
Hebron to Jerusalem, passes not far from these places, and
yet leaves them entirely untouched. The able accounts of
such men as von- Schubert, Russegger, Wilson, Tischendorf,
and even of Seetzen and Burckhardt, throw no light upon
this region, and Pococke and Irby and Mangles have touched
it only here and there. Passing from the neighbourhood of
the celebrated Pools of Solomon, now el-Burok of the Arabs,
near Bethlehem, the beginning of a large aqueduct which
did much in ancient times to supply Jerusalem with water,
and which has not ceased to fulfil that function even yet, the
traveller reaches the deep Wadi Urtas, running eastward, and
forming the basin for a fine brook, by whose waters many
gardens in the vale are made fruitful. It takes its name
from the little ruined village of Urtas.[1] Above the spring the
beginning of the valley is altogether barren. The abundance
of water found in the vale, so near to the pools which were
employed not merely to supply the city of Jerusalem with
water, but also to irrigate the neighbouring district, in which,
according to Josephus, king Solomon laid out the gardens of
Etam,[2] where Rehoboam built the cities of Bethlehem, Etam,
and Tekoa, and where, according to the Talmud, were the
springs of Etham, so often named in connection with the Pools
of Solomon, make it probable that, in the place now known as
Urtas, we may locate the spot anciently known by the names
of Etam, Etham, and Aitam. The fine abundant spring which

---

[1] Robinson, *Bib. Research.* i. pp. 474, 477 ; Wolcott, *Excursion to Masada*, in *Bib. Sacra*, 1843, p. 43.

[2] Lightfoot, in Robinson, ii. p. 167, Note.

forms the first murmuring which Robinson discovered in Palestine, was certainly once a not unfrequented region, and one well worthy to be spoken of as it is in the Song of Solomon, as a " garden enclosed." Down the valley were to be seen, at the time of Robinson's visit, the countless flocks of the Ta'amireh Arabs. On the way to visit them he passed the ruined village of Menehtisheh, in whose neighbourhood he detected traces of the ancient Canaanite terrace culture. In an hour he reached the foot of Jebel el Fureidis,[1] or the " Little Paradise," a word which evidently hints at a time long past, when it was admired for its beauty and fertility. The mountain rises to the height of three or four hundred feet as a flattened and entirely isolated cone, standing on the level table-land, and high above the lowest portion of Wadi Urtas. Its base displays traces of ancient terrace culture, and was apparently more used for purposes of tillage than of defence. Remains of ditches, a church, and road, which Pococke asserts that he saw, were not observed by Robinson, but there were clear traces of terraces, of cisterns, and the remains of walls. In ten minutes he had reached the top of the hill, where he found a wall circling the entire summit; the stones composing it were of tolerably large size : there were magazines, cisterns, and four massive towers looking towards the cardinal points. Among the recent travellers who have visited the place, which is best known in modern times under the name of the Frank Mountain, are Irby[2] and Wolcott.[3] Their accounts are, however, brief. The latter came from a south-east direction, and observed an ancient road twelve feet wide leading up the hill on the north-east side, near the lower portion of which there were the clear traces of former terrace culture. This discovery has been fully confirmed by the later observations of Gadow and Wolff.[4] Before their day, Pococke, Mariti, Berggren, and von Raumer[5] had shown the identity of the Frank Mountain with the Herodium or burial-place of Herod the Great, described by Josephus. Irby considered the architectural traces hardly extensive enough

---

[1] Robinson, *Bib. Research.* i. p. 478.
[2] Irby and Mangles, *Trav.* p. 339.
[3] Wolcott, *Excursion, l.c.* pp. 69, 70.
[4] Ph. Wolff, *Reise in das Gelobte Land,* p. 121.
[5] Von Raumer, *Paläst.* pp. 219, 220.

to have been a fortress, but he recognised the remains at the
foot as Roman work. Wolcott entirely coincides with this,
although he confesses that there is very little coherence in the
ruins; and of the two hundred polished stones of which Josephus
speaks, as forming a magnificent staircase to the top, no trace
whatever remains. Wolff, however, noticed stones which he
thought might have had such a use. Yet, notwithstanding that
Wolcott did not remark what Wolff was so fortunate as to do,
he was struck with the close agreement of the description given
by Josephus of the Herodium with this place, and asserts that
it gives him great confidence in his accuracy as a historical
guide; for although in some points he may be inclined to
exaggerate, yet in this description at least he speaks of that of
which he had been an eye-witness.

Robinson[1] found, on ascending the Frank Mountain, that
the prospect from the summit was not nearly so extensive as
he expected to find it : the view was tolerably extensive towards
the north, but towards the east and the Dead Sea it was very
contracted, neither the northern nor the southern ends being
in sight, and not much more of the surface being visible than
could be discerned from the Mount of Olives. Robinson
found that the name commonly given to this mountain sprang
from an entirely groundless tradition, that the Franks fled to
this place for security at the time of the Crusades, and long
defended themselves here against the Saracens. The tradition
was first made current by Felix Fabri,[2] who does not, however,
name the place as the Frank Mountain, but as Rama. On the
other hand, Robinson declares himself decisively in favour of
the conjecture that that place is to be identified with the ancient
Herodium ; and not less strong in this is Reland. According
to Josephus, it was sixty stadia or three hours' distance, and
therefore not far from Tekoah. Here, upon a mountain of
moderate height, as we are told on the same authority, Herod
erected a fortress with rounded towers, and containing apartments suitable for the pomp and revelry which he loved. In
order more coveniently to ascend, he constructed a staircase of
two hundred steps, and at the base he built a costly palace,

[1] Robinson, *Bib. Research.* ii. pp. 393, 398.

[2] Fel. Fabri, *Evagatorium : de monte Rama et ejus oppido,* T. ii. pp.
335-337.

laying out beautiful gardens around it, and supplying it liberally with water. Wolff observed a cistern in a good state of
preservation, and about the size of the Pool of Hezekiah[1] at
Jerusalem, near the north-west corner of the ruins. The whole
plain displays the relics of a large city; and we know that the
place was once of so great consequence, that it gave the name
to one of the toparchies of Judæa. The place is not mentioned
by Ptolemy, Eusebius, nor Jerome. Reland, as I have already
remarked, regards this as the true Herodium, and as not to be
confounded with one east of the Dead Sea, and mentioned by
Josephus. It was in this Herodium west of the Dead Sea
that the body of Herod was interred, although recent travellers
have not been able to discover the place of the sepulture: inscriptions and sculptures are utterly wanting. The conjecture
that on this mountain, prior to the erection of the structures of
Herod, was the watch-tower of Beth-haccerem referred to in
Jer. vi. 1, is not destitute of inherent probability, but data are
wanting to enable us to substantiate it.

A narrow and picturesque gorge runs along the north-east
side of the Frank Mountain to Wadi Urtas, displaying high
precipitous rocks on both sides, on whose crest may be seen the
remains of a square tower of the village of Khureitun,[2] a little
beyond which is the opening to an immense cave, which can
be entered on foot. Eli Smith, as well as Irby and Mangles,
have described it under the name of the Labyrinth.[3] They
dismounted from their horses, and followed a long and winding
passage until they reached some natural chambers and caverns
on both sides. At length they came to a large chamber with
high natural arches; from this there ran galleries in several
directions, forming a perfect labyrinth, and said by their guide
never to have been thoroughly investigated. The galleries, so
far as they explored them, they estimated to be about four feet
high, three feet wide, and free from rubbish; the air was sweet
and pure. In one apartment were to be seen fragments of
pottery, and on the walls the names of English travellers who
had been there, written with coal. The caverns seemed to have
once been inhabited; the legend calls them the caves of Adullam,

[1] Wolff, *Reise in das Gelobte Land*, p. 122.
[2] Robinson, *Bib. Research.* ii. p. 398.
[3] Irby and Mangles, *Trav.* p. 340.

in which David once concealed himself for fear of Saul (1 Sam. xxii. 1) : in 2 Sam. xxiii. 13, it is mentioned in connection with the valley of Rephaim and the well of Bethlehem.

In the book of Joshua, where the king of Adullam[1] is mentioned among the princes of Judæa, and in connection with those of Jericho, Jerusalem, and Jarmuth, and others whom Joshua conquered, the last-named place is connected with Adullam, Socoh, and other places among the lowlands, according to which its situation has been supposed to be farther west. According to the *Onomasticon*, it was ten Roman miles east of Eleutheropolis : this would be north-east of Beit Jibrin, in the neighbourhood of Shuweikeh (Socoh) and Yurmuk (Jarmuth), and would agree well with the statement of Joshua. As the region, too, is not destitute of caves, it is not probable that the so-called Labyrinth of Khureitun is identical with the ancient Adullam.

The most careful exploration of this network of caverns near the village of Chörbet Chareitun, or Khureitun, was made by Tobler[2] in December 1845. Though called by Europeans the Labyrinth, it is never known by the Arabs as anything but the Caves of Chareitun. His purpose was to explore the place in all directions; and in spite of great difficulties and some dangers, he fully accomplished the object. After climbing up to the almost inaccessible passage, he followed the opening in a direction running first north-west and then north. The roof of the cave he found thickly peopled by bats. Soon he discovered several side passages. Passing the first cavern, he entered one bearing the name of John Gordon, an Englishman who explored it in 1804. Soon he advanced to a third, which had been explored by Franciscan monks, and bore their appellation. From this place ran two paths, a shorter one running northward, and a longer one bearing to the right. This one Tobler[3] chose for his special exploration, as the most recent visitors had entered the one most easily examined. With the entrance of the less accessible gallery began the process of fresh discovery in this interesting subterranean world. Countless passages opened

[1] Robinson, *Bib. Research.*; Keil, *Comment. zu Josua*, p. 234.
[2] In *Ausland*, 1847, Nos. 179–181.
[3] F. A. Strauss, *Sinai und Golgotha*, p. 343.

before him, many of them offering great difficulties in his path; but the greater the obstacles, the more delight did the bold and enthusiastic Tobler take in overcoming them. The main gallery was soon followed to the end, and then came the successive side passages which led to the places of sepulture. In one place he found a cistern containing water, and along the sides of the galleries there were brown marks, which seemed to him to indicate the height at which water had stood in the rainy season.

The excavation of stone effected by human hands did not seem to him to have had for its object the piercing of the whole mountain, but merely the reaching of a place where the remains of the dead might lie in all possible quiet. Inscriptions were very numerous, but they were not cut deeply into the rock. He copied several of them, and considered the characters to be those in use among the Samaritans. Here and there he found fragments of stone coffins and sarcophagi. All the graves seemed to have been injured by violence. From the entrance to the first deep cavern Tobler found the distance to be four hundred and twenty feet; thence to the John Gordon cave, seventy feet; thence to the Franciscan cave, three hundred and three feet; and thence to the end, two hundred and seventeen,—making an aggregate of more than a thousand feet. The warmth he found to be great, although it was late in December, the thermometer standing at 20° Reaumur. The investigation of the hitherto unknown labyrinth consumed two hours. The object of the exploration was fully accomplished: for it was clear the place was originally intended to be a place of sepulture. Tobler adds to his account some valuable details regarding St Chariton,[1] from whom this place derives its name.

Only about a half-hour's distance southward from this spot, on a slight eminence,[2] from which the sea can be descried in many places, the whole plain is covered with ruins, which bear the name Tekua,[3] conjectured by Pococke, and held since his day, to be the Tekoa of the Bible. Robinson speaks of the great extent of the remains, among which he noticed those of

---

[1] Bollandi *Acta Sanctorum*, 28 *Sept.* p. 615 ; *Vita Charitonis*, comp. *Vita Kyriakus*, 29 *Sept.*

[2] Irby and Mangles, *Trav.* p. 407.

[3] Robinson, *Bib. Research.* i. pp. 486, 489.

a square tower or ancient castle, and by their side the fragments
of a Greek church, with pillars and baptismal font of rose-
coloured marble, near which were many cisterns hewn in the
rock, and a fine spring of water. Irby discovered the pillars,
but none of the other remains.

In 2 Chron. xi. 5, 6, it is stated that Rehoboam, who
resided in Jerusalem, built the cities of Bethlehem, Etham,
and Tekoa as fortresses; but these places had an existence
much earlier: for at the time of David, Tekoa is mentioned
in connection with the story of Joab and Absalom. Under
Jehoshaphat the district east of the city is called the wilderness of Tekoa. The name survives in the modern Tekua,[1]
as is the case with so many places on the west shore of the
Dead Sea, such as Ziph in Siph, Main in Maon, Usdom in
Sodom, Ain Jiddi in Engeddi. Besides this, which is in
itself decisive, the distance assigned to Tekoa from Jerusalem
by Jerome and Eusebius agrees precisely with the facts as
shown by modern travellers. It is not improbable that the
Eltekon mentioned in Josh. xv. 59 is an ancient name of
Tekoa,[2] and that the place was thus known among the
Canaanites. In the sixth century St Saba founded a new
laura in connection with the more celebrated one already
described; and we find it held by Christians at the time of
St Willibald's visit in 765. At the time of the Crusades, too,
Tekoa was inhabited, and gave assistance on the occasion of
the assault on Jerusalem. Still later the place was made over
to the canons of the Church of the Holy Sepulchre in exchange
for Bethany.[3] It is possible that the octagonal font discovered
by Wolcott at Tekoa[4] in 1842 may date back to this recent
time. He also saw the capitals of the pillars which Irby and
Mangles observed. In the year 1138 the place was plundered
by a horde of Turks, and most of the inhabitants took refuge
in the neighbouring caves of Kureitun, then held to be those
of Adullam.[5] Nothing is heard of the place subsequently to
that time; and even in Jerusalem, such was the panic there,

---

[1] Von Raumer, p. 219.
[2] Keil, *Comment. zu Josua*, p. 304.
[3] Robinson, *Bib. Research.* i. p. 432.
[4] Wolcott, *Excursion*, in *Bib. Sacra*, p. 69.
[5] Will. Tyr. xv.; Wilken, *Gesch. d. Kreuz.* Pt. ii. p. 682.

that the Turkish robbery at Tekoa was unheard of,—a fact all the more singular, as the place was one of note for its connection with the birth of the prophet Amos. It is only in modern times that its site has been examined. In the opening verse of the prophecy of Amos, we learn that he was one of the herdsmen of Tekoa at the time of Uzziah the king of Judah, and Jeroboam the son of Joash king of Israel. At the time of the Maccabees this district was called the wilderness of Tekoe; and Jerome alludes to it as a broad desert, only inhabited by herdsmen, and once the home of the prophet Amos. And such it remains to the present day. Here the camps of the Taamireh and the Jehalin are found, extending from the great central line of watershed to the shores of the Dead Sea. Between these two chief tribes in the north and the south, there are found other smaller ones scattered here and there, whose mode of life and habits do not vary materially from what they were in the time of the prophet Amos. The desert region lying between the line of fixed habitations and the coast of the Dead Sea, forms a natural transition from the wild life of the Beduins to that of the agricultural people who live in villages and huts. The tribes inhabiting this intermediate tract hold a singular position: they are viewed with equal distrust by those less and those more wild than themselves, and are usually known by the scornful appellation of Israelites. In order to reach the western shores of the Dead Sea, it is necessary to put one's self under the guidance of these tribes. Robinson[1] passed a night in the camp of the Taamirah at Tekua, consisting of only six tents, and learned that the whole tribe reckoned three hundred armed men, who pasture their herds between Bethlehem, Tekoa, and the Dead Sea. They have but a single village, but they do not live there much, and use it mainly as a convenient place for storing the few agricultural products which they raise. The women went without veils, and were busily engaged in kneading thin cakes and baking them in the ashes, in making butter by shaking cream well together in sheep-skin bottles, and in turning the hand-mills, which seemed to be identical in construction with those often mentioned in the Bible, and to be turned now as then by

[1] Robinson, *Bib. Research.* ii. pp. 482, 487; Wolcott, *Excursion, l.c.* p. 55.

women, who lighten their arduous labour by singing. The men were far differently employed: they were away on their predatory expeditions, gaining a worse name, if possible, than they had already acquired in the land. In the year 1834 they took a formidable part in the rebellion against the Egyptian authority; but being at length thoroughly put down, they were disarmed, and reduced to a tolerable degree of subjection. Among this restless race Robinson[1] found himself as safe as he had done elsewhere among other Arabs, when they had pledged themselves to serve him; and both the sheikh and the men would have offered their lives in his defence, although lying and cheating were as familiar to them as to all their Beduin fellows. The sheikh was a sacred personage among the Arabs, and his protection was no less valuable to Robinson than that of another fakir had been to the missionary Smith[2] among the mountains of Moab and Heshbon.

DISCURSION V.

WEST SHORE OF THE DEAD SEA CONTINUED: ROBINSON'S ROUTE FROM THE CAMP OF THE TAAMIRAH VIA BENI NAIM (KAPHAR BARUCHA) AND TELL ZIF (ZIPH) TO MAEIN (MAON) AND KURMUL (CARMEL) ; THENCE TO AIN JIDDY (ENGEDI) AND AIN TERABEH. WOLCOTT'S VISIT TO SEBBEH, MASADA.

1. *From the Camp of the Taamirah and Beni Naim by way of Tell Zif to Kurmul.*

A half-day's march brought Robinson from the Taamirah camp to the village Beni Naîm, one and a quarter hours north-east of Hebron. The tract which he crossed is intersected by numerous wadis which run towards the south-east, and unite in the neighbourhood of Ain Jiddi.[3] Still westward, and between Tekoa and Hebron,[4] lies the village of Sair, surrounded by arbutus trees, dwarf oaks, small firs, and with the ground overgrown with the fragrant zater (*thymus serpillum*). Not far away upon the hill lies a cistern, Bir es Zaferaneh, on the side of a rocky tract, where three trees form a landmark observable

---

[1] Robinson, *Bib. Research.* ii. pp. 482, 487 ; Wolcott, *Excursion*, p. 55.
[2] Eli Smith, *On Bedawin Tribes*, in *Miss. Herald*, vol. xxxv. p. 87.
[3] Robinson, *Bib. Research.* i. pp. 487–520.
[4] Wolcott, *Excursion*, *l.c.* p. 55.

at a long distance. While the guides went to Hebron to get
barley, Robinson continued his researches along the high line
of watershed till he reached Beni Naim, which seemed to be
the loftiest point in the whole Judæan range. The whole of
the road which he followed, although very desolate, yet showed
almost everywhere traces of the terrace culture which was once
so flourishing throughout this whole district. The Moslems
pay veneration to a place there which they suppose to be the
burial-place of Lot, above which a mosque is now built: the
tradition is mentioned by Maundeville[1] as existing five hundred
years ago. The building has very strikingly the appearance
of a castle. The most of the houses are constructed of large
hewn stones of ancient origin: many of the cisterns hewn in
the rock were covered with large stones, in order to guard them
from the encroachments of strangers, and it required the efforts
of two or three men to remove one from its place. The arrangement was almost identical with that at the time of Abraham
and Jacob, and recalled to Robinson's mind the patriarchal
times at almost every step. He cites, in confirmation of this,
Gen. xxix. 2, 3 : " And he looked, and behold, a well in the
field, and, lo, there were three flocks of sheep lying by it ; for
out of that well they watered the flocks : and a great stone
was upon the well's mouth. And thither were all the flocks
gathered : and they rolled the stone from the well's mouth,
and watered the sheep, and put the stone again upon the well's
mouth in its place." The prospect from the roof of the mosque
northward is limited within a short distance by the mountain
land, on the west by the Hebron range : eastward the ridge
east of the Dead Sea is plainly to be seen ; while southward
the country slopes gradually towards the southernmost spurs
of the Judæan mountains and to the Ghor. Many traces of
ancient places are to be seen whose old names are still often
to be found reproduced, though slightly changed, in those by
which they are now designated.

    This locality would on many accounts correspond with the
situation of Kaphar Barucha, the *villa benedictionis,* or city of
blessings. Reland[2] supposed that this was the site of the Vallis
Beraca, in which, at the time of the Ammonites and Moabites

[1] Sir John Maundeville, *The Voiage and Travaille,* ed. Halliwell, p. 68.
[2] Reland, *Pal.* pp. 356, 685.

who came up from Engedi, and who were threatening Jerusalem, a complete victory was gained over the enemies of Israel. This gave the name Baracha to the place. The eminence which was ·described above is probably not to be considered as the place originally called the Valley of Praise ; the primitive name appearing in the appellation of a place discovered by Robinson[1] in the neighbourhood, and called Bereikût. Wolcott's investigations in 1843 confirmed this, and made it certain that the ancient name Berachah[2] survives in the word Bereikût, and that it was at an early period wrongly supposed to be not in the valley, but upon the high land near by, of which Jerome speaks in his account of the journeys of Paula.

Robinson, much encouraged and stimulated by the success which he met in this region in throwing light upon the lands of Scripture, resolved, after resting a short time at the mosque of Beni Naim, to visit Kurmul, Zif, Main, and Yutta, on the road to Engaddi.

One and a half hours towards the south-south-west he came to the western base of the hill of Zif, a round eminence lying in the plain, about a hundred feet in height, and on the road from Hebron to Kurmul.[3] The ruins of the ancient city of Ziph mentioned in Josh. xv. 55 lie about ten minutes east of the hill, on a low ridge between two little wadis, which have their beginnings here, and run on towards Masada. Broken walls composed of massive stones are scattered around ; and Robinson also noticed[4] a large square structure with arches, cisterns, and a hewn entrance, which seemed to lead to a subterranean magazine. The top of the hill is also surrounded with a wall, and provided with cisterns. This Ziph is not identical with the one mentioned in Josh. xv. 24, whose position is still unknown. The one discovered by Robinson is mentioned in the third group of cities mentioned in the chapter just cited, and is conjoined with Maon, Carmel, and Juttah : it is the place also to which David fled from the persecutions of

---

[1] Robinson, *Bib. Research.* i. p. 491.

[2] Wolcott, *Excursion*, p. 43.

[3] Robinson, *Bib. Research.* ii. p. 97, and i. p. 492 ; comp. Rödiger, *Rec. i.a.l.* p. 566.

[4] Robinson, *Bib. Research.* ii. p. 101, Note 1.

Saul : the account is contained in 1 Sam. xxiii. 14, 25, and following verses. The fifty-fourth Psalm is supposed to be a prayer for deliverance while David was in danger of his life. It was in Ziph, too, that that friendship was contracted between David and Jonathan, which is one of the most touching episodes in the Bible. It is probable that this is the Ziph which is mentioned in 2 Chron. xi. 8 as rebuilt by king Rehoboam. Jerome mentions its distance from Hebron as eight Roman miles, which, however, does not agree with the location of the place to which I refer, which is but five Roman miles thence.

From Tell Ziph[1] the Hebron road runs for several hours through the finest district, according to Robinson, which he had seen in the mountain land in Judæa. It is skirted on both sides by basin-shaped plateaus surrounded by mountains, which, though not so high as those of Dhoheriyeh[2] in the west, on the road from et-Tih, yet rise to an altitude of fifteen hundred feet above the Mediterranean. The summits, free from rocks, and with a waving surface, are mostly devoted to the cultivation of wheat. The grain was nearly ripe at the time of Robinson's visit, and the hungry Arabs were plucking the ears, rubbing them with their hands, and eating them : they asserted, moreover, that it was an old usage to do this with impunity, and that the owner of the grain could not remonstrate with them for so doing. This seems to throw some light upon the act of the disciples referred to in Matt. xii. 1–6 and Luke vi. 1, and shows why the Master called His disciples innocent. The Pharisees, too, it will be noticed, did not condemn the taking of the corn, but the doing so on the Sabbath-day, by which the temple was desecrated. The reader will recall the answer which shows the grandeur of the speaker : "But I say to you, that in this place is One greater than the temple."

Passing two little places which were both called Ziph by the Arabs, Robinson passed upon the left a collection of ruins called Um el Amad, or Mother of Souls,[3] the name being derived, it may be, from a church which seems once to have been there. At six o'clock he reached the site of Kurmul[4] (Carmel), lying three hours directly south from Hebron. In its neighbourhood

---

[1] Robinson, *Bib. Research.* i. pp. 208–211.   [2] *Ibid.* p. 492.
[3] *Ibid.* ii. p. 206.   [4] *Ibid.* pp. 96, 97.

he discovered the village of Main, a little farther south. There were caves and sheepfolds to be seen there. A crowd of herdsmen from the village of Yutta were tending flocks, and sheltering them in the caves around. They showed themselves willing to serve the strangers; for they supposed that they were Franks who had come to rescue them from the yoke of their Egyptian masters. They were under the delusion that their guests were in possession of valuable documents, and that they had come to seek information regarding the property held by the Arab tenants.

This Main is unquestionably Maon, the home of the rich but selfish Nabal, and of Abigail his wife. Here he found pasture for the three thousand sheep which he possessed at the time when David met him.

I have elsewhere[1] had occasion to allude to the site of the Kurmul of the Arabs, the Carmel of southern Judæa, a place by no means to be confounded with the Carmel range south of the plain of Esdraelon. It has been carefully observed by Robinson and Wolcott. There are the ruins[2] of a solitary church, and of an ancient city, lying just at the opening, and along the two sides of a tolerably broad and long valley, whose commencement forms a semicircular amphitheatre surrounded by rocks, from which the vale extends about two hundred paces towards the Dead Sea. The bottom of this amphitheatre is now occupied by a fine grass plot, at whose centre is an artificial reservoir a hundred and seventeen feet long and seventy-four wide : this is fed by a spring in the rock, but was dry at the time of the American's visit. The chief ruins of Kurmul lie west of the amphitheatre, on a level spot where once a castle stood, whose walls may yet be seen lying in wild confusion on all sides, scattered among the ruins of many houses, including those of a little church. An open entrance leads to a natural cave, as at Ziph : this seems intended to have served either as a place of sepulture or as a storehouse for provisions. At the east of the castle there is a second cave, but not a natural one, leading into the rock. The site of the castle in the midst of the city, with its walls rising to a height of thirty feet, is almost as unmistakeably a monument of antiquity as the Hippicus tower

[1] Seetzen, in *Mon. Corresp.* vol. xvii. p. 134.
[2] Robinson, *Bib. Research.* i. pp. 496-500.

at Jerusalem. The walls, which are nine or ten feet in thickness, consist of two storeys; the arches of the windows have been unquestionably added within a modern period. At the north side of the castle there are the foundations of a round tower, at the east side the remains of a little church.

On the east side of the valley, opposite the castle, lay a small part of the ancient city, perhaps a suburb of it; remains of a tower appeared ten minutes farther on; and upon the summit of a hill were to be seen the ruins of a large church: all proofs of the importance of this border city of Palestine at the time of Jerome. The place is mentioned as existing as early even as the time of Joshua, and it is mentioned still later in the account of Nabal and Abigail. At the time of the Crusades and of Saladin it appears as a small place, but as containing a castle which had been restored by the crusaders:[1] the time of its entire destruction is unknown. Wolcott, who visited the place, March 11, 1842, found the tower composed of small slightly hewn stones, with a Greek cross upon the northern arch, and therefore not ancient: the external wall had no relation to the internal one. He confirms the existence even now of the ruins of three churches,[2] evidently built at different times; he discovered tombs in the rock with round arches, and seemingly dating from the Byzantine period. From the remains, the crusaders appear to have built the castle with arches, which is seen in the neighbourhood of the three churches. From the greatest eminence, on which the scanty ruins of Maon lie, a mere square castle with cisterns, the view ranges away over the wilderness, taking in several places whose ancient names have been preserved with slightly changed forms for nearly three thousand years. A part of these Seetzen[3] learned and entered upon his map; but the topography of the district was first carefully studied by Robinson, Eli Smith,[4] and a few other recent travellers. Wilson,[5] who also traversed the region, was thoroughly surprised at finding that, although, since the time of Jerome, hardly any single one of the ancient places

[1] Wilken, *Gesch. der Kreuzzüge*, Pt. iii. p. 151, Note 162.
[2] Wolcott, *Excursion*, in *Bib. Sacra*, 1843, p. 61.
[3] Seetzen, *Mon. Corresp.* xvii. pp. 134–138.
[4] Robinson, *Bib. Research.* i. pp. 494–496.
[5] Wilson, *Lands of the Bible*, i. p. 380.

has been mentioned by any historian, the names which were current in Joshua's time still live on in that south-eastern corner of Judæa.

Semua[1] is probably the ancient Esmua, and the Eshtemoh of Josh. xv. 50, xxi. 14, which belonged to the tribe of Judah. It was made over to the sons of Aaron; and its castle, whose masonry is well preserved, seems to date back to the period of the Crusades. From its tower Yutta and Tell Tawaneh can be seen. Kinnear[2] recognised here the remains of Roman architecture. Yutta, a large village lying towards the north-west, is the Juttah of Josh. xv. 55. Seetzen visited it on his journey from Hebron to Madara,[3] and found it inhabited by Mohammedans. He considered it identical with that city of Judah to which Mary went when visiting Elisabeth in the house of Zacharias. Reland recognised this place, which was near to Hebron and Carmel, as the πόλις 'Ιούδα of the New Testament, the *urbs sacerdotalis et patria Johannis Baptistæ.* Rosenmüller and von Raumer are of the same opinion. One reason for coming to this conclusion is, that nowhere can the home of Zacharias, the father of John the Baptist, be more fitly looked for, than in one of the cities appropriated to the priests; and such Juttah was.

Tawaneh[4] seems not to be an ancient name. But Altir's ruins, south of Semua, may possibly indicate the site of Jattir, which at the time of Jerome was a great village, inhabited by Christians. It was twenty Roman miles from Eleutheropolis, *in interiore Daramæ juxta Malatham,*[5] which seems to correspond well with the places newly discovered.

Sufiah is a spot lying farther north-west : it has many pillars, but no remains of houses. Anab, west of Carmul, retains unchanged the name which it had at the time of Joshua; it appears in Jerome[6] under the designations Anam and Anim : the place, however, has not been visited. In the name

[1] Keil, *Comment. zu Josua,* p. 301.
[2] J. Kinnear, *Cairo, Petra, etc.,* p. 191.
[3] Seetzen, *Mon. Corresp.* xvii. p. 134 ; comp. Rosenmüller, *Bibl. Alterth.* vol. ii. p. 317 ; and von Raumer, *Pal.* p. 206. See also Keil, *Comment. zu Josua,* p. 302.
[4] Robinson, *Bibl. Research.* ii. p. 205.
[5] Keil, *Comment. zu Josua,* p. 300.   [6] *Ibid.* p. 301.

Shuweikeh, a village south-west of Kurmul and Semua, may be recognised the diminutive of Shaukeh, and the ancient Socoh,[1] a mountain' city mentioned in Josh. xv. 48. Certainly a careful examination of that neighbourhood would throw much light upon other cities not yet identified, and show the sites of very many of the cities spoken of in Josh. xv. 48–61, as belonging to the territory of the tribe of Judah. Even the comparatively slight investigations made by Robinson[2] yielded results astonishingly great, far beyond any which he had ventured to expect.

2. *Route from Kurmul (Carmel) through Wadi el Ghor to Ain Jiddi (Engedi).*

From this region, so full of monuments of the Mosaic times, Robinson took his way from Kurmul directly eastward to Ain Jiddi,[3] which he reached after a march of seven or eight hours through a wild and romantic district, lying directly upon the western shore of the Dead Sea. As Robinson is the only traveller who has described this route with full details, he will be our guide.

Leaving Kurmul, and passing the ruins of Tell Tawaneh, his course led him at first through a tract of arable land to an encampment of Kaabineh Arabs, consisting of thirty tents, which gave shelter to a hundred men. The way was constantly a descending one; the air grew hotter as he left the high land. At Kurmul the grass was green; two hours farther on it was scorched, and the district assumed more and more the appearance of a waste. After a four hours' march, Robinson found himself in a desolate tract, where a limestone soil alternated with a chalky and a pebbly one. On every side rose cone-shaped hills to a height of from two to four hundred feet. The most of these were overgrown with bushes. Soon, however, as he passed on, even this scanty vegetation ceased, and there was little left beside the scanty shrubs which grow upon the desert of the Sinai Peninsula. Passing some very steep mountain ridges, Robinson reached a water cistern called Bir Selhub, and afterwards arrived at a precipice about two hundred feet high, down which he had to make his way. Half an hour later he

---

[1] Robinson, *Bib. Research.* passim; Keil, *Comment.* p. 301.
[2] Robinson, *Bib. Research.* i. pp. 495, 496. [3] *Ibid.* p. 499 et sq.

met a similar abrupt slope, after descending which he found himself at the opening of a very difficult pass leading to the Wadi el Ghor. Caves, crags, and dangerous abysses were visible on every side. He had reached the wilderness of Engedi where Saul went out with three thousand men against David, and into one of whose caverns the king entered to cover his feet, when his life was spared by his young antagonist, who had him completely in his power. Here, too, took place the reconciliation between Saul and David, shortly before the death of Samuel.

The Wadi el Ghor becomes narrower and narrower, the perpendicular crags being at last but about fifty feet apart. They serve as a refuge for innumerable doves. Soon Robinson found the way entirely impassable, and was compelled to leave the ravine and betake himself to the high plateau. He here discovered the road leading directly from Jerusalem to Ain Jiddy. The locality which he had just left he supposed, as Rödiger[1] has also done, to be the place in which the army of Jehoshaphat laid their ambuscade at the time of the invasion of the combined forces of Moab, Ammon, and Seir. Here seems to be the brook mentioned in 2 Chron. xx. 16, and the precipice of Ziz. Here it was, in all probability, that that easy victory was gained over forces altogether outnumbering those of Judah ; and here the high priest ordered the hymn of praise to be sung to the glory of God, who had given them so easy and yet so complete a victory.

From the high lands above the pass, the Dead Sea can be so clearly seen that it seems to be but a very short distance away ; and yet so many obstacles lay in the way, that Robinson found it a journey of some hours to arrive there. The whole southern portion of the sea was to be seen with perfect distinctness ; the view of the northern half was hidden by the projecting crag of Mersed. Especially striking was the great number of little tongues running out into the southern portion of the sea. Burckhardt,[2] who gained a good view of the Dead Sea at Kerak, was particularly struck by this feature, and speaks of the number of sand-banks which he saw, which seemed in some cases to form perfect islands, encrusted over

---

[1] Robinson, *Bib. Research.* i. p. 508.
[2] Burckhardt, *Trav.* p. 395.

with salt. At the southern extremity of the lake Robinson saw the salt pillar of Sodom, the Usdum of the Arabs; Kerak, with its castle, was visible to the south-east; the mouth of the Arnon and Serka Maein were seen to the east. Southward, half-way to Usdum, and below Wadi es Seyal, the valley next south of Khuberah, there was to be seen a high pyramidal crag which the guide called Sebbeh. Seetzen had noticed it, and entered it upon his map under the name Szebby; but it was never visited until Wolcott explored it some years subsequently to Robinson's investigations. He ascertained that it was the site of the ancient fortress of Masada.

After taking a thorough survey of the scene, he began to make the toilsome descent down the zig-zag pass,[1] over masses of red limestone, smooth as glass, but with irregular surfaces. Only in a few places had human skill done anything to lessen the difficulties, which Eli Smith declares to have been greater than he had encountered in the mountains of Persia, and Robinson to have surpassed those of Switzerland. During the descent the travellers noticed an optical illusion—a dark yellow island seeming to be lying in the middle of the lake,—a phenomenon to which Seetzen,[2] Irby, Mangles, and other recent travellers have alluded, and of which Josephus also speaks as peculiar to the Dead Sea.

After a descent of three-quarters of an hour, Robinson reached the fine spring of Ain Jiddy, which breaks forth from the surface of a small spur of the mountain range, more than four hundred feet above the level of the sea. The stream which flows from it rushes down through a thicket of trees and bushes. It was impossible to clamber down the rocks at this place, and a long detour was needed. At the spring there were several remains of ancient buildings,[3] although the site of Engedi is some distance below. The spring is clear, sparkling, and profuse, but not cold, the temperature of the water being 21¾° Reaumur.

Among the trees around the spring were the Arabian gum acacia, the seyāl, and the semur, natives of the Sinai Peninsula; but Robinson also saw several which are found at

---

[1] Robinson, *Bib. Research.* i. p. 504.

[2] Seetzen, *Mon. Corresp.* xviii. p. 438; Irby and Mangles, *Trav.* p. 457.

[3] Robinson, *Bib. Research.* i. p. 505.

Jericho,—the nabk, the asher, the fustak, and even a few palms. The latter may have given the proud name Hazezontamar, *i.e. Amputatio palmarum*,[1] derived perhaps from the custom which prevailed here of increasing the fruitfulness of the trees by cutting off the fructified pistils. The date palm is now no longer found at Engedi. So, too, the balsam trees and vineyards which are mentioned in Josephus, the Song of Solomon, and Pliny. The vineyards mentioned by Hasselquist[2] are not those alluded to in the Song of Solomon, since at the time of the Swedish naturalist the location of Engedi was not known. An ancient legend caused the Christians of Hebron to locate Engedi[3] and the cave of David there,—an error which some of the most recent writers[4] have fallen into, and which, looked at superficially, has some show of probability, from the fact that in ancient times the land bordering upon the brook of Eshcol yielded the finest grapes, and even now the largest raisins,[5] while Robinson did not discover a single vine at Engedi.[6] On Seetzen's map the location of the place is given correctly for the first time. It was seen by him from the mouth of the Arnon opposite. Reland, D'Anville, Pococke, and Arrowsmith (even in the second decennium of the present century), place it at the northern extremity[7] of the Dead Sea.

It required a half-hour to clamber down through the thicket to the sea-shore, passing over a succession of terraces once used as gardens.[8] At their foot Robinson discovered the ruins of an ancient city. They offered no features of special interest, the stones being all rough and unhewn. From the base of the steep descent, a fine fruitful plain extends for a space of a quarter of an hour to the coast-line. Through this plain runs the water of the brook, which serves as the outlet of the spring above. At the time of Robinson's visit, how-

[1] Rosenmüller, *Bib. Alterthk.* ii. p. 162 ; Winer, *Bibl. Realw.* i. p. 537.

[2] Hasselquist, *Reise nach Palästina*, p. 256.

[3] Quaresmius, *Elucidat. Terr. Sanctæ*, tom. ii. lib. vi. c. 10, fol. 691–695; Pococke, *Trav.* Pt. ii. p. 62.

[4] *Syrien, Pal. und Klein Asien*, vol. ii. p. 62.

[5] Robinson, *Bib. Research.* ii. p. 80.   [6] *Ibid.* p. 509.

[7] Roberts, *La Terre Sainte*, liv. vii. tab. xix.

[8] Robinson, *Bib. Research.* ii. p. 506.

ever, the land was so dry that it absorbed all the water before it reached the sea. As far as the influence of the brook extended, the ground was plentifully covered with cucumbers, belonging to the Arabs living in the neighbourhood. The soil seemed to be of uncommon fertility, and to be capable of yielding large returns. The plain is about a quarter of an hour's length on every side. On the south it is bounded by the narrow ravine, Wadi el Ghor, and on the north by the short but steep and narrow gorge of Wadi Sudeir. The crag on the northern side, el-Mersed, seems to be the highest upon the whole western shore, and projects so as to entirely impede the progress of those who might wish to walk along by the side of the sea. Close to the coast-line there is a gravel-bank six or eight feet above the level of the water. It is encrusted over with a saline substance, which Seetzen[1] compared to a coating of lime and gypsum. The water of the sea Robinson found to be of a greenish colour, not entirely transparent, extremely salt and bitter, and with a taste of sulphate of soda. The depth increased very gradually, and it was necessary to wade out forty or fifty steps before the water came up to the shoulders: the bottom was good, and free from mud. The bath, which was at first refreshing, left a very oily feeling upon the skin, which was not pleasant. Drift-wood lay scattered about upon the shore, brought down the neighbouring wadis, doubtless, during the rainy seasons. Robinson measured a base line fifteen hundred feet in length, and then took the bearings of most of the conspicuous localities in sight. The great fruitfulness, the abundant water, and the tropical climate, seemed to Robinson to make it certain that, with proper tillage, the place might be made a paradise. On the 10th of May, at sunrise, the thermometer stood on the high land of Kurmul at $8\frac{1}{2}°$ Reaum.; on the plateau above the pass, at two o'clock in the afternoon, it was $22\frac{1}{3}°$; on the sea-shore at sunset it was $21\frac{1}{3}°$; and on the following morning at sunrise it was $16°$. In such a climate the productions of Egypt would flourish, as it is plain that they did before the destruction of Sodom and Gomorrah, when the whole land was a garden of the Lord, like Egypt. Then it was the possession of the Amalekites, and the Amorites lived at Hazezon-tamar: here Lot was regarded as a stranger

[1] Seetzen, *Mon. Corresp.* xviii. p. 444.

and an intruder. As early as in the book of Joshua, instead of the ancient name, it is called by its later appellation of Engedi, *i.e.* the Goat's Spring. At the time of Josephus, however, the place was renowned for its fine palms and its balm trees. There is only a single Engedi mentioned. The statement that there were two or three places bearing this name is not confirmed. Jerome[1] is the last author who alludes to Engedi as a place of any importance. It is a remarkable fact that at the time of the Crusades it is not mentioned. Brocardus[2] in 1280 is the first who speaks of Mount Engedi rising above the Dead Sea, and couples it with the wilderness of Tekoa. He locates it, however, at the southern extremity of the lake, only a leuca distant from Segor (Zoar), and at the pass where was the balsam garden, whose trees Cleopatra transferred to Egypt. He makes no further allusion to a place of this name; and the time of the destruction and extinction of Engedi is unknown. The legends of the monks, instead of assisting in determining the location of Engedi, only obscured the matter by transferring it to the neighbourhood of Bethlehem; and Quaresmius states that it was only six Roman miles thence, and about seven from the Dead Sea. This would make it lie on the road to Mar Saba. He speaks of the vineyards of the place as if they had some connection with those of Bethlehem. This probably misled Hasselquist, as it did other Christian pilgrims; and the place remained unvisited till Robinson[3] explored the place. He supposed, however, that Seetzen had preceded him, which was not the case; and the American has the undisputed honour of having discovered the site of the scriptural Engedi.

3. *Northern Route along the coast from Ain Jiddi past Ain Terabeh, Ain Ghuweir, and the mouth of the Kishon to Ras el Feshkhah.*

The morning after Robinson arrived at Ain Jiddi, he was surprised at the welcome which he received at waking from the

---

[1] Rödiger, art. *Engeddi* in *Encyclop.;* Robinson, *Bib. Research.* i. p. 508, Note; Keil, *Comment. zu Jos.* p. 306 ; Winer, *Bib. Realw.* i. pp. 325-327.

[2] Brocardus, *Terr. Sct. Descrip.* ed. S. Grynæus in *Novus Orbis*, 1532, fol. 311, 312.

[3] Robinson, *Bib. Research.* ii. p. 448.

countless[1] birds which thronged the spot. The trees, the rocks, and the air seemed to be filled with song. The trill of the lark, the drum-like beat of the quail, the call of the partridge, were readily recognised; while many little unknown songsters flew around on every side, and birds of prey hovered over the mountain-tops, or clambered down from the crags.

Robinson ascended again to the high pass in order to gain another view down into the deep depression. The sea had just motion enough to send a slight wave against the shore: the sound was inexpressibly gratifying to the ear, and tended to remove the almost painful impression of loneliness which the whole scene would have otherwise left upon the mind. From this height the view southward fell on a distant ruin, situated upon a conical hill close to the sea-shore. Seetzen had entered it upon his map as Szebby: the Taamirah Arabs called it Sebbeh. Smith and Robinson conjectured that it was the site of the city of Masada, a stronghold described by Josephus; and the suspicion was subsequently confirmed by the results of Wolcott's exploration of the place.

Turning to the north, the American travellers directed their steps northward to Jericho. They first crossed Wadi Sudeir, which has been already mentioned, through which runs the brook that enters the sea near the towering cliff of Mersed.[2] The road passes onward, traversing naked ridges, and then an extensive flat region, called Husasah. It slopes gently to the east, and is a perfect waste, exhibiting scarcely a trace of culture, and no vegetation, excepting a few bushes. It is used merely as the camping-ground of a few feeble Arab tribes.[3] It is traversed by several small wadis, which all run from west to east, coming down from the Frank Mountain and the Pools of Solomon. All of these wadis were dry at the time of Robinson's visit, even the Taamirah which begins at Bethlehem. In the latter there were merely a few places where water was found among the rocks.

The desert, covered as it was with fragments of limestone and chalk, and destitute of the faintest traces of vegetation, was a fearful spectacle of desolation. Robinson took his course over the high tract along the shore till he arrived at Ain Tera-

---

[1] Robinson, *Bib. Research.* i. p. 524.　　　　[2] *Ibid.* p. 527.
[3] *Ibid.* ii. pp. 18, 98.

beh. The descent to this spring was through a pass as steep as that at Ain Jiddi, but not so high. He did not go down, however, to the sea-shore, but continued to go northward over a plateau about a thousand feet above the level of the sea. From this path there was a very extensive view, Kerak being distinctly visible. To reach this place had required five full hours since leaving the spot where the path to Jericho branches off from that to Jerusalem, although the distance had been but about seven English miles, reckoning even from the starting-point at Ain Jiddi.[1]

The spring lying near the sea at the point to which Robinson had now come was but a scanty one, and its water saltish. The region was exceedingly solitary; and as the moon arose that evening over the scene, the impression was solemn in the extreme. The place seemed like a valley of graves, and the travellers could not fail to think of the fate of the thousands who had perished in that valley of desolation when the ill-fated cities of the past were overthrown.

The next morning[2] Robinson crossed Wadi Ras el Ghuweir, and came soon afterward to the small spring Ain Ghuweir near the mouth of the Kedron, reaching Jericho late in the evening of the same day. The two springs Ghuweir and Terabeh lie in the territory of the Taamirah: these, together with those south of Wadi Sudeir, Ain Jiddy, Wadi Areijeh, and el-Ghor, were the only places known to his guides where water was to be found.[3]

4. *Wolcott's Route from Kurmul to Sebbeh (Masada); description of the latter, and its ruins.*

Wolcott,[4] also an American, after making a long sojourn in Hebron, rode eastward, passing Kurmul, Tell Tawanah, Wadi el Fedhul, and Bir esh Shurky, at length entering on the evening of the same day the mountain land of extreme eastern Judæa. The next day he began to study the general physical character of the landscape. He found that there

[1] Robinson, *Bib. Research.* i. p. 529.   [2] *Ibid.* p. 531 et sq.
[3] *Ibid.* ii. p. 492.
[4] Wolcott and Tipping, *Excursion to Masada*, in *Bib. Sacra*, 1843, pp. 61–68. See supplementary paper, *The Coast of the Dead Sea*, in *Bib. Sacra*, vol. iii. pp. 398–402.

were three distinct divisions of nearly equal breadth, the first of which was waving land, green at the time of his visit, and affording excellent pasturage for the herds of the Beduins. The second division was composed of a chain of white cone-shaped hills, almost all of them naked; while the third was the immediate border of the sea—a rough, rocky tract, intersected with frequent ravine-like wadis. Sometimes these physical forms ran into each other, but in general they were easily discriminated. After a march of two hours, Wadi Seyal, an appalling gorge, was encountered, two English miles to the east of which the massive cliff of Sebbeh was to be seen. The pass which led down to the base of this great cliff was of similar character to that at Ain Jiddy.

Sebbeh lies directly opposite the promontory already mentioned, on the eastern side of the Dead Sea. It is separated from the waters of the lake by a sand-bank two or three miles in length. The mountains on the south side, of equal height with the Sebbeh rock, are separated from it by the deep ravine of Wadi Sinein. In the winter time the water streams down these gorges in torrents, bringing with it large quantities of mud and drift-wood, whose position in the summer time shows the height of the lake when it is in the most swollen state.

After a short rest, Wolcott ascended the crag on the west side, and examined the ruins, which are the same which were minutely described by Josephus, and called by its ancient name of Masada. The ascent was so steep, that it was necessary to climb up on hands and feet. An artificial approach, which the Jewish historian speaks of as having been on the west side, seems to be no longer existing. The height to which one is compelled to climb is a giddy one; it cannot be less than a thousand feet: the loftiest points are on the north and south-west sides, the least elevated one at the south-east. The area on the top is about three-quarters of a mile in length, and a third of a mile in breadth, and is destitute of every trace of vegetation.

Approaching the west side, Wolcott discovered the outlying spur of the mountain, the place where the city was assaulted. Before and behind could be seen the wall which was built by Herod the Great, of which the lower part now is standing. It is of a dark-red colour, occasioned, as Wolcott supposed, by a conflagration. In the remainder of the ruins can be seen what seem to have been barracks or storehouses; the wall was all uniform in its character, and seemed to be of Roman origin. Higher up there was a much more modern structure to be seen, the only one of its kind, with a portal of hewn stones and arches, together with a few rounded steps, a circular tower, and window-like openings in the rock, which seem to have led to cisterns which are now in a shattered state. One of these had a depth of fifty feet, a length of a hundred, and a breadth of forty feet.

The most interesting historical monument, says Wolcott, was the wall, which was built around the outside of the rock, erected by the Roman general Flavius Silva at the time of his investment of the city. From the extreme top the whole place came into sight, and the site of the Roman camp was distinctly visible. It lay at the south-east, towards the Dead Sea. The wall was six feet in thickness, more roughly built than those higher up, but thoroughly well planned, and so solidly constructed, as to display clearly at the present day the determined character of the efforts then made to reduce the powerful citadel.

The description given by Josephus was found by Wolcott to coincide very closely with the appearance of the place. Masada was first erected by Jonathan Maccabæus; it afterwards became a refuge of Herod and his family, who sought to make it impregnable. It was a place of such strength, that at the time of the destruction of Jerusalem, it, together with Herodium and Machaerus, were the only places which were not conquered. The two last named could only be taken by treachery; but Masada met with a singular and most tragic fate. After the destiny of the fortress was certain, and there was no longer a doubt that the Romans would obtain possession of it, the entire population remaining died by one another's hand. Almost a thousand thus perished, and only seven persons escaped with their lives. Thus were fulfilled literally, says Wolcott, the words recorded in Matt. xxvii. 25, " His blood be on us, and on our children."[1]

[1] See Tristram's interesting account of his explorations, *Land of Israel*, p. 303.

5. *Wolcott's Journey from Sebbeh to Ain Jiddy, and back to Tekua.*[1]

This return trip supplied the deficiencies in the survey of the coast, and cannot therefore be wholly passed over. Leaving the wild crags around Sebbeh, Wolcott came to Wadi Seyal, crossing it two miles from the shore of the lake. An hour brought him to Wadi Khubarah, north of which the water comes close to the foot of the cliffs. Here there is a great hollow, called Birket el Khalil, from which the Arabs picked little pieces of asphaltum. A little later Wolcott passed Wadi Areijeh, which lies only a quarter of an hour's distance from Ain Jiddi. His course back to Tekua was over ground which has already been described, and did not yield fresh discoveries to Wolcott, Robinson having so thoroughly examined the field already.

DISCURSION VI.

THE SOUTHERN EXTREMITY OF THE DEAD SEA—KERAK AND ITS NEIGHBOUR-
HOOD—THE GHOR ES SAFIEH AND THE WADI EL AHSA.

In the course of the preceding pages, I have had occasion to allude to both of Seetzen's explorations around the southern end of the Dead Sea,[2] as well as the careful explorations made by Robinson, and the discoveries effected by Burckhardt, and by Irby and Mangles. It remains that I should speak more freely than I have yet done of Kerak, a city which has been repeatedly mentioned, and which was formerly one of the chief local centres of civilisation. Seetzen was the first European to explore this place, but the account which he has given of it is but fragmentary : it has been supplemented, however, by the narrative of Burckhardt,[3] who spent three weeks there. The deficiencies which then remained in our knowledge of the place, were made good by the subsequent explorations of Irby,[4] Mangles, Legh, and Banks.

[1] Wolcott, *Excursion, l.c.* p. 69.

[2] Seetzen, in *Mon. Corresp.* xviii. pp. 433–435.

[3] Burckhardt, *Trav.* pp. 378–396.

[4] Irby and Mangles, *Trav.* pp. 338–367 ; Legh, *Route in Syria,* in Macmichael, *Journ.* pp. 200–210.

1. *Kerek or Kerak, Crac, Petra Deserti, the chief city in ancient Moab.*

Burckhardt found this city to lie about six hours south of the ruins of Rabba, the ancient Rabbath Moab, or Areopolis. North of the place is the deep and precipitous gorge called Wadi Sassaf. The southern wall of this ravine, indented with caves, displays blocks of limestone, of extraordinary size. A very difficult zig-zag path winds to the top of the citadel, which, like that of Szalt, may be seen from a great distance, while the houses of the city, on the other hand, being very low, are not seen. The height of Kerak can be seen from Bethlehem,[1] from Jerusalem, and even from the heights of Jericho. From the castle of the Moabite city, on the other hand, the Dead Sea may be distinctly seen. The ruins of this castle, viewed from the north, are seen to consist of two parts,[2] a large mass on the south corner of the city, and another farther to the north : between the two is the only entrance on the north-west side. To this Irby ascended, and found it to consist of a simple narrow arch, with an Arabic inscription. This entrance is very remarkable, since the arch adjoins the entrance to a natural cavern, which runs in a winding course through the crag, and forms the chief entrance to the fortress. The position of the place as a stronghold is not a particularly good one, the city being surrounded by eminences on every side. The stream which lies on the north side of the city, and flows to the Dead Sea, is called Wadi Sassaf, as I have already observed ; that on the west side is called Wadi Kobeyshe ; while one on the south side bears the name Wadi Franshi, an appellation which evidently hints at the possession of the city by the Franks at a former period. These unite north-west of the city, and form the Kerek river, which drives four mills, and enters the Dead Sea near the ruins of Zoar, through a wadi called el-Deraah.[3] Besides the streams already mentioned, which cause the soil around Kerek to be uncommonly fertile, and water the excellent olive groves of the neighbourhood,

[1] Wilson, *Lands of the Bible*, i. p. 395. See also Burckhardt, *Trav.* p. 378 ; and Seetzen, *Mon. Corresp.* xviii. p. 433.
[2] Irby and Mangles, *Trav.* p. 361 ; Legh, p. 207.
[3] Irby and Mangles, *Trav.* p. 446.

there is yet another prominent spring, Ain Sara, lying in a very romantic spot, where once stood a mosque. The city wall, which has fallen in many places, is defended by six or seven great towers, the most northern one of which is in good condition, and displays a long Arabic inscription,[1] which was too high, however, to be read.

Besides that dark passage through the rock, on the northwest side of the city, there is one yet darker on the south side, forty paces long, and, like the other, opening through the solid rock. The castle, like others in Syria, Burckhardt considered to date from the time of the Crusades. On the side towards the city, it is protected by a deep moat, in which even now may be seen several pillars of grey and red granite. The southern side of the whole eminence on which the castle stands, is wholly bordered with hewn stones. On the west side a high wall has been built directly across the wadi, to some high rocks which rise in that quarter. In the castle there is a deep well: many private houses have the same; but the water in them is not good, being tinctured with salt. At the time of Seetzen's visit, he found the castle very much in decay, yet he identified the ruins of a church, which were used as a sheepfold. Irby and Mangles considered the ditch[2] which has been alluded to, on the south side of the castle, as the quarry from which the stone was taken to build the structure. The church spoken of above displayed a far less striking architectural character than that of the great castle proper: it was evidently of more recent origin than the Byzantine epoch; for there is to be seen an Arabic inscription, which is inserted in the wall, with the wrong side up, showing a much more modern origin of the place. Among the figures on the walls, there were observed an armed king, the martyrdom of a saint, and some illegible Gothic inscriptions. Besides these, Irby and Mangles discovered the sculptured wing of an eagle, which they at length concluded to be the representative of the Roman sovereignty. These writers wrongly ascribe the building of the castle to King Baldwin I.; and the same authorities confound the Mons Regalis, *i.e.* Shobak, with this more northern Kerek, or Petra Deserti,— a mistake which was all the more easy, from the fact that the word *kerek* signifies fortification, and is probably the Oreb of

[1] Burckhardt, *Trav.* p. 379.   [2] Irby and Mangles, *Trav.* p. 644.

the Midianites, mentioned in Judg. vii. 25, viii. 3, Ps. lxxxiii. 12, Isa. x. 26 : it is also the Hisnalgorab of Jemaleddin.[1] Irby and Mangles assert that they discovered no architectural antiquities of any special interest here, but that they saw several foundation walls and fragments, which seemed to have been the work of the primitive population of the place. They may be the remains of that ancient city, which is called in Judg. vii. 25 the rock of Oreb, on which the Midianite chieftain was killed by Gideon. It seems subsequently to have taken the name of Charak or Karak, and has been in comparatively modern times the seat of an episcopate.[2]

The houses of the city[3] are in general built in the manner of those in the Hauran :[4] they are only one storey in height, built of earth, with flat roofs, which in many of the houses lies on the near side, level with the ascending ground, so that one in going up the slope often passes over the houses themselves. The chief apartment of the best houses has two arches, on which the beams rest. These are often black with smoke, there being only a very small aperture for its escape. The walls are smeared with black and red, and covered with rough figures, such as horsemen, camels, and the like. On the east and west sides of the city Seetzen as well as Burckhardt discovered a great number of rough tombs excavated in the rock, some of which seemed to owe their origin to the very earliest Midianite times.

Seetzen reckoned eighty Christian houses and twice as many of Moslems in the city, in every one of which several families dwell side by side. He thought the Christians of the place could put four hundred armed men, and the Mohammedans seven hundred, into the field. Burckhardt reckoned a hundred and fifty Christian and four hundred Turkish families in the place, the latter of whom could muster eight hundred muskets, and the former two hundred and fifty.[5] The Greeks were said to come from all parts of Syria, but particularly from Hebron and Nablus, while the other Christians were reputed to be mostly

---

[1] E. Quatremère, Makrizi, *Hist. des Sultans Mamelouks*, T. ii. Append. p. 236.
[2] *Ibid.* pp. 238–246.   [3] Burckhardt, *Trav.* p. 388.
[4] Irby and Mangles, *Trav.* p. 363 ; Legh, p. 208.
[5] Burckhardt, *Trav.* p. 381.

from Jerusalem, Bethlehem, and Beit Jade. They chose this home because here they could live free from oppression, and on equal terms with the Turks.

The Kerekein, or Arabs of the place, marry the daughters of Beduins; and even the Anezeh give their children in marriage to the local Arabs, in consideration of the payment of six hundred, eight hundred, or a thousand piastres, to which are added a few special gifts, such as a gun and a hanger. Whoever has no money, must work out his debt for his wife; and as Jacob toiled for Rachel seven years, so it is the custom to labour five and six years for a wife at the present day. Among the genuine Beduins, however, no mixed marriages take place at all; for although they may be clothed in mere rags, they believe themselves to be of royal blood, and superior to all with whom they come in contact, and they scorn to intermarry with those whom they consider their inferiors.

Kerek owes to its towering Mons Regalis the consideration in which it has always been held as the key of the desert,[1] for it stands in such a position as to command all the caravan routes connecting Egypt and Arabia with Syria. Whoever holds this place has it in his power not only to drive his enemies back, but to cut off their supplies, and plunder all caravans which are not thoroughly protected. Through its dominating power, the sultans of Egypt were rendered unable to communicate with Syria, and the pilgrim trains to Mecca were placed in the greatest peril. This was the reason why the Egyptian sultans, as well as Saladin the Kurd and his followers, risked everything in order to come again into possession of this stronghold. The commanding position of the place was the reason why the Franks made such strenuous efforts to obtain possession of it, and why, when they were driven out, the Arabs have been no less zealous to hold it. Different tribes of these have had transitory possession of it since the time of the Franks, those having control of it for the longest time being apparently the Beni Sachars.[2] During the possession of the place by various Arab tribes, it has apparently enjoyed a kind of prosperity, owing in great measure doubtless to the happy manner

[1] Quatremère, *l.c.* p. 240; De Guignes, *Gesch. der Mongolen,* vol. iv. pp. 150—157; Reinaud, Note 1 to p. 309, in Michaud, *Bib. des Croisades.*
[2] Quatremère, *l.c.* p. 246.

in which the Mohammedans and Christians live together, and
to the peaceful relations which the whole community maintains
in its intercourse with the people of the neighbouring country.
The condition of the place, prosperous as it is, is not to be
compared with that enjoyed by Petra at the time of the Naba-
thæans, or with that which was displayed in Kerek itself at the
time of the Crusades.[1] Yet even now there are extensive vineyards, groves of olive and nut trees, and gardens of all sorts,
and the traffic carried on by the place with the adjacent country
is by no means insignificant. A large part of the products goes
to Jerusalem,[2] but the greater part to Hebron. Kerek seems
to stand in no immediate connection with Suez, Egypt, or Gaza,
in which it differs from Shobak, farther south. Seetzen[3]
was of the opinion, that the best way to visit the place was in
company with pedlars from Hebron, who traverse these wild
tracts in all directions.

2. *Approach to the southern extremity of the Dead Sea on the*
   west side, through the Hebron road, past the Camp of the
   Jehalin, the Zuweirah Pass, and the Salt Mountain of
   Usdum (Sodom); then through the Ghor es Safieh, the huts
   of Ghawarineh, and along the Wadi Derah'ah, or the River
   of Kerek.

I have yet to speak of the two approaches to Kerek on the
south : the one leading from the peninsula of el-Mezraah south-
westwardly along the Kerek river; and that coming from the
west, from the land of the Jehalin Arabs, and the salt peaks of
Usdum, through the Ghor es Safieh, and over the ancient barrier
river of el-Ahsa. These routes have been more fully described
by Irby and Mangles than by Seetzen, while Robinson has
given us the description of the route through the Zuweirah Pass,
and over the Usdum mountains, and thence southward to Wadi
Jeib and Jerafeh. The route from Kerek southward has been
portrayed by Burckhardt and Irby. Robinson, Schubert,
Russegger, and others have all pursued very much the same

---

[1] Quatremère, *l.c.* p. 241.

[2] Seetzen, MS. *Erste Reise*, 1806 ; Burckhardt, *Trav.* p. 387.

[3] Seetzen, MS. *Erste Reise*, 1806 ; Legh, p. 240; Irby and Mangles, *Trav.*
p. 455.

course in turning from the road to Kerek, and entering Palestine by way of the Hebron mountains.   Bertou has traversed the same district; but his itinerary fails to be of much service, from the want which it displays ᴻf precision in the use of Arabic geographical terms.

DISCURSION VII.

THE VARIOUS EFFORTS TO NAVIGATE THE DEAD SEA, FROM THE EARLIEST TIMES
DOWN TO THE LAST SCIENTIFIC EXPEDITIONS THITHER.

To what has already been said regarding the district bordering on the Dead Sea, it is necessary to add yet one chapter more, relating to the various efforts which have been made to examine this bitter lake in all its characteristics,—a work still by no means completed, and leaving much to be attempted by those who shall follow up the results already gained.

Ancient history is silent concerning navigation in the territory of Palestine, and it is only in the Gospels that we obtain glimpses of the boats which once traversed the waters of the Sea of Galilee.   Strabo makes mention of the fact, however, that from time to time the people who lived in the neighbourhood of the Dead Sea made use of rafts for the purpose of collecting the masses of asphaltum which were seen floating on the surface of the lake.   And yet Diodorus Siculus gives us to understand that these rafts were the slightest affairs possible, being composed merely of light reeds, which would enable the people to accomplish very little with them, and which were in no way worthy of being dignified with any appellation which would convey the idea that they were used in navigating the Dead Sea.   I have alluded on a preceding page to the use of boats which was made by Vespasian on the Sea of Galilee, and of the fearful slaughter which occurred.   The Jews who escaped that massacre fled in all directions, some to Machaerus, some to Masada, others elsewhere.   Many pressed down the Jordan valley, and took boats at the mouth, intending to embark on the Dead Sea; but their murderous conqueror followed closely upon them, and the same scene of bloodshed which had reddened the waters of Tiberias filled the mouth of the Jordan with blood.   After that occurrence we have no allusion to the presence of boats on the Dead Sea till the time of Edrisi. The historians of the Crusades make no allusions to attempts to navigate its waters, nor have the Turks and Arabs of the last two centuries made any endeavour to do so. Edrisi[1] asserts that in his time (1150 years after Christ) there were from time to time small expeditions upon the Dead Sea, from Zara (Zoghar) and Dora (perhaps the mouth of the Deraah river) to Jericho, in order to bring corn from the Ghor thither. How long this traffic was continued we do not know. It is singular that that statement of Edrisi's should have been overlooked as much as it has been,—a fact which I can account for only on the supposition that other oriental authors, whose works are unknown to us, have mentioned the same circumstance. Within our own time five successive expeditions have followed one another, the last three of which have great scientific value, while the first two are by no means to be overlooked or spoken lightly of, since they gave an impetus to that spirit of inquiry whose results have been reached by the subsequent expeditions. Irishmen, Englishmen, and Americans have brought this interesting geographical field into view, and it is to them that the world owes its thanks.

1. *First attempt—that of Costigan in* 1835.

The first modern attempt to navigate the Dead Sea was made by Costigan,[2] an Irishman, in 1835. An inscription in the Latin Cemetery at Jerusalem commemorates the fate of this man, and perpetuates the memory of his bold, heroic, but romantic and ill-planned, adventure. Embarking in an open boat, which he had caused to be brought from the Mediterranean to Lake Tiberias, he undertook, in company with a Maltese servant alone, to descend the Jordan and explore the Dead Sea. He succeeded in doing so, and even in reaching the southern extremity of the lake : he crossed it several times, and made repeated soundings ; but as he had laid in a store of provisions sufficient for only five days, he yielded to the intense heat, and was carried to Jerusalem to die. He left no account but some illegible lines upon the margin of the books which he

---

[1] Edrisi, ed. Jaubert, T. i. p. 338.

[2] H. Stebbing, *The Christian in Palestine*, illustrated by Bartlett, pp. 182, 183 ; Kitto, *Palestine*, vol. ii. p. clxxxv.

had with him ; and unfortunately the account of the servant, although taken from his lips by Mr Paxton, was so disconnected and loose as to be of little worth. He states that they sailed for eight days upon the lake, going ashore every night to sleep, excepting in one case, when they did not land for fear of the Arabs whom they saw on the hills. At one place they found no bottom at a depth of 1050 feet. Along the shore they discovered three spots where were hewn stones, which apparently denoted the existence of former cities there, and at one spot there was a hot sulphur spring. During the night the servant said that the waves ran as high as in the Gulf of Lyons.

2. *Attempt of Moore and Beke in* 1837.

The second attempt, made by G. H. Moore [1] and W. G. Beke in 1837, was not carried out with that fulness which was contemplated, since these gentlemen went thither prepared to make a trigonometrical survey of the Dead Sea, to examine its depth carefully, and to collect specimens of all the productions of its shores. When Schubert [2] approached Jericho, in March 1837, he was surprised by finding upon the lake a boat bearing the English flag. It had been brought with great difficulty from Jaffa to Jericho, had been liberally supplied with provisions, and was well fitted to make a thorough exploration of the sea,—a thing, however, which the jealousy of the Government authorities prevented. They were allowed, however, to spend nineteen days in running along the coasts; they examined the breadth of the sea, and took its soundings at several places, finding the maximum to be 300 fathoms, or 1800 English feet. The length of the sea they found to be less than had been generally supposed. The measurements with boiling water displayed a greater depression than that of the surface of the ocean, but the explorers did not ascertain how great it is. Moore was compelled to go to Egypt to seek permission of the Pasha to continue his explorations, which was refused, while Beke was driven back to England by the precarious state of his health. The results of this expedition are therefore briefly

[1] *On the Dead Sea and some Positions in Syria,* in *Journ. of the Roy. Geog. Soc. of London,* 1837, vol. vii. p. 456.

[2] Von Schubert, *Reise,* iii. p. 93.

told. The latitude of several places is given in their report, but they may be more conveniently found by the reader in the appropriate table.[1]

3. *Lieut. Symonds' Exploration of the Jordan and the Dead Sea.*

The expedition undertaken by the English Admiralty in 1840 and 1841, under the command of Major Scott and Lieut. (now Captain) Symonds, to survey the entire coast of Syria, and to include the shores of the Dead Sea, as well as its depth, has been alluded to on preceding pages. Its results are not yet made public;[2] and all that I have been permitted to use has been the map of Jerusalem,[3] though it is to be hoped that ere long other charts will be published. The accounts of that expedition, as we have them in the public journals, are contradictory and unreliable. The best notice which has been made of them has been in the notes to Humboldt's[4] work on Central Asia. These are not to be passed over by the student, to whom also I commend the other documents referred to below, all of which have a direct bearing upon the subject. I will here merely give the general result, contenting myself with the simple statement that Symonds ascertained the surface of the Dead Sea to be 1231 Paris feet below the Mediterranean, and

---

[1] The reader's attention ought to be called particularly to the fact that it is to this expedition that we owe the direct discovery of the depression of the Dead Sea. Robinson cast doubts upon its possibility as recently as 1847, and the weight of his great authority was a heavy burden to lift. It was proved in the most conclusive manner also by my esteemed friend Dr Petermann, that so many were the windings of the Jordan between Lake Tiberias and the Dead Sea, that it would require no greater fall per mile than many English rivers exhibit, to reach the supposed depression of the Dead Sea. See *Journ. of the Roy. Geog. Soc.* vol. xviii. P. ii. pp. 89–104. This view fully confirmed the startling discoveries of Moore and Beke.—ED.

[2] W. R. Hamilton, *Address to the Geog. Soc. of Lond.* March 22, 1843, p. lxxiv. ; Murchison, *Address*, May 27, 1844, vol. xiv. p. cxxiii.

[3] *Plan of the Town and Environs of Jerusalem, copied from the Original Drawing of the Survey made in March* 1841 *by Lieuts. Aldrich and Symonds,* in Williams, *Holy City,* vol. i.

[4] A. v. Humboldt, *Central Asien,* in *Asie Centrale,* ii. pp. 319–324. See *Kosmos,* vol. i. p. 314, and Not. pp. 473, 474 ; Mahlmann, in *Monatsber. der Berliner Geog. Ges.* 1846, vol. iii. pp. 163–167 ; von Wildenbruch, in the same, vol. iv. p. 141 ; Jameson, *Edinb. N. Phil. Journ.* 1843, p. 178 ; *Bib. Sacra,* 1843, pp. 15–17 ; Aug. Petermann, *On the Fall of the Jordan,* in *Journ. of the Roy. Geog. Soc. of London,* xviii. pp. 89–104.

its greatest depth to be 350 fathoms, or 2100 English feet, *i.e.*
1970 Paris feet, below the ocean. Its bottom is therefore 3201
Paris feet below the general level of the sea, using that expression in the usual geographical sense.

4. *The attempt made by Lieut. Molyneux to explore the Jordan and the Dead Sea in* 1847.

I have spoken fully on another page of the efforts made by
this young officer[1] to reach the Dead Sea : it remains to devote
a few lines to the result of his brief examination of the lake
itself.

Accompanied by only two servants,[2] Molyneux, after the
loss of all the sailors who accompanied him, ventured at six
o'clock in the evening of September 3, 1847, to sail out from
the Jordan into the Dead Sea. A favourable wind soon arose,
and in a few minutes he was borne beyond the sight of land.
The breeze strengthened, however, and soon threw up high
foam-crested waves, which at first he took to be breakers. Not
experiencing any danger from them, he pressed on hour after
hour, and between two and three o'clock the next morning he
was sure that he had reached the southern extremity of the
lake. He sailed towards the western shore, and awaited the day,
which at length showed him that he was about five miles from
the great peninsula, and only two miles from the crags which
hem in the sea on the west. About seven o'clock the wind
went down, and intense heat followed. He estimated the height
of the mountains on the western side, extending from Ras el
Feshchah southward, to be from 1200 to 1500 feet ; they were
all destitute of verdure, excepting in the neighbourhood of Ain
Jiddy, where he saw a little greenness. He was afraid to land,
lest he should be attacked by Beduins. The mountains on the
east side seemed far more lofty than those on the west : they
were more broken, however, and did not rise so precipitously
from the sea, but gradually, like a flight of colossal stairs.
After examining the contour of the coast as well as he could
without landing, he turned the prow of his boat towards the
spot where he thought he should find the depth of the sea the

---

[1] W. J. Hamilton, *Address to the Roy. Geog. Soc.* 1848, p. 16.

[2] Lieut. Molyneux, *Exped.* in *Journ. of the Roy. Geog. Soc.* 1848, vol.
xviii. pp. 126-130.

greatest. He reached no bottom at 1350 Eng. feet. The drawing up of the lead was a work of the greatest difficulty, in consequence of the oppressive heat. The wind prevented his examining the coast of the peninsula as much as he wished, and drove him directly north. He states, however, that the peninsula came two-thirds across the whole breadth of the lake, and the shores did not seem to rise higher above the water than do the Jordan banks. Everywhere he saw the same sandy colour which he had observed in the Jordan, and noticed that the water had a disagreeable smell, that it caused an oily feeling on the skin, and that it was very corrosive, especially in its action on metals. At eleven o'clock he threw the lead a second time, and found the depth 1068 Eng. feet. At one o'clock the soundings gave 1098 feet, and the lead brought up a blue mud.

The wind died away ; it was necessary to row, although the men were nearly powerless. Yet to proceed was absolutely essential, for the boat had sprung a leak. At half-past five in the afternoon a stiff wind sprang up, causing the little shell to ship water badly, and compelling Molyneux to begin to throw the heavy articles overboard. He let the boat drive, bailing water, and making every effort to keep her afloat and to reach the shore. At daybreak Ras el Feshchah was two miles away. The wind fell, however, and the men had to resort again to their oars. At eleven they espied the white cloth of their tent, and in an hour more reached the shore, thankful enough for their preservation. The whole interior of the boat was lined with a thick crust of salt; whatever was made of iron was badly rusted, and the skin of the sailors was pricking and sore : they had involuntarily swallowed so much of the water, too, that all appetite was gone, while a burning thirst followed, which was hard to assuage. Birds had been seen, including ducks, and some had come within gunshot; but not a fish nor a living creature had been discovered in the water. The whole length of the sea was covered with a strip of foam, which did not begin at the mouth of the Jordan, but was first seen some miles away. It seemed to be like that produced by rushing water, but had great permanency. Molyneux gave to three noticeable promontories which come down to the Dead Sea from the east, the names Ras el Balkah, Ras el Tafila, and Ras el Kerah : on the west side he mentions only Ras el Feshchah. The shores seemed to him to rise precipitously, and to display heights upon heights ; he discovered no ruins upon them, however. Towards the north end he found the bottom of the lake more muddy than farther south, but towards the west the waters were not so shallow, and the shores were more abrupt. They were encrusted, Molyneux noticed, with salt.

The night after his return to shore, he slept so soundly, that the next day he was able to go on to Jericho; thence he journeyed to Jerusalem and to Beirut, and joined his ship ; but the heat and his own efforts had proved too much for him, and he soon died, greatly to the loss of his friends and of science, for he survived his labours not long enough to prepare a full account of his exploration.[1]

5. *Fifth Expedition ; that undertaken by the United States, under the command of Lieut. Lynch, to descend the Jordan, and to examine the Dead Sea.*[2]

At 1.45 P.M., April 18, 1848, started with the boats, the caravan making a direct line for Ain el Feshkhah (Fountain of the Stride), on the north-west shore of the Dead Sea, a few hours distant. The course of the river, at first circuitous, preserved more of a southern direction than heretofore. At 1.52 stopped to fill the India rubber water-bags, and at 2.22 started again. The banks, at first lined with tamarisks and willow, became gradually fringed with the cane, and the river was wider and deeper, with a more sluggish current as it descended; passed a small stream with a fœtid sulphureous odour flowing in on the left. At 3.16 the water brackish, but with no un-

[1] He prepared a sketch, however, which may be found in vol. xviii. of the *Trans. of the Roy. Geog. Soc.* It is well worth the perusal, for the reader cannot fail to be struck with the remarkably fine qualities of this young hero, and even now to mourn his loss. It is from this sketch that Ritter has digested the above account.—ED.

[2] I have inserted in a preceding passage a portion of Lieut. Lynch's narrative relating to the valley of the Jordan. When Ritter prepared that portion of the work, neither Lynch's popular book nor the report for the U.S. Government had been published. At the time that Ritter had advanced in the *Erdkunde* to this point, the well-known *Narrative* of Lieut. Lynch, published both in England and America, had come to hand, but not the scientific report. From that narrative the author extracted in his skilful way about fifty pages of matter, giving it in the form of a digest. The report to Hon. J. Y. Mason, Secretary of the U.S.

pleasant smell. The banks, red clay and mud, becoming lower and lower, and bare of all vegetation. The river eighty yards wide, seven feet deep, muddy bottom, current three knots. Saw the Dead Sea over the flat, bearing south. At the mouth of the river were three mud islands, subject to overflow. At 3.25 P.M. passed by the extreme point where the Jordan is one hundred and eighty yards wide and three feet deep, and entered upon the Dead Sea. The river, where it enters the sea, is inclined towards the eastern shore, pretty much as repre-sented in the map of Messrs Robinson and Smith, which is the most exact of any we have seen.

A fresh north-west wind was blowing as we rounded the point. The wind soon freshened into a gale, and caused a heavy sea, in which the boats laboured excessively. The spray was painful to the eyes and skin, and, evaporating as it fell, left encrustations of salt upon our faces, hands, and clothing. At 5.40 P.M., unable to stem the sea, kept away for the northern shore, with the intention of endeavouring to beach the boats to save them. At 5.58, a gunshot distance from the shore, the wind instantaneously abated, and with it the sea as rapidly fell,—the water, from its ponderous quality, settling as soon as the agitating cause had ceased to act. The sun went down, leaving beautiful islands of rose-coloured clouds over the coast of Judæa, but above the yet more sterile mountains of Moab all was gloomy and obscure.

The northern shore is an extensive mud flat, with a sandy plain beyond, and is the very type of desolation : branches and trunks of trees were scattered in every direction, some charred

Navy, came too late to be at all available to Prof. Ritter. As it is not published, but is only to be consulted in large libraries to which it has been presented by the U.S. Government, and as Lynch's popular work is everywhere to be had, I have thought it best to incorporate from the official report the pages relating to the Dead Sea, which, if lacking the picturesque and somewhat diffuse detail of the *Narrative*, will be found better suited to the character of a scientific work. Those who may wish to go further, will find in Lynch's official report the exhaustive geological report of Dr Anderson, geologist to the expedition, tables of products, an ornithological report by Mr Cassin, a botanical report by Dr Griffith, and full chronometrical and meteorological tables. See *Official Report of the United States Expedition to explore the Dead Sea and the River Jordan*, by Lieut. W. F. Lynch, U.S.N., published at the National Observatory—Lieut. M. F. Maury, super-intendent.—ED.

and blackened as by fire, others white with an encrustation of salt. These were collected at high-water mark, designating the line which the water had reached prior to our arrival. The north-western shore is an unmixed bed of gravel, coming in a gradual slope from the mountains to the sea. The eastern coast is a rugged line of mountains, bare of all vegetation, coming from the north, and extending south beyond the scope of vision, and throwing out three marked and seemingly equal distant promontories from its south-eastern extremity.

At 7.58 P.M., wet and weary, reached the beach below Ain el Feshkhah, where the caravan had arrived and pitched the tents. The camp was in a cane-brake, beside a fœtid and brackish spring.

On their route from Meshraa, the shore party crossed a sandy tract of damp ravines, and over a plain encrusted with salt, and sparsely covered with sour and saline bushes, where it was difficult for the camels to march without slipping. Some of the bushes were dead and withered, and snapped on the slightest touch given them in passing. They noticed many cavernous excavations in the hill-sides, the dwelling-places of the Israelites, of early Christians, and of hermits during the Crusades. They at length reached a sloping, dark-brown sand, forming the beach of the Dead Sea, and followed it to Ain el Feshkhah.

In descending the Ghor, Mr Dale sketched the topography of the country, and took compass bearings as he proceeded. The route of the caravan was on the bank of the upper terrace, on the west side, every day except one, when it travelled on the eastern side. That elevated plain was at first covered with fields of grain, but became more barren as they journeyed south. The terrace was strongly marked, particularly in the southern portion, where there was a continued range of perpendicular cliffs of limestone and conglomerate. This terrace averaged about five hundred feet above the flat of the Jordan, the latter mostly covered with trees and grass. They descended each day to the lower plain to meet the boats.

Wednesday, April 19.—The wind sprang up in the night, and blew fresh from the southward. At early daylight we were awakened with the intelligence, that, from the high sea running, the boats were nearly filled with water. We hastened immediately down to dry them, and secure our effects. I here discharged the scouts and camel-drivers, and engaged 'Akil to go to the tribes on the Arabian shore to announce our coming, and make arrangements for supplying us with provisions in the country of Moab. In the course of the day a partridge was heard up in the cliffs, and a small bird twittered in the canebrake.

We gathered some fresh-water shells and specimens of conglomerate, and noticed an entire absence of sea-shells or of round pebbles upon the beach, which was covered with minute fragments of flint. There was no vegetation except the cane, and some dead trees on the margin of the sea.

Thursday, April 20.—Sounded over the sea in east and south-east lines towards Wadi Zerka in one direction, and a little below the mouth of the Jordan in another. Returned at 10.45 P.M., the soundings towards the chasm giving a hundred and sixteen fathoms (696 feet) as the greatest depth. The south-east line gave 170 fathoms (1020 feet), the bottom blue mud and sand, and a number of rectangular crystals of salt. For many casts in succession there was no variation in the depth. In the evening some of the tribe Rashayideh came in to serve as guides, and as messengers to procure provisions.

Difference of level between the Mediterranean and the Dead Sea, by barometrical measurement, 1234·589 feet.

Friday, April 21.—A light wind from the westward ; the weather clear but warm, and the sea smooth. Lofty arid mountains on both sides, a low flat shore to the northward and to the southward ; the eastern and the western shores converge in the last direction, leaving only water visible between them. In that direction, too, a light veil of mist was drawn over the sea.

At 11 A.M. broke up camp, sent Sherîf to Jerusalem to assist in forwarding provisions, and embarked to make an excursion to the southward, the precipitous limestone mountains towering high above us. At 1.36 P.M. stopped at the mouth of Wady en Nar (Ravine of Fire), with the Convent of Mar Saba midway up the ravine, and the city of Jerusalem at its head, where it takes the name of the valley of Jehoshaphat—the torrent bed perfectly dry, and covered with fragments of rock. The mountain sides and summits, and the shores of the sea, are almost entirely devoid of vegetation, and the rocks are of a burnt, brown colour.

At 3.30 P.M. low land visible to southward. At 4.15 threw over the drag in ten fathoms of water. It brought up nothing but mud. At 4.43 rounded a low, gravelly point, with some drift-wood upon it, and landed and pitched our tents in a small bay, by the fountain Ain Turabeh,—a spring of pure, clear, and comparatively cool water, issuing out upon the beach a few rods from the sea. Near by was a thicket of canes, and a line of ghurrah and tamarisk trees skirted the shores. The temperature of the spring 75°. The pebbles along the beach, and the stones in the torrent-beds, to-day were coated with a saline encrustation. We found here a pistachio in full bloom, and in the stream of the fountain were several lily stalks. The sand bordering the fountain and stream were discoloured by a sulphureous deposit, as at Ain el Feshkhah. We found also here the yellow henbane, with narcotic properties ; the night-shade (*anit et dil*), or wolf grape, supposed by Hasselquist to be the wild grape alluded to by Isaiah ; the lamb's quarter, used in the manufacture of barilla, and a species of kalo— *Salicornea-Europea.* This last plant is found wherever saline formations appear. It was here upon the shore of the Dead Sea ; and Fremont saw it on the borders of the Great Salt Lake, west of the Mississippi. The tamarisk trees around the fountain were in full bloom, the flowers small, and of a dull white colour. The wood of this tree makes excellent charcoal, and in the season the branches bear galls almost as acrid as the oak.

Soon after our arrival, one of the party fired at a duck, with a dark-grey body and black head and wings, a short distance from the beach. The startled bird flew a short distance out to sea, where it alighted, and again directed its course towards the shore. We therefore inferred that its haunt was among the sedges of the fountain.

At sunset, the temperature of the air 70°, with light variable airs. The night was clear, and passed away quietly.

Saturday, April 22.—Early in the morning it was quite cold. We here gathered some flowers for preservation, and an Arab brought us several specimens of sulphur picked up on the banks of the Jordan.

At 7.51 A.M. started from Ain Turabeh, with a light wind

from south-east. At 8.20 passed Wady Taamirah, at the head
of which is Bethlehem. At 8.30 a thin haze over the southern
sea; appearance of an island between the two shores; the sun
intensely hot. At 9.50 passed throug'. a line of foam, coloured
brown by floating particles of decomposed wood. At 12.10
stopped at Wady Sudeir, below Ain Jidy (Engaddi), Fountain
of the Kid, and pitched our tents upon the shore, about a mile
distant from the fountain, which is four hundred feet up the
cliff. Our camp was upon a broad sloping delta, its surface
covered with dust and coarse pebbles, or small angular pieces
of rock, mostly flint. We found here the nubk (*Spina Christi*
of Hasselquist) and the osher—supposed to bear the celebrated
apple of Sodom. The nubk has small, thick, glossy leaves;
its branches are covered with sharp thorns, and it bears a berry
with a large stone. The fruit has a pleasant sub-acid taste,
and is much relished by the Arabs. The osher is a small tree,
its bark ribbed like that of the sassafras; the leaves are long,
thick, smooth, and oval-shaped. The flower is delicate, white
and purple, growing in clusters. The fruit is the size of a very
large peach; it is very nearly hollow, is puffy and elastic to
the touch, and the skin very thin, and when unripe, of a light
green colour. The fruit and the young branches emit a viscous
milky fluid when cut or broken. The nubk is called by the
Arabs the dhom, and its fruit the dhom apple. On the upper
part of the plain were the remains of former terraces, and a
few cucumber beds, destroyed a short time since by an in-
cursion of hostile Arabs; also a few patches of barley still
standing. The whole aspect of the country parched and desolate. The mountains, with caverns in their perpendicular faces,
towering fifteen hundred feet above us.

Examined the boats for repairs; found them very much
battered, and their keels and stem and stern posts broken.

There were tamarisk trees in the bed of the ravine, besides
many pink oleanders. About the plain we found the rock
rose, from one of the species of which the gum ladanum is
procured; also the common pink, the Aleppo senna, which
is used in medicine, the common mallow, and the scentless
mignonette.

Commenced a series of barometrical and thermometrical
observations, and measured a base line of 3350 feet across the

plain, and angled upon all possible points. Several of the Rashadiyeh and the Taamirah Arabs came in, and we found them very useful in bringing water and procuring provisions. They were very poor, and frequently solicited charity. We established our depot here ; here we proposed to leave our tents, and everything we could dispense with, and this would be our home while on the sea.

The wind blew strongly from the north during the night, and brought with it a foetid smell of sulphuretted hydrogen.

Sunday, April 23.—A clear warm day, given to rest; a light breeze from the southward during the forenoon, which towards evening shifted to the north and blew fresh, again bringing the foetid smell. At 3.30 P.M. Dr Anderson and the Sherîf arrived with the provisions, and brought with them four soldiers to assist the latter in guarding the camp during our absence. Calm and sultry throughout the night ; the air impregnated with a sulphureous smell, but less strong than when the north wind blew.

Monday, April 24.—At 6.38 one boat started to sound diagonally across to the peninsula, and the other directly across to a black chasm on the opposite coast, while the third party remained at the camp to make observations for determining its position. The greatest depth in the diagonal line was 137 fathoms (822 feet) ; of the direct one, 188 fathoms (1128 feet); the bottom in both cases light-coloured slimy mud, with rectangular crystals of salt, some of them perfect cubes.

The peninsula is a broad promontory from forty to sixty feet high, with a sharp angular central ridge some twenty feet above it. Between it and the sea is a broad flat margin of sand. The shore was encrusted with salt and bitumen, and there were a few dead bushes at the water's edge, and much drift-wood strewed upon the beach, together with myriads of dead locusts. The frequent indications of salt, sulphur, nitre, and gypsum, presented, in the opinion of Dr Anderson, a most interesting field of investigation.

To the northward of the point is a deep bay, indenting the peninsula from the north. The black chasm opposite to the camp is Wadi Mojeb, the mouth of the river Arnon of the Old Testament.

In the afternoon we again noticed a current setting to the

northward along the shore, and one farther out setting to the southward ; the last, no doubt, the impetus given by the Jordan, and the former its eddy, deflected by Usdum and the southern shore of the sea.

On our first arrival here, I despatched a messenger to the tribes along the southern coast. He returned this evening, and reported that they have all been driven away, and that the country is frequented only by robbers.

Secured a stone-coloured partridge and several insects for our collection, and gathered a specimen of every variety of flower for our herbarium. There were several large fires seen on the peninsula. In the night killed a tarantula and a scorpion.

Tuesday, April 25.—A foetid sulphureous odour in the night. At daybreak a fine invigorating breeze from the north ; air over the sea very misty.

At 8 A.M. completed a set of observations, and started, leaving Sherîf in charge of the camp. Weather very warm ; at 9 the thermometer 89°. The limestone strata of the western mountains are horizontal. We sounded every five minutes, and occasionally pulled out in search of the northern ford laid down in the map of Messrs Robinson and Smith, but could not find it. At 1.58 P.M. abreast of Wadi Sêyâl (Ravine of Acacias). On the cliff above, which is that of Sebbeh, are the ruins of the fortress Massada, built by Herod. This fortress, constructed by Herod, and successfully beleaguered by Silva, had a commanding prospect overlooking the deep chasm of this mysterious sea. Our Arabs could give no other account of it, than that there were ruins of large buildings on the summit.

The cliff is perpendicular, 1200 to 1500 feet high, with a deep ravine breaking down on each side, so as to leave it isolated. On the level summit, visible from the sea, is a line of broken walls, pierced in one place with an arch. The cliff is removed some distance from the margin of the sea by an intervening delta of sand and *detritus* of more than two miles in width. A mass of rock, regularly laminated and isolated from the surrounding hills, its aspect from the sea is one of solemn grandeur, and seems in harmony with the fearful records of its past history.

At 4.45 P.M. stopped for the night in a little cave five or six miles north of the Salt Mountain of Usdum. From Ain Jidy to this place, the patent log marked 13⅛ nautical miles, which is less than the actual distance, the log not working sometimes from the shallowness of the water.

We paid particular attention to-day to the disposition of the ancient terraces and abutments of the tertiary limestone and marls, and to the geological construction of the western shore, for which I refer you to the Geological Report.

There was no variety in the scenery to-day. High barren cliffs, and dry torrent-beds, opening upon arid plains or deltas, with now and then a shrub or stunted tree, were all that the land view presented. The sea was mostly calm, and looked sluggish and greasy. The beach where we were encamped was bordered with innumerable dead locusts. There were also encrustations of lime and salt, and bitumen in occasional lumps. The latter presented a bright smooth surface where fractured, and looked like a consolidated fluid. The Arabs called it " Hagar Mousa" (Moses' stone).

Near our camp were several nubk and tamarisk trees, and three kinds of shrubs and some flowers, which were gathered for preservation. On a slight eminence we discovered the ruins of a building, the foundation walls alone remaining, and a line of low wall running down to a ravine; near it was a rude canal. There were many remains of terraces. Here Costigan thought that he had found the ruins of Gomorrah.

We had seven Aràbs with us, and they were of three tribes —the Rashâyideh, Ta'âmirah, and the Kabêneh. Being beyond the limits of their territories, they were very fearful of an attack. We found here the ruins of an aqueduct, and part of the walls of a stone building. The wind during the night blew fresh from the north, and was so hot that we could not lie with our heads under the awning, which had been stretched along the shore, but crawled out and slept upon the open beach. On this, as on every other occasion, there was an officer and two men always on post, and the blunderbuss was ever mounted immediately in front.

Wednesday, April 26.—At 5.30 A.M. we started and stood for Ras Hîsh (Cape Thicket), north point of Usdum; sounding as yesterday in quest of the ford. At 8.12 landed on the point—a broad, flat, marshy delta, of adhesive mud. There were many dead bushes encrusted with salt at the margin of the sea. At 8.30 started again. At 9, the water shoaling, hauled more off shore. Soon after, saw on the eastern side of Usdum, one-third the distance from its northern cape, a lofty round pillar standing detached from the general mass, at the head of a deep, narrow, and abrupt chasm. It proved to be a large pillar of salt, cylindrical in front and pyramidal behind, capped with carbonate of lime. The upper, or rounded part, about forty feet high, resting on a kind of oval pedestal, from forty to sixty feet above the level of the sea. We procured specimens from it. It slightly decreases in size upwards, crumbles at the top, and is one entire mass of crystallization. A prop or buttress connects it with the mountain behind, and the whole is coated with a dust of the colour of ashes. From the surrounding configuration, its peculiar shape is perhaps attributable to the action of the winter rains. The shore was soft and yielding to the foot, and the footprints we made on landing were at our return, an hour after, encrusted with salt. Some of the Arabs, when they came up, brought an oblong, ribbed-green melon, exceedingly bitter to the taste. They had gathered it on the north spit of Usdum.

Intending to explore the southern shore of the sea, and then proceed to the eastern or Arabian side, I here dismissed all the Arabs but one, and gave them provisions and water.

At 11.28 we were unable to proceed farther south, from shallowness of the water. With great difficulty landed to take a meridian altitude; but the sextant would not measure it. The southern shore of the sea presented a mud flat, which is terminated by the hills which bound the Ghor to the southward. A very extensive plain or delta, low and marshy towards the sea, but rising gently farther back, and covered with luxuriant green, is the outlet of the Wadi es Safieh (Clear Ravine). We coasted as close to the shore as possible, the inner ones turning up the mud, but found it impossible to land. The line of demarcation between the sea and the shore, full three-fourths of a mile distant, indistinctly traced, from the stillness of the water and the shining surface of the mud.

While in full view of the peninsula, I named its northern extremity "Point Costigan," and its southern one "Point Moly-

neux," as a tribute to the memories of the two gallant men who
lost their lives in attempting to explore this sea.

At 11.42 there was much frothy scum upon the water.
Soon after, we picked up a dead bird resembling a quail.
Sounding every five minutes. At 11.50 depth four feet,
firmer bottom : the only ford must be about here.

At 12.21 there was a very loud reverberating noise as of
thunder, and a cloud of smoke and dust on the western shore,
most probably a huge rock fallen from a high cliff.

At 3.30 P.M., calm and exceedingly sultry : temperature of
the air, 79°; of the water, twelve inches below the surface, 90°.
The sea and shore covered with a thin purple haze. I appre-
hended a thunder-gust or an earthquake, and took in the sail.
At 3.50 we were struck with a hot, blistering hurricane, that for
some time threatened to sweep us to sea. At 4.30 reached the
shore, all hands exhausted. We landed near Wadi Humeir,
under the mountains of Moab. The sirocco blew fiercely until
midnight, during which time we lay upon the ground, with
our heads wrapped up to screen them from the blistering
wind. A little after midnight the wind shifted and blew
lightly from the north, and the thermometer, which had stood
at 106° at 8 P.M., fell to 82° before daybreak.

Thursday, April 27.—We bivouacked last night on the shore
of an inlet on the south side of the peninsula.

This morning about forty fellahin or agricultural Arabs,
armed with swords, guns, and cudgels, came out from the
thicket. I drew our men up, and there, with the interpreter,
advanced to meet them. Finding us too strong to be attacked,
they began to beg, and I gave food to some that seemed on the
point of starvation.

At 8.45 we started, one boat sounding directly across ; the
other skirting the peninsula, to sketch the topography. Weather
warm, air 92°, water 85° at 9 A.M.; every one oppressed by an
almost overwhelming sensation of drowsiness. At 12.52 P.M.
landed on the western shore at Wadi Muhariwat, where a shallow salt stream ran down the bank into the sea.

At 1.15 P.M. started again, and pulled parallel with the
western shore. At 3.5 encountered a very irregular, heavy
swell from north-west, and at 3.20 were struck with a hot
hurricane, which lasted three-quarters of an hour.

At 4.15 P.M. we stopped for the night in a spacious bay under Rubtat el Jâmus, a high and desolate cliff, where we could procure no water. Our provisions were also nearly exhausted, but our supper was helped out by some dhom apples brought by our Arab guide.

The Arabs were our guides and messengers; they brought us food when nearly famished, and water when parched with thirst. They had thus far been perfectly tractable, and I know not what we should have done without them.

Friday, April 28.—Light airs from the north-east, and cloudy. Took a small cup of coffee each, and started at 5.58 A.M. Steered the course for Ain Jidy, with the intention of crossing over to Wadi Mojeb if the wind should spring up favourable, but to keep on to the camp should it continue light, or prove adverse. At 7.30 the wind freshened up from northeast, which left us no alternative, as we were out of water; and were we to attempt to cross the sea, we might be kept out all night, or driven ashore, where, as last night, water could not be procured. Unlike on all other seas, there was no fear of drowning here: neither the boats nor those who were in them could be made to sink; but its inhospitable shores afford no food, and very little wholesome water.

Notwithstanding the high wind, the sun was very hot, and the tendency to drowsiness almost irresistible. The men pulled mechanically with half-closed lids; and besides them and myself, every one in my boat was fast asleep. The necessity of steering, and observing all that transpired, alone kept me awake.

At 1.35 P.M. arrived at the camp; Sherîf was overjoyed to see us, and we were gratified to learn that he had not been molested. In the evening we went up Wadi Sudeir, and found a small stream of cool and refreshing water. We were also surprised to see evidences of former habitations in the rocks; roughly hewn caverns and natural excavations we had before seen, but none before evincing so much art. We concluded that they were the dwellings of Essenes prior to, and of hermits in, the early days of Christianity.

About sunset we tried the buoyancy of the water of the sea, by driving a horse and a donkey into it. When beyond their depth, the animals could with difficulty keep from turning over.

A muscular man, without exertion, floated breast-high out of the water. Picked up a large piece of bitumen on the shore; and some of the blossom, and green and dried fruit of the osher, were gathered for preservation.

At one time to-day the sea assumed an aspect peculiarly sombre; unstirred by the wind, it lay as unruffled as an inland lake. The great evaporation curtained it with a thin transparent vapour, its purple tinge contrasting strangely with the extraordinary colour of the sea beneath, and where they blended in the distance, gave it the appearance of smoke from burning sulphur. It seemed a vast cauldron of metal, fused, but motionless.

A pleasant breeze from the west during the night, without unpleasant odour; but towards morning it shifted to the north and blew freshly, bringing the sulphureous smell with it.

Saturday, April 29.—At daylight despatched Lieutenant Dale, Dr Anderson, and Mr Bedlow, with the interpreter, a Turkish soldier, and some Arab guides, to Sebbeh.

Soon after breakfast, sent Mr Aulick in one of the boats to sound in a north and south line between the peninsula and the western shore. At 1 P.M. he returned, having sounded up a gradual ascent to thirteen fathoms.

Protected by our presence, some of the Ta'âmireh to-day harvested their small patches of barley. They used their swords for reaping-hooks, and the grain was trodden out by three diminutive donkeys driven round the threshing-floor in a line abreast. I purchased the grain for distribution at home.

In the afternoon visited the fountain, which is four hundred feet up the mountain. It is shaded by a grove of the *Spina Christi*, and the course of its water is marked by a long line of green. At sunset the party to Sebbeh returned. Their observations confirmed the supposition of Messrs Robinson and Smith, that the ruins are those of Masada, where nine hundred and sixty-seven Sicarii under Eleazer preferred self-immolation to falling alive into the hands of the Romans.

On their return they noticed a fœtid smell in passing Berket el Khulîl, a pool of stagnant water.

Sunday, April 30.—Weather quite warm. The forenoon given to rest. The faces of nearly all the party looked swollen and inflamed, and our bodies were covered with minute pustules. They caused me great uneasiness, although I could not tell of what they might be the symptoms, whether of improved health or coming sickness.

This was the day appointed to meet or hear from 'Akil on the Arabian shore, and in the afternoon we sailed over to the peninsula, leaving the faithful Sherîf again in charge of the camp. On reaching the shore near Mezra'a, we met Jumâh, one of 'Akil's followers, sent down in the morning from Kerak, where 'Akil arrived the day before. We learned from Jumâh, that on his way from 'Ain el Feshkhah, 'Akil and his party stopped at an encampment of Beni Sukrs, and that they were surprised by the hostile tribe of Beni 'Adwans, and forced to retreat, 'Akil losing his camel with all his baggage ; subsequently reinforced, they became in turn the aggressors, and after a warm engagement came off victorious. Twelve of the Beni Sukrs, including 'Akil's party, were wounded, and twenty-two of the Beni 'Adwans were reported to have been killed. The son of the sheikh of the latter tribe was among the slain, and his double-barrelled gun was given to the younger Sherîf, nephew of Sherîf Hazaa, for his gallantry in the action.

A little after sunset, a deputation of five Christian Arabs, headed by the son of the Christian sheikh, brought us an invitation to visit Kerak. The town of Kerak is occupied by about two hundred Christian and one hundred Muslim families. The former are of the tribe Beni Khallas (sons of invincible), and number about one hundred and fifty fighting men. The latter are of the Kerakiyeh tribe, which musters about seven hundred and fifty warriors. The great body of the last-named tribe live in black tents a short distance from the town. The Christians are subservient to, and much tyrannized over by them.

The deputation of Christians expressed great delight in seeing fellow-Christians upon this sea. They said that we were brothers, and that however we might differ in forms, our faith was the same.

An invitation was also received from the Muslim sheikh. I accepted it with a full sense of the risk incurred ; but the whole party was so much debilitated by the sirocco we had encountered on the south side of the peninsula, and by the subsequent heat, that it became absolutely necessary to reinvigorate it at all hazards.

In the course of the evening many of the Ghauwarîneh from Mezra'a came in. They as well as the Christians looked with amazement upon our boats, and were very inquisitive as to the position of the legs.

The wind was fresh from north-west during the night, the thermometer ranging from 82° down to 70°; at the latter temperature we felt quite cold. There was a bright meteor from zenith, shooting to the north-east towards morning.

Monday, May 1.—A calm and warm, but not unpleasant morning. Sent Mr Dale and Mr Aulick in one of the boats to complete the topographical sketch of the shore-lines of the bay, verify the position of the mouth of Wadi Kerak, and sound down the middle of the bay on their return.

There was much of the nubk and some osher trees upon the plains, and some patches of dhoura or millet, which is now a few inches high. About meridian the boat returned.

P.M.—I rode out upon the plain, accompanied by two Arabs, to look for the ruins of Zoar. Saw a number of heaps of stone, but I could not tell whether they had been building stones, or collected by the fellahin when clearing the ground for cultivation. Farther on, about the position indicated by Irby and Mangles as the site of Zoar, there were the ruins of a large and very ancient building. The word "large" is used in a relative sense, as compared with most of the buildings we have seen since we left St Jean d'Acre.

In the evening the Christian sheikh of Kerak, accompanied by the son of the Muslim sheikh, arrived with horses and mules for our visit to-morrow. They brought a letter from 'Akil, apologizing for not coming himself in consequence of the wounds of one of his followers, and the weakness of his horses.

A little after nightfall another party of fourteen came in, singing their war-cry, and bearing a tufted spear. There were about forty of these Arabs around us at night; and being uncertain of their disposition, we kept a more vigilant watch than usual.

The night was sultry, although the wind blew fresh; the thermometer 81°, with a heavy dew.

Tuesday, May 2.—A cloudy morning; started at 5.30 A.M. with the whole party for Kerak, except one seaman, left at his own request with Jumâh, who had charge of the boats. Our route was up a steep and rugged bridle-path on the southern bank of the deep chasm of Wadi Kerak.

We reached the town, which was seventeen miles distant, a little after noon. It is enclosed within high walls, and seated on the summit of the mountain : the country around, a high rolling plain, now brown and parched from the devastation of the locusts and the hot blasts of the sirocco. The streets are narrow, lined with low, square, mud-roofed stone huts. At the north-west angle of the wall there was a large ruined tower with a rich cornice, and at the south-west angle the ruins of an extensive castle, apparently built by the crusaders, and subsequently repaired by the Saracens. About ten years since it was partly blown up by Ibrahim Pasha.

The Christians of Kerak received us kindly, but were too poor to furnish anything but milk and a few eggs. The Muslims from the first demanded *backshish*, which being refused, they became surly and disobliging.

Instead of hospitality, we met with nothing but rude demands, which were invariably refused. We kept by our arms, and it was at some risk that we contrived by turns to visit the town and the ruins.

We were quartered in a room without furniture of any kind, and but for the exertions of the Christian sheikh, could not have procured a morsel of food. This conduct of the Muslims determined me at all hazards to give them nothing whatever, and to this I stedfastly adhered.

Throughout the day our room was crowded by Arabs coming in to look at us, and the stairway was thronged with coming and returning visitors.

At night we placed a board against the door, that its fall might apprise us of an attempted entrance, and slept with our arms in our hands.

Wednesday, May 3.—It was exceedingly cold during the night, the wind whistling shrill through the casements, and we were tormented by fleas. Still we were invigorated by the mountain air.

We started on our return at 6.30 A.M., with the Christian sheikh mounted and a few of his men on foot, leaving the Muslim Arabs in a surly mood. In about half an hour Mohammed overtook us, and demanded various articles—a watch, a gun, etc. etc.—intimating that if we did not give them as a *backshish*, there would be a hundred men in our path to compel us. Whereupon I made him prisoner, and placing an officer and one of the most trusty men by him, with orders to shoot him on the first symptom of treachery, I held him as a hostage for the good behaviour of his tribe. This measure had the desired effect, and we reached our boats unmolested.

That evening we proceeded to Wadi Môjeb (the river Arnon), and camped upon the southern side of its delta, on a fine pebbly beach, in a little cove.

The Arabian shore from the peninsula to the Arnon presented a barren aspect of lofty perpendicular cliffs of red sandstone, and here and there a ravine with patches of cane, indicating the immediate or recent presence of water.

The Arnon, now eighty-two feet wide and four feet deep, flows through a chasm with perpendicular sides of red, brown, and yellow sandstone ninety-seven feet wide; the cliffs on each side so fantastically worn, as to resemble Egyptian architecture. After leaving the chasm the river runs through a delta in a south-westerly course, narrowing as it goes, and is ten feet deep where it debouches into the sea; on its banks were the castor bean, the tamarisk, and the cane. George Overstock, seaman, had a chill to-day. Wind cool from north-west during the night.

Thursday, May 4.—A warm but pleasant morning; Overstock better; sent Mr Dale in one of the boats to sound across to 'Ain Turâbeh: just before starting heard two gunshots, and voices in the cliffs above. Proceeded in the other boat to Wadi Zerka Main, the outlet of the hot springs of Callirhoe, sketching the topography as we went: the shore the same as yesterday, except that in one place the mountain-side was covered with huge boulders of trap and tufa, and every evidence of volcanic formation.

The sides of the chasm through which the Zerka flows are equally high and precipitous as those of the Arnon, but are not worn into such fantastic shapes. The chasm is one hundred and twenty-two feet wide, and the sides eighty feet high at the mouth, but much higher within. In the bed of the chasm were two streams, one eight feet wide and two deep, and the other six feet wide and two and a half deep, running down at the rate of eight knots per hour; the water at the temperature of 94°, and one mile up 95°, while that of the sea was 78°; the taste not unpleasant, although a little sulphureous; there was a saline deposit on the rocks.

It was quite cool in the night, the thermometer ranging from 70° to 68°, and there was a large fire on the Judæan shore in the direction of Feshkhah.

Friday, May 5.—Wind from the north; air quite chilly this morning. It is this change of temperature which makes the heat of the day so oppressive. I wished very much to have visited the ruins of Machaerus, upon this singular hot-water stream, and to have excavated one of the ancient tombs mentioned by Irby and Mangles; but fear for the health of the men, who are beginning to complain, warned us to lose no time in completing our reconnaisance and exploration.

At 3.40 A.M. started for 'Ain Turâbeh, sounding as we proceeded. Two furlongs from the land there were 27 fathoms (162 feet); the second cast, five minutes after, gave 174 fathoms (1044 feet), gradually deepening to 218 fathoms (1308 feet): the bottom soft brown mud, with rectangular crystals of salt.

At 8 met the other boat sounding also. Put passed-midshipman Aulick and Dr Anderson in her, and directed them to complete the topography of the Arabian shore, and determine the position of the mouth of the Jordan, while we continued on to 'Ain Turâbeh. On the way, made a series of experiments with the self-registering thermometer, to ascertain the temperature of the sea at various depths. That of the surface was 76°, and at 174 fathoms (1044 feet) it was 62°, with a regular gradation between, except at ten fathoms, where we invariably found a stratum at the temperature of 59°.

In the afternoon, reconnoitred the pass over the cliffs here, to see if it be practicable to carry up the level. It proved very steep and difficult, but less so than those of 'Ain el Feshkhah and Ain Jidy, and I determined to attempt it; for the advancing season, and the present state of the southern desert, prohibited the route from near Usdum across to Gaza. Made arrangements for camels to transport the boats in sections across to Jaffa *via* Jerusalem. Weather very warm through the night.

Saturday, May 6.—A warm morning, the sea curtained

with a mist; commenced levelling, which duty I assigned to Lieutenant Dale, who was fully competent to the task.

At 9 A.M. the thermometer in the shade standing at 100°. At 11 Mr Aulick and Dr Anderson returned. The latter had collected many specimens in his department. Sent Mr Aulick out to make experiments with the self-registering thermometer at various depths. The result the same as yesterday, both with regard to the gradual decrease of temperature, and the cold stratum at ten fathoms. The increase of temperature below ten fathoms is perhaps attributable to heat being evolved in the process of crystallization.

Light flickering airs, and very sultry during the night. Noticed, what we have often before observed, a central current of about one knot per hour setting to the southward, and another of less velocity setting to the north, along the shore; the last, no doubt, an eddy.

Sunday, May 7.—This day given to rest. The weather exceedingly warm and oppressive. At 8.30 A.M. the thermometer stood at 106°; the clouds motionless, the sea unruffled, the rugged surface of the rocks without a shadow.

At 6 P.M. a hot hurricane, sweeping in currents from north-west to south-east, which blew down the tents, and broke our last barometer. In two hours it gradually subsided to a perfect calm. All were suffering very much with languor, and prudence warned us to be gone.

The temperature of the night was lower than that of the day, and we slept soundly the sleep of exhaustion.

Monday, May 8.—A cloudy, sultry morning. At 5 A.M. the levelling party proceeded to work up the pass. Constructed a large float, and carried it out and moored it, with the American flag flying, off 'Ain Ghuweir, in eighty fathoms water, too far from the shore to be molested by the Arabs.

The heat continued to increase as the day advanced, and at meridian the thermometer stood at 110° in the shade, and we were compelled to discontinue work. At 1.30 P.M. a light breeze sprang up, which gradually freshened and hauled to the northward. In the afternoon went to 'Ain Ghuweir, a short distance to the north, and found the water sweet, and not brackish, as it had been represented.

At 4 P.M. the levelling party returned, having worked up

the pass, and three hundred feet beyond, into the Desert of Judæa. Light airs, and sultry during the night.

Tuesday, May 9.—Sent Mr Dale at early daylight to reconnoitre the route from the pass to the Convent of Mar Saba. Sent also George Overstock and Henry Loveland, sick seamen, to the same convent to recruit. Took the boats apart, in six sections each, and sent them on camels to Jerusalem.

Tried the relative density of the water of this sea and some from the Atlantic, procured in latitude 25° north, and longitude 52° west. Distilled water being as 1, the water of the Atlantic was 1·02, and that of this sea 1·13.

The last dissolved 1-11th of its weight of muriate of soda, the water of the Atlantic 1-6th, and distilled water 5-17ths, or nearly one-third of its weight. The salt was a little damp, for which a small allowance should be made.

The exploration of this sea was now complete. We had carefully sounded its depths, determined its geographical position, taken topographical sketches of its shores; ascertained the temperature, width and depth, and velocity of its tributaries; collected specimens of its own and its tributary waters, and of every kind of mineral, plant, and flower; and noted the winds, currents, changes of weather, and all atmospheric phenomena. These notes, with a succinct account of events exactly as they transpired, will give a correct idea of this sea as it appeared to us. The same remarks hold with respect to the Jordan, and the country through which it flows. Unless when prevented by high winds, we have on no occasion, day or night, omitted taking astronomical, barometrical, and thermometrical observations.

Wednesday, May 10.—At daylight, sent the levelling party ahead; at 9.30 A.M. struck the tents for the last time on the shores of this sea; and at 10, started and ascended the pass. From time to time, as we slowly moved up the rugged path, we turned to look upon our flag, floating far off upon the sea.

The greatest depth we had found in the sea was 1308 feet, directly across from 'Ain Turâbeh; and the height of the summit of its pass was 1305·75 feet, or nearly the exact measure of its depth.

On the 17th we reached Jerusalem *via* Mar Saba, and found it to be 3927·24 feet above the Dead Sea.

Resuming the level on the 22d, we proceeded slowly and

laboriously to the west, until we reached the plain of Sharon, which presented no other impediments than frequent cactus hedges; and on the 29th reached the Mediterranean Sea, a little south of Jaffa.

The results give 1316·7 feet as the depression of the level of the Dead Sea below the Mediterranean. Jerusalem is 2610·5 feet above the latter, and 3927·24 feet above the former sea; its elevation above the Dead Sea being almost exactly the multiple of its height above the Mediterranean, and the difference of level of the two seas.

DISCURSION VIII.

GENERAL RESULTS REGARDING THE NATURE OF THE DEAD SEA—THE DEPRESSION AND SOUNDINGS—THE PRODUCTS, ASPHALTUM AND SULPHUR—THE HOT SPRINGS, SALT SPRINGS, TRIBUTARY STREAMS—DRIFT-WOOD—ADJACENT MOUNTAINS—EVAPORATION, VAPOUR CLOUDS—CHANGES IN COLOUR —ROCK-SALT, SALT ZONES, AND SALT MEASURES—THE OLD TRADITIONS OF THE ORIGIN OF THE DEAD SEA—THE GREAT DEPTH OF THE NORTHERN PORTION, AND THE SHALLOWNESS OF THE SOUTHERN.

From the preceding pages, it appears that many things which were entirely unknown regarding this singular sea, have within our time been quite cleared up ; and yet it is only right to confess that many questions remain still unanswered. At the present time, the depression of the surface of the Dead Sea below the general ocean-level may be stated in round numbers to be unquestionably over a thousand feet, but there is as yet no accord among the observers. Symonds gives the number of feet 1231; De Bertou, 1290 ; Russegger, 1341; Wildenbruch, but slightly different, 1351 ; Lynch a little more than 1300,[1] or 1220 Paris feet. The depression of the Sea of Tiberias is even more variously stated, and has never been[2] thoroughly ascertained.

Regarding the elevation of the mountains on the west above the sea-level, there is also a tolerable degree of unanimity ;

---

[1] Lynch, *Narr.* p. 140. See also *Central Asien*, Note by Mahlmann, Pt. ii. p. 457 ; and Lynch, *Narr.* p. 467.

[2] According to the Duc de Luynes, the depression of the Sea of Tiberias is 620 Eng. feet, or 189 metres ; that of the Dead Sea, 1286 feet, or 392 metres.—ED.

and it is certain that the range is not far from 3500 feet above the surface of the Dead Sea, while according to Lynch the plateau south-west of St Saba is over 2000 feet. The height of the mountains on the east side seems to be no less, but it has never been ascertained with exactitude, excepting at one place, Jerash (Gerasa), where Moore and Beke ascertained the elevation to be 2000 feet. The depth of the Dead Sea at different places varies considerably, and the statements regarding the results of soundings seem to be widely discordant. Moore gives us 1800 Eng. feet as the greatest depth noticed by him; Symonds, 1970 Paris feet; Molyneux, 1350; and Lynch, 1227, or 218 Eng. fathoms. At all events, it is over a thousand feet; and if the mountain range be estimated as having an altitude of 2500 feet above the Mediterranean, there is a descent of 3500 feet at least to the surface of the Dead Sea, whose bottom must lie certainly[1] 2200 feet below the surface of the ocean.

It certainly is calculated to strike us with surprise, that in the accounts which have been given by modern explorers of the Dead Sea, so little has been said regarding the bitumen and naphtha about which so much is recorded in ancient writers. The ominous names Sodom (found in Usdum) and Hemar (Shinar), or Chemar, in the Hebrew,[2] and Hommar in the Arabic, *i.e. asphaltum* or *bitumen*, still found in the neighbourhood of the Dead Sea, carry us back to the remotest history, as does the name Bahr Lut, telling us as it does of Lot, and mentioned even by Edrisi, in whose time there existed also the ancient name of Zoar. We find an allusion to Hemar or Shinar in the most ancient times, and read that the ground there, as at Babylon, was suitable to the manufacture of bricks and mortar. Even at the time of Chedorlaomer, before the great catastrophe which befell the cities of the plain, we read that there were many slime-pits there; and also that the region was so abundantly watered, that it was as fruitful as a garden, and could be compared only to Egypt. In the account of the

---

[1] For an admirable *résumé* of the characteristics of the Dead Sea, the reader is referred to the posthumous volume of Dr Robinson, the *Phys. Geog. of the Holy Land.* It contains little, however, which is not more fully given in Ritter.—ED.

[2] Rosenmüller, *Bib. Arch.* iv. p. 12 ; Wilson, *Lands of the Bible*, ii. 22.

destruction of the cities, we read only of the rain of fire and
brimstone; but elsewhere there are allusions to convulsions
which shook the whole district, and to a smoke which ascended
like the smoke of a furnace. These all indicate the action
of volcanic forces, in which the many slime-pits spoken of in
Scripture played no unimportant part. Hence the expression in Josephus, φρέατα ἀσφάλτου, quia isto tempore locus
iste puteis abundabat. The appearance of asphaltum in large
masses from Hasbeya all the way down the Jordan valley has
been alluded to repeatedly, and in composition with sulphur
and salt it has often been collected by Arabs and travellers.
That the same substance was abundant in ancient times, is
sufficiently well testified by the name *Lacus Asphalticus*, or
Ἀσφαλτηφόρος λίμνη, of which Pliny says, " Asphaltites nihil
præter bitumen gignit, unde et nomen," and on which, according to the same writer, a viscid substance used at times to be
seen swimming.

Strabo and Diodorus Siculus have both given full accounts
of the appearance of the asphaltum and bitumen of the Dead
Sea; and the most distinguished mineralogists of the present
day suppose that asphaltum, bituminous resin, petroleum, and
naphtha are very similar in character, and that they are to
be regarded as the results of separate stages in a common
process.[1]

Although Strabo or his copyist has confounded the *Lacus
Sirbonis* on the Egyptian frontier with the *Lacus Asphalticus*
in Judæa, yet there is not lacking in his account many valuable and trustworthy statements, which are corroborated by the
report given by Diodorus Siculus. The waters of the lake,
says Strabo, are very deep, and so heavy that it is hard to swim
in them. It is rich in asphaltum, which at certain periods is
thrown to the surface; and the masses which emerge collect
and form floating islands. Diodorus adds that that takes place
every year, and that some of the combined masses comprise
two or three acres. They are compared by the barbarous
tribes living on the shores to swimming oxen and calves.
These reports agree in one important particular, namely,
that the appearance of the asphaltum masses was periodical;
and in the rarity of their production at the present time, it is

[1] Hausmann, *Handbuch der Mineralogie*, vol. ii. p. 1512, Note.

only reasonable to suppose that the volcanic forces to which they owed their origin have in the course of time greatly diminished in intensity. Josephus speaks of black masses being thrown to the surface at certain times, continuing to swim, and assuming the appearance and size of the backs of headless cattle. The appearance of these masses, according to Diodorus, may be predicted some twenty days in advance, by the diffusion over the lake of a strong smell of asphaltum. So powerful is the gas which is so unpleasantly apparent, that it tarnishes all metals exposed to it. The effect of the water upon the metallic boats which have traversed the Dead Sea confirms this statement. Strabo speaks also of this dulling of bright metals, and also of the sooty fumes which proceed from the asphaltum masses. According to Diodorus, the barbarians were accustomed to bind together bundles of reeds (as is still done in crossing the Euphrates), and then venturing forth, three men on each rude raft. Two rowed, while the third bore a bow and arrows, to ward off any attacks which might be made upon them. Arriving at the unctuous masses, they hacked off as well as they could such pieces as were capable of being detached, and brought them to the shore. In case the rafts broke into pieces, there was little loss either of life or of property, and the men easily made their way to the land. The proceeds of the traffic were not inconsiderable, however; for the asphaltum was in much demand in Egypt for purposes of embalming. When none of this substance was mixed with the spices which were used, the bodies would not long resist the natural corruption. The use of asphaltum was so great in Egypt, therefore, that Edrisi calls the substance itself *mumia*. Josephus tells us that it was in use for the caulking of ships, and also for the preparation of medicaments for the treatment of wounds. It was also employed as a wash for grape vines,[1] to prevent the depredations of worms. Strabo gives a hypothesis regarding the origin of this substance, evidently in accordance with the popular belief of his time: for it is still that of the rude inhabitants of the district adjoining the lake. The asphaltum, he says, is a kind of resin, which is made fluid by the heat which exists beneath the sea. It blows up to the surface of the ground, and is there coagulated by

---

[1] S. de Sacy, in Abd-Allatif, *Relat. de l'Egypte*, pp. 273–276, Note.

coming in contact with the cold salt water. It thus becomes viscous and tough, so as to be broken into pieces only by the agency of an axe. It swims easily on the surface, after being detached from the masses at the bottom of the sea. He thinks it more than probable that the most of the productive activities which give rise to the asphaltum exist where the depth of the sea is the greatest, and that the irregular appearance of the bitumen affords certain proof that the submarine forces are not continuous in their action. He compares the Dead Sea in this respect with the Nymphæum in Epirus. In confirmation of his view, that the whole district rests upon a volcanic basis, he cites the calcined rocks of Masada, and also the various crives which are found in the neighbouring country, where bitumen is seen exuding, and whence a disagreeable smell proceeds, which is discernible a long way off. In his days there existed a tradition that thirteen cities had been destroyed; among them Sodom, whose ruins were still to be seen, covering a district sixty stadia in circuit. Maundrell assures[1] us that he had never seen them, but that he had heard from several trustworthy men that architectural remains were in existence, and that at low water they could be seen. More recent observers have reported nothing in confirmation of this, if we except a few words dropped by Costigan, and referred to on a preceding page. Strabo asserts that earthquakes and other powerful volcanic forces had somewhat changed the limits of the lake in his day; he also asserts that there were rocks in its neighbourhood which were of so bituminous a character that they would burn.[2] The existence of what was called the Moses stone, and which had an inflammable character, is mentioned by Maundrell.

Josephus alludes to the destruction which came upon the five cities, the Pentapolis, in almost the same language with the book of Wisdom. In Gen. xix. 24 only Sodom and Gomorrah, however, are mentioned as being destroyed, while in Deut. xxix. 23 Admah and Zeboim are added to the list. In the book of Wisdom five cities are alluded to as having perished, but no names are given; in Strabo, thirteen are spoken of.

Regarding the weight or specific gravity of the water, Josephus asserts that Vespasian, after his victory on the lower

---

[1] Maundrell, *Journey from Aleppo to Jerusalem*, p. 84.

[2] *Traduc. de Strabon*, T. v. p. 246, Note 2, and T. i. p. 92.

Jordan, tested the matter thoroughly, by binding the arms of several of the prisoners behind their backs, and casting them into the sea. They could not sink, he says; for whenever they were pushed under, they rose to the surface. Such exaggerated language is repeated in several ancient authors. They were first fairly met, however, by Maundrell, who quoted Tacitus against them, in the following words: "Periti imperitique nandi, perinde adtolluntur." Not all the accounts of the wonderful properties of the Dead Sea, however, which found their way into the legends and traditions, are to be rejected; for it may with good reason be supposed, that in the course of time the physical character of the sea has changed; and that just as the springs at Tiberias are evidently widely different from what they were two thousand years ago, so the Dead Sea may have been equally transformed.

Edrisi,[1] for example, tells us that in his time the water of this lake was hot, and sent forth an offensive odour; and this may indeed have been the case, for the sulphureous gas which Lynch mentions may not then have arisen from springs as now, but may have been thrown into the sea first. And we have the authority of the American explorer for believing that there is hot mud at the southern extremity of the sea. Said Termini, a physician of Jerusalem in the tenth century, asserts that he enjoyed excellent opportunities of examining asphaltum, or homar: he says that the winter storms[2] threw it up to the surface, that it bore the name of anotanon, and that it was different in its character from that which is found by digging, and which is mixed with salt and gravel. Is it not possible that the cold of winter, affecting the water of the sea as much as it does, may account for the coagulation of the masses of homar or asphaltum which are then brought to the surface? And does not the heat of summer occasion that free flowing of the oil which causes it to give its character so far to the sea, that, as all travellers agree, no living thing can inhabit its waters?

Passing over Seetzen's account of the reports which he heard on the east side of the Dead Sea regarding the formation of asphaltum,[3] and the large quantities which were gathered

[1] Edrisi, in Jaubert, i. p. 338.
[2] Abd-Allatif, *Relation de l'Egypte*, ed. S. de Sacy, pp. 273–277.
[3] Seetzen, in *Mon. Corresp.* xviii. p. 441, and his *Zweite Reise*, MS.

there by the Arabs, all of which he found on personal investigation to be unfounded, I come to Russegger, who, together with Robinson, have paid particular attention to the subject. The asphaltum or bitumen[1] of this sea is, according to Russegger, of two very different kinds, being both hard and soft, perfectly pure, also mixed with chalk and clay. The places where the pure hard bitumen exists, had never been visited by any European before him. They lie on the east side of the lake in Jebel Belka, opposite Ain Jiddy, probably at the Tur el Hammera of Seetzen. It gushes from the layers of chalk, and collects itself at the foot of the rocks. When exposed to the direct rays of the sun, it loses its petroleum character, and becomes a shining, extremely black, firm and brittle substance, which at last forms large masses, and falls into the water. Being lighter than the latter, it floats, and becomes the prey of the Arabs. After the earthquake of 1837, much of it was brought to the surface, and sold at the bazaar of Jerusalem at the rate of three pounds sterling the hundredweight. Russegger holds that at the bottom of the sea there are far greater accumulations than along the rocks on the shores, and that these are detached from the bottom by violent earthquakes, and brought to the surface. Bitumen is often found largely filled with organic remains, as well as with earthy substances. The conglomerate burns freely, emitting a great deal of smoke and a strong bituminous smell. The fire which is said to have come down from heaven, may be taken literally as lightning; and Tacitus says expressly : " haud procul inde campi, quos ferunt olim uberes, magnisque urbibus habitatos, fulminum jactu arsisse," etc. The rocks whence the bitumen proceeds could be readily kindled by the lightning, and the punishment inflicted by a divine hand[2] upon Sodom and Gomorrah would be entirely consistent with the working of natural law. Russegger discovered bituminous layers in the Jura formation, some of which were from two to three feet in thickness. The Arabs break off pieces for fuel, but carry on

---

[1] Russegger, *Reise*, iii. p. 253.

[2] Robinson enunciates the same theory in his posthumous volume, the *Phys. Geog. of the Holy Land*, p. 214, holding, with Ritter, that the *ordinary* method of miracle is to engraft upon a natural growth the more unusual and striking elements which God wishes to exhibit.—ED.

no traffic in it, as the transportation of it is beyond their power
and skill. The inhabitants of Bethlehem make use of the solid
bitumen in the manufacture of little articles, which they sell to
pilgrims, such as rosaries, crosses, and the like.
Robinson,[1] who himself discovered small bits of asphaltum
on the shores of the Dead Sea, heard from the lips of the
sheikh accompanying him the same report regarding the existence of large masses on the east coast that Seetzen and Burckhardt report ; and another sheikh told him that it was to be
found at a place north of the peninsula, to which Irby and
Mangles did not penetrate. Lynch has given no special description of the place. The Arabs do not report the existence of
this commodity on the west side of the sea ; but after the earthquake of 1834, there was so much thrown up from the bottom at
the south-west side, that the Jehalin Arabs carried away about
6000 pounds, selling the most of it at Beirut. After the great
convulsion of 1837 there was another great mass thrown up, as
large as a house, some said, others as large as an island. It
emerged not far from Usdum, where Lynch reports that the
mud is hot even at the present day. The Jehalin and the
people of Jutta swam out to it, and hewed off fragments with
their axes, just as they used to do in the time of Diodorus.
The Taamirah wanted to take part in the work also, but they
found seventy men already engaged. The bitumen was
carried away through the Ain Jiddy pass, and brought four
piastres a pound.

These instances of the sudden appearance of vast masses of
asphaltum on the surface of the sea directly after a great
natural convulsion, hardly leave us free to accept the explanation offered by Strabo, that the fluid discharges of submarine
springs are hardened by contact with the water ; but they make
it more probable that vast masses of bitumen are submerged,
and are subsequently detached by the action of the earthquake.
Regarding this, however, we must wait till the results of future
soundings in the southern part of the sea shall enlighten us.
Robinson was the first to advance the theory that large masses
of asphaltum occupied the site of the lower part of the sea,
that it was kindled by lightning, and that the result of this
terrible conflagration was not only the destruction of the cities

[1] Robinson, *Bib. Research.* ii. 188-193 ; and ii. p. 524, Note xxxviii.

of the plain, but the filling up of the whole locality by the waters of the sea.

The ease with which the asphaltum swims is owing to the great specific gravity of the sea, as compared with the ocean. Lynch found that his metal boats sank an inch deeper in the Jordan, when equally heavily laden, than they did in the Dead Sea. A comparison of the relative density of the two showed, that if distilled water be 1, that of the ocean is 1·02, and that of the Dead Sea 1·13 : distilled water takes 5-17ths of its weight in salt, that of the ocean 1-6th, and that of the Dead Sea only 1-11th. Microscopic examinations did not disclose to the American explorer any traces of animal life, not even the existence of *infusoriæ ;* but the trained eye of Ehrenberg discovered these in some Dead Sea water which was brought to him by Lepsius. This, however, was from the northern end, and it remains a question how much may have depended upon the influx of the fresh water of the Jordan. A piece of coral which the Countess Hahn-Hahn brought from the Dead Sea to Humboldt establishes nothing, for it evidently belongs to the adjacent chalk formation, and may have been swept from the shores into the lake. The influx of fresh water during the winter season and after long storms must be very great, for Lynch found water-marks which showed that even at the end of April the water had already fallen seven feet; and if it is true that Irby and Mangles were able to ford from the peninsula of el-Mezraah to the south-western part of the sea, a place where the water was eighteen feet deep at the time of Lynch's visit was then not more than five.[1] The great amount of drift-wood[2] found along the shore shows, as was noticed by Robinson, a change of level along the shores of the lake amounting to ten or fifteen feet. The result is, that the water rises at times so much that it runs far into the wadis, and then receding, leaves a pestilential marsh. It needs no special proof to cause us to believe that the whole rim of the lake is a barren desert. It is very probable, too, that in the southern portion

---

[1] Lartet, the geologist, who accompanied the Duc de Luynes' expedition, discovered that, since the last geological changes in the basin of the Dead Sea, the fall of water, owing to evaporation, has been more than a hundred metres, or 328 feet.—ED.

[2] Robinson, *Bib. Research.* i. p. 515.

of the sea there are submerged hot springs, as Burckhardt and Dr Anderson suspected, the latter testing the heat by wading through the water. There may be also in the same region naphtha, but of its existence we have not as yet any facts. The long line of foam which Molyneux observed was not discovered by Lynch. The waters of Ain Terabeh, Ain Jiddy, and of the salt fountain of Muhariwat, were all absorbed by the ground before reaching the sea ; so, too, were the waters of Sudeir, Seyal, Muboghghik, and Wadi Humeir ; and Wadi Kerak was dry when Lynch visited it. His efforts to ascertain the amount of water annually poured into the Jordan, in order to test its relation to the amount carried off by evaporation, cannot be accepted as settling the question.[1]

I cannot omit alluding to the extraordinary masses of vapour which rise from the Dead Sea, in consequence both of the direct influence of the sun, and of the powerful hot winds from the south. These carry away the thick heavy clouds to other places ; or in case they are not experienced, the opaque clouds hang over the lake, and produce the most singular effects in their action on the light. Sometimes they give the appearance of huge waterspouts, as was observed by Irby and Mangles ; and now and then these overhanging clouds discharge their contents with such an extraordinary fall of water, that it resembles the overturning of a cistern rather than rain. Sometimes the clouds which overhang the Dead Sea are entirely cleared away ; and when this is the case, it is generally to be ascribed to powerful winds from the north. The singular effect of light upon the surface of the lake, which has been often described in glowing colours, and which has in some cases been supposed to be merely fanciful exaggeration, is to be explained as the effect of the layer of mist which almost always overhangs the Dead Sea. I have already alluded to the possibility of deception in the atmosphere of the Dead Sea ; but yet, such is the uniformity of testimony regarding the singular qualities of this lake, that we can go back with confidence to Josephus, and accept his words, in which he speaks of the wonderful variety of colours which are observable there, and which are manifested with every change of the light. Gadow,[2]

---

[1] Lynch, *Narrative*, p. 378.

[2] Gadow, in *Zeits. d. Deutsch. Morgenl. Ges.* ii. p. 61.

who stood on the northern shore, and watched the play of colours for an hour, was amazed at the number which he observed, both far away and close at hand : near him the atmosphere was blue, transparent, and as clear as crystal ; it shaded away into grey, then took on a greenish tint, intermixed with masses of white. There can hardly fail to be other colours manifested at different hours of the day, and in the various seasons of the year. My honoured friend, Dr Parthey,[1] noticed that the layer of mist which overhangs the Dead Sea is entirely different in character from the morning and evening clouds which rest upon the surface of other seas. These come and go with the changes of temperature : they depend upon the rays of the sun for their existence, and their dispersion as well : they depend entirely upon the temperature of the water and the air. But it is not so in the Dead Sea : there the vapour clouds remain permanent : they stand like an unshaken wall over the sea ; and sometimes whole years pass without allowing the inhabitants of Jericho to look down the Ghor valley, and see the pillar of Usdum at the southern extremity, although there are occasional times when it can be seen with perfect distinctness. The waters of the Dead Sea do not ripple lightly, as do those of other lakes, and of the ocean : they lie smoothly, like molten lead ; and owing to the peculiar form of the basin, the surface is protected from many of the winds which sweep over it. When, however, they do descend so far as to strike the water, the waves have such a power, owing to the great specific gravity of the water, that their blows on the bows of his boats were only to be compared to those of powerful hammers.

The play of colours in the vapour clouds overhanging the Dead Sea is very beautiful. Sometimes there is to be seen an incomparably deep blue, which, with the advance of the sun, is transformed into a milk white or into a violet hue. Seen from Jericho, this violet shade sometimes attains an intensity greater than can be seen at any other place, particularly towards the close of the day. The sun's rays, which fall perpendicularly, appear to occasion the greatest amount of evaporation ; for when the sun is highest, the southern part of the sea is observed to swim in mist to a greater extent than at any other time,

[1] Dr G. Parthey, MS. *Mitth.* 1838.

except night and morning. The continued exhalations from the Dead Sea, and the silence which reigns around it, and as far as Jerusalem, had caused the belief to be common, that no earthquake will ever disturb the quiet of the region again. Although this has not proved to be the case, yet it is very probable that this gorge, 3000 feet in depth, has been the conductor, so to speak, to relieve the whole district of the powerful action of the volcanic forces which were once at work there on so great a scale. The many hot springs which are found in the neighbourhood all testify to the action of those forces ; and it may be, that if it were possible to close all the places which now serve to give the volcanic action vent, an immediate eruption would ensue.[1]

The salt contained in the Dead Sea, and found upon its shores, is connected with phenomena which have not a mere local interest, but which affect the whole surface of the globe. The salt cubes, which are found isolated, and which Lynch discovered in large numbers upon the bottom of the lake, or floating around freely in the water, may be a secondary product of hot springs at the bottom. It is interesting to observe, that such isolated salt crystals are found elsewhere in salt measures, as in the Hehlen mines,[2] on the banks of the Weser, showing that there a process has ended which in the brine of the Dead Sea is still going forward. An accurate examination of the crystals found there would be interesting. According to the most recent observations in northern Africa, there are found there three great salt zones, extending across almost the whole of the continent in parallel lines, the northern one of which, according to Fournel,[3] extends along the Atlas plateau, near the sea, from Fez, over Constantine and Tunis, to the southern cape of Sicily. The second is more inland, and runs parallel with the first in a general direction, from south-west to north-east, from Datt or Daumas, which is so rich in rock-salt, to Tripoli ; and the third, the one most remote from the sea of all, begins at the Cape Verd Islands, appears in the celebrated Tegazza salt

---

[1] A. v. Humboldt, *Cosmos,* i. p. 222, etc.

[2] Hausmann, *Ueber eine von Kochsalz herrührende pseudo-morphische Bildung in Muschelkalk der Wesergegend,* in *Götting. Noch.* Nos. 8 and 17.

[3] H. Fournel, *Sur le Gisement de Muriate de Souda de l'Algérie,* Bona 1846, in *Annales des Mines,* 1846, T. ix. p. 565 et seq.

measures, and continues north-eastward till it ends at Usdum, on the southern shore of the Dead Sea. This arrangement of salt belts changes the whole face of the globe. It stands in the closest correspondence with the main axis of the central Alpine system, and probably owes its existence to the upheaval which gave them their origin. The great valley which once intervened between these salt zones and the Alps has been filled with the waters of the Mediterranean.

From the laws which have been educed by Humboldt,[1] as controlling the rise of parallel chains of mountains, and which have been laid down by him in his *Cosmos*, it would appear that the rock-salt formation which is found at the southern extremity of the Dead Sea, stands in no vital connection, in respect to its origin, with the period when the great depression of the Ghor took place, and that it is to be merely regarded as contiguous to that depression at a single point; and the extremely salt character which the lake now has, may be regarded as not having been peculiar to it from the very first. What is said of the fertility of the country adjoining it, the comparison of it with the garden-like valley of the Nile, the allusions made to its attractiveness in the eyes of Lot as well as of king Chedorlaomer, could hardly be said of a country blasted by the contact of such a mass of brine as the Dead Sea now is : it could only have been true of a tract laved by fresh water.

This seems to make it certain, that if we accept Fournel's views regarding the belts of salt which span northern Africa, we must at least consider the pillar of Usdum as the extreme limit of one of these. In Robinson's volumes may be found a valuable letter from Leopold von Buch.[2] According to him, fossil salt is a product of volcanic action along a fissure occurring between two parallel chains of mountains which have been upheaved at the same time. So, too, are fountains of bitumen. The fertility of the soil depends largely upon the intermixture of the ingredients found in it, and it is not probable that the fertility would be augmented by an admixture of bitumen. An earthquake in the neighbourhood of the Ghor may, too,

---

[1] A. v. Humboldt, *Cosmos*, i. p. 168.

[2] L. v. Buch's letter to E. Robinson, dated April 20, 1839, in *Bib. Research.* ii. pp. 191, 524.

have brought out a larger mass of fossil salt, which, being carried by the waters to the bottom of the valley, would suffice to take away its productive power. And, thinks von Buch, Lot would hardly have been so struck with the fossil salt as to suppose his wife was changed into salt, had there been any knowledge of its existence between the layers of the mountain before the remarkable catastrophe.

Regarding the great fissure of the Jordan valley from the Lebanon mountains to the Dead Sea, the distinguished geologist says further, in the same letter: Such "long fissures, especially frequent among limestone mountains, give the configuration to our continents. If they are very large and deep, they afford passage to the primitive mountains, which for that reason form chains in the direction which the fissure prescribes. We might therefore expect a greater development of the volcanic agents at the bottom of this fissure than upon the heights.

"The asphaltum of the Dead Sea is probably nothing more than bitumen consolidated at the bottom of the lake, which, not being able to flow off, forms by consequence a layer at the bottom. It is quite probable that this accumulation may have taken place in remote times as well as in our day; and if some volcanic action, an elevation of the soil, or shocks of earthquakes, have brought to light masses of asphaltum analogous to that which you describe (a phenomenon of the highest importance, hitherto unknown), we can very well conceive of the conflagration of entire cities by the inflammation of materials so eminently combustible.

"Could some mass of basalt be discovered in the southern part or towards the southern extremity of the Dead Sea, one might believe that a basaltic dyke had been upheaved at the time of the celebrated catastrophe. The movements which accompany the breaking out of such a dyke are of a character to produce all the phenomena which have changed this interesting region, without exercising any very marked influence upon the form and configuration of the mountains round about." Von Buch, however, candidly says that it is impossible to pass judgment upon the whole subject before some experienced geologist has carefully examined the whole geological constitution both of Mount Lebanon and of the valley of the Jordan, from Tiberias quite to Akaba.

Of the two classes of observations which it was necessary to make upon the Dead Sea, one, by the labours of Symonds, Molyneux, and Lynch, has been brought to a considerable degree of perfection—namely, those relating to the question of depth; but regarding the geological character of the basin, much remains to be examined, though, in view of the cinders, lava, tufa, and sulphur which have been discovered in the neighbourhood of the Dead Sea, there is little doubt that the region was a volcanic one; and it does not need the proof afforded by the three mountains discovered by Burckhardt and Irby and Mangles between Shobek and Kerak, to show that plutonic agencies were once at work in that region.

When the fact that there was a continuous cleft from the Lebanon mountains to the Ælanitic Gulf had been confirmed, the hypsometrical measurements by De Bertou produced an irresistible impression upon Callier[1] and Letronne,[2] that this cleft once served as a channel to allow the waters of the Jordan to pass to the Red Sea. But Russegger and Humboldt have both asserted that it is an impossibility that the Jordan, under the conditions which now govern its course, should ever have poured its waters through the lower Ghor into the Red Sea. Humboldt's language[3] is decisive as usual on this point.

And, indeed, it may now be admitted on all sides, that in the present physical constitution of the Ghor it would be impossible for the waters of the Jordan to pass over the watershed which lies between the southern extremity of the Dead Sea and the Gulf of Akaba, and which occurs in what is known among the Arabs as Wadi Araba, and has since the time of Burckhardt been known to us by that title mainly. The course of the wadis northward demonstrates this fact indisputably, they being traced almost as far south as the latitude of Akaba, but farther west—that is, from the high

---

[1] Callier, Note in *Bullet. de la Soc. Geogr.* T. x. pp. 85–100.

[2] Letronne, Rev. of ˜Laborde and Linant, in *Journ. des Savans*, 1835, Aug. pp. 466–474, and Oct. pp. 596–602; Letronne, *Sur la separation primitive des Bassins de la Mer rouge et la Mediterr.*

[3] Humboldt, *Central Asien, i.a.l.* vol. i. Pt. ii. p. 545. See also Leake, pref. to Burckhardt, *Trav. in Syria*, pp. v. vi.; v. Hoff, *Gesch. der Veranderungen d. Erdoberfläche*, Pt. ii. p. 118.

Tih plateau, tending towards the Dead Sea, and not towards the neighbouring Ælanitic Gulf.

My own view is essentially this. I discriminate between the primitive vast Jordan fissure running from the Lebanon to the Gulf of Akaba, regarding whose formation we have no historical account, and a' later and secondary modification of the same, connected with which was a great catastrophe, of which we have a historical record, because it took place in the territory under the immediate observation of the patriarchs. That catastrophe may have been at the close of the great secondary modification of the primitive Ghor. In the letter of Leopold von Buch to Robinson,[1] already quoted, he says : " Could some mass of basalt be discovered in the southern part or towards the southern extremity of the Dead Sea, one might believe that a basaltic dyke had been upheaved at the time of the celebrated catastrophe. The movements which accompany the breaking out of such a dyke are of a character to produce all the phenomena which have changed this interesting region, without exercising any very marked influence upon the form and configuration of the mountains round about." At the time when these words were written, the porphyry-formations with sandstones above them had not been discovered running through the centre of the district lying east of Wadi Araba, whose existence, now known, makes it probable that the lower portion of the watershed described by Burckhardt plays the part of that dyke, having run directly across the long fissure of the Ghor in direct coincidence with the upheaval of the porphyry. A geological examination into the age of that region would throw much light upon the matter.

With the upheaval of such a porphyritic or basaltic dyke, possibly connected with other geological forms, and forming together a massive watershed, which, extending farther eastward, expanded into the towering forms which have been discovered there, a tending of the wadis northward toward the Dead Sea would be but a natural consequence.

Such an upheaval of the soil may have been going on for many hundred years, and with such quietness that the successive generations of men did not mark its progress. In its gradual development it may have checked the course of the Jordan, and

[1] Robinson, *Bib. Research.* ii. p. 192.

begun to convert it into a salt sea before that great catastrophe recorded in the Bible took place, and brought sudden desolation upon its shores. The great depression of the Dead Sea is no good reason for believing that the waters of the Jordan did not once run into the Red Sea; for it is very reasonable to suppose that the depressed surface of the lake is the result of an excess of evaporation, as in the case of the Caspian. Arago's parallel[1] between the latter sea and the Mediterranean throws much light upon the history of the Dead Sea. If we imagine, he says, an island to rise and close the Straits of Gibraltar, the current flowing from the ocean into the Mediterranean must of course cease. From that moment the surface of the latter must begin to fall; for all the rivers which flow into it do not compensate for the vast quantity of water removed by evaporation. During this gradual sinking, parts of the soil which are now beneath the surface would begin to appear.[2] Arago thinks this the solution of the Caspian Sea problem; and according to my own conviction, it throws great light[3] upon the Dead Sea as well, to which the history of the great biblical catastrophe can be conjoined as one of the elements of change. Daubeny has wrought this theme out with singular clearness and force, and has shown that, as water was chosen as the minister of God at the time of the Deluge, so volcanic agencies may have been ordained to the same mission at the time of the destruction of the cities of the plain,—a conviction in which I heartily coincide, and which does no violence to the statements of Scripture. Russegger confirms what has already been

---

[1] Arago, in *Annuaire du Bureau des Longitudes*, 1832, pp. 352–354 ; and *Central Asien*, vol. i. p. 540.

[2] Dr Anderson, geologist to the U.S. Exploring Expedition, thinks that the saltness of the Dead Sea is an inevitable consequence of these conditions. The saline ingredients being continually introduced, and never running out, the brine is of course brought at length to a state of saturation. It requires, in fact, nothing but a higher temperature to dry up or to convert into salt seas the contents of any great inland basin—the North American lakes, for example. Dr Anderson's opinion regarding the cause of the great depression will be quoted in another place, as his paper, being only issued in connection with Government documents, is not accessible to the general reader.—ED.

[3] A. v. Humboldt, *Central Asien*, i. p. 544. See also Dr Daubeny, *On Volcanoes; the Destruction of Sodom and Gomorrah*, in *Jameson's Edin. Journ.* 1826, pp. 361–372.

advanced,[1] and thinks it not impossible that there may have been a time when the Dead Sea stood so high as to flow up the whole valley of the Jordan, and to stand on the same level with the Red Sea. They may, he thinks, have then been connected, and only separated by the rising of the land which now forms the watershed between the two seas. But whatever may be thought of this, it is unquestionable that we have to deal here with a long fissure which was originally formed by volcanic action. If we wish to connect this remarkable phenomenon with the account given in the Bible, the theory that the fissure was thus created gains a probability; and after the valley thus formed had become habitable, a depression, itself the result of later volcanic action, would occasion the present relief. And yet, even with this later action, there is no reason to doubt or to deny that the sea was once much larger than it is now, and that active evaporation has both lowered its surface and increased its saline qualities.[2] I may close this part of the subject by stating that Sir R. I. Murchison,[3] in an address delivered before the Birmingham Association in 1849, has endorsed the views which I have briefly presented above. See also the authorities cited below.[4]

It remains to be noticed that there exists an ancient tradition found in Justinus, and relating to the Sidonians, that the Phœnicians were driven by earthquakes from their primitive home, and that they then settled in the neighbourhood of the Assyrian marshes, but afterwards removed to the sea-shore and

---

[1] Russegger, in Poggendorf's *Annal. der Physick*, 1841, No. 5, p. 183 ; comp. *Reise*, Pt. iii. p. 108.

[2] See Reland, *Pal.* cap. xxxviii. pp. 238-258 ; Rosenmüller, *Bib. Alterth.* Pt. ii. pp. 180–190 ; Robinson, *Bib. Research.* ii. pp. 188–193; *Kenaan*, i. p. 45, and pp. 278-788 ; Winer, *Bib. Realw.* i. p. 101 ; also pp. 73-76, and p. 479.

[3] *Athenæum*, 1849, No. 1114, p. 992.

[4] The reader who may wish to prosecute this subject further is referred to a lecture delivered by Prof. Ritter before the Berlin Academy in 1850, in which his theory is yet more fully developed. The title is, *Der Jordan und die Beschiffung des Todten Meers.* It would be impossible to close this subject without incorporating the condensed language of Dr Anderson, the accomplished geologist who accompanied the U.S. Exploring Expedition under Lynch. It will be found at the end of the present chapter. —ED.

founded the city of Sidon. The language of the original text is: "Tyriorum gens condita a Phœnicibus fuit, qui terræ motu vexati, relicto patriæ solo, Assyrium stagnum primo, mox mari proximum litus incoluerunt, condita ibi urbe, quam a piscium ubertate Sidona appellaverunt, nam pisces Phœnices Sidon vocant." Reland supposes that, by the expression "Assyrian marshes," nothing else is to be understood than the Asphaltic Sea. Movers[1] supposes, however, that the Dead Sea and the Red Sea are here confounded together, and questions the historical truth of the tradition; and yet here is a distinct tradition, not biblical in its origin, and possibly Babylonish, of the expulsion of Phœnicians (people of Canaanitic extraction) from their primitive homes through the agency of earthquakes. In the name Siddim (Sedom) there may be traces of the ancient word Sidon, or perhaps of Shedim, the devils mentioned in Deut. xxxii. 17, to whom the sacrifices were offered which Moses was so zealous to put away. And if this tradition runs back to a period so remote as even to precede the sundering of the Dead Sea from the Gulf of Akaba, it would be still more probable that the Phœnicians were dispossessed and driven from these regions by the same earthquakes which may have subsequently effected such changes in the Ghor. Regarding the existence of real volcanoes, we have only the statements of Aulick[2] relating to the north-east corner of the Dead Sea, in the neighbourhood of Wadi Ghuweir, and those of Irby and Mangles relative to three between Kerak and Shobak; yet it is unquestionable that there is not a single well-defined crater in the neighbourhood of the sea. It is to be hoped, however, that ere long geologists who are familiar with the Arabic language will thoroughly examine the problems suggested in the preceding pages, and be able to solve some of the interesting questions which have been propounded rather than settled.

I close with a condensed summary of facts relating to the depth of the Dead Sea, and the configuration of the lower Ghor. The basin of the Dead Sea consists of two divisions, entirely distinct and unlike,—a larger and deeper one at the north, and a smaller and shallower one at the south. The two

---

[1] Movers, *über Herkunft der Phönizier,* in *Z. für Philos.* v. pp. 28-32.

[2] Lynch, *Dead Sea Expedition,* p. 280.

are partly separated by the flat peninsula of el-Mesraa, being connected by a narrow channel which bears the name of its first explorer, Lynch. The northern basin seems to owe its origin to depressing volcanic agencies, the southern one to elevating ones. The two do not vary much in respect to width, and both are closely hemmed in by the lofty walls of rock which rise on the east and west, the former of which tower a thousand feet higher above the level of the sea than the latter. The depths of these two basins are widely different; that of the southern not surpassing sixteen Paris feet, and generally much shallower than that; that of the northern seldom less than a thousand feet in the middle, and not shelving up towards the western shore to a depth less than five hundred feet, and generally nearer seven and eight hundred. In the northern third there is a considerable extent running from north to south, where the depth is about 1227 Paris feet. Throughout the northern portion of the sea, navigation may extend without danger to the very shores themselves ; and at the romantic bay at the mouth of the Arnon, it was found that there was water having the extraordinary depth of over 1050 feet.[1] The great diversity which exists between the two seems to make it certain that the two basins do not owe their present form to similar physical conditions. The southern one is so shallow, that in very many places the water is not more than five feet deep ; and sometimes Lynch's party, when wishing to land, could not get the boats within half an hour's walk of the beach, and were compelled to wade to the shore through mud which was ankle-deep.

NOTE.—Prof. Ehrenberg's researches have opened a new field of inquiry regarding the animal life of the Dead Sea.[2] This has always been denied to exist; and although not much

[1] The Duc de Luynes, in his recent expedition, found the deepest place sounded by him to be 350 metres, or 1248 Eng. feet. Lynch, it will be remembered, found 400 fathoms, or 1312 feet.—ED.

[2] Vergnes, one of the officers of the Duc de Luynes' expedition, reports that, in spite of all efforts, no living creatures were found in the waters of the Dead Sea proper. Near the mouth of the rivers which flow into it, a few specimens of crustaceæ and some fish were seen, but they instantly died on coming in contact with the saturated waters beyond.—ED.

has yet been ascertained, still the subject is brought before naturalists, and some interesting facts have already been adduced. These have been communicated by Prof. Ehrenberg to the Berlin Royal Academy, and are the result of microscopic observations on water and earthy deposits brought to Europe by Prof. Lepsius.

It appears, as the result of these inquiries, that the waters of the Dead Sea are not entirely destitute of life, but that there are minute creatures peculiar both to fresh and salt water which maintain their existence there, and propagate their species, although none of the larger varieties of living things have been discovered there. A considerable portion of the deposits taken from the bottom consists of microscopic chalk polythalamia, which leave it uncertain whether they ever were able to live in the water of the sea, only their shells being found, as indeed they are in the chalk formation of the Lebanon. But these are fresh-water creatures, and probably have been swept into the lake, and there perished. The bottom seems to be composed to a large extent of chalk debris; and the Dead Sea appears to have once been a brackish lake, having no analogy with genuine seas, as the real living creatures of the sea are lacking there, or are very feebly represented. On the other hand, however, living creatures have been found in that part of the lake nearest the mouth of the Jordan, and it appears probable that a longer search would be rewarded with greater results. Among the creatures discovered, there were some which continued to live. The clear water of the Jordan is thickly peopled with animated forms which thrive in fresh water. But it is a very striking fact, that there are found in the fresh water of the Jordan salt-water forms, such as might be expected in the sea, but not in the river,—such, for example, as Ehrenberg had discovered at Cuxhaven at the mouth of the Elbe. This led him to the conclusion that their true home may have been in the sea, and that they have been driven up the river by storms and like causes, just as living marine creatures are found at Hamburgh and at London, being carried up by the tide. In the Dead Sea water he found eleven varieties of polygastera, five phytolitharia, two polythalamia, and a few crystals which seemed to be of volcanic origin. In the waters of the Jordan he discovered twenty-five polygastera, eleven phytolitharia, and three varieties of chalk polythalamia. Most of these varieties were familiar to him, but six were new, and peculiar to the Jordan.

———◆———

SUPPLEMENTARY NOTE.

THE brief and condensed remarks of Dr Anderson, geologist of the Lynch Expedition, should not be omitted, to complete the discussion of the origin of the Dead Sea. They may be found in his official report submitted to the United States Government.

To account for such depressions, we are reduced at present to two hypotheses, neither of them very promising. The first assumes a fissure or series of fissures to have taken place in one of the early geological eras, and unequal denudations or partial accumulations subsequent to these, to have imparted gradually the present relief. The second supposes the *carina* to have been once one of continuous descent, so that no lakes in the course of the river existed at that time. The dislevelling agencies have then in the course of geological ages disturbed the line of the *carina* by their effects on the whole embracing platform, depressing and uplifting its various sections according to the laws of the disturbing forces. The depressed areas became the cavities which hold lakes ; the elevated portions separate these completely or not, according to the depths of the connecting valleys and the still deeper excavation.

The fissure theory is favoured in the Jordan case by the volcanic character of some of the neighbouring districts, by the straightness of the Ghor, and by that diversity of structure on opposite sides of the valley which might be expected where a *fissure* is modified into a *fault*. On the other hand, it is liable to the serious objection, that it cannot explain the origin of curvilinearly winding valleys, which are far more numerous than the rectilinear excavations.

The theory of a pre-existing continuity of descending water discharging itself at some remote era of geological antiquity into the Gulf of Akabah, if that gulf itself, and even the Red

Sea, were not then a continuation of the Ghor, is met by the usual difficulty of accounting for the change *since* made in the levels of the stream-bed, and by the still more formidable objection, that to admit of a subsidence of three thousand feet at the latitude of the Dead Sea, we must accept a corresponding depression of the whole platform east and west of it; whereas the land on both sides is just as elevated opposite to the deepest part of the sea, as north of its northern or south of its southern extremities. The objection is strengthened at first sight by the fact that this comparative horizontality of lake districts is found to prevail, with few exceptions, wherever these very remarkable cavities are found.

Another consideration pressing with equal force against the theory of a once continuous descent from Wady et Teim to the Red Sea, is the absence of all south-tending valleys south of the point now at least of the great depression; showing very conclusively that the present system of wadis had their origin subsequently to the sinking of the area which embraces the Dead Sea. But the disappearance of the more ancient valleys would still remain to be explained.

To these objections the only answer appears to be, that as the lake districts have been depressed beneath the sea subsequently to the first excavations of the river-beds, their disturbed re-emergence has subjected the whole area in which they were destined to lie to the levelling detrition due to the incessant grinding of the upper or moveable stratum of the ocean, which, in instances innumerable, has, by its long-continued and unsparing planing down of local unevennesses, quite worn away the principal undulations of the re-emerging lands. Without such an hypothesis, indeed, it would seem impossible to account for the remarkable horizontality to which the upturned edges of plunging strata are sometimes worn away for many hundred miles. And with such an hypothesis, the disappearance of the valleys formed before the submergence, and the growth of new ones with different directions subsequent to the re-emergence, become a portion of the changes to be expected on the freshly exposed plane, even supposing no other forces to concur than those which are now allowed to subsist.

One fact appears well established: that whether we ascribe the formation of the Ghor to a fissure or to a water-current

excavation, with subsequent disturbance, the necessity exists
equally in both cases, of supposing that the Ghor and some of
its tributary wadis already existed long before the tertiary era,
—a fact which is but an instance of a general law, and corroborated by the frequent occurrence of tertiary accumulations in
the broader and deeper valleys of every part of the globe. In
the Jordan-Akaba Ghor these tertiaries have taken possession of the whole valley-bottom, and line the hill-sides from
Hâsbeiya to Wadi Wetû.

In the event of the adoption of the hypothesis of a sectional
excavation of the jurassic platform, followed by a gradual
submarine depression of the whole district of which the Jordan
is the axis, and ending in an imperfect re-emergence with a
watershed far south of the Dead Sea, we are to suppose that
the destructive process which has obliterated the secondary
tributaries to the river-bed now ascending towards the south,
began as soon as the first submersal, and was repeated long
afterwards, when the emerging district had brought its still
remaining inequalities successively in subjection to the levelling
operation of the upper and moveable stratum of the tertiary
seas.

The effect of this obliteration of valleys existing before the
submersion, would not extend to their entire destruction, but
would leave a portion near the mouths of these excavations
still much depressed below the partially abraded platform; but
the upper valleys would have disappeared, and would in time
be replaced by others having directions determined by the new
order of levels.

[To this may be added a few words from the pen of M.
Lartet, geologist to the Duc de Luynes' expedition : " Pour
l'observateur qui cherche à se rendre compte de l'âge géolo-
gique et du mode de formation des reliefs limitant le bassin de
la mer Morte, et qui, d'autre part, s'est assuré que ses anciens
sédimens ne renferment aucune trace fossile d'organismes
marins, il devient évident que cette dépression continentale
n'a été, de l'origine, rien de plus qu'un réservoir d'eau atmo-
spherique, dont la salure, empruntée à des circonstances, en-
vironnantes, s'est de plus en plus accrue sous l'influence d'une
incessante évaporation."]

PART II.

SEC. I.—INTRODUCTION.

I. THE ANCIENT BOUNDARIES OF THE PROMISED LAND—THE
DIVISION AMONG THE TWELVE TRIBES, AND THE CHECKS
WHICH THEY SUFFERED IN THE NORTH AT THE HANDS
OF THE PHŒNICIANS.

AVING thus far studied with some closeness the valley of the Jordan, and having made ourselves acquainted with the general outlines of territory known as Palestine proper, the task is now before us to investigate the geography of the district lying between the basin of the Jordan and the Mediterranean, and extending from the great desert region traversed by the children of Israel, and the mountain ranges of Lebanon and Anti-Lebanon. This district, which is very rich in its diversities of geographical characteristics, is broken up in the New Testament narratives into three parts, different in physical structure, and bearing the names of Judæa, Samaria, and Galilee. These designations, although not the oldest known to us, and although not continuing to be used in modern times, have yet acquired a certain classical authority, and have a historical value even at the present time. The names given to the territories distributed among the Israelitish tribes by lot, never won a vitality that preserved them amid all the changes of time : nor did those political re-arrangements effected by David and Solomon harden into binding and traditional habits of speech. Equally ephemeral were the later divisions of the country between the kingdoms of Judah and Israel. Yet we cannot entirely pass over the primitive allotment of the country among the twelve tribes, although the student, should he wish to study the subject exhaustively, must consult the pages of the most learned commentaries on the Old Testament, and the writings of those geographers who, like Reland and Raumer, have laboured with such loving and patient care to interpret the topography of the Bible. But some knowledge of the primitive geographical divisions of Palestine is a necessary preface to the study of its present condition ; and only by its acquisition can we rid ourselves of the countless errors with which an ignorant, and in part a lying tradition, has for centuries veiled that country.

In a manner entirely peculiar, the apportionment of Palestine, after its conquest from the Canaanites, was effected by the casting of lots. Despite the numerous names which are given in the record, we lack from the very beginning an accurate specification of the geographical boundaries; and even where they have been given, the changes made in the old landmarks, as time rolled on, tend to perplex us : still there remain data enough to guide to a tolerably correct estimate of the early geography of the Promised Land.

The territorial limits of Canaan, as it existed during the sway of the ancient tribes who were dispossessed of their domain, did not coincide with those which bounded the country held by the Israelites, and of which I have already spoken. The real possessions of the Hebrews were always less extensive than the promises made by Moses indicated that they would be. Not even in the time of David's grand military exploits, and Solomon's splendid diplomatic and commercial achievements, when the power of the Jewish name was honoured as far as to the Euphrates at Tiphsah or Thapsacus (1 Kings iv. 24), to Gaza and to Æla on the Red Sea, did the Israelitish territory extend to the limits which, it was hoped by Moses and Joshua, would bound the future possessions of their countrymen.

To what has been said on a preceding page regarding the boundaries of the territory granted to the nine and a half tribes, there is but little to be added here, excepting this remark : the accounts as recorded in Num. xxxiv. and that given later in Ezek. xlvii. do not exactly harmonize. The western boundary was to be the " great sea," by which the Mediterranean alone can be meant. The northern limit, according to Num. xxxiv. 7, was to extend from the " great sea" to Mount Hor, thence to Hamath, and thence to Zedad. In this passage the Mount

Hor referred to, cannot refer, as I have incorrectly stated on a previous page, to Hermon, although the name Hor is applied in Scripture to this mighty mountain. Hermon stands too far eastward to answer the conditions of the problem : a peak near the sea, lying, like Casius, south of the mouth of the Orontes, must be meant, although I cannot think that Casius itself, the centre of the ancient Phœnician idolatry, was the mountain[1] meant to be a point in the frontier of the kingdom of Jehovah. Still it is probable that the Mount Hor of Num. xxxiv. indicates a peak very near the Mediterranean. The name has been sought along the coast in vain : von Raumer says very justly of it that its situation is unknown, but that it was probably one of the outlying peaks west of the Lebanon and belonging to it, and discernible from Sidon. The learned Jewish geographer, Esthori B. Mode da-Parchi, a Provençal, and a contemporary of Abulfeda, spent many years in wandering through Palestine, and finished his description of the country in 1322, calling his work by the title *Khafthor va-ferach*.[2] He took great pains, with the assistance of the Midrash, the Mishna, and the Talmud, to determine the boundaries of the land promised to his countrymen at the time of their conquest. He did not discover the name of Hor in the neighbourhood of the northern frontier, but he believed that he had found[3] the place designated by that name in a mountain which lies between Mount Casius (the present Okra) and the ancient city of Laodicea ; a spot which, after the destruction of the temple, was a place of refuge for many of the Jews driven from their own land. There are frequent allusions to this mountain in the Talmud : it lies a half-hour's distance from the sea, and seems to be the western spur of a small range, Jebel Rieha, which runs northwesterly, and through which the Orontes breaks in the narrow defile called Jissr Shogher. Burckhardt[4] ascended the eastern slope, and Thomson[5] appears to have traversed the wild tracts

---

[1] Movers, *Die Phönizier*, vol. i. p. 668.

[2] Zunz, *On the Geog. of Pal. from Jewish Sources*, in Asher, *Itin. of Ben. of Tudela*, ii. pp. 393–448 ; comp. Bernhadi, *Discurs.* in *Annal. Acad. Livorensis*, p. 11.

[3] See the same, pp. 414–420.

[4] Burckhardt, Gesenius' ed. i. pp. 225–231.

[5] Thomson, *Journ.* in *Miss. Herald*, 1841, vol. xxxvii. p. 233.

on the western side, on his very laborious tour from Latakia to Mount Casius. The Jewish author to whom I have referred, bases his conjecture that the mountain here indicated[1] was the Mount Hor referred to in Num. xxxiv., on the fact that many of the old Jewish cities belonging to the tribe of Asher, and which were in that neighbourhood, like Ummah, mentioned in Josh. xix. 30, have been discovered within a day's march of the eminence which he identifies with Hor. It strengthens his position, that the location of this mountain in relation to Hamath, three days' march south-eastward, corresponds well with the scriptural account of the northern border of Palestine. In his time the country between these two points was a tract of continuous heath. The termination of the first section of the northern boundary is found a little more to the south-east, in the desert, and is indicated with great particularity in the accounts both of Numbers and Ezekiel. This Zedad can be no other than the present Sadad,[2] lying on a southerly road from Hamath to Tadmor (Palmyra). The place lay on the routes taken by David and Solomon in their military expeditions, and has been repeatedly visited by recent travellers, who have explored the ruins of the once famous city just mentioned.

The northern boundary was then continued past the yet unknown Ziphron to the village of Enan or Hazar-enan (Num. xxxiv. 9), a place which, according to Jerome, indicated the limits of the Damascus territory, but of which nothing was ascertained in his day, or has been in ours. The Jewish geographer already mentioned, thinks that he has discovered this Hazar-enan in a city lying upon a low mountain west of Homs, and bearing in his time the name of Hessn Alakrad.[3] It was three days' journey north of Damascus. In addition to what I have said on a previous page regarding the eastern boundary, which extended from Enan past the also unknown Zephan to Riblah, Ain, and Lake Chinnereth, I need only add that no further allusion was made to the possessions of Reuben, Gad, and the half tribe of Manasseh on the east side of the Jordan, because those tribes had received their allotment already from Moses

---

[1] Keil, *Comment. zu Josua*, p. 350.
[2] Wood and Dawkins, *Ruins of Palmyra*. See Wilson, *Lands of the Bible*, vol. ii. pp. 358, 644.
[3] Benj. v. Tudela, *l.c.* ii. p. 418.

himself. See Josh. xiii. 15-32, Num. xxxiv. 14, and Ezek. xlvii. 14. Still, in a general sense, the district held by these eastern tribes was included in the Israelitish domain ; and hence the eastern boundary had to be drawn from Hamath and Damascus through Gilead and Hauran to the Dead Sea. The southern boundary has been already sufficiently commented upon ; and to what has been said, I need only add that Ezekiel alludes to a place called Tamar, not mentioned in Moses' account. The line ran from the Dead Sea to the river of Egypt, *i.e.* Wadi el Arish. The present position of the ruins of Kurnub seemed to Robinson to correspond to the location of the Roman garrison city of Thamaro, which is mentioned by Ptolemy, and which seems to be the Hazazon-thamar of Jerome. This place lay a day's journey south of Hebron. If the ruins of Kurnub do correspond to the Tamar of the Israelites, " the waters of strife in Kadesh " would not be sought to the east of it, but to the west, since in the account given in Ezekiel the order of places is, first the Dead Sea, then Tamar,[1] then Kadesh, and lastly the Mediterranean.

One account of the entire extent of the country remaining to be possessed by the Israelites, after Joshua was obliged by reason of his age to abandon the attempt of conquering it all himself (Josh. xiii. 2-6), breaks up all the unsubdued region into three different districts, which must be passed in review before we can understand the account given by Moses of the whole area of the country which he promised to the Israelites, under condition of their continued loyalty to Jehovah, but which they never succeeded in bringing under their own sway. The southern portion was to embrace " all the borders of the Philistines, and all Geshuri," from the brook Sichor, *i.e.* " river of Egypt," or the present stream el-Arish, northward to the city of Ekron, the most northerly city of Philistia. The second district (Josh. xiii. 4) embraced the " land of the Canaanites, and Mearah (or place of caverns) that is beside the Sidonians, unto Aphek, to the borders of the Amorites." This land had not been all conquered at the time when the words just quoted were written, and the location of the region meant by Mearah is not yet determined. The crusaders discovered a cave in the district, called the Cavea de Tyro, and held it to be the Mearah

[1] Wilson, *Lands of the Bible*, i. p. 343.

of Scripture, yet without sufficient reason; and although Keil, the learned commentator on Joshua, is of the opinion that that Mearah is not the appellation of a specific locality, but is used in its general signification of a "place of caverns," yet the question remains, whether the expression does not refer primarily to the deep and cave-like ravines which characterize the Lebanon mountains near Sidon and the city of Lais or Leshem, or whether it may not be a method of conveying the same conception which afterwards found expression in the words Κοίλη Συρία, the ancient Cœle-Syria. The situation of Aphek, which in Josh. xix. 30 is included in the domain of Asher, is likewise unknown. Nor have we the data which allow us to determine where the "borders of the Amorites" lay. The northern district is described as also comprising "the land of the Giblites, and all Lebanon, toward the sun-rising, from Baal-gad under mount Hermon, unto the entering in of Hamath." This refers to the whole district extending from Gebel and Byblos on the sea to the neighbourhood of Hamath, the Epiphania of the Greeks, on the Orontes. Baal-gad is hardly to be understood as Baalbec (Heliopolis), or as the site of Cæsarea Philippi, but rather a place near the head waters of the Jordan, and in the vicinity of the present village of Hasbeya, at the foot of Jebel es Sheikh, immemorially a mountain sacred to the worship of such divinities as Baal.

The southern boundary of the tribe of Judah, which coincides, speaking [1] in general terms, with the southern frontier of the Promised Land, and which is characterized in more specific language in the account contained in Josh. xv. 1–5, is still shrouded from our knowledge, since modern investigation has not been able to ascertain the location of many of the places connected with that boundary in the scriptural narrative.

In the first and second verses of the chapter just cited, we are told that the "lot of the tribe of the children of Judah" was as follows: "Even to the border of Edom, the wilderness of Zin, southward, was the uttermost part of the south coast. And their south border was from the shore of the salt sea, from the bay that looketh southward." These localities have all been

---

[1] Car. Chr. S. Bernhardt, *Dissert. causæ quibus effectum sit, ut Regnum Judæ diutius persisteret quam Regnum Israel*, in *Annal. Acad. Lovan.* 1825, p. 9.

alluded to in preceding pages of this work;[1] but it may be remarked here, that the exactness of this description, especially in its closing verses, gives an unmistakeable indication of the place where the line commenced, and whence it advanced to Akrabbim, Zin, and Kadesh, places whose location is now ascertained. Although it states further, that the line passed afterwards through Hezron, Adar, Karkaa, and Azmon; yet, with the exception of Adar, the situation of these places is still unascertained.

The same is the case with the boundaries of many other of the tribes: the special topography cannot now be determined with exactness, from the fact that many of the places named as landmarks in the Old Testament have so utterly passed away as to leave not a trace behind. There is also another difficulty to be encountered in the effort to identify the ancient bounds of Israel, namely, that the actual conquests were never commensurate with the conditional promises and apportionment of the land by Joshua. Even Josephus was unable in his day to determine the ancient limits of the tribes with any degree of exactness, and has left us a mere general description, far short in point of particularity of the details given in the book of Joshua. Modern commentators have been led, by the lack of knowledge at their command, to suppose that the difficulties just hinted at are insuperable, and that they implicate and render doubtful the authenticity of the narrative, and have rejected the whole story of the division of the land among the tribes; but the main source of their difficulties has been, that they have never penetrated to the full significance of the lot as employed among the children of Israel, entirely different as it is from its use among the moderns. In the former case the whole destiny of a nation was made dependent upon it. It was the method in which Jehovah, acting through the agency of His servant Moses, the deliverer of the people from the hardships of servitude and the perils of the desert, would bring them into the land which was appointed for their home, and indicate to them with unerring precision the portion which it was determined for them by Divine Providence that they should occupy. The lot meant all this to the Israelites; but not at all, with the human and natural interpretation of it, that it was ever intended

[1] Keil, *Comment. zu Josua*, p. 279.

that an equal distribution should be effected among the tribes, and all claims balanced, and all causes for strife about the inferior and superior allotments be taken away from the tribes. On the contrary, it was understood that there was, and that there was to be, a great deal of inequality in the distribution of the land; but the portion of each tribe was to be received with thankfulness and submission as the direct gift of Jehovah. Yet, as it is evident that the tribes of Reuben, Gad, and the half tribe of Manasseh had their apportionment [1] assigned to them on the east side of the Jordan, because they had a great number of flocks and herds, and needed fine pasture land, the inference from this is fairly drawn, that the nature of the soil and the general physical character of the country west of the Jordan were consulted in the assigning of territory to the remaining nine and a half tribes, and that it was never purposed to break the whole land up into parts of equal area, which should be drawn for as in the modern method of casting lots. It was entirely different with the Hebrews, when the will of Jehovah was read in the assignment of territory through the agency of Joshua and Eleazar. There were weak tribes which must be cherished and protected by the stronger ones; there were powerful ones which must be stationed on the north and south to defend the country from the fierce enemies on both frontiers. As there was pasture land in the east, so there were fertile 'plains along the sea-coast for the small and peaceful tribe of Zebulon; at the north there was the country to be conquered from the Phœnicians, for the powerful tribes of Asher and Naphtali; at the south there was the broad desert, over which the Egyptians and the Edomites could freely range, and on this side a powerful tribe like Judah must be placed, like a strong and sure wall of defence. And that this was the character of Judah, is sufficiently well proved by Jacob's blessing (Gen. xlix. 9), beginning, "Judah is a lion's whelp," and by that of Moses in Deut. xxxiii. 7.

To think of exercising any personal influence in our time, when lots are cast, is absurd, unless there be fraud employed; and no one would think it at all needful to make any inquiries, in case land were to be distributed in this way, as to the nature of the district in question. All would be left to the simple

[1] Keil, *Comment. zu Buch Josua*, pp. 262-279.

arbitration of the lot. But it is plain that Moses wished to know what sort of a country it was which the tribes were to possess, and that for this reason he sent the spies to carefully examine every part, and to bring back their report to him.

Nor did the division of the land by lot take place all at once; for after Judah and Ephraim and the half tribe of Manasseh had received their portions, and Caleb had been invested with the personal possession of Hebron (Josh. xiv. 14, xv. 16, 17), the camp of Joshua was transferred from Gilgal on the Jordan to Shiloh, where the tabernacle was set up (Josh. xviii. 1). The great leader being now "stricken in years," there yet remained, before the whole great work should be accomplished, that the remaining seven tribes should subdue the land which was to be their home. Their remissness in undertaking the task called out this remonstrance from Joshua (Josh. xviii. 3): "How long are ye slack to go to possess the land which the Lord God of your fathers hath given you?" A new division of the unconquered territory was then made; and in order to effect it, three men from each one of the seven remaining tribes were sent to explore it and bring back a full report. The result of this examination, which was unquestionably a much more careful one than that made by the spies of Moses, was that the unsubdued territory was found to be too small for the wants of seven tribes, while that apportioned to Judah was seen to be disproportionately large. To remedy this difficulty, a place was found for Benjamin between Judah and Ephraim: both had to give up some cities also to Dan, and the portion of Simeon was taken out of the southern part of Judah. Josh. xix. 9: "Out of the portion of the children of Judah was the inheritance of the children of Simeon; for the part of the children of Judah was too much for them: therefore the children of Simeon had their inheritance within the inheritance of them." This was all effected at Shiloh under the direction of Joshua. Josh. xviii. 10: "And Joshua cast lots for them in Shiloh before the Lord; and there Joshua divided the land unto the children of Israel, according to their divisions." This was accomplished in part by the counsels of the great military leader, the high priest, and the chief men of each tribe, as we learn from Josh. xix. 51. The five remaining tribes then received their portions—Zebulon, Issachar, Asher, Naphtali,

and Dan; for Levi had no apportionment made to them, excepting certain cities in which to live, and the suburbs for their
flocks and cattle (Josh. xviii. 7, xiii. 14, xxi. 2). In accordance,
too, with a custom common among the Phœnicians, Carthagi-
nians, and Canaanites, they received a tenth part of the produce
of the land, as Abraham and Jacob had promised long before[1]
(Gen. xiv. 20, xxviii. 22). These tithes the Levites collected for
the offerings on the altar, and also for their own use, reserving
the tenth of the tenth part for the high priest. The settlement of the actual boundary could only be indicated in general
terms, or accomplished after a lapse of time, after the tribe had
fairly dispossessed the primitive population. This in some
cases was never entirely effected, in others only after centuries
had passed. This was the case, for example, with the Jebusites,
who were not driven from their capital—the site of Jerusalem
—until the time of David. That, at the time of the apportionment, the land was not all ready to be possessed, but that the
task still remained to conquer it, and drive out or exterminate
the original population, is shown by the complaint of the house
of Joseph (Ephraim and half Manasseh) made to Joshua, that
their portion was too small. They were told upon this, to make
room for themselves in the mountains of Gilboa by cutting
down the forests and exterminating the Perizzites; and this
they effected thoroughly, driving them westward as far as
Gezer (between Joppa and Ramleh), and making them pay
tribute to the tribe of Ephraim (Josh. xvi. 10). The descendants of Dan enlarged their inheritance, which extended northward from Joppa (Japho) along the sea-coast, by receiving
some of the cities originally assigned to Judah: afterwards
the victorious course of their arms northward gave them
possession of Leshem, or Lais, near Sidon, where they built
the city of Dan, and pressed close upon the borders of the
Phœnicians (Josh. xix. 47; Judg. xviii. 29). Asher, on the
other hand, was not able to conquer all the land allotted to it,
and was never strong enough to take Accho (Acco), north
of Carmel, Sidon, or Tyre (Josh. xix. 28, 29). Judg. i. 31
says: "Neither did Asher drive out the inhabitants of Accho,
nor the inhabitants of Zidon, nor of Ahlab, nor of Achzib,
nor of Helbah, nor of Aphik, nor of Rehob." But the most

[1] Ewald, *Die Alterth. des Volks Israel*, p. 314.

stubborn and able opposition to the victorious progress of the Israelites was made by the warlike coast tribes of the Philistines, which pressed into the territory of the Hebrew tribes, especially that of Judah, and were felt from Gaza to Jezreel in the land of Issachar (1 Sam. xxix. 1, 11). For centuries they made their power felt: they were crippled during the reign of David; but they remained in possession of some portions of the Promised Land down to the time of the Maccabees, and of Alexander the Great. At a period subsequent to this, their name dropped out of history.[1]

The boundaries of the tribes are given with great fulness of detail in the book of Joshua: those of Judah in chap. xv.; of the house of Joseph, *i.e.* of Ephraim and half Manasseh, in chaps. xvi. and xvii.; of the tribe of Benjamin in chap. xviii.; and of the remaining seven in chap. xix. The identification of these lines can only be effected at the present day by studying the topography of the whole country, and by comparing the ancient names with those which are now found attached to the ruins which are scattered over the land. The reader who wishes to examine into this subject exhaustively, is referred to Reland's *Palästina,* cap. xxviii. (*de partitione Terræ Israeliticæ facta inter tribus duodecim*),[2] von Raumer,[3] and in particular, the commentary of Keil on Joshua.[4] The maps of Kiepert (*Bibel Atlas*) will be of great service also. But I need not enter into details here regarding those primitive divisions among the tribes.[5] They will be discussed with a far more lively interest when we shall come to pass the different parts of the country in review.

The importance of this division of the conquered land was much greater directly after the invasion and the taking possession than it was when the territory had been materially enlarged[6] by the victories of David and Solomon. It grew less and less apparent; and at last, the feebleness of the feeling,

---

[1] Hitzig, *Urgeschichte und Mythologie der Philistaer,* p. 26.

[2] Reland, *Palästina,* pp. 142–168.

[3] Von Raumer, *Paläst.* pp. 98–103.

[4] Keil, *Comment. zu Josua,* pp. 279–326. (Translated in Clark's For. Theol. Library.)

[5] Kiepert, *Bibel Atlas,* Plate iii.

[6] Bernhadi, *Diss.* in *Annal. Acad. Lovan.* p. 5.

which had once been so strong, produced the division into the two rival kingdoms,—that of Judah, embracing the tribes of Judah and Benjamin ; and that of Israel, embracing the other ten. The first named of the new monarchies clung more to the worship of Jehovah ; the second, with Jeroboam at its head, erected its capital at Shechem, on Mount Ephraim,[1] and began to cultivate the worship of heathen gods. Their king, in order to wean his people away from their pilgrimage to Jerusalem, set up at the northern and southern extremities of his kingdom two golden calves, such as he had seen during his sojourn in Egypt.[2] All this, of course, had its natural effect : the people began to set their heathenish idols above the God whom they had been bidden to serve (1 Kings xii.).

Although there must be considerable obscurity regarding the primitive boundaries of the tribes, since the means of identifying many of the places mentioned in the book of Joshua are wanting to us, yet there are some ethnographical characteristics which are connected with the early settlement of the country, which it will be well to glance at before we go on to speak of its more modern geography, since they exerted the greatest influence on the condition of the Israelitish people for centuries, and even to the time of its extinction as a nation. The study of the connection between the country, as it was when held by the primitive inhabitants and the victorious nation which entered it, is a theme of wide interest.

Although the ancient Canaanitish population, numbering, it is probable, some millions of people, were driven at once from their former possessions, yet they were not so wholly expelled, that some traces did not remain in the country, very gradually to disappear. But in the north it was very different from what it was in the south and east, where the nature of the boundary lines, and the decisive battles which were fought there, at once established a fixed frontier; whereas in the north the efforts made against the Phœnicians were always without complete success ; and in the west, new and hitherto unexperienced difficulties arose, particularly those with the warlike Philistines, whose influence was discernible for centuries.

Incomplete as are the Hebrew records regarding the rela-

---

[1] Movers, *Phönizier*, Pt. i. p. 667.
[2] Lepsius, *Chronologie der Egyptüer*, Pt. i. p. 326.

tions with the powerful race on the north, yet it appears to be put beyond a doubt, that the Israelites were never engaged in real war with the great Phœnician maritime states, although, in the early stages of the invasion of the country, it is unquestionable that the subjugation of the whole length and breadth of the land was contemplated, including Phœnicia and the land of the Giblites (see Josh. xiii. 5). In the account of the conflicts with the minor Canaanitish kings who joined themselves to king Hazor in the north country, and who were overcome by Joshua at the waters of Merom, we do not read that either Tyre or Sidon took an active part; and the evidence seems very strong, that these two maritime powers, following their usual custom, expressed in Judg. xviii. 7, dwelling "careless, quiet, and secure," *i.e.* busied with their industries and commerce, thought it the most desirable course to take no active part in the war of their allies against Israel, the more as it was impossible for these new and powerful invaders to interfere successfully with their own domain. The old unity and fiery valour of the twelve tribes had been much lessened when the powerful ones, who were to possess the district east of the Jordan and the southern part of the Promised Land, had conquered and taken possession of their territory; and independently of this, it was necessary for a large number of men to be detained there to defend the borders, and to settle all the arrangements necessary to be made in a newly conquered territory; and the great advantage enjoyed at the outset was lost to the smaller and weaker tribes of Asher, Zebulon, Naphtali, and Issachar, which had a longer series of hard-contested battles than the tribes which took possession of the interior of the country. This slackened the tie which bound them to their brethren in the south, and led to their easy transfer of allegiance to the idols worshipped just beyond the northern frontier. According to Judg. iv. 3, Israel was for twenty years tributary to Hazor, before the Lord gave them the victory over him.

It seems to have been considered preferable by the great commercial states along the northern coast, to institute friendly relations with the enemy, when they saw that the most of their own inland domain was hemmed in on all sides, and almost surrounded by the Israelites, and that their own roads to Egypt, Arabia, and the lands on the Euphrates were shut up against them. The compensation which they enjoyed for the loss of so much power, and such a high-handed prerogative, will appear in the considerations which I shall now present, and which are drawn, not from the direct words of the Old Testament, but from its implication. It is to the admirable studies of the ingenious Movers[1] that we are indebted for several valuable inferences relative to this subject, which had never been drawn by any who have gone before him in this field. It was seen that a great portion of the northern tribes of Israel, falling away from a rigid observance of the injunctions of Moses, settled down peacefully as *metoikoi*, or fellow-citizens by adoption and naturalization, in the territory belonging to the Phœnician cities, dividing the land between themselves and the original inhabitants, under certain fixed regulations. Out of this mixed state of society great modifications must have been made in the polity of the northern tribes. How large this influence must have been upon Asher, Naphtali, Zebulon, Issachar, and still later upon Dan, and how lasting that influence must have been, can be seen by glancing at the localities which they occupied, and the gradual unfolding of the history of those northern branches of the great Israelitish stock. There are many little details which have been gleaned by Movers, which, when put together, make up a body of evidence which seems indisputable, in support of the theory that the Hebrews were adopted or naturalized as *metoikoi* in the Phœnician territory.

The tribe of Asher, as we have already learned from Judg. i. 31, did not succeed in driving the Phœnicians out of the territory apportioned to it ; and yet its people lived in the cities already cited, which probably belonged collectively—Ahlab, Achzib, Helbah, Aphik, and Rehob—to the territory of Sidon. This explains the 32d verse : " But the Asherites dwelt among the Canaanites, the inhabitants of the land." It implies the same relation, though conversely turned, which existed between the tribes of Manasseh, Zebulon, Naphtali, and Ephraim, excepting that in the case of the latter the Canaanites were the dependent ones, and paid tribute, and became villeins or serfs, or subject aliens, so to speak, to the new possessors of the land. In Phœnicia, on the contrary, the Israelites, though not nominally or even really a subject people, were so thoroughly

[1] Movers, *Die Phönizier*, Pt. i. pp. 306–311.

checked in their plans of conquest, and dashed their strength so uselessly against the strong rock of Phœnician power, that in the shock of failure they settled down as a people admitted to be strong, and allowed to exist side by side with the Phœnicians, under certain statutes and arrangements mutually entered into.

At the most remote period, when the conquered Canaanites who lived in the midst of the Israelites enjoyed a great degree of freedom, there may have been the same absence of an oppressive spirit on the part of the Phœnicians towards the Asherites who settled among them, and enjoyed a certain degree of civic favour. It appears, indeed, from the song of Deborah, that this tribe was too prosperous to continue true to the heroic spirit which had been displayed by the brother tribes of Zebulon, Naphtali, and Issachar, against the oppressions of Hazor, and in the effort to free themselves from the payment of tribute to him. In Judg. v. 17 we read : " Asher continued on the sea-shore, and abode in his breaches." In the blessing of Jacob, which pictures the condition of the tribes as it would be after the occupation of Canaan, and made undoubtedly with a thorough knowledge of the country to be possessed, and with a shrewd forecasting of the effect of the locality which each tribe should possess upon the formation of the tribal character, the future of Asher is depicted thus (Gen. xlix. 19) : " Out of Asher his bread shall be fat, and he shall yield royal dainties." By this can scarcely anything else be meant than the productive harvests of wheat, which Solomon afterwards turned to good account in exchange for the cedars and workmen of Hiram of Tyre (see 1 Kings v. 11 and 2 Chron. ii. 15, where wheat, barley, and oil are spoken of). The stipulations which were entered into by the Asherites with the Phœnicians may have made them despised among the other tribes ; and that may be the secret reason why the twenty cities which were given by Solomon to Hiram were looked at so disdainfully, and counted as a worthless gift (1 Kings ix. 13 ; Josh. xix. 27).

Yet in the other tribes there was the same villeinage rendered to the Phœnicians as among the Asherites, though less marked ; for we know that the tribe of Dan, which had at the outset pressed so hard upon the Sidonian power, and had wrested from it the city of Lais or Leshem, was chided in the song of Deborah for not pushing forward with the old daring spirit, and for "remaining in ships" (Judg. v. 17), meaning thereby their entering the Sidonian service as helpers in lading and unlading ships, and in doing the rough work which had to be done in the harbours which communicated with the great roads to the Euphrates, leading directly over the territory of Dan.

The expression used by Jacob regarding Issachar is fruitful in lessons regarding the position of almost slavish servitude which the people of that tribe assumed in relation to the Phœnicians, becoming their common carriers, mule-drivers, and servants of all work. His words, recorded in Gen. xlix. 14, run: "Issachar is a strong ass crouching down between two burdens: and he saw that rest is good, and the land that it was pleasant; and bowed his shoulder to bear, and became a servant unto tribute." This depicts very clearly the condition of the nomadic races which collected their caravans in the neighbourhood of the Phœnician cities, and entered the service of that rich nation as the carriers of their goods. In Deut. xxxiii. 18 we read, "Rejoice, Issachar, in thy tents;" and with reason, for the territory which belonged to that tribe (including the great plain of Jezreel near Beisan) lay upon the great caravan road between Phœnicia and the Jordan, and extending onward to Damascus and Arabia. Even the two minor tribes of Zebulon and Naphtali, having their possessions partly within the Phœnician limits, and farther north than the country of Issachar, could not escape the influence of the powerful Phœnicians. In the blessing of Jacob it was said of Zebulon: "He shall dwell at the haven of the sea; and he shall be for an haven of ships: and his border shall be to Zidon;" and in the blessing of Moses the same implication is found (Deut. xxxiii. 19): "They shall suck of the abundance of the sea, and of treasures hid in the sand." This refers probably to the capture of the oyster which yielded the Tyrian purple, and to the manufacture of glass, both of which preparations were peculiar to Tyre; and it seems fairly to be inferred that the Israelitish neighbours were employed in the rude service of a nation so cultivated and renowned. In Judg. i. 33 we are expressly told that Naphtali "dwelt among the Canaanites," although the latter paid tribute; and we know from such passages as that in 1 Kings vii. 14, referring to the son of a widow of the tribe of Naphtali, whose husband was a famous Tyrian worker in brass, that marriages were effected between people of the different nations.

Thus it appears that all the Israelites in the immediate vicinity of the Phœnicians came into close relations with this people ignorant of Jehovah, and served them in the humble capacity of farm labourers, drivers of their caravans, and stevedores on their wharves. How it was possible for the Israelites to settle down in this quiet way in a country so thickly peopled with the original inhabitants as the coast land of Phœnicia was, can only be understood by considering what the nature of the system of colonization employed by that maritime nation was, and that it was continually thinning out its own population by sending all its own discontented subjects away to settle in distant lands, and therefore needed fresh supplies of labour for its rougher work. There is not the slightest trace of evidence that the Israelites were ever transported to help to form new colonies ; it may have been among the original stipulations that this should not be done. The formidable might of the Israelites during the reign of Samuel, and the peaceful relations between Solomon and Hiram, may have contributed to defend the Hebrew tribes from the Sidonians, although in the time of the judges the latter were reckoned among the oppressors of Israel, at least of the northern tribes (Judg. x. 12). At a still later period the oppressions of the Phœnicians must have become more grievous ; for in the time of Uzziah, the prophet Amos breaks out in complaint against Tyre, " because they delivered up the whole captivity to Edom, and remembered not the brotherly covenant." And Joel tells us that the inhabitants of Tyre and Sidon sold the Israelites as slaves in foreign lands, and threatens the severest judgment upon them in consequence. The expression " the brotherly covenant" presupposes such a stipulation as that which Solomon entered into when he delivered the twenty cities of Galilee over to Hiram king of Tyre (1 Kings ix. 11). I need not enter into any statement of the natural effect which the mutual relations between the Phœnicians and the Hebrews had upon the introduction of idolatry among the latter.

II. THE THREE LATER DIVISIONS OF THE COUNTRY INTO JUDÆA, SAMARIA, AND GALILEE, AND THE PHYSICAL BASIS OF THIS PARTITION.

At the period of the Maccabees, and subsequently to the building of the second temple, the division of Palestine, not as before, among twelve tribes, but into three different portions, Judæa, Samaria, and Galilee, begins to come into vogue, especially in all legal documents; but at the outset it is not intended to designate sections sharply defined, but rather to hint at the triple character of the whole domain known as Palestine. The earliest indication that some such triple division was recognised is found in Josh. xx. 7, where the arrangement was made, that certain free cities should be established as places of refuge for those who had accidentally, and without any malice, taken human life. The three cities designated were Kedesh in Galilee, Shechem on Mount Ephraim, and Hebron in Judah.

Galilee then comprised only the northern portion of the later province bearing the same name. It was a small tract, known sometimes as the " circle of the Gentiles," and embraced the twenty cities which were given by Solomon to the king of Tyre. At the time of Josephus, Tiberias was the capital of Galilee, the third important district in the kingdom of Herod, and lay at about the centre of the province. In like manner, Shechem was very near the middle of Samaria, and Hebron was at the very heart of Judah ; for such an arrangement was necessary, in order that those who were fleeing to the cities of refuge should have all possible advantage in escaping from the bloodthirsty vengeance of the pursuers.[1] The forms of the three mountain systems which characterize Palestine determined the central place which should be in each the city of refuge.

The physical character of these three districts was the prime cause for that radical diversity in the population of each, which followed the primitive and necessary union when the country was conquered by the combined efforts of the children of Israel. At the time when the New Testament was given that diversity was so great, that Galilee was scorned, Samaria was wholly beyond the lines of Jewish comity and trade, and

[1] Keil, *Comment. zu Josua*, p. 363.

Judæa held herself disdainfully aloof from both. The division into these three provinces, which did not supersede that of the Idumæan Herods into tetrarchates and toparchates,[1] was the one generally recognised during the later days of the Jewish history (see Acts ix. 31), and was that which Josephus followed in describing his country for the information of the Greeks and Romans. A glance at the map will do away with the necessity, for the present, of entering into a lengthy description of the topography of these three districts; for this will best be learned when we shall pass on to traverse the length and breadth of the land, and study the monuments of its history, and all its physical characteristics. It is well known to the reader that Judæa embraced all the country from the desert of Arabia Petræa on the south, northward to the Samarian boundary, and comprising the territories of Simeon, Judah, Benjamin, and Dan. Further on I shall have occasion to indicate the nature of the southern boundary of Samaria; but this province extended northward across the middle third of Palestine, and as far as to the celebrated plain of Jezreel.

Galilee extended from this plain and from Mount Carmel northward as far as to Hermon and the boundaries of Tyre, and embraced the district lying between Lake Tiberias and the Mediterranean.

Thus much for the general limits of the three provinces. One glance remains to be taken at the most striking points of difference between them before we come to the study of the topographical peculiarities which presuppose an acquaintance with the general geography of the land, and which receive their clearest explanation from it.

I have already had occasion to indicate the three roads which lead up from the desert into southern Palestine, the land which we have now to traverse and study in detail. The desert is left behind; the distinctive character of Arabia Petræa exchanged for a landscape entirely different—that of the Syrian mountain land, extending from south to north in a great diversity of combinations, and, notwithstanding all the unity which the system exhibits, with an individuality stamped upon every locality which communicates itself to all the forms of

[1] Reland, *Pal.* cap. xxx. *de Partitione, etc.;* and cap. xxxi. *de Partibus majoribus, etc.,* pp. 173–177, and 178–184.

life which cluster around it. As soon as the last wearisome leagues of the arid desert are passed, there appear beyond the grass plains and scattered fields of Wadi Chalil, the first out-lying mountains of Judæa rising up on both sides, and which follow the valley all the way up to Chalil or Hebron. Round-topped hills, with short side-vales separating them, and their sides covered with grey masses of shattered rock, of jurassic limestone and of chalk, appear on all sides, the clefts filled with a scanty but hardy growth of grass and low bushes. The very crevices between the scattered rock-heaps sustain some living things, and a network of green is woven over the whole labyrinth. Only here and there is a tree seen, and nowhere are there any which attain to any considerable height.[1]

The first place of any importance in Palestine is the village ed-Dhoheriyeh, five or six hours south-west of Hebron. It derives its interest from the fact that here converge the west road leading through Wadi es Seba and Beersheba, the great highway to Gaza and Egypt, and the great eastern road from Petra and Sinai. The place becomes therefore a kind of haven where the ships of the desert may find refreshment after escaping the perils of the sand ocean. On the way from the desert thither there may be seen along the sides of the valleys traces of former terraces built once to the hill-tops, as is done now on the slopes of the Lebanon; gazelles are seen, and a ranker growth of shrubs; for in September there the rains begin to fill up the springs, and exercise a lasting influence upon the verdure of ed-Dhoheriyeh, since the hills which sur-round it are higher than that on which it stands, itself no mean eminence, it being 2040 Paris feet above the sea. Thick fogs and heavy dews[2]—phenomena utterly unknown in Edom—tell the traveller that he has completely left the desert behind, and arrived at a land which gives a foretaste of the one which flowed with milk and honey. Still the thick carpet of verdure is not seen as yet: the grass shoots forth only in scattered bunches; but here and there can be seen wild oats, clover, tulips, and other varieties of the flora known in Europe, in such abun-dance as fairly to surprise Dr Wilson, a Scot, who, after his long absence in India, felt almost transported to his home when

---

[1] Russegger, *Reise*, iii. p. 71.
[2] Wilson, *Lands of the Bible*, i. p. 344.

he saw the familiar growths of Palestine, and passed through the country with the words of the Psalm, " Praise the Lord, O my soul," continually rising to his lips. This southern extremity of the Syrian mountain region, which closes on the side of the desert with the Jebel Chalil and the outlying hills of ed-Dhoheriyeh, runs off towards the south and south-west, with a gradual lessening of the altitude, and with here and there bold steep cliffs, till it is lost in the plains of Gaza and in the sandy tracts of the isthmus. Towards the south-east the physical character is not unlike the south-western offshoot, the range declining by successive terraces till it reaches the Ghor, and ceases in the deep basin of the Dead Sea. Northward the mountains of Chalil are seen, and beyond them Jebel el Kods (the heights of Jerusalem) and the summits of Ephraim falling away on the east to the valley of the Jordan, and declining by gradual steps on the west till they are lost in the plain of Jaffa.

The fruitful coast plain begins with the southern frontier of Judæa at Gaza, up to which point I have already traced the celebrated ancient road from Pelusium. From Gaza it extends northward, a uniform tract of level land as far as to the promontory of Carmel; thence it begins anew, and continues with some breaks, and within narrower limits, passing the side spurs of the Lebanon and Beirut till it reaches the mountain region of Jebal, where it seems to be closed by Mount Okra, the Casius of the ancients. This plain in the portion south of Carmel is one of the most fruitful and fairest districts of Syria; and the northern section of it, the plain of Sharon, under proper cultivation, would supply the entire population of Palestine with food. All that is wanted is industry, to give this land, not wrongly called by the term blessed, a tropical richness of vegetation, since all the nobler products of the Mediterranean basin flourish there: the wild date palm even thrives in the southern portion of the plain,[1] and when cultivated, bears fruit as far north as to Khaifa, at the northern foot of Carmel. Still by far the greater part of this plain lies untilled, a mere pasture for cattle to range over, and producing little but cucumbers and melons.[2]

[1] Von Schubert, *Reise*, iii. p. 114.
[2] Wilson, *Lands of the Bible*, ii. p. 254.

The Judæan mountains are broad,[1] arched, and for the most part waste and bare, cultivated only here and there in the valleys which lie between them. For the most part, the broad, elevated plains, never over from two to three thousand feet above the sea-level, which form the summits of the ridgy mountains, are capable of being made very productive, and were unquestionably places of great fertility in those earlier times when Palestine sustained that great population which has left its traces in the countless ruins on all the hills of the land. The relative heights are rather higher as we approach the Jordan than as we go westward: the cliffs there are therefore steeper than on the western side of the country, where all the physical features assume a gentler type: the valleys are longer, and the gorges less wild.

The line of watershed runs from south to north, not in a continuous and direct line, but in a wavy one, passing from peak to peak, and taking in here and there some well-known summits. It is always nearer the Jordan than the Mediterranean. Among the mountains which lie in its course are those on which Hebron and Jerusalem are built, the former 2644 Paris feet, the latter 2349, above the sea; the Mount of Olives, 2509 feet high; Gerizim, near Nablus, 2398 feet; and others, which, though of considerable altitude compared with the sea-level, rise only a few hundred feet above the plateau on which they stand. The gorges which they present, and the abrupt cliffs, are of no inconsiderable magnitude, especially on the east. The most convenient and direct line of communication extends along the watershed, running from Hebron to Jerusalem, thence to the Samarian mountains, and so on to Tabor. This is, in fact, almost the only great highway through the country at the present time. It was the same in ancient times, and on it stood the most important cities of the land. From this central highway there were the side-paths turning to the right and left, which could be taken by those who sought the more secluded spots. The other routes running north and south have always been shunned, so inaccessible are they. Of all the highways in Palestine, that leading from Jerusalem to Nablus has been most exhaustively described; but regarding the roads which lead off from the great central road, much remains to be learned.

[1] Russegger, *Reise*, iii. p. 200; Buckingham, *Palestine*, ii. p. 390.

Notwithstanding the general unity in the physical structure of the whole country, there is a considerable degree of diversity in the landscape of the north and the south of Palestine. And yet the geological character is everywhere the same—soft chalky limestone[1] of the upper Jura formation, containing few but very perceptible organic remains. The stone lies mostly in horizontal strata, and externally terrace is seen rising above terrace. Out of these strata the violent rains of the country have gullied shallow strata, producing on the higher and level spots some slight inequalities of surface, and below some of the wildest and most rugged of ravines. The streams which pour over the rocks in the rainy seasons have worn away the soil, and left the surface of the rocks bare, or covered with a scanty growth of yellow or brown lichens, which deceive the European eye, used as it is to a covering of a rich dark green, and give an impression of barrenness which does not exist; for although there is a great want of skilful agriculture, yet in the localities which are the most sheltered and sequestered, there is a rankness of vegetation which is full of promise, and which would ensure abundant provision for the needs of a large population. Where the holm oak and the mountain juniper are found, they sometimes cover broad tracts of ground. But in general the central mountains of Judæa[2] have a wild, more rocky, and more sterile look than the more moist regions in the neighbourhood of the sea-coast, including the mountains of Ephraim and Samaria. It is true that the immediate vicinity of the desert of Edom on the south, with its burning sun, its dry winds, and its rainlessness, displays the terrible influence of all these agents; yet in the few places where springs are abundant, and there is a little shade, the advantages of the dry climate for maturing fruit are so great, that some of the finest of grapes are found near Hebron (the old Eshcol valley),[3] the finest of dates[4] near Gaza, and the most juicy of olives in the groves on the gentle western slopes of the hill country about Askelon.

The character of the more northerly landscape of Samaria is, on the whole, far more pleasing than that of Judæa: the

---

[1] Wilson, *Lands of the Bible*, i. p. 383.
[2] Russegger, *Reise*, iii. p. 204.
[3] Robinson, *Bib. Research.* i. p. 216.
[4] Robinson, *Bib. Research.* ii. p. 35 ; Dr H. Barth, *Diary*, MS.

mountains of Ephraim, which extend from the northern frontier
of Judæa, or more definitely from Bethel to Shechem, 2 Chron.
xix. 4 (the last-named city being built upon one of them), were
more strictly a succession of high plateaus and terrace-like
slopes than a true range of peaks. These mountains constitute
a large portion of Samaria. The province extends as far as to
Carmel, which, with its central summit and outlying spurs,
bounds it on the north-west. Eastward it declines into the
valley of Jenin, at the southern part of the deep plain of Jezreel
or Esdraelon, rising again still farther to the east in the mountains of Gilboa. This great plain, which lies between these
two ranges, with its red and black loam, is the richest tract in
all Palestine. It forms the natural barrier between Samaria
on the south and Galilee on the north : in my description of it
as an unbroken tract of level land reaching from the Beisan
valley of the Jordan westward to the Gulf of Akko on the
Mediterranean, I have termed it the Open Gate, and through
it runs the celebrated brook of Kishon. Schubert's measurements have revealed to us the slight elevation of this plain above
the level of the sea, and have shown us that it is but about
four hundred and thirty-eight feet; that of Gerizim being 2398,
and that of Nazareth 1161. In the neighbourhood of the
sand-dunes, at the mouth of the Kishon, the elevation above the
level of the sea is only a few feet.

In the beautiful province[1] of Samaria, lying south of this
fertile plain, all organic life is more abundant and more varied
than in Judæa ; several of the mountains are adorned, not
only on their summits, but upon their sides, with fair forests ;
even the Carmel ridge, which on account of its neighbourhood
to the sea has a more imposing appearance than its height
actually justifies—its elevation being but 1200 feet—was once
covered with woods. The valleys are almost all abundantly
watered and skilfully cultivated, particularly towards the west ;
gardens, groves of olive trees, and forests of fruit trees, adorn
the vales, while springs and fountains carry verdure everywhere, and give a picturesqueness to the entire scene. Here,
upon this fruitful soil, the Ephraimites, according to Zech. ix. 10,
once drove their chariots, full of pride and defiance, while the
people of Judah were obliged to content themselves with horses,

---

[1] Russegger, *Reise*, iii. p. 205 ; Buckingham, *Trav. in Pal.* ii. p. 390.

the nature of the country forbidding the employment of wheeled carriages. In the highly picturesque words with which Jacob blessed his sons, and which unquestionably picture the condition of the tribes directly after the occupation of Canaan, the prophecy regarding Judah refers evidently to the special character of the employment of its people, and indicates that they should pay less attention to agriculture than to the rearing of cattle, and the culture of the grape and fruit trees: "binding his foal unto the vine, and his ass's colt unto the choice vine ; he washed his garments in wine, and his clothes in the blood of grapes : his eyes shall be red with wine, and his teeth white with milk" (Gen. xlix. 11, 12). Compare this with the blessing of Ephraim: " Joseph is a fruitful bough by a well, whose branches run over the wall.'

As one comes out from the hilly land of Samaria and enters into the plain of Esdraelon, where it loops down between the mountains of Ephraim and those of Gilead, there is seen the full length and breadth of this fertile tract, with the Carmel ridge on the west and the south-west, with Little Hermon on the north-east, and in the distant north the cone-like Tabor. So uniform is the surface, that it seems like the basin of a former lake, which has found its way to the Mediterranean, and left behind it the dark rich soil which characterizes the valley of Esdraelon, and which gives such a rich yield of barley, wheat, and even of cotton.[1]   This fertile plain[2] now exhibits hardly a single village, although once covered with towns and cities, whose abundant ruins display their former number ; but the tall grass waves over its broad expanse, so well watered by the Kishon and its tributary rivulets.

The third and most northerly province, Galilee, rises with its mountains of Little Hermon and Tabor, and those about Nazareth, above the plain of Esdraelon, and extends northward to the sources of the Jordan above Banias, embracing those near Hasbeya, between Hermon (Jebel es Sheikh) and Lebanon ; north-westward it embraces the fine valley of Merj Ayun, and is bounded on the north by the wild and gorge-like channel of the Litany, and on the west by the Tyrian frontier.   The whole eastern side is limited by the lakes of el-Huleh and

---

[1] Wilson, *Lands of the Bible*, ii. pp. 85, 86, 302.
[2] Buckingham, *Trav. in Pal.* ii. p. 384.

Galilee, and by the valley of the Jordan. The portion which is now to be brought particularly under our study is the western slope towards the Mediterranean, and extending from Akko (Acre, Ptolemais) to the southern limit of the coast of Phœnicia. The wooded ridge of Carmel, running out into the naked and bald promontory, forms the sharp barrier between the two great sections of the Palestine coast, the northern one of which is much more closely related to the Phœnician form of shore line than the southern one from Carmel to Gaza is. In front of Carmel, and to the north of it, lies the great coast plain, extending from Haifa to Akko.[1] The stone which underlies the deep soil consists of very recent deposits of sandstone, the result of the consolidation of the sand once washed up : this is intermingled to a certain extent with the chalk and Jura limestone of the neighbouring mountain ridge. Sand-dunes are sometimes seen running down to the very sea-shore. Such coast plains are found repeatedly as we go northward, but they become constantly smaller in proportion as they occur on the border of Phœnicia, at Tyre (Sur), Sidon (Saida), and Beirut; and at last the Lebanon pushes its spurs so far westward as to cause them to disappear almost entirely, leaving only a mere rim of level land along the shore. This affords picturesque scenery, but it also produces inaccessible roads, and gives rise to those plunging rapids which break through the deep ravines of Lebanon, and which have no long level plain to stay their course, and bid them meander gently along. These mountain streams are very full in winter, and in summer they retain much of their water, being fed by the perennial snows of the mountains. The waḍis in the south country, on the contrary, having no such similar supply, are dry in summer. The violent floods of the north carry much devastation with them; but their very violence compelled the people to the practice of industry, and drove them to construct some means of defence against the ravages of the mountain floods. These have been neglected within recent years, and the people have turned their attention to terrace culture rather than to that of the valleys, their reason being, that there is a degree of security on the mountains not known below, where there is no certainty that they will enjoy the fruits of their labour.

[1] Russegger, *Reise*, iii. p. 201.

In Galilee the forms of nature are more charming than in Samaria and in Judæa, although they are presented on a scale equally large; for although the mountains are not absolutely higher, yet their forms are sharper and bolder, their highest portions are more thickly wooded, and covered with a denser carpet of verdure. The beauty of Tabor is a subject of universal praise; and the grandeur of Hermon, the northern keystone of the whole land, has been the theme of song for ages. The little lakes of Galilee, with their blue transparent waters, contribute not a little to the charming beauty of the northern province. The valleys found in it are not, as farther south, mere arid wadis, but fruitful vales, capable of being cultivated even to the mountain-top. And if the country were only blessed with an industrious population and a well-administered government, Galilee would become one of the most favoured and most densely populated mountain lands in the world.

PART III.

SEC. 2.—JUDÆA, THE MOST SOUTHERN PROVINCE OF
PALESTINE;

INCLUDING THE PLAINS ALONG THE COAST, AND THE MOUNTAIN RANGES BETWEEN
EGYPT AND EDOM ON THE SOUTH, AND SAMARIA ON THE NORTH.

 HAVE already alluded on previous pages to the
two main roads which lead up into Judæa from
Egypt, and from the Sinai Peninsula : one of them
following the coast from Pelusium and the Isthmus
of Suez, passing el-Arish, the ancient Rhinocolura, and terminating at Gaza ; the other crossing the desert and the mounts
of et-Tih, passing the ancient wells of Beersheba, and the outlying green hills which lie south of Hebron, and which mediate
between the fertile land of Palestine and the barren wastes of
Arabia Petræa. The natural course will henceforward be to
study first the regular route along the plain from Gaza to
Joppa; then to take the road which runs from Hebron northward, following the watershed between the Mediterranean and
the Dead Sea. And although this was not the route which
was taken by the children of Israel, yet it is connected with
great expeditions, and has a great name in history. I need
only allude incidentally to the fact that this central road was
an important route as far back as the times of the Sesostridæ
and the Hyksos, and that it assumed importance in all the
great wars which determined the destinies of all the great
monarchs who essayed to dictate laws to two continents. Pelusium, at the extremity of the eastern arm of the Nile, was the
necessary point of departure for all Egyptian armies starting
for Syria. The only available way from Mesopotamia and

Syria to Egypt passed over Rhinocolura, Mons Casium, and by the side of Lake Sirbonis, and thence to Pelusium. It was over this road that Sesostris passed on his way from his career of conquest in Asia back to Daphnæ near Pelusium, where his treacherous brother met him. From here to Heliopolis, Sesostris is said to have fortified his outposts strongly against the incursions of any foe from the east. Near Pelusium, Sethos, the priest of Phtha (the Hephæstos of Herod. ii. 141), met the powerful army of Sennacherib the king of Assyria, " because this was the key to Egypt" (ταύτῃ γὰρ εἰσιν αἱ ἐσβολαί).

There, near the Pelusian mouth of the Nile, and below Bubastis, the Ionians and Carians were placed by Psammeticus on both sides of the stream, at the place which afterwards bore the name Στρατόπεδα, and near the spot where the prophets locate a tower bearing the name of Migdol, the same place which afterwards was known as Magdolo. It may have been the same fortress near which Pharaoh Necho conquered the Assyrian hosts which were invading Egypt. In the history of the overthrow of the Hyksos, who passed over the same road on their way from Syria as early as 2100 years B.C., there is mention made of one of the shepherd kings, Salatis,[1] who laid the foundation of the strong city of Abaris, in the Sethroitic Nomos, as a protection against those Syrian invaders who at a later period were welcomed as auxiliaries and allies, and gave assistance to Egypt at the time that all leprous people were expelled from the land. Among the latter were included the Israelites, who, however, in withdrawing from their temporary home, did not take the regular road leading into Canaan, but turned southward to Sinai. The importance of the great highway of which I am speaking, at the time of Cambyses, Alexander, and Amru, is known to every reader, and need not be dwelt upon.

[1] Lepsius, *Die Chronologie der Egyptäer*, Pt. i. pp. 339, 340.

CHAPTER I.

THE COAST ROUTE THROUGH THE LAND OF THE PHILISTINES, FROM EL-ARISH THROUGH GAZA TO JAFFA.

THE WADI SYSTEMS OF PHILISTIA, WITH THEIR TOWNS AND PEOPLE.

SOUTHERN PHILISTIA.

DISCURSION I.

FROM WADI EL ARISH, THE FRONTIER OF EGYPT, TO GAZA : THE CITY OF GAZA, AND ITS PORT MAJUMAS.

THE road from Egypt to Palestine has always been a travelled one, although the children of Israel did not take it, for fear of encountering enemies in that direction whom they, a shepherd people, would not be able to subdue (Ex. xiii. 17). Yet, notwithstanding the great amount of travel which has passed over this route since that day, very few distinct architectural traces are to be found between the Nile and Wadi el Arish, the site of the ancient important Nabathæan commercial city of Rhinocolura, whence to Gaza it is a two days' journey. This Wadi el Arish is spoken of in Josh. xiii. 3 under the name Sihor, as the brook " which is before Egypt," and which is elsewhere alluded to as the southern or south-western boundary of the Promised Land (see Num. xxxiv. 5). The name Sihor[1] signifies black water, a term which in its Greek form was applied to the Pelusian mouth of the Nile, and which was justified by the black mud which discoloured the waters. Hence many commentators on the Bible have fallen into the error of supposing that the Sihor, or " river of Egypt," was the Nile,—a position which is un-

[1] Keil, *Commentar zu Josua*, p. 240.

tenable, as the Promised Land never extended, even theoretically, so far westward.

The abundant supply of water in Wadi el Arish, which commences in the heart of the Tih plateau, and serves to drain a large tract of territory, always allowed the region which lies at its lower or northern extremity, and on the sea, to be inhabitable; for although there is not always a brook with running water,[1] yet there is such an abundance in the wet season that it sinks down into the ground, and by sinking shafts a few feet it is possible to procure sweet water every season of the year. It is from that fact that Wadi el Arish has always been a place of such importance to the travellers between Syria and Egypt.

This "river of Egypt" has served as the frontier between the two countries just mentioned from the earliest times to the present day; for it is a boundary drawn by nature, on the north of which is cultivation, on the south desert. Fogs are very often encountered here, which frequently condense into light rains. After leaving the wadi, and entering on the tract farther north, the arid sand of the southern side begins to be modified, and to assume by degrees the character of loam. The present town of el-Arish lies on a moderate eminence, about ten minutes' walk from the sea; and among its sand-dunes, wells, and palm trees, it exhibits a few relics of antiquity, in the form of fragments of Roman pillars. The place has some historical interest and importance as the scene of Baldwin's death, the second Christian king of Jerusalem, who expired of wounds and exhaustion in 1118, after pressing southward as far as to the city of Forama, near the Tanis and the Pelusian Nile. His entrails were buried at el-Arish; and even yet the place of interment is called by the Arabs Baldwin's stone, and the territory around Baldwin's Salt Desert.

Northward of this point, as has been already stated, the country wears a better look: the soil improves in quality, and bears good crops of millet, the most profitable article which can be raised for the market there. Here and there signs of water are seen: the camel is sometimes observed yoked to the plough, and the cactus is seen. The first signs of cultivation are accompanied by those of the jerboa, a creature which lives

[1] Irby and Mangles, *Travels,* p. 174 ; Bové, *Recit. d'un Voy.* in *Bullet. Geogr.* T. iii. p. 331.

only where there are roots in the earth. Seven hours north of el-Arish is the tomb of a sheikh, Abu Zueid, where good water may be found one and a half hours from the sea. Before reaching this place, however, Dr Barth[1] discovered the remains of an ancient city, said to bear the name of Rafia. This would indicate that here was the site of the ancient Raphia, of which Josephus says that it was the first Syrian city as one comes up from Egypt. Polybius speaks of the place as the one where king Antiochus iii. was conquered by Ptolemy iv. of Egypt,— an event which placed Syria for a time under the dominion of Egypt.

Gaza and its Port Majumas.

The row of sand-dunes which follows the sea-coast from el-Arish conducts one to the beautifully situated and ancient city of Gaza, lying in the midst of olive groves, which the people claim to be as old as the time of Alexander, and which extend as far from the town proper as the Shech Muntar, the ridge which commands Gaza on the east, and whose south-eastern eminence bears the name of Samson, one of his feats being said to have been performed there. The centre of the city rises in an imposing manner from the plain, and resembles an amphi-theatre in appearance :[2] from the eminence many views of sur-passing beauty can be obtained. Dr Barth spent the month of January 1847 in Gaza, and reports seventeen rainy days out of thirty-six. This has, of course, the most favourable effect upon the vegetation of Gaza, and gives the place the aspect of a paradise.[3]

The present eminence in the heart of the town must be regarded as the true centre, although only the southern part of it is at present covered with houses. The main portion of the city lies at the foot of this eminence, and reaches away towards the north and east. The houses on the hill are mostly made of stone ; those on the lower ground of sun-dried brick, and mud. These present a pitiful Egyptian aspect ; differing from the houses of Egypt in this, however, that in consequence of the great amount of rain, they are better roofed than is necessary

---

[1] Dr H. Barth, *Reise*, MS.
[2] Dr H. Barth, Manuscript account of his stay in Gaza.
[3] See Roberts' *Holy Land*, Book viii. No. 45.

on the Nile. The ancient Gaza, the Philistine stronghold, unquestionably lay upon the very picturesque hill which still forms the most prominent feature of the place.[1] All traces of the ancient high walls which made Gaza so strong at the time of Alexander have disappeared,[2] although Kinnear thought that he was able to identify them; and the city has no longer any gates even. At the time of the Crusades, however, it was so strongly fortified as to be capable of the most energetic defence against the assaults of Saladin. Yet even at the present day the people point out the position of some of the old gates at the foot of the hill,—among them the one on the south-east, which Samson bore on his shoulders to a hill near Hebron. Between the houses of the suburbs and the many outlying gardens Robinson saw here and there fragments of wrought marble and blocks of granite, the latter of which must have been strangers to the soil of Palestine, and were doubtless brought from Egypt. Kinnear discovered in one of the houses that the roof was supported by five Corinthian columns laid one upon another; and Roberts assures us that he saw capitals of the most admirable workmanship worked into the rude masonry of the most pitiful huts. The seven mosques of Gaza are mostly built, he says, of the fragments of ancient architecture. The chief one is an important building, and was once a Christian church; Turner assigns its construction to the Empress Helena. The tasteless Turkish architects have made many changes in this structure, as they have elsewhere, and not for the better.[3] The bazaars of Gaza are spacious and well filled; the streets are narrow and disagreeable; the residence of the governor is a spacious building surrounded by extensive gardens. In the seventeenth century this officer had control over all Palestine, and Gaza was the acknowledged capital of the land;[4] at the commencement of the nineteenth century, a Turkish aga had jurisdiction over the place, and his authority did not extend farther than to Khan

---

[1] J. Fr. Burscher, P. P. in Stephani Byzantii *de Gaza Narratio*, Diss. Lipsiæ, p. v. Comp. Godofr. Siberus, *de Gaza Palestinæ oppido;* and Reland, *Pal.* pp. 787–801.

[2] Kinnear, *Cairo, Petra, and Damascus in* 1839, p. 209.

[3] Ali Bey, *Trav.* ii. p. 207.

[4] D'Arvieux, *Reise*, Pt. ii. p. 19.

Yunes, three hours south of Gaza: he, too, was under the authority of Jaffa, which in its turn was subject to the Pasha of Acre. At the time of Robinson's visit, the power of the governor of Gaza extended over Hœoron, and as far into the Sinai Peninsula as Petra: so mutable have the conditions of power at this place always been. It follows that the population is a very mixed one, being composed of Turks, Arabs, Fellahs, Beduins from Egypt, Syria, and Petra, with the most varied costumes, languages, habits, and morals. The number of inhabitants must be as mutable as that of the nationalities: for Ali Bey, at the beginning of the present century, reports finding but 5000; while Robinson, and subsequently Barth, state that they found it to be between fifteen and sixteen thousand, —a population larger than that even of Jerusalem.

The prosperity of the city depends not so much upon the mere fact that it lies upon the sea-coast, and that it is surrounded by fruitful gardens, as upon the peculiarly advantageous position which it occupies in relation to the caravan routes which connect Palestine, Syria, Arabia Petræa, and Egypt. For although the Sinai pilgrims no longer go, as they did in the thirteenth century,[1] by way of Gaza, and although the great caravans which go from Egypt to Mecca pass directly across the Tih desert from Suez to Akaba, yet Gaza remains the chief depot of supplies for Petra, Maon, and the inland stations generally. The bazaars of this place are therefore better supplied with goods than those of Jerusalem, and the aggregate of sales is large, and the profits not inconsiderable. These flow, however, into the pockets of a few wealthy merchants, while the majority of the people, as in most eastern cities, are very poor. The chief articles manufactured at Gaza are some varieties of coarse silk goods and soaps, the latter of which are made of the ashes of certain shrubs collected by the Beduins. These have the same large sale now that they had at the time of Volney's visit.[2] The manufacture of silk was formerly so extensive here, that Father Morone tells us that in his day the pasha planted 40,000 mulberry trees for the manufacture of silk; but within the last

---

[1] Fratris Fabri, *Evagatorium, etc.*, ii. p. 378; L. de Suchem, *Libell.* c. lxvi.

[2] Volney, *Trav. in Syria*, Ger. ed. ii. pp. 233, 254; Morone da Maleo, p. 473.

few years we do not hear of this article being produced there. I have already alluded to the fact, that before the Arabs of the Peninsula were brought under their present check, Gaza was the place to which they brought the spoils which they had taken, many of which were of great value. All this has given Gaza more of a commercial character than Jerusalem has, although the place, notwithstanding its position on the sea, has scarcely more marine interests than the mountain capital. Regarding the beauty of the Gaza gardens there is only one opinion among travellers. Pierre ·Belon,[1] who was here in 1548, alludes to the excellent fruits of the place—the figs, olives, pomegranates, apples, and grapes ; and Robinson tells us that the productions of Gaza are not widely different from the Egyptian flora.[2]

The middle of the seventeenth century appears to have been a season of unexampled prosperity to Gaza, it having been then the capital of Palestine, and the residence of a pasha who was independent of the Ottoman Porte. He was lord, it is said, of a hundred and sixty cities, and was a mild and sagacious ruler, bringing the city in which he lived into a state of opulence which it has not enjoyed since under the blighting Turkish influence. From the Chevalier D'Arvieux,[3] who was there as the agent of France, and from Father Morone,[4] we have detailed pictures of the splendour of Gaza at that time, the luxuriousness of its palaces, the extent of its gardens, the elegance of its baths, its mosques, and its other public buildings. Many remains, too, of its ancient Roman magnificence were then existing ; and, indeed, not a few of the most splendid of the structures erected in the seventeenth century, owed their finest charms to the elegant marbles which were found in great abundance. So profusely scattered around were they, indeed, that a ·small present to the cadi was all that was needed to secure the possession of elegant marble columns and other architectural remains. Besides the chief mosque, which had formerly been the Church of St John, D'Arvieux speaks of six other places of Mohammedan worship, all adorned with marble

[1] Pierre Belon du Mons, *Observations*, liv. ii. c. 79, fol. 139.
[2] Bové, *Recit.* in *Bullet. Geogr.* iii. p. 333.
[3] D'Arvieux, *Report of his Journey*, ii. pp. 19-59.
[4] P. Morone da Maleo, *Terra Santa*, cap. xiv.-xvii. pp. 472-474.

columns. There were, in addition to these, an Armenian and a Greek church, the latter the largest of all. It was a very attractive object to pilgrims, and had, even from Fabri's time, been reputed to stand upon the place where Joseph and Mary rested, as they were fleeing with their little child into Egypt.[1]

Even as early as the time of Fabri,[2] Gaza was a place of much repute. He says (writing in 1483) that he noticed two things there of special interest: one was, that it was twice as large and densely peopled as Jerusalem, and so rich, that the expression *fossa butyri* applied to it had come to be a proverb. Never, he declares, had he seen a place at whose market the pilgrim could provide himself at so little expense with all that he might need when on a long journey. In the second place, it was a very peaceable town : no obstacles were put in the way of Christian pilgrims, and he was able to walk the streets, even unattended, without hearing a single word of scorn addressed to him, even although he wore upon his back an embroidered cross. The population of the place was very mixed even at that time, consisting of Arabs, Ethiopians, Egyptians, Syrians, Indians, and oriental Christians : there were no Latin Christians, however. As long ago as the Byzantine time, and before Mohammedanism had exercised its blighting influence upon Gaza, the place appears to have had the peaceful character of a great and opulent commercial metropolis; and as early as 600 A.D. Antoninus Martyr says[3] of it : Gaza civitas est splendidissima et deliciosa, et homines in ea honestissimi, facie libera, decori et amatores peregrinorum. Even in a far earlier day the city was in excellent repute ; and Polybius, referring to the reputation which it had in the time of Alexander the Great, speaks of the place as a very model for cities.

The history of Gaza deserves, therefore, a more careful attention from students than it has yet received. Its whole past has been one of change : reduced by Pharaoh Necho (Jer. xlvii. 1), besieged by Alexander the Great for five months, and at last taken by storm, taken by the Moslems under Amru, A.D. 634, it has played a part in many of the great wars of the

---

[1] Fratris Fabri, *Evagatorium*, ii. p. 403.   [2] *Ibid.* p. 379.

[3] *Itinerar. B. Antonini Martyr. ex Mus. Cl. Menardi*, fol. 25.

world. Unfortunately but little has come down to us regarding the history of Gaza, excepting incoherent fragments: these have been collected and exhibited in their most available form by Reland,[1] Robinson,[2] Rosenmüller,[3] and Quatremère,[4] to whom I will refer the reader who wishes to master the subject. It needs here only to be remarked, that Gaza, the Azzah of the Hebrews, *i.e.* the strong, was one of the oldest cities of the land, and that before the invasion of the Israelites it was in the possession of the Avites or Avims. This was prior to the time when the Philistines had possessed themselves of this territory, and driven out the ancient inhabitants (Deut. ii. 23). The name itself may have been given to the place by the earlier Avite inhabitants, as it appears to be of Semitic origin,[5] yet Gaza did not begin to be a powerful and well-known city till it came into the possession of the Philistines. At the time of the distribution of territory by lot to the twelve tribes, Gaza with its tributary towns and villages, as far as to the Wadi el Arish, the "river of Egypt," were made over to the tribe of Judah (Josh. xv. 47), and were taken possession of without delay (Judg. i. 18). After the rise of the five allied Philistine princes, however (Judg. iii. 3), the place fell into the possession of the inhabitants (Judg. xvi. 1; 1 Sam. vi. 17), and was a Philistine stronghold till it was taken by Pharaoh Necho. It is uncertain whether Herodotus refers to Gaza in his account of Pharaoh's expedition into Syria : he speaks of a certain Cadytis, and places it in power and wealth not below Sardes;[6] but whether he refers to Gath,[7] as Reland and Valckenaer suppose, or to Gaza, as Gesenius holds, is a difficult question to decide. In my own opinion, the latter is more probably meant, since this would coincide more fully with the allusion in Jer. xlvii. 1. It is impossible for it to be Jerusalem, as some have asserted, misled by a fanciful etymology; for none of the characteristics

[1] Reland, *Pal.* pp. 787–801.

[2] Robinson, *Bib. Research.* ii. pp. 34–43.

[3] Rosenmüller, *Bibl. Alterthk.* ii. Pt. i. pp. 384–390.

[4] Quatremère, in Macrizi, *Hist. des Sultans Mamelouks de l'Egypte*, T. i. App. pp. 228-239.

[5] Hitzig, *Die Philistäer*, p. 6 et sq.

[6] Hecataei Milesii *Fragm.* ed. Klausen, No. 261, p. 115.

[7] L. C. Valckenaer, *Specimina Academica; Schediasma de Herodotea urbe Cadyti*, p. 22.

attributed by Herodotus to Cadytis[1] are attributable to the Jewish capital. The fortunes of Gaza are, however, intimately connected with those of the Israelites, as is shown by the repeated allusions found in the books of Judges, Samuel, the Kings, and Chronicles. The repeated devastations which the people of this strong city carried into the Israelite territory found an avenger at last in Samson, and the place ultimately fell into the hands of David, and was included among the territories which he quietly conveyed over to the hands of his son Solomon (2 Sam. v. 19, viii. 1, xxi. 15; 1 Kings iv. 24).

With Cambyses' expedition against Egypt, Gaza fell into the hands of the Persians, from whom it was taken by Alexander, who carried the women and children away into slavery, and established a new colony in Gaza. The place was not destroyed, and did not pass into a state of desolation, as has been inferred from a gloss in Strabo; for in the subsequent wars of the Syrians, the Maccabees, and the other princes of Palestine, it appears as still a stronghold. It was destroyed, however, ninety-six years B.C., by Jannæus, but was rebuilt in greater splendour by the Roman general Gabinius at the command of Pompey. Augustus made over Gaza to Herod; and after the destruction of Jerusalem by Titus, and subsequently under Hadrian and his successors, it remained a Roman city, as may still be seen by the coins which were struck in honour of the emperors. At the time of Hadrian, Gaza appears to have been a great mart for the sale of slaves.

In the passage, Acts viii. 26, the word "desert" used to be connected with Gaza by the earlier commentators; and the notion was prevalent, that the expression was in fulfilment of the prophecy contained in Jer. xlvii. 5: "Baldness is come upon Gaza; Ashkelon is cut off with the remnant of their valley;" but the meaning is not that Gaza was desert, but that as one went southward over the road from Jerusalem to Gaza, it was desert or solitary. And even in this light it might be a source of difficulty, that the great road which connected these two places should be spoken of as solitary; but in subsequent pages I shall have occasion, in alluding to the supposed identification of Beth-zur, to point out another[2] and far less travelled

[1] Lord Lindsay, *Letters on Edom and the Holy Land*, vol. ii. p. 52.
[2] Comp. Winer, *Bibl. Realw.* i. p. 395.

road from Jerusalem to Gaza, which it is not improbable may have been the one taken by Philip and the eunuch.[1] Strabo states that Gaza had a harbour distant from the city seven stadia, or a half-hour's walk; and there is no question that Alexander shipped the war engines hither, which he had already employed at the capture of Tyre. Earlier writers have made no allusion, however, to any harbour at Gaza; and there is no question that all the important cities as far northward as Joppa lay some distance from the sea, and in the rear of the high sand-dunes. The whole coast is, in fact, defenceless against the violence of the sea winds; and it has always been perilous to approach that shore. This affected the whole character and habits of the inhabitants of that district, making them as little maritime as though they lived inland, and converting them into a farming and cattle-raising population. The difference between the coast cities of Philistia and those of Phœnicia, protected as are the latter by outrunning promontories, can be seen at a glance. And though it appears that the cities of the southern coast had some harbours at a very early period, to protect them from the unexpected attacks of the corsairs which infested those seas, yet the Phœnicians, jealous of the rise of a commercial spirit among the Philistines, appear to have so successfully intrigued as to possess themselves of them, and make them really Phœnician ports. No collision took place between these two nations, however : their common hostility to the Israelites served to bind them together. This mutual understanding between the Phœnicians and Philistines raised Dor, Joppa, and Ashkelon[2] into places of some slight importance as seaports, which they lost, however, directly after the decline of the great cities of Phœnicia. The ports of Gaza and Ashkelon bore the common name of Majuma,—a word which Movers and Petermann believe to be of Egyptian origin,[3] and to signify " the place on the sea." Gaza lies so far from the strand, however, that the sea cannot be seen even from the summit of the hills, and there is no travelled path leading down at the present time. Robinson gives the distance from the city to the shore as an hour. The older writers speak with no cer-

---

[1] Von Raumer, *Pal.* p. 164, Note ; Keil, *Comment. zu Josua,* p. 304.

[2] Movers, *Die Phönizier,* ii. p. 175.

[3] Quatremère, Hist. in Macrizi, T. i. App. 229 ; Movers, *Die Phön.* ii. p. 178.

tainty upon the matter. Yet it is certain, upon the authority of Sozomenos, that ancient Gaza had a harbour which bore the name above quoted,—a place which, though near, was separated in some things so widely from the main city, that when the latter was still adhering to an idolatrous worship, the former accepted the Christian faith. This took place under Constantine, who commemorated the event by changing the name of the port to Constantia.

DISCURSION II.

ROUTE FROM GAZA TO ASKULAN (ASKELON), AND ITS RUINS.

From Gaza it is a two days' or two and a half days' journey to Jaffa, on the direct route by way of Esdud and Yebna. Yet it is not a pleasant road, and the camel or mule drivers very unwillingly leave the well-trodden road which leads up to Jerusalem, for the sandy and hilly path which runs along the coast to Askulan and el-Mejel.[1]

Following this route, however, we pass through the following cities of the ancient Philistines : Ashkelon, Ashdod, Ekron ; and only Gath, the fifth city of the ancient allied princes, lies off from the road, and is reached by taking the road which leads up into the eastern hills. In visiting these cities, we traverse the entire territory occupied by the ancient Philistines, and taken possession of by them only a short time before the Israelites invaded Canaan.

The road from Gaza runs for an hour and a half northward, through agreeable gardens, and one of the largest olive plantations in all Palestine :[2] westward of the beaten thoroughfare there is a sandy plain, an hour in width, extending to the sea. This would need only water to make it fertile, as is shown by the greenness which it puts on in the rainy season. The direct road to Ramlah turns to the right, at the village of Daer Senin, while the one which runs to Eshdod continues northward, and that to Askulan, the ancient Ashkelon, bears to the north-west towards the sea.

[1] See M. Baptistin Poujoulat, *Voy. dans l'Asie Mineure, en Palestine et en Egypte*, T. ii. p. 477.

[2] Robinson, *Bib. Research.* ii. p. 35.

The ruins of Ashkelon have attracted the attention of travellers since the middle of the seventeenth century. D'Arvieux,[1] who passed along the sea-coast in 1660, on his return from Gaza, was filled with amazement at the thick walls and the shattered towers which had once given strength to Ashkelon. He says that the place was then desolate, destitute of any harbour, and about as large in extent as Gaza. In the heart of the ruins he discovered a well, surrounded by seven or eight upright columns, the remains, apparently, of an earlier building erected there. What is now the neighbouring village of Mejel (a name which reminds one of the biblical Migdol), was, at the time of his visit, a large and populous city. His contemporary, Father Morone,[2] adds to this account, that the walls of Ashkelon were strongly cemented together by means of an excellent mortar made of sea-sand and lime, but that they had suffered much from the ravages of soldiery, and more from the violence of earthquakes. Close by the sea he was able to count twenty-two elegant marble columns, partly covered by sand, partly submerged by the waves. All around he saw only ruins, and here and there among them the pitiful huts of the Arabs. These reports were repeated in slightly changed form by subsequent travellers;[3] yet many who wished to explore the ruins of Ashkelon were unable, owing to the jealousy of the Arabs, to discover their site; and even Irby and Mangles, as late as 1818, did not succeed in reaching the most interesting part of them. They owe their subsequent celebrity, in great part, to the efforts of the eccentric Lady Hester Stanhope,[4] the niece of Pitt, who caused extensive excavations to be made there, in the hope of reaching treasures which she believed to be buried at Ashkelon. A copy of an ancient document, said to have been discovered in a Frank convent of Syria, and sent to her in a mysterious manner, spoke with great definiteness of certain treasures concealed in the ruins of Ashkelon, and indicated the precise spot where it would be necessary to look for them. The universal belief of the people of the East, that Europeans visit their ruins for the purpose of discovering treasure, together with the obvious sin-

---

[1] D'Arvieux, *Reise*, Pt. ii. p. 59.
[2] Padre Morone da Maleo, p. 471.
[3] Joliffe, *Reise in Palästina*, pp. 270–279.
[4] *Trav. of Lady Hester Stanhope*, iii. pp. 87-94.

gularities of Lady Stanhope's mode of living, made the authorities very suspicious of her; and it was considered doubtful whether she was a person who was searching for treasures, or was a spy of England. She considered it her best course, therefore, to make a proposition which should be evidently disinterested; and therefore conveyed her wish to the Turkish Government, that she might be permitted to undertake the investigations at her sole expense, the entire sums discovered to be surrendered to the authorities, while she should have the honour of the undertaking. This arrangement was willingly assented to, and she commenced her labours. A force ranging from a hundred to a hundred and fifty men was employed; and such was the confidence felt in the enterprise, that the work was prosecuted with the greatest energy for several days. Not a single gold piece was discovered, however. Day after day the excavations were continued, and fragments of marble and granite pillars were constantly exhumed. The massive foundations of a building, which had evidently been one of great splendour, were reached. It was first supposed to have once been a mosque; then it appeared to have more probably been a church; and subsequent excavations still revealed the aspect of a Roman temple. On the fourth day a colossal marble statue of great elegance was discovered, seemingly perpetuating the memory of an emperor or a distinguished general : the habiliments in which it was arrayed had evidently been rich; the pedestal was of white marble; and beneath all was an accumulation of granite pillars, which presented the appearance of having been overthrown by a party of marauders on a plundering expedition. Lady Stanhope continued her excavations faithfully, and at length reached the underlying ground, beyond which it was hopeless to go. The results had been meagre, even in an antiquarian light. A copy of the statue was made by the physician of Lady Stanhope; but it was impossible to procure the original for the British Museum. It was supposed to contain the treasures which were sought; and the fanatical and foolish Turk who directed the search, caused it to be broken into a hundred pieces, to see what the contents of the interior were. The failure of the enterprise did not bring that discredit to Lady Stanhope which one might suppose : on the contrary, it was merely thought that some more fortunate explorer than she had already removed the treasures; and rumour pointed to the unscrupulous Pasha of Acre as the man. This at least is true, that he took advantage of the excavations which Lady Stanhope made, in sending schooner after schooner from Acre to Ashkelon, to transport the fine architectural fragments which were turned up to his own city, and used them freely in his own building enterprises. The statue which was discovered resembled in its style the best works of the Cæsarian epoch, and is thought to have been one of the works of art which Herod set up, in his slavish sycophancy to Augustus, to decorate one of the temples built by him. We know that Ashkelon was one of the cities which Herod extended and beautified, erecting temples, palaces, theatres, and bazaars. These tokens of his love of architectural display were left at Byblos, Berytus, Laodicea, Tripolis, Tyre, Ptolemais, Cæsarea, Anthedon, Antipatris, and elsewhere. At Ashkelon, Herod's father, Antipater, a man of Idumæan family,[1] lived for a considerable time, when a man without extensive influence or authority; and according to Eusebius, Herod was born there of an Arabian mother, and was dedicated by his father to service in the temple of Apollo at Ashkelon. In consequence of his early connection with this place, Herod always showed it special favour. As the statue spoken of above was found at a depth of eighteen feet from the surface, it is not improbable that it dates back to the Herodian days of the city; for before that time it had not been celebrated as a home of art, but as a stronghold. Yet the antiquity of its temples is unquestionable, for the earliest records allude to the heathenish worship celebrated there; and Herodotus tells us, that when the Scythians, after ravaging Syria and attacking Egypt, were compelled to fall back from the frontier of the latter country, they plundered the temple of Aphrodite at Ashkelon. This temple Herodotus thinks to have been the most ancient of all the temples of this goddess, even antedating those of Cyprus and Cythera.[2] Other authorities confirm the great antiquity of Ashkelon; and Justinus[3] makes it older than Tyre. Indeed, according to him,

---

[1] Euseb. *Hist. Eccles.* lib. i. c. 6, ed. Zimmermann, p. 32.

[2] C. Ritter, *Die Vorhalle Europäischer Völkergesch. vor Herodotus*, p. 423.

[3] Movers, *Die Phönizier*, ii. p. 315.

it was the founder of Tyre, it having sent a colony thither as early as 1209 B.C.

Ashkelon was formerly noted for the excellence of its onions, both Theophrastus and Pliny making mention of them. The quality of this vegetable appears to remain unimpaired down to the present day, and the physician of Lady Stanhope speaks of their being a favourite dish still among the labouring people of that region.[1]

The only traveller who has brought much additional information respecting the ruins of Ashkelon since the time of Lady Stanhope, is Mr Kinnear, who visited[2] the place in 1839. He found the excavation still open which had been made in search of lost treasure, and believed that further search might reveal many interesting architectural relics. He himself identified the traces of a former fosse, but it had been mostly filled up with sand. The walls of the city were composed in great measure of fragments of Roman architecture, among which were several granite columns. This observation is valuable, as showing that the powerful fortifications even now to be seen, were probably composed of the fragments of earlier Roman walls, dating back in their present condition to the time anterior to the Crusades, when the Egyptian sultans held this place as their strongest protection on the north. During the short period that the Christians held Ashkelon, these walls may have been strengthened, but not materially changed. The place was besieged for eight months by Baldwin III., it being regarded the strongest place in Palestine. The narrative is given by William of Tyre, from whose account it is clear that the present arrangement of the walls corresponds closely with that at the time of its possession by the Egyptian sultans. In the detailed account given by the Archbishop of Tyre, and confirmed by Abulfeda, it is stated that Ashkelon had no harbour, and was a very unsafe station for ships. The truth of the last assertion is made the more sure by the loss of the great fleet of the crusaders before Ashkelon in 1169. And yet the statement must be partially untrue; for at the time of the Council of Constantinople there must have been a port connected with the place, since mention is

---

[1] Lady Hester Stanhope, *Trav.* iii. p. 156; comp. Steph. Byz. ed. Berkel, fol. 180.

[2] J. Kinnear, *Cairo, Petra, and Damascus*, pp. 211–214.

made in the records of Stephanus Episcopus Majumas Ascalonis; the port Majuma, *i.e.* place by the sea, being distinguished from the main city. Ashkelon itself was wrung from the crusaders by treachery subsequently to the victory of Saladin at Hattin in 1187; but the fiery attacks of King Richard of England during the next four years[1] compelled Saladin to destroy his prize in 1191, in order to save it from again becoming a powerful auxiliary to his enemies. Then the glory and splendour of Ashkelon passed away. Richard did indeed attempt in the subsequent years to rebuild it, re-erecting the walls and no less than fifty-three towers; but it fell again into the power of Saladin, and was this time so thoroughly demolished, that even rocks were cast into the sea to close the harbour. Thus it seems, that although William of Tyre does not appear to have been aware that there was any approach to the city by sea, the existence of a harbour was recognised, and pains were taken to close it after the third crusade. Kinnear speaks of seeing the remains of a mole: this was probably the traces of the former harbour, and seemed to give sufficient token of capability to encourage Ibrahim Pasha in the plan of creating a new harbour at Ashkelon out of the ancient materials.

Kinnear alludes to a temple of great dimensions lying in the midst of the great field of ruins, the pillars erect, and consisting each of them of a single block of granite. The whole lower storey remains in a perfect state. The capitals and entablatures are all of white marble, the order is Corinthian, and according to Roberts,[2] the skill displayed is of the finest. Near by stands a colossal statue, also of white marble; but as it was secured to the solid masonry on which it stood, it could not be brought away. Friezes, entablatures, and fragments of marble statues, were to be seen scattered in all directions. The ruins of a small church, apparently erected in the fourth century, awakened Kinnear's greatest interest: the walls, the floors, and the pedestals of the pillars guided him to a knowledge of the plan of the church, perhaps the oldest in the Holy Land. Roberts, who accompanied Kinnear, has given an excellent view of these ruins. The church may not unlikely have been one dating from the time of the Byzantine supremacy; for

---

[1] Wilken, *Gesch. der Kreuzzüge*, iv. pp. 427, 468, 569.
[2] Roberts, *Views in the Holy Land*, Book viii. No. 46.

Sabinus, who called himself bishop of Ashkelon, is mentioned as a member of the Council of Nicæa as early as 381. The period of Christian ascendancy in Ashkelon was preceded by a long and severe struggle between the dominant heathenism and the new faith, as would doubtless be testified by the writings of the eminent men who then lived in that city, had they come down to the present time. Eli Smith, who visited the place in 1827, contrasts the savage wildness and desolation of the present Ashkelon with its state of former splendour. Among the names which made this place illustrious, are Antiochus, Antibius, Eubius, Ptolemæus the grammarian, Dorotheus, Apollonius and Artemidorus the historians, Julianus, Eutochius, and Zosimus.[1] The passionate fury with which the old idolatrous spirit of the place raged against the Christian religion, is best shown by the fact, that when Julian the apostate began to persecute the church, the bodies of Christian young women and of priests were opened, filled with barley, and then cast out before swine to be torn to pieces.[2] The church, whose ruins are still seen in Ashkelon, would seem therefore to have been built subsequently to the time of Julian. This structure may then have been converted into a mosque by the Mohammedans, and restored still later to its primitive purpose by Baldwin III.[3]

The fanatical spirit of the Ashkelonites, and their obstinate adherence to their heathenism in spite of the spread of Christianity, may have been strengthened by the antiquity of their allegiance to Dagon. This god appears to have been revered in the ancient days of Philistine supremacy, and to have been acknowledged by the five cities, Gaza, Ashkelon, Ekron, Gath, and Ashdod. In addition to the allegiance paid to Dagon, still greater deference was given to the warlike Ashtaroth, whose worship extended itself from Ashkelon over Phœnicia, Cyprus, as far as to Cythera and Greece.[4] The national deity Dagon,[5] the Sanconiathon of the Phœnicians, was the reputed inventor of the plough and of grain, and was held in the same place of honour among the Philistines in which Melkart was held among the Phœnicians; his temples in Gaza, Ashdod, and some of the

---

[1] *Chronicon Paschale*, i. p. 345.   [2] *Ibid.* i. p. 546.
[3] Wilken, *Gesch. der Kreuzz.* iii. 26.   [4] Movers, *Phönizier*, i. 635,
[5] *Sanconiathonis Berytii Fragmenta de Cosmogenia et Theologia Phœnicum*, ed. Orellius, p. 33.

border cities, were especially famous. The reader will remember that, when Samson the Danite was taken in Gaza by treachery, the five allied princes assembled with a vast concourse of their people in a temple of their god Dagon, to bring him a thank-offering. The building was probably[1] constructed like a Turkish kiosk, its front resting on only four pillars. The story of the strong man's feat is known to every reader.

After the Philistines had carried away the ark of the Israelites, and placed it in triumph in the temple of their god Dagon at Ashdod (1 Sam. v. and vi.), it brought misfortune, pestilence, and distress. The ark was in consequence removed to Gath and other cities, and after seven months was delivered back to the Israelites. In the temple of Dagon at Ashdod, the statue of the god was found prostrate and broken in the presence of the ark, only the stump remaining entire (1 Sam. v. 4). The temple of Dagon was subsequently destroyed by the Maccabees (1 Macc. x. 83, 84). From this description, it is probable that the Dagon of the Old Testament is identical[2] with the divinities which are mentioned by classic authors, and which appear on the Ashkelon coins half woman and half fish. To this goddess fishes were consecrated, and the eating of them was supposed to be followed by the breaking out of running sores. The name of Dagon (which signifies fish) recalls the rites paid to the Assyrian piscine goddess Odakon, mentioned by Berosus.[3] The worship of Dagon was not exclusively Philistian, as is shown by the recurrence of the word Beth-dagon in the tribes of Judah and Asher (Josh. xv. 41, xix. 27).

MIDDLE PHILISTIA.

DISCURSION III.

THE COAST ROAD FROM ASKULAN TO ESDUD (ASHDOD, AZOTUS). THE THREE WADI SYSTEMS OF PHILISTIA : WADI SIMSIN, WADI ASHDOD, AND NAHR RUBIN. WADI ASHDOD FROM TELL ES SAFIEH (BLANCHEGARDE) TO ESDUD.

Pursuing the direct road from Gaza, and passing several minor villages, we reach, after a few hours, the insignificant

---

[1] Winer, *Bib. Realw.* i. 244.   [2] Movers, *Phönizier*, i. 500–592.
[3] Berosus, in Euseb. *Chronic. Armen.* i. p. 12 ; Syncelli, *Chronogr.* ed. Dindorf, i. p. 71.

place bearing the name of Esdûd, a corruption of the ancient Hebrew name Ashdod. The Greek appellation Azotus, mentioned by Herodotus, and first appearing in the Jewish records in 1 Macc. iv. 15, has long since completely passed away. Kinnear heard the name of the place spoken precisely as the Jews pronounced it, and hence called it in his narrative Shdood. The way thither is lined with corn-fields,[1] tobacco plantations, gardens, olive groves ; and the soil is admirably adapted for agriculture. The hills on both sides are dotted with villages having a crowded population, and the people, particularly the women, are of fine build. It was so as early as the visit of Pietro Della Valle[2] in 1616, who, in his account of his journey from Gaza to Esdud says that it is a favoured country, like his own Italy.

If one takes the road leading northward from Ashkelon, after passing the village of Mejdel and the hamlet of Hammameh,[3] he bears away from the coast and towards the right, and in between three and four hours reaches Esdud. Two prominent wadis may be seen upon both Jacotin's and Robinson's maps, both running from east to west, connecting the mountain land of Judæa with the sea. Both are crossed by stone bridges, over which the great caravans must pass on their way northward to Ramleh. The more southern of these wadis, which comes down Tell es Safieh (the Blanchegarde of the crusaders, Alba Specula), at a point south-east of Esdud turns northward, and passes by the north side of this place. The name given to it by the natives not having been stated by travellers, I will venture, for convenience sake, to designate it as Wadi Ashdod, in order to discriminate it from the more northern stream or valley, whose general course may be termed parallel to it. This one has its beginning in Wadi Surar, passes at the foot of the eminence on which Akir lies, turns northward, and enters the sea under the name Nahr Rubin. The more southern of these two wadis receives its main historical importance from the fact that the Philistine city of Ashdod stood upon its left bank, while Nahr Rubin is interesting from its connection with the two cities of Ekron

[1] Ali Bey, *Trav.* ii. p. 208 ; Irby and Mangles, p. 214 ; Kinnear, p. 214.
[2] Petri Della Valle, *Trav.* Geneva ed. Pt. i. p. 136.
[3] Dr Barth, *Reise*, MS.

and Jabneh, between which it ran. The memory of these two cities is perpetuated in the modern names Akir and Yebnah, which are borne by their ruins.

The Wadi of Ashdod commences on the western slope of the mountains of Judah, and near Bethlehem. It begins on both sides of an isolated hill bearing the name Tell es Safieh.[1] Not far from it, towards the south-east, lies the village Ajjur,[2] where the very prominent Wadi Simsin, *i.e.* the Wadi of Askalon,[3] begins to take its south-western course. It was in this neighbourhood that Gath, the Philistine city most distant from the sea, Beit Jibrin, as well as A'dorain, seem to have lain, although neither ruins nor ancient names certainly, so far as Gath is concerned at least, appear to be in existence at present. The situation of Gath on this elevation, above the fruitful plain of ancient Philistia, and connected with it by two natural roads, gives a clue to the reason why this city was so formidable an enemy to the Israelites.

Tell es Safieh, a longish ridge, one of whose rocky sides, covered as it is with olive groves, gives it the appearance of a well-wooded hill, and at whose base the great plain begins to spread itself out, displays no extensive ruins upon its summit, although there are to be seen the foundation walls of a castle. A terrace may still be traced on the western slope of the hill, hinting at a skilful culture of the soil there at an early day: at the foot of the eminence, beneath a solitary palm tree, is a spring whose refreshing waters are flowing for the greater part of the year. From this only moderately elevated but isolated hill an extensive prospect is obtained, and the place is one well adapted to the erection of a military stronghold. Northward one can look across the plain to the tower of Ramleh, five hours away. Towards the north-east, in the direction of Jerusalem, can be discriminated the cone-shaped hill on which lies Amwas, the ancient Emmaus or Nicopolis,—not the Emmaus which was near Jerusalem, mentioned in Luke xxiv. 13, which is often confounded with this, but an Amwas which lies in the neighbourhood of Yalo[4] (Ajalon). Westward, Esdud (Ashdod) may be seen, the wadi bearing its name winding down thither through a

---

[1] Robinson, *Bib. Research.* ii. p. 29 et seq.   [2] *Ibid.* ii. pp. 21, 30.

[3] *Ibid.* ii. p. 24.

[4] *Ibid.* ii. pp. 255, 256 ; comp. in *Bib. Sacra,* 1843, p. 38.

fertile country, thickly dotted with villages, the names of many of which have been as yet entered upon no map. Two and a half hours south-south-east of this Tell, and still farther south than Ajjur, the conjectural Gath, lies Beit Jibrin (Bethogabara or Eleutheroplis), on a southern tributary of the upper Wadi Simsin.

The castle on this hill, which had fallen into complete oblivion since the time of Saladin and the crusaders, Robinson found to be unquestionably the once celebrated fortress of Alba Specula, Alba Custodia, which usually bore the name Blanche-garde[1] among the Franks. It was erected by King Fulco about the year 1138 at Tell es Safieh, to form together with that at Beit Jibrin a protection against the attacks of the Moham-medans at Ashkelon. It was built, as William of Tyre tells us, of enormous stones, and was strengthened with four towers. Notwithstanding the efforts made to keep it in the hands of the Christians, it fell subsequently into those of Saladin, and was razed by him in 1191. In the following year, however, it was re-erected by Richard of England; and some of his most romantic adventures occurred in the neighbourhood of this castle, and on the road between Ashkelon and Ramleh. In the Old Testament there is no allusion to this place, unless it be the Zephatha near Maresha, where king Asa attacked the Ethiopian army under the leadership of Zerah, and routed him with so signal a victory (2 Chron. xiv. 10).

In descending from Tell es Safieh to the plain extending westward from its base, the whole district is seen to be under cultivation,[2] and in the time of harvest a very animated scene is presented. There is a well at the foot of the hill eleven feet in diameter and a hundred and ten feet deep; down to the surface of the water it is nicely walled in; and in the neighbour-hood there are traces of an ancient castle. From this hill can be seen, three hours distant, the village of Esdud, also lying on the side of a gentle eminence, surrounded with olive planta-tions. This was the site of the ancient Ashdod, and to this place we will now direct our attention.

Robinson did not visit Esdud, but Irby and Mangles[3] were there in 1818. The place lies about fourteen hours north of

[1] Wilken, *Gesch. der Kreuzzüge*, Pt. ii. p. 615.
[2] Robinson, *Bib. Research*. ii. p. 33.
[3] Irby and Mangles, *Trav.* pp. 179–182.

Gaza. Before entering it they discovered an open square structure, which seemed to be of ancient origin, but whose later use appeared to have been as a khan. They entered it through an arched passage, passing by spacious piazzas on both sides: in the rear were chambers, and stairs which appeared to lead to an upper storey. One of the side apartments had served in former times as a Christian chapel, and in it an altar and a cross were still to be seen: over the door was an oriental inscription. Portions of other arches—several in partially buried fragments—were discovered still nearer the village of Esdud, in which also there were discovered bits of marble, and the relics of Corinthian capitals. The inhabitants of the place were astonished at the sight of the Europeans: they brought their sick to be cured, and begged for a little of their hair to burn—the ashes of Christians' hair having medicinal potency: they also placed bread and honey before their guests, and would receive nothing in return.

The position of Esdud on a commanding eminence, gave[1] to the ancient city that security which it possessed, and which it needed as the northern stronghold of the Philistines, and almost on the frontier of Dan. All the cities of the Philistines appear, indeed, to have been built on hills; and they stood in marked contrast with the πεδίον of Josephus, the Campestria Philistrum, so often ravaged and burned in the time of the Crusades, while the towns on the hills remained untouched. The fine waving land which surrounds Esdud affords rich pasturage, and is partly cultivated, but in too many places is overgrown with thistles—a sign of the fruitfulness of the soil. Dr Barth considers the eminence on which lies the modern village of Esdud, with its two hundred and fifty houses, to have been a hill once carefully fortified, and although losing in the course of time all the direct traces of the ancient circumvallations, to show enough scattered fragments yet to indicate the great strength of the place. Indeed, Ashdod was once so formidable as to resist the attacks of the Egyptian king Psammeticus for twenty-nine years—the longest recorded in history, and one which Herodotus does not fail to contrast with the more celebrated but not so protracted siege of Troy. And yet even then, the period

[1] Kinnear, p. 214; Dr Barth, *Reise*, MS. See view in Roberts' *Views in the Holy Land*, Book viii. No. 47.

of Ashdod's greatest power and splendour was past; for Psammeticus was a contemporary of Manasseh, Amon, and Josiah
(699 to 611 B.C.).

This city of Ashdod, whose Hebrew name signifies the
"strong," is one of the places which is mentioned (Josh. xv.
46, 47) as having been assigned to Judah in the division of the
Canaanite territory, but which was never conquered by the
Israelites. From a tradition respecting some refugees who
came thither from the Red, Sea and settled at Ashdod, Hitzig[1]
has drawn the inference that the Avim, who occupied the
southern part of Philistia before the Philistines themselves,
settled there, and subdued and subjugated the former possessors (Deut. ii. 23), were the founders of Ashdod. Among the
refugees from the Erythræan Sea, he comprehends as Avim
the people who were termed in the ancient legends οἱ φυγάδες,
a term which would also describe the Phœnicians. This, however, is not a tenable position, for the Avim only occupied the
territory extending from the "river of Egypt" to Gaza. From
this territory they were expelled by the Philistines; and the
only subsequent trace of them appears to be in Avim, the name
of a city within the Benjamite territory (Josh. xviii. 23), where
some of the exiled Avites may have taken up their abode.

During the centuries in which Israel was governed by
judges, and in which continuous wars were waged between the
Israelites and the Philistines, who had, as we read in Judg.
xiv. 4, "dominion over Israel," the inhabitants of this fruitful
coast and these strong cities pressed as far eastward as to
Mount Gilboa, where at last Saul became their victim. During
all these years Ashdod was constantly growing in strength.
After the Philistines had gained so signal a victory over the
Israelites as to carry the ark of the covenant away in triumph,
it was first placed for safe keeping in the temple of Dagon at
Ashdod, and only subsequently, when pestilence broke out
among the Philistines, was it carried to Ekron and Gath. At
the time of the subjection of five Philistine princes, when they
brought tribute to Jehovah and restored the ark to Israel,
Ashdod is again placed in a conspicuous place, as if at the head
of the allied cities (1 Sam. vi. 17). With David's victories òver
the Philistines, and the organization of his body-guard from

[1] Hitzig, *Die Philistäer*, pp. 3, 68.

the warlike Cherethites and Pelethites (1 Sam. xxvii. 7, ii. 3, v. 6, 7), by whose aid he was enabled to gain possession of Jerusalem, which had been up to that time in the possession of the Jebusites, began the decline of the Philistine princes. The goal was then really reached which had been held up in Judg. iii. 1–4, and the Israelites had always been kept a warlike people by the obstinate resistance made by the strong nations whom till David's time they were not able to subdue.

With the triumphs of David as just stated, many of the Philistine cities fell into the hands of the Israelites; yet down to the time of Uzziah Ashdod was still in the hands of its former possessors, as well as Gath and Jabneh. This powerful king conquered them all, however, and razed their walls. Yet, Ashdod was soon re-fortified; for we learn that during the reign of Hezekiah, the Assyrian king Sargon (Sennacherib), while prosecuting his campaign against Egypt, sent his general Tartan to capture Ashdod (Isa. xx. 1). And yet the city strengthened itself anew to such an extent as to hold out for twenty-nine years against Psammeticus. This was, it must be confessed, an honourable termination to the career of this powerful city, to which Jeremiah subsequently alludes (xxv. 20) as only a remnant. Still it is plain that the place was subsequently inhabited; for at the time of the Jews' return from Babylon, and while they were engaged in rebuilding the city, they were attacked by the people of Ashdod, and compelled to prosecute their labour with arms in their hands (Neh. iv. 7–18). This occurred at a time when the Jews had intermarried largely with the daughters of Ammon, Moab, and Ashdod, and when, in fact, half of the young children spoke the Ashdod language. This called out the bitter words of Nehemiah (xiii. 24). The Ashdod dialect must have been different from the Hebrew, it would appear; but can hardly have been not Semitic, although Hitzig[1] holds it to have been a Germanic-Indian language, akin in structure to the Sanscrit. It disappeared utterly, however, when the place was subdued by the Maccabees. Judas Maccabæus destroyed the altar at Ashdod, and burned its idols; the two brothers, Jonathan and Simon, of the same family, completed the annihilation of the place just before the entrance of Pompey into Syria.

[1] Hitzig, *Die Philistäer*, pp. 25, 53.

Although the place appeared again in history under the name Azotus, being rebuilt by Gabinius, Pompey's chief general in Syria, it was no longer a Philistine city, but a Greek and Roman colony, and, together with Jamnia and Phasaelus, was given to Salome as her share of her brother's inheritance.

The expression κατὰ θάλασσαν applied to Ashdod, as it was by Greek writers, does not seem to be applicable to a place which lies inland. But even Jerome says that Ashdod was contiguous to the sea. This led Reland to the suspicion that Ashdod, like Gaza, had a harbour with which it stood in intimate connection, and which sometimes bore the name of the main city itself; for in the *Græca Notitia Patriarchatum* mention is made of an *Azotus maritima* and an *Azotus Hippinus.* This is made all the more probable, from the fact that the neighbouring city of Jamnia had a *majumas*, or harbour; and it is probable that every one of the Mediterranean cities in which the Phœnicians carried on any trade was provided with its port. Still maritime operations formed no considerable part of the business of these southern cities: the people were never spoken of as commercial; on the contrary, their agricultural character was so marked as to become proverbial. Sieber,[1] the botanist, alludes markedly to the productive soil around Ashdod, which bears well even where it is blown over with a thin stratum of sea sand. The strong sea winds have, however, piled up large dunes along the coast, and borne such heavy clouds of sand into the interior, as to very much impoverish the soil at present. This tract of poor land extends to within a half-hour's walk of Esdud; and, in truth, the sand may be traced as far as to the western walls of the town.

In modern times we hear little of Azotus: only a few coins from the Roman times have been discovered, among which is one bearing the image of the sacred goddess of the Azotites. The gospel was preached there at an early day by Philip the deacon, after he had baptized the chamberlain of queen Candace; and from Azotus Philip advanced northward, scattering his message abroad as far as to Cæsarea. In the Byzantine epoch, the place appears to have been the seat of a bishopric; but the names of only four of the bishops are on record between the Council of Nicæa in 325, and that of Jerusalem in 536.

[1] F. W. Sieber, *Reise*, p. 20.

After that followed the irruption of the wild Arab races; and Azotus disappeared so signally, that no mention was made of it by Isthakri, Abulfeda, or Edrisi. The Greek name even was utterly lost; while, as in so many other cases, the more ancient word retained its hold, and in 1616 was discovered but slightly changed by the learned Italian Della Valle.[1] Volney alludes to finding scorpions at the village of Esdud. During the Crusades the place played no part of any importance: the deeds which made Ashkelon and Joppa eminent were not wrought there. The latter is mentioned but once, and this is on the occasion of the return of king Baldwin i. thither in 1101,[2] but not even there is it connected with any important event.

NORTHERN PHILISTIA.

DISCURSION IV.

THE WADI SYSTEM OF NORTHERN PHILISTIA, NAHR RUBIN AND WADI SURAR: THE CHIEF SCENE OF THE CONTESTS OF THE PHILISTINES AND ISRAELITES. WADI BEIT HANINA: EL JIB (GIBEON, THE ROYAL CITY)—NEBY SAMWIL (MIZPEH)—KURIYET EL ENAB (KIRJATH-JEARIM)—SABA (RAMATHAIM ZOPHIM). THE HIGH LAND, THE NATURAL RAMPART OF JUDÆA; THE HILL LAND OF BEIT NETTIF (NETOPHA). WADI SUMT—THE PLACE OF OAKS—THE MEETING-PLACE OF DAVID AND GOLIATH. WADI SURAR AND AIN SHEMS (BETH-SHEMESH). MERJ IBN OMEIR (THE VALLEY OF AJALON). THE NORTHERN PHILISTINE CITIES OF EKRON (NOW AKER), JABNEEL (NOW JABNEH), ON THE NAHR RUBIN.

1. *The Wadi System of Nahr Rubin and Wadi es Surar in Northern Philistia.*

Volney stated this river, Nahr Rubin, to be but about eight English miles long, which is altogether incorrect, as the wadi of which it forms a part is one of the largest in all Philistia. Under the name of Wadi Surar it extends to the very neighbourhood of Jerusalem and Hebron, dividing into many ramifications, to which no common name is given by the Arabs, and which are not a little difficult to study. The only clue to the

[1] Petri Della Valle, Pt. i. p. 136.
[2] Wilken, *Gesch. de Kreuzzüge*, Pt. ii. p. 112; in *Gesta Dei per Francos.* T. i. P. i.

connection is caught from the course of the brooks in the rainy season; but these running waters demonstrate infallibly the unity of the whole system, which I will sum up in the word Wadi es Surar. It is true, not all the waters which flow from these—the side valleys—find their way to the sea; for the soil is a porous one, and absorbs them readily; while irrigation, and the diffusion of water over the bottom of the broad and shallow wadis, make it readily plain why the amount which reaches the sea is not so large as a hasty observer might suppose.

Two or three hours north and north-west of the high ridge on which Jerusalem lies, between el-Bireh[1] (Beeroth), on the watershed separating the Jordan and the Mediterranean, and el-Jib (Gibeon), lies an open plain, which resolves itself at the south into a marked depression, taking the name Wadi Beit Hanina.[2] This great valley—a geographical feature often alluded to—cuts into the great Judæan range in such a way as to divide it into two sections, the southern one of which is called the Mountains of Judah, and the northern the Mountains of Ephraim. The depression which effects this division runs first in a southerly direction, and then sweeps round to the west, entering the western plain under the name of the Wadi Surar, six or eight hours distant from Jerusalem. It then follows the southern road from Ramleh to Joppa, and so becomes in its lower course the thoroughfare of a portion of the travel between Jerusalem and its port. Crossing it near the village of Kulonieh,[3] one comes at once to the high land where stand the important historical localities el-Jib, Neby Samwil, Saba, and a little farther west than these, Kuriyet el Enab, all of which played an important part in the ancient wars between Israel and Philistia. In the Old Testament writings these places correspond to Gibeon,[4] Mizpeh, Ramathaim, and Kirjath-jearim. In the Arabic el-Jib is still to be seen, indeed, the ancient Hebrew word which it has supplanted, as was shown by Pococke and confirmed by Robinson. This moderately large village lies upon the highest part of a ridge consisting of

---

[1] Robinson, *Bib. Research.* i. p. 453. See his map of the neighbourhood of Jerusalem.

[2] *Ibid.* i. p. 259, and ii. pp. 9, 10.

[3] *Ibid.* i. pp. 259, 461.

[4] *Ibid.* i. pp. 454–457.

horizontal layers of limestone, over whose northern slope runs a second road from Jerusalem to Jaffa. This ridge displays in the massive buildings of its present villages, on how grand a scale its former architecture was erected: a large structure is seen, whose foundations and adjoining towers indicate that it was once a castle. In its neighbourhood a profuse spring and cisterns have been discovered. The western slope of this ridge sends its waters towards the sea through Wadi Suleiman, while there is an outlet southward through Beit Hanina to the wadi system of es-Surar.

The village of el-Jib lies in a subordinate watershed, a little west of el-Bireh. The western slope is less rocky than the eastern, and is much better cultivated, and more fruitful. It is, in fact, one of the most productive portions of all Philistia, and there is no diminution in the fertility till the mouth of Nahr Rubin itself is reached.

2. *El-Jib, Gibeon, the Royal City.*

Upon the high land to which I have just alluded, lay, at the time of the Israelite invasion, the great royal city of Gibeon (Josh. x. 2), whose citizens, belonging to the Hivites, and having no king, were a warlike race, and had dominion not only over their own city, but the neighbouring ones of Beeroth and Kirjath-jearim. It is recounted of Gibeon (Josh. ix. 17), that its inhabitants were compelled to save themselves by subterfuge from extinction at the hands of the neighbouring Canaanite tribes, and that, although spared by Joshua's clemency, they were compelled to accept a place as bond-servants to the Israelites, and to be "hewers of wood and drawers of water." This step led to the formidable league of Adoni-zedek king of Jerusalem, Hoham king of Hebron, and other of the native princes; and it was after the Gibeonites had had recourse to their new allies to save themselves from this formidable alliance, that that great battle took place concerning which we are told that the day was prolonged, the sun seeming to tarry in his course at Gibeon, and the moon in the valley of Ajalon,[1] till the extermination of the foe might be complete. The routed kings took refuge in the cave of Makkedah, whose locality has not yet been ascertained with certainty, but which appears to

[1] Keil, *Comment. zu Josua*, x. 12–15, pp. 177–194.

have lain south-west of Aseka. The eminence on which Gibeon stood, which is called in the book of Kings (1 Kings iii. 4) "the great high place," has received a new consecration in connection with Solomon's prayer and dream, in which he expressed his desire, not for riches or long life, but for an "understanding heart," and judgment to discriminate between good and evil. At Gibeon,[1] which belonged to the territory of Benjamin (Josh. xviii. 25), and which was one of the cities of the Levites, the tabernacle was set up for a time during the reigns of David and Solomon, and remained there till the latter transferred it to Jerusalem (1 Kings viii. et sq.). In more recent times this place has been not at all a marked spot; yet Jeremiah alludes to the battle-field at Gibeon where the "great waters" were; and the whole neighbourhood has, in fact, always been well watered. In Josephus and the writers of the age of the Crusades the place is called Gabaon; yet the Arabic author Bahaeddin has preserved the ancient name in el-Jib, the appellation of the spot down to the present time.

3. *Neby Samwil, the ancient Mizpeh.*

Neby Samwil, only a half-hour's distance directly south from el-Jib, is characterized by its towering peak, which rises at least five hundred feet above every surrounding object, and even surpasses in altitude the Mount of Olives, three hours distant to the south-east. At its base lies a little village, and on its summit is a small dilapidated mosque, said by the people living below to cover the remains[2] of the prophet Samuel, whose sepulchre has given, they think, the name to the hill. The shrine is in its present state a pitiful object, but it appears to occupy the site of a Christian church whose walls were laid in the form of a Latin cross. Indeed, traces of more ancient architecture still may be seen: the rock is in some places smoothed off, and three cisterns may be traced excavated from the rock. The local legend claims that here was the Ramah of the mountains of Ephraim, the Ramathaim-zophim of Samuel, the place where the great prophet was born, lived, died, and was buried, and whither David came to take a part in the funeral of the great seer (see 1 Sam. i.-xix., xix. 18, xxv. 1, xxviii. 3). But that the Ramah of Samuel could not have been at Neby

---

[1] Keil, *i.a.l.* p. 175.   [2] Robinson, *Bib. Research.* i. pp. 451-461.

Samwil, is clear from the biblical narrative of Saul's career.[1] The place where Samuel was born, and to which I shall allude further on, appears to have been forgotten at an early day.

Still the tradition in its present state respecting the burial-place of Samuel is not a modern one; for even in the time of Procopius there existed a Convent of St Samuel, which remained down to the time of the Crusades, and was plundered by Saladin. This convent was probably connected with the Latin church referred to above, whose site is now occupied by the so-called tomb of the prophet and the mosque. The people of the neighbourhood call it Neby Samwil, but the monks differ in their appellations, some designating it as Shiloh, some as Ramah. Hence in the narratives of the earlier pilgrims there is the greatest confusion regarding the point. Robinson, struck with the commanding situation, at once recognised that it could have been no other than the hitherto unknown Mizpeh, the "watch-tower," whose situation is not described in detail in the Bible, excepting in 1 Kings xv. 22, where it is spoken of as in the neighbourhood of Ramah. King Asa, the successor of Jeroboam, appears to have fortified Mizpeh with materials which he conveyed thither from Ramah. In 1 Macc. iii. 46 the expression occurs, "Mizpath over against Jerusalem," which presupposes that from Mizpeh Jerusalem was to be seen, which is the case with Neby Samwil; it being not only easy to distinguish the capital two hours away, but to recognise the Frank mountain, those in Belkah beyond the Jordan, the whole western plain dotted with villages, and even Jaffa and the Mediterranean.

Mizpeh signifies in the Hebrew the "watch-tower," and the site well deserves the name; for only a few other places are to be compared with it for the wideness of the view; and of them all, Neby Samwil is by far the one most probably meant, for on it are still to be traced the remains of a not insignificant ancient city. Within this Benjamite stronghold the tribes often assembled; and after their twenty years' vassalage to their Philistine neighbours, they gathered themselves together to forswear their allegiance to Baalim and Ashtaroth, and to turn anew to Jehovah (1 Sam. vii. 5-7). The statement of Eusebius and Jerome, that Mizpeh lay near Kirjath-jearim, was

[1] Robinson, *Bib. Research.* i. pp. 458-460, 473.

confirmed by Robinson's discovery that the latter was but a short distance westward, with which Rödiger[1] and von Raumer coincide.

4. *Kuriyet el Enab, the ancient Kirjath-jearim.*

Kuriyet el Enab lies an hour's distance at the farthest from Neby Samwil, the ancient Mizpeh, and would well answer to what Eusebius and Jerome say about Kirjath-jearim, if other proofs should be cited to confirm their identity. This Robinson[2] has done in calling attention to the physical character of the place, which, as the city where the ark was received on its return from Beth-shemesh (1 Sam. vii. 1, 2), has much interest in its relation to Israelitish history.

The analogy of the name Kirjath with Kuriyet is not to be considered a sufficiently definitive ground for admitting the identity of the two places, since the word merely signifies city, and can serve no further as a guide in this matter than as it indicates that here an ancient city stood. The name Kirjath-jearim signifies the "city of forests," while Kuriyet el Enab means the "city of wine." In the book of Joshua the place is twice mentioned as a border city : once as belonging to the territory of the tribe of Judah, to which it was in fact assigned (Josh. xv. 9) ; and again as appertaining to the tribe of Benjamin, at whose southern corner Kirjath-jearim is said to have lain (Josh. xviii. 14, 15). It is plain, therefore, that it lay upon the ancient frontier of Judah and Benjamin ; but the place fell at last into perfect oblivion. Eusebius and Jerome, however, speak of it as nine or ten Roman miles from Jerusalem, on the way to Diospolis (Lydda). Subsequently no writer has alluded to it, and in Jerusalem Robinson sought in vain to find a trace of this city, and a name that might correspond with the ancient one. Kirjath or Kirjath-jearim is identical with the place mentioned by Joshua under the names of Kirjath-baal,[3] Baalah, and Baalah-jehudah. The modern Kuriyet el Enab corresponds with the statement in the *Onomasticon*, in so far that it lies on the direct road to Ramleh, about nine Roman miles from Jerusalem, west of Neby Samwil, and not far from el Jib (Gibeon). When

---

[1] Rödiger, *Rev.* in *Allgem. Litt. Z.* 1843, p. 566 ; v. Raumer, *Pal.* p. 193.

[2] Robinson, *Bib. Research.* i. pp. 475–478.

[3] Keil, *Comment. zu Josua*, pp. 165, 284, 306.

the people of Kirjath-jearim brought the ark from Beth-
shemesh (Ain Shems) in Wadi Surar, they found a convenient
road leading up this great valley, till they came to the side
wadi, at whose northern commencement lies the modern village
of Kuriyét el Enab[1] (1 Sam. vi. 21, vii. 1). Opposite the
mouth of this wadi, and close by the western extremity of Beit
Hanina, comes in Wadi Bittir from the south, having its
beginning in the neighbourhood of Bethlehem. These three
uniting form Wadi Ismail, which bears this name as far down
as Sanoah, mentioned in Josh. xv. 34, and a different place
from the one of the same name in the mountain land mentioned
in ver. 56, and still unknown. The wadi widens after passing
Sanoah, and takes the name of Wadi es Surar.

The position of this place, corresponding as closely as it
does with the Old Testament accounts, makes[2] the identity of
Kuriyet el Enab and the ancient Kirjath-jearim in the highest
degree probable,[3] even although their names afford no authentic
guide; and, at the same time, we are enabled to learn where
ran the former boundary between the territories of Judah and
Benjamin.[4]

5. *Sobah, the Ramathaim-Zophim in the land of Zuph, the*
   Ramah of the prophet Samuel.

There yet remains one place, Sobah, on the high land north
of Beit Hanina, before we follow Wadi es Surar downwards.
North-west of this great Beit Hanina, which runs south-westward between Jerusalem and Mizpeh to Wadi Ismail, there are
upon two prominent summits the villages Sobah and el-Kustul.[5]
These lie at the southern extremity of the ridge which connects on the north with the mountains of Ephraim. Neither of
these places presents anything essentially striking in its present
aspect; and Sobah derives all that makes it worthy to detain
us now, from the conjecture that it occupies the site of Ramah,
or more fully, Ramathaim (*i.e.* the double peak[6]) Zophim, the

[1] Robinson, *Bib. Research.* i. pp. 482–487 ; Keil, *Comment.* p. 296.
[2] Keil, *Comment.* p. 165.
[3] Olshausen, *Rev.* in *Wiener Jahrb.* 1842, vol. xcviii. p. 152.
[4] Robinson, *Bib. Research.* i. p. 333, ii. pp. 10, 11.
[5] *Ibid.* ii. pp. 6–10.
[6] Ewald, *Gesch. des Volks Israel,* ii. p. 433, Note 2 et sq.

home of Samuel. As such, it became a place of the greatest moment in the history of Israel, and has formed a prominent object of antiquarian research. Robinson[1] has brought forward strong reasons for identifying Ramah with Sobah, while others have stoutly denied his conclusions.

El-Kustul, situated on a cone-shaped hill, only an hour's distance south of Kuriyet el Enab, is evidently the corrupted form of Castellum, which has been located by other travellers at Kassr, on the southern Ramleh road from Jerusalem. Sobah lies upon another cone-shaped hill, near el-Kustul, and towers above Wadi Ismail, which passes on the south. Over against these two lies, towards the south-east, the Convent of St John. Sobah had been incorrectly considered the mountain of Modin, the home of the Maccabæus family; and the inhabitants of the place still boast of discovering bones in the soil, and these the fancies of pilgrims have converted into relics of the Maccabæan kings. If such remains truly exist there, they afford another proof that here once existed a large city, such as the Ramah of Samuel probably was. The Modin of the Maccabæus family unquestionably lay farther west.

Since Neby Samwil is probably Mizpeh, but cannot be the city of the great prophet, antiquarians have been compelled to seek anew for the lost Ramathaim Zuph. The grounds which Robinson has cited to identify the home of Samuel with the modern Sobah, are of a double character : the agreement of the name Sobah with Zuph, and the direction of Saul's journey to Samuel. Saul the son of Kish, a Benjamite, who lived at Gibea, the modern Tuleil el Fulil, a good hour's distance north of Jerusalem,[2] was sent by his father to search for the lost asses (1 Sam. ix. 1–16, x. 2–7). He wandered first through the mountains of Ephraim, and did not discover them; he then passed evidently from north to south, through the Benjamite territory, and reached the land of Zuph and the city of Samuel. Here the prophet met them; and after anointing Saul as king, he directed him to return by way of Rachel's grave, the Benjamite frontier town of Zelzah, the oak of Tabor, and the mountain of God.

---

[1] Robinson, *Bib. Research.* i. p. 215.

[2] Robinson, *Notes on Bib. Geog.*, *Gibeah of Saul*, in *Bib. Sacra*, 1844, pp. 600–602.

The city in which Samuel lived is not mentioned by the name of Ramah in this narrative; but the land of Zuph, whose position is not elsewhere more minutely indicated, must, in order to connect itself with the western course of Saul, have lain south of the mountains of Ephraim. It is there that we find Sobah, on the most southern spur of this mountain district, and separated from the hills of Judah by the deep valley of Beit Hanina. As this region still belonged to the territory of Benjamin, and as no mountains of Benjamin are spoken of specifically in the Old Testament, it is to be inferred that the whole ridge bore the name of the mountains of Ephraim, as far as the territory of Benjamin extended. From the circuitous southward journey which Saul took, the position of Ramah at Sobah[1] has appeared to some inadmissible, on the ground that it would have been folly for Saul to go to a point south of Jerusalem, and then virtually to retrace his own steps. Those who bring this objection have forgotten that this circuitous journey was specifically dictated to Saul by Samuel, for reasons which were not announced to the young king.

Could it be proved that the name Sobah is identical with the ancient Hebrew Zuph, there would be no good ground to doubt the reasonableness of Robinson's conjecture. And so far as the etymology of these names is concerned, no radical objection can be raised; for there is a frequent interchange of the hard and soft consonants. Certainly Robinson's hypothesis is more tenable than others which have been suggested. Gesenius' conjecture, for example, that Ramah was at the Frank mountain, had very little but the etymology of the word Ramah, *i.e.* height, to recommend it.[2]   So, too, the identification of the place with the modern Ramleh, as well as with the still unknown Arimathea,[3] has been successfully disposed of by Robinson himself, as has also the view of Gross,[1] that er-Ram (Ramah), north of Jerusalem, and half-way to Bethel, was the Ramah of Samuel.   The frequent occurrence in Palestine of the same names, renders the solution of such a

---

[1] Olshausen, *Rev.* quoted, p. 151 ; v. Raumer, *Pal.* p. 197, Note 238, *a.*

[2] Rödiger, *Rev.* in *Allg. Lit. Z.* 1842, No. 72, p. 572, and No. 111, p. 178.

[3] *Bib. Sacra*, 1843, Note, p. 565.   [4] *Ibid.* p. 604.

question as this very difficult, and allows a large margin for conjecture. Robinson has discovered a Ramet el Khulil near Hebron. It bears the name of the house of Abraham.[1] Whiting, on examining closely its colossal foundations, heard the Arabs apply the word er-Ram, or Ramah, to the place; and on this slender foundation he based his conjecture that it was the Ramah of Samuel. And in this connection it must be remembered that Samuel's father was from Ephrata, *i.e.* Bethlehem. Still I fall back upon Robinson's results, as on the whole the most probable, and conclude that the family of Samuel had left their old home near Bethlehem before his birth, and had removed to the city whose site is now indicated by Sobah.[2]

6. *The high barricade formed by the mountains of Judah; Wadis Musurr and Surar, and the hill land traversed by them; the battle-field of Goliath and the Philistines.*

All deserted by the spirit of antiquity extends the district lying south of the cradle land of Wadi Rubin, and west of the mountain-land of Judæa, on which are Bethlehem and Jerusalem. This high tract reaches southward as far as Hebron like a mighty barricade,[3] rising about 2800 feet above the level of the sea. West of this comes the hilly country, which is intersected by the various valleys which unite in the deep Wadi es Surar. These valleys all issue from the high mountain land, and take the most varied names, many of them not known to fame. They extend southward as far as to Wadi Musurr, which runs in a south-westward direction towards Ashkelon, and which is crossed diagonally by the ancient Sultana,[4] or great royal highway, from Jerusalem to Gaza. They extend northward as far as to Wadi es Sumt, which runs northwestward from Beit Nussib in the neighbourhood of Hebron, and which passes Shuweikeh and Yurmuk, east of Ajjur (perhaps the site of Gath), and which, after traversing Tibneh (the ancient Timnath), enters Wadi es Surar, in which lies Ain Shems, the Beth-shemesh of Hebrew history.

The hilly district crossed by these numerous wadis, and

---

[1] Wolcott, *Excursion to Hebron, etc.,* in *Bib. Sacra,* 1843, p. 44.
[2] Robinson, in *Bib. Sacra, l.c.* pp. 46-55.
[3] Robinson, *Bib. Research.* ii. pp. 4, 5.   [4] *Ibid.* ii. pp. 13, 15.

lying west of the steep barricade of Judæan mountains, rises in its highest eminences to an altitude of only nine hundred or a thousand feet, and belongs to the best watered and most fertile parts of Palestine. It is full of modern towns and villages, among whose names it is not difficult to detect the appellations applied in the Old Testament times. This was the territory which was so long and so valiantly contended for by the Philistines, whose great object was first to possess this hill country, and then to press up the wadis, and master the mountain land of Judæa. To meet these formidable foes the chief strength of Judah was concentrated around Hebron, and always kept in readiness to meet the valiant warriors of the fruitful plain along the seaboard.

Upon a broken and very marked hill lying in Wadi el Musurr, and connected with the ridge on the south-east side, is the bold site of the modern village of Jebah,[1] which Robinson considers[2] to occupy the position once held by the Gibeah of the Judæan mountain district, although Keil thinks it more likely to have been the Gabatha of Eusebius and Jerome, which was twelve Roman miles from Eleutheropolis. Gibeah is spoken[3] of by Joshua (xv. 7) as one of ten cities comprised in his lists. Still it is difficult to gain any satisfactory clue to its situation, since the name, like Ramah, was so frequently given, that the identification of any special one is not easily effected.

West of Jebah, and upon one of the high ridges between two wadis, lies the modern village of Beit Nettif,[4] from which a fine view is afforded over the whole country as far as to the sea. The plain is traversed by only one large wadi, Surar : all the other valleys are subordinate to this, and are all tillable, and covered with corn-fields. The rolling hills are studded with olive groves, and the summits are crowned with villages and the remains of ancient towns. One misses here the steep declivities which characterize the mountain land farther east, and only here and there are solitary peaks and spurs seen which descend abruptly to the fertile plain.[5] From a single

---

[1] Robinson, *Bib. Research.* ii. pp. 5, 6, 13.
[2] Keil, *Comment. zu Josua*, p. 303.
[3] Robinson, *Bib. Research.* i. p. 465. [4] *Ibid.* ii. pp. 15, 19.
[5] *Ibid.* ii. p. 223.

spot Robinson counted twenty-five villages, more than a half of which bear the same names, with only slight changes, which they had in the Old Testament times. Beyond the plain, and in the extreme west, he could see the blue waves of the Mediterranean. North of and beyond Sanoa (the Sanoah of Josh. xv. 56) was to be descried, on the farther side of Wadi Surar, the village of Surah (Zorah, the birthplace of Samson, Judg. xiii. 1); while west of this, and at the confluence of Wadi Surar and Wadi Sumt, he could see Tibneh, the ancient Timnath, whence Samson brought his wife, and the place to which he was going down when he met and tore in pieces the young lion (Judg. xiv. 5). Still nearer, in Wadi Surar, Ain Shems was to be discerned, the Beth-shemesh to which the ark was brought back from the country of the Philistines. From the point where Robinson stood was to be seen, in a word, the whole arena where the deeds of Samson's prowess were done, and the chief battle-fields of the Israelites and the Philistines. Still nearer, and westward, at the mouth of Wadi Sumt (the Valley of Acacias), Robinson could descry Jurmuk (the Jarmuth of Josh. xv. 25, and the Jermus of Eusebius), and farther up the same wadi, Shuweikeh (the Socoh of the Israelitish history). Beyond this, and still westward, were the heights of Ajjur, the conjectural Gath, and Tell es Safieh, the Blanchegarde of the crusaders. Southward the eye reaches as far as to Beit Nusib (Nezib of Josh. xv. 43),[1] lying near the commencement of Wadi Sumt, and only seven Roman miles from Eleutheropolis.

7. *The Village of Beit Nettif, Netopha, Wadi Sumt, and the Valley of Beth-shemesh.*

The name of Beit Nettif, whence this comprehensive view is gained, is probably the same which we have in the ancient Netopha, a place mentioned in Ezra ii. 22, and in Neh. vii. 26. It is now only a small village, lying on the western border of the district of Arkub, which forms the south-western part of the province of Jerusalem. The inhabitants belong to the party of the Keisiyeh, which stands in a strife of long standing with the Yemanijeh.[2] Towards the American strangers

---

[1] Keil, *Comment. zu Josua*, p. 298.
[2] Robinson, *Bib. Research.* ii. pp. 18, 19.

who visited them they showed great kindness, and Robinson alludes particularly to their great hospitality, and to their unwillingness to receive any pecuniary return for it.

The names met in the neighbourhood of this village of Beit Nettif were the same which are mentioned in the Scriptures as having been borne by places in the immediate neighbourhood of the celebrated Eleutheropolis, whose situation remained unknown till it was discovered by Robinson and Smith at the modern village of Beit Jibrin (Bethogabra). As this lies outside of the wadi system of Nahr Rubin, and upon the road from Gaza to Hebron, I shall have occasion to speak of it at another place. For the present, it must content the reader to follow the course of Wadi Sumt, the southern tributary of Wadi Surar. The way will pass by one or two places of much historical interest. From Beit Nettif the road leads south-westward for twenty minutes over an olive-covered slope to Wadi Sumt, which is here crossed by the Sultana, the great royal road which runs from Wadi Musurr past Beit Jibrin to Gaza. Very near it, on the north-west side, in a hollow, lie the ruins of Shuweikeh, the Socoh of the Old Testament (Josh. xv. 48). Wadi Sumt is here a fine fertile plain, with hills of moderate height on both sides. Shuweikeh is the diminutive of Shaukeh,[1] a word which is not very unlike the ancient Socoh. The many mimosa or acacia trees (the sumt or sunt of the Arabs and Egyptians) give this wadi its modern name. Colossal butm or terebinth trees[2] stand there even to the present day; and it was from these that the valley took the name of Elah in the time of the Philistines, El and Elah signifying terebinth in Hebrew (1 Sam. xvii. 2, 19). The monks' legend has retained the name "Valley of Terebinths" down to the present time, but has transferred the spot from its primitive and rightful position to the immediate neighbourhood of Jerusalem. Here,[3] where was located the first group of the cities which were assigned to Judah, as recounted in the catalogue of Joshua (Josh. xv. 33–36), and where Sanoah, Jarmuth, Socoh, and Asekah lay, are still to be found the names of the places[4] which

---

[1] Keil, *Comment. zu Josua*, p. 301.
[2] Rosenmüller, *Bibl. Alterthk.* Pt. iv. p. 229.
[3] Keil, *Comment. zu Josua*, pp. 294–300.
[4] Robinson, *Bib. Research.* ii. pp. 20, 21.

once gave this plain such historic interest, in connection not
only with the battles of the Philistines and the Israelites, but
more particularly the contest between the fiery David and
Goliath of Gath, hard by. In 1 Sam. xvii. 1–4 we read:
"Now the Philistines gathered together their armies for battle,
and were gathered together at Shochoh, which belongeth to
Judah, and pitched between Shochoh and Azekah, in Ephes-
dammim.[1] And the men of Israel were gathered together, and
pitched by the valley of Elah (Wadi Sumt), and set the battle
in array against the Philistines. And the Philistines stood on
a mountain on the one side (*i.e.* to the west), and Israel stood
on a mountain on the other side: and there was a valley between
them. And there went out a champion out of the camp of the
Philistines, named Goliath, of Gath," etc. This Wadi Sumt
unites itself a little to the north-west, after passing the ruins
of Shuweikeh and Tibneh, the ancient Timnath, with the great
valley of Wadi Surar which comes down from the east. Lying
in this valley, and east of the confluence of the two, lay Beth-
shemesh, *i.e.* the City of the Sun, the place rendered famous in
Jewish history for its reception of the ark from the Philistines.
Not only its distance from the ancient Eleutheropolis, but also
the name still given to the well[2] in the valley, Ain Shems, the
Fountain of the Sun, confirmed Robinson's conjecture that here
lay the ancient Beth-shemesh. The village of Ain Shems, with
its wely or sanctuary, is built of ancient materials; and the
remains of a city of antiquity are to be seen in many foundation
walls, which consist in part of hewn stone, and cover a considerable tract of ground. They lie a little west of the present village,
on the summit of a low hill, situated between a small wadi at
the south and the larger Wadi es Surar at the north. Much
of the material formerly belonging to this place has been used
for the building of modern villages in the neighbourhood: the
well, which has preserved the name of the place, was without
water at the time of Robinson's visit. Beth-shemesh is spoken
of in Josh. xv. 10 as lying on the border of Judah; it was one

---

[1] The Dammim mentioned in this passage has since been identified by
Van der Velde in the ruins of Khirbet Damûn, on the high northern brow
of Wadi Masur.—ED.

[2] Robinson, *Bib. Research.* ii. pp. 11, 12, 223–226. Comp. Olshausen,
Rev. cited, p. 152.

of the places given to the Levites (Josh. xxi. 16). From a comparison of the boundaries specified in Josh. xv. 11 with those of Josh. xix. 41–43, where Ir-shemesh is mentioned, von Raumer[1] has conjectured with the greatest probability that Beth-shemesh and Ir-shemesh were identical. The western border of Judah ran from Beth-shemesh past Timnath and Ekron (now Akir) to Jabneel (now Jebnah) and the sea (Josh. xv. 11); following, therefore, the general course of Wadi Surar to the coast. At a later period, however, the boundary was drawn farther east; and the shore district extending from this wadi northward to Japho (Joppa) was assigned to Dan (Josh. xix. 41), while the boundary between Judah and Benjamin ran in the direction of Mizpeh.

At a later period, Beth-shemesh was one of the places appointed to provide Solomon's household with provisions, each for a month (1 Kings iv. 9); subsequently it fell a prey of factions; and at last disappeared entirely, until the learned American travellers discovered its site. We do not doubt that this place is the Bir Sama of the *Notit. Dignitat.*[2] *Orientis,* and the Bezamma of the *Notit. Eccles.,* where, at the time of the Emperor Justinian, a garrison of Illyrian cavalry was stationed. The place derives its highest interest, however, as the locality where the graphic scene pictured in 1 Sam. vi. occurred, and which presents to us the striking figure of Samuel receiving back the ark of the covenant, after its long detention by the Philistines. In the next chapter, we are told that the inhabitants of the neighbouring Kirjath-jearim, the modern Kuriyet el Enab, came down to bring the ark up to their city, where it remained twenty years.

8. *Akir (Ekron) and Jebnah, or Jabneh (Jamnia), on the Nahr Rubin.*

Ekron is the last great Philistine city, and was easily reached by Robinson in a half-day's journey from Ain Shems. Lying as it does in the lower course of Wadi Surar, and therefore in the direct path up into the mountain country of Judæa, its strategic value must always have been great. Nevertheless Akir or Ekron had passed into entire oblivion when its site

[1] Von Raumer, *Pal.* p. 163, Note 160.
[2] *Notit. Dign.* ed Böcking, i. pp. 78, 345.

was discovered by Robinson.[1] The place lies only an hour's distance north-west from Wadi Surar, and is situated on a hill of moderate height. As Robinson passed back from Ramleh to Jerusalem, he traversed the broad plain bearing the name Merj Ibn Omeir, on whose southern border lies Yalo, whose situation corresponds to that of Ajalon, where Joshua called the sun and moon to his aid in his contest with the five Philistine kings. The account given in Jerome, Robinson found to confirm his own discovery of the site of the valley of Ajalon. Whatever was lacking to make Robinson's hypothesis certain, was supplied by the results of Wilson's[2] researches in 1843. Akir is now a large village, from which a row of sand-hills shuts off the view of Jebnah on the west, and of Ramleh one and a half hours northward.

Akir, the Akkaron of the Greeks as well as of Fabri,[3] has preserved the name Ekron down to the present time in very much the same form which it had when it, with its adjacent cities, was allotted to Judah. Subsequently, as we learn from Judg. i. 18 and Josh. xix. 43, Ekron, together with Gaza, Ashkelon, and Ajalon, were conveyed to the tribe of Dan. We are told, however, that in spite of this formal conveyance, the Israelites did not come into possession of the low country during the life of Joshua and under the judges ; for the people there used iron chariots in battle,—an engine of war with which the Jews were unable to contend. Nor were the Danites able to take Ekron, so strongly entrenched were the Philistines within it. While the other four great cities of Philistia lay more in the interior of that district, Ekron formed the outpost on the northern frontier (Josh. xv. 11). This place, with its dependent villages, is mentioned in the fourth group of cities in the lowland (Josh. xv. 45–47).[4] Here was a celebrated oracle of Baal Zebub, the defender against uncleanness, to which Ahaziah the king of Israel sent messengers from Samaria to learn whether he could recover from his disease. This caused Elijah to threaten him with death, because, instead of consulting a heathen god, he had not turned to the God of Israel (2 Kings

---

[1] Robinson, *Bib. Research.* ii. pp. 226–229.
[2] Wilson, *Lands of the Bible,* ii. p. 260.
[3] Fel. Fabri, *Evagatorium,* ed. Hassler, ii. p. 356.
[4] Keil, *Comment. zu Josua,* p. 299.

i. 16). Under the Maccabees, the city of Akkaron, together with all the Philistine strongholds, came under the Jewish sway. At the time of Jerome the place was a large village, inhabited by Jews: also in the time of the Crusades, during the many contests with the Saracens along the Mediterranean coast, Akkaron is often mentioned; but since then it has been mentioned by no traveller, there being no ruins there which date from antiquity. Still the Sheikh of Akir believed that the place occupied the site of Ekron, and told Robinson that cisterns have been found there, and some stones which were used in hand-mills. The whole plain before the place is very fertile, and yields abundant crops—millet, wheat, and barley.

Jebna or Yebna, the Jabneh of Reland, the Jabneel of Josh. xv. 11, and the Jamnia of the Greeks and Romans, is the most northern place in the territory of Philistia. Together with Ekron, it was allotted to Judah, and was subject to the same fate that Ekron underwent.

Despite the various methods of writing the name of this place, which, in the account of the destruction of its walls by Uzziah, is written Jabneh, and in Jerome Jamneel, all these various readings probably refer to the same place, regarding which the Old Testament has given us no full account.[1] In Philo's time the place was a populous city, mostly inhabited by Jews; and although these were often subjected to bitter persecution, they formed here a celebrated Jewish school and a sanhedrim. Josephus, Strabo, and Pliny mention the place: the last named places it between Azotus and Joppa, and says that there was a double Jamnia, one portion of which lay in the interior, while the town proper lay away back from the sea, as we have seen was the case at Ashkelon and Gaza. The harbour with all its ships was destroyed by Judas Maccabæus, and the conflagration is said to have been discernible as far away as Jerusalem.

During the middle ages there is very little mention made of Jabneh, whose name may still be seen in the appellation of the modern village which marks the spot. The crusaders[2] built there the castle of Ibelin, whose site Felix Fabri in 1443, and

---

[1] Keil, *Comment. zu Josua*, p. 285.

[2] Wilken, *Gesch. der Kreuzzüge*, ii. p. 615; Robinson, *Bib. Research.* ii. p. 66, Note; Fel. Fabri, *Evagatorium*, ii. p. 356.

other pilgrims, have held to be that of the Philistian city of Gath. Recent travellers have very seldom visited the place. Volney[1] mentions seeing a hill there, but this does not appear to be confirmed. Irby and Mangles[2] noticed a ruin which appeared to them to be the relics of a Roman aqueduct. They did not visit the village of Jabne. On the same day they passed by a Roman bridge which crosses the Nahr Rubin, then dry. On the east bank of this watercourse they discovered one of those burial-places which are so common throughout all Syria, where the remains of a canonized sheikh were said to lie. It was whitewashed, and could not fail to remind the travellers of those "whited sepulchres" spoken of in Matt. xxiii. 27. Two hours distant from this wely lies the town of Jaffa, with its beautiful vineyard and gardens. Between Jabne and Jaffa Dr Barth discovered a village bearing the name Jesor (Yazur of Robinson), which he conjectures to mark the site of the ancient Azor. According to Jerome, this place lay near the coast, and eastward of Ascalon, a position which harmonizes with Barth's conjecture.

[1] Volney, *Reise*, i. p. 251.
[2] Irby and Mangles, *Trav.* p. 182.

CHAPTER II.

THE ROUTE RUNNING DIAGONALLY FROM GAZA TO HEBRON:

FROM THE PLAIN OF SOUTHERN PHILISTIA TO THE MOUNTAIN LAND OF SOUTHERN JUDÆA, AND PASSING ELEUTHEROPOLIS (BEIT JIBRIN), JEDNA (IDNA), AND ADORAIM (DURA).

THE road running north-eastward from Gaza to Hebron presents different features from the coast route, which has been followed northward, from Gaza to Joppa, in the preceding chapter, and makes us acquainted with the mountain-land of Judæa. The general features are much the same, whether we take the route from Gaza to Hebron or that to Bethlehem. Both conduct us up from the plain to the top of that natural rampart which formed the natural, and at the same time the best, defence of the Israelites.

DISCURSION I.

THE ROAD FROM GAZA BY WAY OF HUJ, BUREIR, UM-LAKIS, AJLAN (EGLON), TELL EL HASY, AND SUKKARIYEH TO BEIT JIBRIN, THE ANCIENT BETHA-GABRA OR ELEUTHEROPOLIS.

A journey of two and a half hours north-east from Gaza brings one to the deserted village of Huj, with its two or three hundreds of inhabitants. The whole region, once, doubtless, well-peopled and prosperous, is now desolate and sterile—the result of the feuds of two Arab tribes. Farther on is the village of Bureir,[1] with a better soil and more prosperity, notwithstanding the heavy exactions made from it by the government. The road passes on, skirting Tell el Hasy, to Sukkariyeh,

---

[1] Robinson, *Bib. Research.* ii. p. 45.

and one hour more brings the traveller to Um-Lakis, lying at one side on a round hill scattered with bits of marble, and overgrown with thistles. Several pillars were seen by Robinson[1] on the south side. Eusebius speaks of a certain Lakis[2] as known in his time, but it cannot be the Um-Lakis discovered by the great American explorer of Palestine. The Lakis of Robinson appears to indicate the site of the ancient city of Lachish, mentioned in Josh. x. 3–5, in immediate connection with Eglon, as cities which were in close league with the five allied Philistine princes.

Only three-quarters of an hour west of Um Lakis lies Ajlan,[3] the ancient Eglon, south of the regular beaten road. Both Lachish and Eglon belong to the cities of the lowland mentioned in the catalogue of Joshua, they being included in a list of fifteen (Josh. xv. 37–41), few of which can be identi-fied at the present day.

Tell el Hasy lies a half-hour's distance farther on. It is a truncated cone, rising about two hundred feet above the plain, and in a situation well adapted for a stronghold. There are no traces of ruins to be seen there, however, at least according to the testimony of Robinson. The place is thought, however, to have once been a well-known site; and, according to opinions of many of the best judges, the hill once was crowned by the city of Ziklag. The first pilgrim who conjectured that Tell Hasy was the site of the ancient town was Felix Fabri,[4] who visited the place in 1483, and whose eye was first caught by the admirable advantages which it offers for defence. On the hill he discovered the ruins of a castle and of an ancient city, which he concluded to be Ziklag, the place which Achish of Gath gave to David while he was a refugee harboured by the Philistines (1 Sam. xxvii. 6). Jerome adds to this, that this place was in Daroma, to the south of Judah and Simeon. This agrees well with the position where Fabri locates it; for in Josh. xv. 31 Ziklag is alluded to among the twenty cities in the south of Judah which lay near the borders of the Edomites,[5]

---

[1] Robinson, *Bib. Research.* ii. p. 516.
[2] Keil, *Comment. zu Josua*, p. 172, Not. 4.
[3] *Ibid.* pp. 173, 297, 298.
[4] Fel. Fabri, *Evag.* ed. Hassler, ii. p. 359.
[5] Keil, *Comment. zu Josua*, pp. 290, 293.

and which, in connection with Beersheba, were given to Simeon. From the hill Fabri had a fine view westward to the sea, eastward to the mountains of Ephraim, northward to those of Ephraim, and southward to the Egyptian plain. This position seems to me to correspond well with the situation of Ziklag, as it is hinted at in the Bible. The place was advantageous for making attacks upon the Geshurites on the brook Sichor, against the Girgesites and the Amalekites, the ancient inhabitants of the district on whose border it lay.[1] This proximity was the cause of its being burned by the Amalekites directly after David had taken possession of it, out of Achish's kindness. After the city had been destroyed, David pursued the Amalekites to the brook Besor, *i.e.* the Wadi Sheriah, which lay south of Ziklag, as it now lies south of Tell Hasy. At this brook David's two hundred men sank down exhausted; but he pressed on with four hundred others, under the guidance of an Egyptian, whom he found by the way, and, surprising the Amalekites intoxicated with their success, gained an easy victory over them (1 Sam. xxvii. 6, xxx. 1). It was when David was returning to Ziklag that he received the tidings of the death of Saul, and on the way he uttered his famous dirge over the fate of the king and Jonathan (2 Sam. i. 1). From Ziklag he returned to Hebron, where he was anointed king (2 Sam. ii. 3). It was here, on this very hill el-Hasy, that David spent a year of exile, banished from the presence of Saul; and from this circumstance it wins a new interest, and deserves more careful attention from travellers than it has received. According to Nehemiah, Ziklag received an influx of Jewish population after the return from Babylon.

A half-hour's distance north of Tell el Hasy, Robinson discovered the ruins of Ajlan, the site of which is very similar to Um-Lakis, but which corresponds well with the Eglon of the Old Testament (Josh. xv. 39). On the way to Beit Jibrin, the only places passed subsequently to those already mentioned are the villages of Sukkariyeh and Kubeibeh. Here the plain is distinctively exchanged for the mountain-land : here and there single fields are seen, but no more the rich lowlands of the coast region.[2] At the time of Robinson's visit the harvest was

---

[1] Ewald, *Gesch. d. Volkes Israel,* ii. p. 558.

[2] See Fel. Fabri, *Evagatorium,* ii. p. 355.

going forward, the reapers were busy; and he witnessed a scene which recalled the account of Ruth, of the gleaners roasting the scattered ears of grain, and eating them as they laboured (Ruth ii. 3–18).

Robinson's first visit[1] to Beit Jibrin led him to the conviction that the place is no other than the ancient Eleutheropolis, an important episcopal residence during the fourth and fifth centuries, and according to Eusebius and Jerome, the central point of southern Palestine in their day. According to the Peutinger Tables, the ancient Betogabra (supposed to be the same place as Eleutheropolis) lay thirteen Roman miles from Ashkelon. As all trace of the Greek name seemed to have disappeared, and as there were said to be no other important ruins in the neighbourhood excepting those of Beit Jibrin, the American travellers Smith and Robinson spared no pains to examine this, and made them the object of repeated visits. And so competent an authority as Olshausen[2] does not hesitate to say that the efforts of the two scholars have been crowned with perfect success, and they have fully identified Beit Jibrin with the ancient Eleutheropolis.

I have already said that many of the local names in this neighbourhood bearing the impress of an Old Testament origin, have been confounded with the ancient Betogabra of Ptolemy, the Beygeberin of the *Notit. Eccles.*, the Bethgeberin of the Crusades. In these local appellations, on the other hand, Robinson was not so fortunate as to discover the name Lachish, Ziklag, Gerar, Gath, and other designations of biblical cities. He was unacquainted, it would seem, with Fabri's account of his conjectural discovery of Ziklag. After a march of an hour and three-quarters, Robinson came south-westward as far as to Deir Dubban, making inquiries for caves which might answer to the account of the Makkedah to which the five Amorite kings fled after their defeat at Gibeon (Josh. x. 16). One was discovered near Deir Dubban, and several west of that place. They seemed, indeed, to be a marked characteristic of this part of Palestine. Yet the Americans failed to discover[3] any one

---

[1] Robinson, *Bib. Research.* ii. pp. 51–55.

[2] Olshausen, Rev. already cited, p. 153.

[3] Robinson, *Bib. Research.* ii. p. 29.

bearing a name similar to Makkedah. Hans Tucher,[1] the Nuremberg pilgrim, on his way from Bethlehem to Gaza in 1479, discovered a place which he called a " ditch excavated from the rock." Near the spot evidently described by him, Robinson met several ditches, of which it was hard to say whether they were the work of nature or of art. From some of these passages led caves or bell-shaped grottos, a portion of which open at the top in a narrow aperture: they were generally met in groups of three or four together. Indeed, one of these groups numbered no less than sixteen, many of the caves being excavated with great care. In some, niches appeared to have been cut to adorn them.

The neighbourhood of Deir Dubban appeared to Robinson to be the site of the ancient city of Gath; the Philistine stronghold, lying, according to his conjecture, between this place and the village of Ajjur on the north. All architectural traces of the place appear to have passed away, as has the name itself. Felix Fabri believes that this location was not only the home of the ancient Philistine giants, but also of St Christopher,[2] and asserts that in his time the inhabitants of this place were larger, stronger, and more warlike, than any others in this neighbourhood. Not only the name Gath appears in the books of Joshua, Judges, Samuel, and the prophets, but in Joshua (xix. 45) mention is made of a Gath-rimmon as a place belonging to the territory of Dan; and in the same book (xxi. 24) the same place is connected with Ajalon as belonging to the Levites. Jerome subsequently gives the distance of the Levite city of Dan as five Roman miles north of Eleutheropolis, and on the way to Diospolis, *i.e.* Lydda near Ramleh.[3] This agrees well with the distance of the locality of caves near Deir Dubban from the present Beit Jibrin. The distance of these caves from Diospolis, about twelve Roman miles, agrees well with the statements of Jerome. The Philistine city of Gath, to which the ark of the covenant was carried from Ashdod (1 Sam. v. 8), and the residence of Goliath (1 Sam. xvii. 4, 23), appears to have been wrested from its rightful possessors at a very early day,

---

[1] Hans Tucher, *Reise in Gelobte Land.* See extract in *Reyssb. des heil. Landes;* and compare Fel. Fabri, *Evagatorium,* ii. p. 338.

[2] Fel. Fabri, *Evagatorium,* ed. Hassler, ii. p. 356.

[3] Reland, *Pal.* pp. 785, 786, 809.

probably directly after Uzziah's victory, recorded in 2 Chron. xxvi. 6. This is to be partly inferred from the fact that the name of Gath is mentioned in connection with other neighbouring cities of the Judæan mountain-land, such as Shoco, Mareshah, Adoraim, and others, as having been re-erected by king Rehoboam, and converted into strongholds (2 Chron. xi. 8). Ewald[1] has conjectured, from the fact that the ark was carried from Ashdod to Gath and thence to Ekron, that we may conclude that Gath lay between Ashdod and Ekron, somewhere in the neighbourhood of the spot marked Tell el Turmus on Robinson's map. It is doubtless probable that the Philistine city of Gath was early destroyed, for Amos and several of the other prophets allude to only four Philistine chief cities, and pass over this one. Jerome, how-ever, in his second mention of Gath, alludes to it as one of the five Philistine cities that lay on the border of the Judæan mountain-land between Eleutheropolis and Diospolis: in his time it was a mere village. Keil[2] has shown that the two different statements made by Jerome conflict with each other: he thinks, moreover, that the site of Gath could not have been near the present Deir Dubban, in support of which view Thenius cites 1 Sam. xvii. 52; yet no more probable site has been assigned than the one between Deir Dubban and Ajjur on the north of it. And this thing is certain, that Gath must have been situated in a vine-producing country, for the name signifies a wine-press.[3] The word is the same as the first syllable of Gethsemane, which means a vineyard.

The crusaders, following the untrustworthy legends of the country, located Gath at places where the error was palpably absurd, some of their writers assuming that it was at Jamnia, others on a hill near Lydda:[4] near the former of these two places, moreover, they located the ancient Beersheba. These errors, gross as they are, perpetuated themselves till Reland first, and Robinson subsequently, showed their want of evidence; and although not showing with entire certainty where Gath lay, yet made its location in the highest degree probable. The

---

[1] Ewald, *Gesch. des Volks Israel*, ii. p. 427, Note 3.
[2] Keil, *Comment. zu Josua*, p. 219.
[3] Rosenmüller, *Bib. Alterthums.* Pt. ii. p. 371.
[4] Wilken, *Gesch. der Kreuz.* Pt. ii. p. 615.

site of the ancient Mareshah,[1] which was in the neighbourhood of Gath, has not been fixed, and remains yet a doubtful question.

About a quarter of an hour's distance south of Deir Dubban lies the village of Rana, around which tobacco and cotton grow. After passing this spot Kudna is reached, where a wall a hundred and fifty feet in length is seen, built of large stones, and not disclosing its real object. Here one passes the frontier of the hilly country, and enters broad wadis running in the most varied directions, and very hard to follow. In one of these, where traces of ancient walls are still seen, and where pillars indicate the barriers of former fields, lies the village of Beit Jibrin, between low hills at the commencement of a broad wadi running north-west by way of Kudna and Rana to upper Wadi Simsin.

Beit Jibrin, the Bethgebrin of the Arabs and the crusaders, the Βαιτογάβρα of Ptolemy, the Betogabra of the Peutinger Tables, and the Eleutheropolis or episcopal seat[2] of the primitive church, lies in the midst of olive-covered hills. The place is not mentioned in the Old Testament, but in the later years of the Byzantine power it became a place of great prominence. The present village displays extensive ruins bearing the marks of a varied origin, and, according to Robinson, the most massive of any which he saw in all Palestine, with the exception of the foundation of the temple at Jerusalem, and the Haram at Hebron. Here are to be seen the remains of a fortress[3] of great strength, situated on an irregular rounded plain, once surrounded by a very thick wall. The latter is composed of large stones laid without mortar; and although fallen on almost every side, still the original course is easily traced. It is evidently of Roman construction. In the middle of the area is an irregular castle, whose lower portion appears to have been built at the same time with the wall, while the upper part is of more recent origin. An inscription over the gate declares that this was effected in 1551, ten years after the latest constructed walls at Jerusalem were put up. Only the north and north-west sides are entire. The court within was planted with

---

[1] Robinson, *Bib. Research.* ii. pp. 67-69.
[2] *Ibid.* pp. 25-29, 51-54, 67-69.
[3] See Roberts, *Views in the Holy Land,* Book vii. Plate 43.

tobacco at the time of Robinson's visit. The many arches, vaults, walls, and marble columns are partly free from rubbish, and in part surrounded by it. The inner court around the castle is occupied by the huts of the modern village. The northern and eastern quarters are full of stone heaps and remains of walls.

The situation of this fortress was low, between two great wadis, beyond which hills arise. The ancient city appears to have extended up the valley towards the north-west, where many walls may even now be seen. In the village lies a large open well.

The extensive ruins found here, together with the distances assigned by ancient authors from Eleutheropolis to other important places, fully confirmed Robinson's conjecture that Beit Jibrin occupies the site of the once noted episcopal city. The six places mentioned by Jerome and Eusebius are found to be precisely the same distance from Beit Jibrin that they are stated in the *Onomasticon* to have been. These places are: Zareah and Beth-shemesh, lying on the north, and ten Roman miles away; Jarmuk and Socoh, N.N.E., nine or ten Roman miles on the road to Jerusalem; and Jednah and Nazib on the road leading south-eastward to Hebron, and nine miles respectively from Eleutheropolis. The statement of Antoninus, that the episcopal city was twenty-four Roman miles from Ashkelon, agrees tolerably with these data, as the situation of some twenty places could be compared with the statements contained in ancient documents. Robinson and Smith, who spared no pains, were able to arrive at a tolerable degree of certainty. Still the result must be confessed as one resting upon probability, though of the highest degree, since no authentic and direct historical evidence has been cited, either by Reland or Robinson,[1] to show the identity of Eleutheropolis, Betogabra, and the modern Beit Jibrin. The oldest mention of Betogabra in Ptolemy dates from the beginning of the second century; all others are later. Reland suspects that the place took its high-sounding name of Eleutheropolis, or the free city, from the Romans, as did Diospolis, Nicopolis, and Cæsarea. Eusebius of Cæsarea, writing about the year 330, is the first who mentions the place as an episcopal centre. The last writer

1 Robinson, *Bib. Research.* ii. p. 60.

who refers to it before the Saracens swept over Palestine, appears to be Antoninus Martyr, who wrote about 600. He makes no special mention of the place, however. Stephen, a monk of Marsaba, tells us that in the year 1796 Eleutheropolis was entirely destroyed, and its population banished. The city appears to have never risen since that time; even the Greek name has utterly perished. The modern name Beit Jibrin appears to have no relation to the ancient Eleutheropolis.

A decisive historical proof of the identity of the ancient Bethogabra and the modern Beit Jibrin with the ancient Eleutheropolis, has been recently discovered by Rödiger,[1] in *Assemani Acta Sanctor. Martyr. Oriental.* T. ii. p. 209. In the Greek, Syriac, and Latin text of the narrative of Martyr Peter Abselama, it is said: " He was born at Anea, in the district of Beth-Gubrin, or as the Greeks and Latins call it, Eleutheropolis." This almost certain conclusion is confirmed[2] by another which is still stronger in Rödiger's opinion,[3] namely, that in two lists of ancient bishops Eleutheropolis and Beit-jerbein (evidently Beit-jibrin) refer to the same place. More recent discoveries seem to have confirmed what appeared already so sure.[4]

The crusaders[5] found the place in ruins, although not given over to desolation. Among their chroniclers the Arabic name Bethgibrin occurs. Many supposed it to be the ancient Beer-sheba. Edrisi names the place Beit-jibril. In the year 1187 it passed into the hands of the Moslems, and an inscription still existing shows that the place was then fortified by the Saracens.

I have already alluded to the extensive caverns which exist in the neighbourhood of Deir Dubban. Robinson[6] discovered that near Eleutheropolis they are no less so; indeed, not far from the Church of St Ann, he found them on a very large scale. They had all the appearance of having been the work of art which those at Deir Dubban have, yet they are far more

---

[1] *Allgem. Lit. Zeitung*, 1843, No. 72, p. 571; comp. Robinson, *Bib. Sacra*, 1843, p. 204, vol. ii. pp. 217-220.

[2] Rödiger, in *Allg. Lit.* iii. 1843, No. 110, p. 268; von Raumer, *Beitr. zur Bibl. Geogr.* pp. 39-41; comp. *Bib. Sacra*, 1844, vol. ii. p. 218.

[3] Leo Allatius, *de Nilis*, App. in Fabri *Bibl. Græca*, T. v.

[4] Von Raumer, *Pal.* p. 167.

[5] G. Cedrinus, *Hist.*, comp. ed. Bekker, i. pp. 58, 19.

[6] Robinson, *Bib. Research.* ii. pp. 51-53.

elaborate. One of the caves was no less than a hundred feet long. Another was fifty feet long, and from fifteen to twenty wide. Some were bell-shaped, and had a height of no less than twenty or thirty feet. From some of them it seemed as if building materials had been extensively taken for the construction of Beit Jibrin. In some, inscriptions were found ; but they did not throw much light upon the use or character or origin of these extensive subterranean chambers. In one place, where Robinson descended under the guidance of a thoroughly competent Arab, he found not a single cavern alone, but an entire labyrinth of apartments leading one to another, and extending far into the heart of the mountain, forming altogether a complete troglodyte city. The massive ruins of the church in the village hard by, and the great Church of St Ann on the neighbouring hill, leave no doubt that here was once the centre of a large population of which we have no history.[1]

A little light may be thrown upon this place by a commentary of Jerome upon the first chapter of the prophecy of Obadiah, where Edom is spoken of. He says the district of Eleutheropolis, southward to Petra and Aila, the possession of Esau, was inhabited by Idumæans, who dwelt in caves. The earliest population of this region of which we have authentic evidence were the Horites, who were driven from their homes at a very remote period. The subsequent Idumæans extended themselves northward into southern Judæa to such an extent, that the name Idumæa is sometimes applied by Josephus to a tract altogether north of its true location. These people, although not the primitive population, used in their rudeness to escape from the heat of the sun, which is really great in the summer time there, and take refuge in the cool caverns of the hills.

The question much disputed formerly, whether these hiding-places, which are so abundant and so extensive in the neighbourhood of Eleutheropolis, are natural or artificial, has been fairly settled by the discoveries of caverns no less capacious and labyrinthine in the neighbourhood of Paris. This has been shown in a masterly way by von Raumer,[2] a most com-

---

[1] Robinson, *Bib. Research.* ii. p. 26.

[2] K. v. Raumer, *Pal.* pp. 433-437.

petent authority, who, from his own researches in the chalk formations of northern France, pronounces authoritatively against the conjecture that the caves of Judæa owe their existence to the hand of man. The very niches and supposed ornamentation which used to puzzle observers are found in the French caverns; and although the inscriptions indicate the hand of man within the grottos around Eleutheropolis, yet the structures in all their essential features owe nothing to human skill. The bell-shaped chambers, the lofty arches, the long passage-ways, the numerous chambers, all are as they were left by the hand of God himself.

DISCURSION II.

THE ROADS FROM BEIT JIBRIN TO HEBRON : THE NORTHERN ONE, BY WAY OF TERKUMIEH ; A SOUTHERN ONE, BY WAY OF DAWAIMEH AND EL-BURJ ; ONE STILL FARTHER SOUTH, BY WAY OF DEBIR AND ZIKLAG (TELL EL HASY) ; ANOTHER AND A MORE DIRECT ROUTE, BY WAY OF IDNA AND TEFFUH.

Of these roads,[1] the northern one, which runs by Terkumieh, is the most comfortable, and the one oftenest chosen. It passes the village of Beit Nusib, the ancient Nezib of Judah (Josh. xv. 43), which lay, according to Eusebius and Jerome, on the way from Eleutheropolis to Hebron, and seven Roman miles from the former. A road lying more to the south passes through the valley of St Anna, and by the village of Idna, the Jedna of Eusebius and Jerome, which lay six Roman miles from Eleutheropolis. Another road, still farther south, and passing Tell el Hasy and the village of Sukkariyeh, was taken by Felix Fabri[2] in his journey from Hebron to Gaza in 1483. It cannot be said in entire strictness to connect Beit Jibrin and Hebron, for it leaves the latter a little to the north. This route has been taken within modern times by the French traveller Baptistin Poujoulat, in 1838, whose narrative, however, is very meagre. Fabri, however, is more full. Leaving Hebron, he passed through a valley running west, which he calls the Vale of Hebron. He heard of a place lying near this valley, and bearing the name of Debir, but did not visit it. The spot

---

[1] Robinson, *Bib. Research.* ii. pp. 54–56.
[2] Fel. Fabri, *Evagator.* ed. Hassler, ii. p. 338.

seemed to him necessarily identical with the Kirjath-sepher, the *civitas literarum,* which was given to Caleb as a part of his possessions (Josh. xv. 15). We learn from Josh. xxi. 11, that Debir once bore the name Kirjath-sepher, as did Hebron that of Kirjath-arba. Both of these cities were given to the Levites. The former of the two was sometimes called Kirjath-sannah, as we learn from Josh. xv. 49 : the overthrow of the Anakim at Debir is confirmed by the same writer (xi. 21). Subsequently there is no allusion to this place ; and Eusebius and Jerome know nothing further about it, than that it lay in the territory of Judah. Nothing has been learned by modern travellers regarding its situation. In the account of the capture of Debir by Othniel, the younger brother of Caleb (Josh. xv. 17), a circumstance is mentioned, connected with the request made by Achsah, which may throw some light upon the situation of the place. Caleb's daughter begged her father to add some watered land to her dowry ; on which her father gave her the upper and the lower springs.[1] According to Keil, the description refers to a place definitely described by this language, and ought to be looked for now as a sign of the location of Debir. Following this hint, Wilson[2] in 1843 discovered, on the road from Dhoheriyeh to Hebron, and therefore not far from the ancient Debir, several fine springs, which seemed to him to correspond well with the statements of the Bible ; yet not a name could be discovered which bore the traces of an Old Testament origin. The very ancient appellation, Kirjath-sepher, which the Septuagint renders πόλις γραμματέων, *i.e.* the *Urbs archivorum,* and which the meaning of *sannah,* found in the word Kirjath-sannah, only strengthens, has lately called much attention to itself, it having been assumed that it is a proof that the ancient Canaanites were acquainted with writing and with books. Yet although the name of a single city may have had this signification, it does not follow that the inhabitants generally[3] were acquainted with art and science. Quatremère[4] considers that this place was the depository of the archives of the ancient

---

[1] Keil, *Comment. zu Josua,* pp. 287–289.
[2] Wilson, *Lands of the Bible,* i. p. 386.
[3] Ewald, *Gesch. des Volks Israel,* i. p. 287, Note.
[4] Quatremère, Gesenius, *Phœniciæ Monumenta,* in *Journ. des Savans,* 1842, p. 513 ; comp. Rosenmüller, *Alterthk.* Pt. i. pp. 280, 297, Note 14.

Canaanites ; and instances, as parallels, the caves of Ecbatana, where, according to Ezra vi. 2, the public papers of Cyrus[1] were preserved ; and Tyre, where the Phœnician archives are said to have been preserved. In the accounts of Joshua's contests with the original Canaanite kings, mention is made of Debir, a king of Eglon (Josh. x. 3), as being one of those who were vanquished and put to death ; and Ewald[2] propounds the conjecture, that this king took his name from the place near Hebron.

From his bivouac near the conjectural Kirjath-sepher, which was but a couple of hours distant from Hebron, Fabri[3] journeyed on through the fruitful Hebron valley, displaying traces of ancient gardens and terraces on both sides, to a spot where another valley runs down from the north, and bears westward. This he calls Eshcol, whose fertility called forth wonder in the time of Moses (Num. xiii. 23). Whether the valley which bore that name in the most ancient times is the one which Fabri mentions, is hard to ascertain ; but the fertility of the soil, and its former cultivation, make it not impossible.

Fabri considered the road down to Gaza which he was taking to be the route which Jacob and the brothers of Joseph took on their way down to Egypt,—a view which does not seem at all improbable. The most important object, and indeed the only one of interest reached by Fabri after emerging from the valley which he conjectured to be Eshcol, was the hill, which he considered the site of Ziklag, to which I have referred on a preceding page.

Robinson, in one of his visits to Beit Jibrin, returned to Hebron by way of the village of Idna. He passed near the villages of Dura and Taiyibeh, but did not visit them till a subsequent period. Dura is reached from Hebron, by passing in a generally south-westerly direction for about three hours. It lies on the eastern slope of a cultivated hill, lying between corn-fields and olive-groves. It is the residence of an important sheikh of the house of Ibn Omar, which formerly ruled all the villages in this district. The village is large, but there are no

---

[1] Joseph. *contr. Apion.* ii. p. 447.

[2] Ewald, *Gesch. d. Volks Israel*, ii. p. 289, Note 4 ; Keil, *Comment. zu Josua*, p. 200, Note 22.

[3] Fel. Fabri, *Evagatorium*, ii. p. 355.

ruins to be seen. Still it occupies the site of Adoraim, which was built by king Rehoboam, in conjunction with fifteen other cities — Bethlehem, Tekoa, Socoh, Gath, Mareshah, Ziph, Lachish, etc. It was erected as a stronghold (2 Chron. xi. 9): later, as we learn from Josephus, it having been spoiled and ravaged by Hyrcanus, it was rebuilt by the Roman emperor Gabinius.

DISCURSION III.

THE ORIGIN OF THE PHILISTINES : THEIR DIVISION INTO TWO DIFFERENT SEC-
TIONS, THE CAPHTHORIM (CRETANS) AND PHILISTIM (SEMITIC LUDITES ;
PRIMITIVE ARABIANS, ERYTHRÆANS). THE CHERETHITES AND PELETHITES :
THEIR INSULAR AND CONTINENTAL ORIGIN ; THEIR RELATION TO THE AGE
OF THE HYKSOS ; THE TIME OF THEIR SETTLEMENT IN PHILISTIA.

Having studied the land of the Philistines in its entire extent, —that district which, at a later period, was wholly absorbed in southern and western Judæa, losing its own population and receiving a Jewish one,—we have now, before coming to the study of the interior of the mountain-land of Judæa, to cast a glance at that Philistine race which has now wholly disappeared, but which for more than half a thousand years, from the invasion under Moses and Joshua to the division of the kingdom of Solomon into Judah and Israel, received, in consequence of the alliance of its princes and the gallant defence which it offered, a more honourable place in history than the Canaanitic tribes, bound together by no ties of alliance, and therefore speedily conquered as far northward as Phœnicia and the Lebanon range; that Philistine race which exerted the greatest influence upon the whole course of Jewish history. Without the resistance which they offered, Israel never would have had such a succession of heroes as the times of the judges afforded; would have given birth to no such deliverer as David; would have advanced to no such splendid estate as was exhibited in the reign of Solomon, its glory lingering long, and throwing a lustrous splendour over the ruptured kingdom which was soon to be. That peculiar intensity which in the beginning was called forth by the religious institutions of the Israelites, by the glowing promises made to them, and by their first brilliant suc-cesses, soon softened in the various tribes, even while in the very

presence of their enemies; not foes, indeed, like the later ones
of Syria and Assyria, but those whose victories were but temporary, alternating speedily with equally temporary ill success.
But on the west border of the country, and even within the
very limits of the land which had been promised to the Israelites,
the brave and thoroughly trained Philistines, their princes
bound together in an alliance not known elsewhere, threatened
repeatedly to sweep the Israelitish nation from the face of the
earth.[1] This necessarily compelled their adversaries, who were
far superior in number, to enter upon a warlike discipline
hitherto unknown to their peaceful habits, and to fortify all
their towns and hill-tops. It was a fortunate circumstance for
Israel, that Judah—the most powerful tribe of all, its strength
early augmented by the absorption of the smaller and weaker
tribe of Simeon[2]—occupied the country best adapted by nature
as a place of defence. And this tribe it was which should give
birth to the hero and king of the whole nation, who should
commence his wonderful series of victories by his signal defeat
of Goliath, while a mere shepherd boy, and standing on
Philistine soil. Later, while pursued by the hatred of Saul, he
gathered six hundred brave Philistines around him, and was
hospitably received by the Philistine king Achish at Ziklag.
Afterwards, when chosen king of Israel, the skill which he
gained while the guest of Achish was of the greatest service to
him; and he was able to impart to his own countrymen, little
skilled as yet in the arts of war, the results of his experience
among their most bitter enemies.

The real origin of this Philistine race, like all historical
beginnings, is veiled in darkness, although they are mentioned
in the list of tribes contained in Genesis. Among the descendants of Ham, and in the direct lineage of Mizraim, the founder
of the Egyptian race, there are mentioned the Pathrusim and
the Casluhim, from whom the Scripture says further came
the Philistim and Caphthorim (Gen. x. 14).

The Egyptian race of Casluchim has been held, in view of
their name and their location, to be the inhabitants of Casiotis,
i.e. the neighbourhood of Mount Casius, east of Pelusium. In
the Coptic language, a mountain is called *ghas*, or *cas*, and a

---

[1] Ewald, *Gesch. des Volks Israel*, vol. ii. pp. 268, 308.
[2] *Ibid.* pp. 291, 309.

desert *lokh;*[1] the two—*caslokh* (*caslokhim, casluchim*)—signifying, therefore, the mountain near the desert,—a phrase which exactly characterizes the mountain of Casiotis and the barren country around it, when brought into contrast with the fertile valley of the Nile. From these *Casluchim,* the celebrated Egyptian colony of Colchians, who settled on the Euxine, is thought to have sprung, and their name is but a changed form of that of their ancestors. It was from the locality which they occupied that the expression which we find in the Scripture, "out of whom came," was derived. It was formerly erroneously thought to have indicated genealogical descent; but the Hebrew word translated "out of whom" can only refer to a place.

The former destructive inundations of Lake Sirbonis referred to by Eratosthenes, probably was one cause of the emigration of the earlier inhabitants of Mount Casius. It is possible that the Philistines were driven eastward by an occurrence similar to that to which Justinus attributes the emigration of the Tyrians from their primitive home. And it is probable that the withdrawing of the Philistines from the neighbourhood of Pelusium was the oldest event in their history known to the compiler of the list of tribes in Genesis, and was therefore intercalated by him in the genealogical record.

In the name of the Pelusiac mouth of the Nile, the primitive home of the ancient race to which I am referring, there seems to be a philological monument testifying to their emigration westward; since the word Πηλούσιον, according to Lepsius,[2] does not originate in πηλός, alluvium, low swampy land, although the Arabs, in their subsequent translation of the word, assigned it this fanciful derivation. It is much more probable that it goes back to the ancient name of the Philistines, Pelistim, since a story current in that part of Lower Egypt about a certain bold leader, Παλαιστινός or Πηλούσιος, proves that Pelusium was the chief city of the Philistines or Palæstinians. With this, another name found in the immediate vicinity, that of the city of Abarim, closely agrees. This Abarim was a fortified place built by Salatis, *i.e.* "the Lord," the first of the Hykso dynasty; and, according to the conjecture of Ewald, the name signifies nothing else than the city of

---

[1] Knobel, *Die Volkertafel des Genesis,* pp. 290–292.
[2] Lepsius, *Die Chronologie d. Ægypter,* Pt. i. p. 341.

Ebrews or Hebrews, the descendants of Eber mentioned in Gen. x. 21,—a race widely scattered, and which had found its way so far south-westward as the Nile.[1] The Philistines were therefore a nation of immigrants[2] into their home in Palestine ; and the Hebrew etymology of the district which they settled, Peleshet,[3] confirms the fact,—a name which, according to Josephus, was afterwards transferred to Palestine, and indeed was enlarged even beyond the boundaries of that country. This term given them by aliens has clung even to the present day to a tribe of cognate origin, inhabiting the Abyssinian mountains,—a tribe which was formerly considered as of Jewish or Semitic origin.[4] Before the Philistines invaded Palestine—an event of which there are no chronological proofs that it occurred after the time of Moses— the country was occupied by a tribe mentioned in the Bible, and called there Avim or Avites. In Josh. xiii. 4, the expression " from the south " ought to be connected[5] with the word Avites which closes ver. 3 ; and in Deut. ii. 23 we have a detailed historical fact relating to them, namely, that they were conquered by the Caphthorim, " which came forth out of Caphthor, destroyed them, and dwelt in their stead." These Avites have been considered the primitive inhabitants of Palestine, but of this there is no direct proof. In Gen. x. 19, it is expressly stated[6] that a Canaanitish population occupied the territory afterwards possessed by the Philistines : " The border of the Canaanites was from Sidon, as thou comest to Gerar, unto Gaza; as thou goest unto Sodom, and Gomorrah, and Admah, and Zeboim, even unto Lasha." It is not impossible that the foundations of the cities of Ekron, Gaza, and Gath, were laid by the ancient Avim; and the Semitic nature[7] of the names seems to afford a support to that view. The ancient city of Ashkelon runs back, according to Justinus, to the founding of Tyre ; and, according to another account, Askelos

[1] Ewald, *Gesch. des Volks Israel,* i. pp. 327–329, 451.

[2] Movers, *Phönizier,* i. p. 3.

[3] Rosenmüller, *Bibl. Alterthk.* ii. p. 74.

[4] Knobel, *Die Völkertafel d. Genesis,* p. 220.

[5] Ewald, *Gesch. d. Volks Israel,* i. p. 289, ii. p. 290 ; Winer, *Bib. Realw.* ii. p. 251.

[6] Keil, *Comment. zu Josua, i.a.l.* p. 243.

[7] Ewald, *Gesch.* i. pp. 315, 450.

of the Ludites, that is, of the primitive Arabians in the broadest sense, belonged to one of the most ancient and unbroken Semitic races of the west, the descendants of Amalek.

Looked at in this light, thus much is certain, that the Caphthorim were preceded by other races, not Jewish in their character, but probably of a very ancient Semitic or Old Hebrew type (using the word in the very broad way above alluded to in connection with Abarim and the descendants of Eber or Heber). And it was in consequence of the subsequent domination of the Philistines in the territory once held by these people of Semitic origin, that the name Abarim, given to his frontier city by the founder of the Hykso dynasty,[1] was finally given up, and became the Pelusium of the Philistines.

From Amos ix. 7 we learn that it was the Philistines who came from Caphtor ; in Jer. xlvii. 4 the same fact is repeated, but with Caphtor is united a word which may mean either island or coast-land. As no closely descriptive word is used to designate what this "country" of Caphtor was, a number of conjectures have been raised regarding its situation. On account of the similarity of names, Gesenius supposed it to be Cappadocia ; Schulthes presumes that it was Cyprus ; Rosenmüller thinks that it was Crete, drawing his inference from the existence of the city of Aptera, and some other causes. The most recent inquirers in this field—Movers, Hitzig, Knobel —support the last-named conjecture.[2]

Accepting this theory of the origin of the Caphthorim, *i.e.* of the Philistines, granting that they came from a land situated on the sea-coast, even if it were not the island of Crete, and laying much stress upon the connection of Philistines and Cretans in the body-guard of David, Hitzig[3] has with rare learning and acuteness laid down a conjectural history of the Philistines, which differs widely from that which has been laid down by other authorities. Into this, however, we cannot enter, as the subject is foreign to what we have directly in view.[4]

The statements made in the list of tribes contained in

[1] Lepsius, *i.a.l.* p. 338.
[2] Winer, *Bibl. Realw.* i. p. 210.
[3] Hitzig, *Urgeschichte der Philistäer*, p. 15.
[4] Keil, *Comment.* p. 312, Note ; Knobel, *Völkertafel*, p. 224 ; Winer, ii. p. 254.

Gen. x. regarding the origin of the Philistines, seem to me to harmonize with the recent investigations regarding the origin of the Phœnicians. Moreover, Hitzig solves the contradiction [1] which has so long been noticed in the earlier data regarding the Philistines, whose derivation he does not derive from Egypt, but from Crete, which he assumes to be the Caphtor of the Bible, by assuming that there were two great divisions in the nation, but that, when taken together, the name Philistine was generally applied to both.

The two divisions are, however, spoken of as separate, as in Ezek. xxv. 16: " Behold, I will stretch out my hand upon the Philistines, and I will cut off the Cherethim, and destroy the remnant of the sea-coast." So, too, in Zeph. ii. 5: " Woe unto the inhabitants of the sea-coast, the nation of the Cherethites! the word of the Lord is against you; O Canaan, the land of the Philistines, I will even destroy thee, that there shall be no inhabitant." And just as Cherethites and Philistines are mentioned together in this place, in the times of Samuel and David the Cherethites and the Pelethites occur in close connection, as the six hundred chosen men of war whom David selected as his trusty body-guard when he was attacked by the Amalekites in Ziklag, and his stronghold plundered and burned. When driven as an exile into the land of the Philistines, David took his six hundred warriors with him to Achish, and established them and their wives, as well as his own, first in Gath and then in Ziklag. When, at a later period, he in turn attacked the Amalekites on the farther side of the brook Besor, the Egyptian youth who was his guide, and who had been left behind by the Amalekites in consequence of sickness, said to him, as recorded in 1 Sam. xxx. 14, " We made an invasion upon the south of the Cherethites, and upon the coast which belongeth to Judah, and upon the south of Caleb; and we burned Ziklag with fire." Here the Philistine territory is spoken of, as on both sides of Ziklag is named after its lords the Cherethites, as Hebron is named after its possessors the successors of Caleb. With the warriors referred to above, and with their wives, David betook himself after the death of Saul to Hebron, and gave every man a house to live in (2 Sam. ii. 3).

[1] Knobel, *Völkertafel der Genesis,* p. 216; Movers, *Phönizier,* i. pp. 3-17, ii. p. 258.

Thence he marched in company with his trustworthy followers, who had been joined by six hundred Gittites, against the Jebusites, and captured their stronghold of Zion, *i.e.* the City of David, of Jerusalem, according to 2 Sam. v. 6, 7. When he had been anointed as king, he set his officers over all Israel, making them military governors, priests, and scribes. Benaiah, the son of Jehoiada, and a hero of great renown, he set over the Cherethites and the Pelethites, who remained true to him. (See 2 Sam. viii. 18, xv. 19.)

These two distinct appellations, Philistim and Caphthorim, carry us back to the time when there were two radically different branches of the same stock; one of which, the Plethi, must unquestionably be regarded as the superior, and in time transferred its name to the whole tribe and to the country of Palestine (Peleshet), where it had its home. The name Cherethites or Caphthorim, on the contrary, gradually passed out of use, and at last wholly disappeared.

Both of the two divisions have a common end, but a different origin : the Philistim, or the true Philistines, and the Caphthorim, came out of various places and over various ways; and therefore, when in their Canaanitish home, they appear as radically different in stock; but in the course of time they assimilated to each other, and assumed that unity of character which is generally observable in the history of the Philistines. Yet there still survived the tradition of an emigration of one portion from a former island home, which had contributed its strength and youth to the invigoration of the larger portion in which it was incorporated.

1. *The Caphthorim, or Cherethites, the later immigrants from over sea.*

It was the Cretans,[1] the biblical Cherethites, who, according to Deut. ii. 23, came from Caphtor and drove out the Avites, who lived at Gaza, near Gerar, which was a little way farther inland. A dark and curious passage in Tacitus (*Hist.* v. 2 : " Judæos [so called from the false etymology which traced the name to Mount Ida] Creta insula profugos novissima Libyæ insedisse") confirms the account in the sacred record; for Tacitus does not mean the Jews, but the Caphthorim, who

[1] Knobel, *Völkertafel der Genesis*, pp. 221-225.

established themselves between Gaza and Gerar (novissima Libyæ). The end of the Saturnian age, to which Tacitus attributes these events, dates back as far as to that time. At the epoch in which Tacitus lived, Libya embraced the cities of Ostracine and Rhinocolura, and extended to Anthedon, where was the boundary separating it from Judæa on the north and Arabia Petræa on the east. Since Anthedon is the next place south of Gaza, this statement of Tacitus coincides exactly with the locality which the Caphthorim took from the Avim : the same district of which the young Egyptian who served as David's guide spoke as the country south of the Cherethites. But since the neighbouring city of Gaza bore a Cretan name, Steph. Byz. calling it *Μινώα*, the inference seems just, that the influence of the Cherethites or Cretans extended as far northward as to this the most southern of the Philistine cities; of which influence farther north there is not the slightest trace. The localities taken possession of by the Cretan portion of the afterwards united Philistine population are thus shown to have been on the extreme southern frontier. It is, however, a matter of uncertainty when the time of the Cretan immigration occurred; but, at all events, it was at the time of the judges, for during the lifetime of Moses the Avim were still dwelling in the neighbourhood of Gaza (Deut. ii. 23), or they had been so recently subdued by the warlike Caphthorim, that the event was held in fresh remembrance, and had an influence in controlling the choice of Israel on a way into the Promised Land— whether westward through the country recently seized by the powerful Cretans or Cherethites, or the route east of the Dead Sea. The sharp turn eastward which the Israelites took in the neighbourhood of the Red Sea, and which carried them through the country of the Moabites, may have been the result of these considerations. If Abimelech, the king of Gerar, the friend of Abraham, was really the king of the Philistines, as we might infer from Gen. xxvi. 1, 8, the immigration of the Cretans must have been long subsequent to that of the Philistines proper; for even in the time of Joshua there were living Avim in the southern part of Philistia who were yet unsubdued. The accession made to the strength of the Philistines by the incorporation with them of the Cherethites, is manifest from the fact, that at the close of the epoch of the judges, the enemies on the south-west of Israel had been so strong as to surpass it in power, and to hold it in continual alarm. The growth to which the Cherethites had attained then, and which gave such new vigour to the Philistine hosts, is hinted at by the equal prominence given to both the Cherethites and the `Pelethites in the sacred narrative.

There is an obscurity, however, resting upon the origin of the insular Cretans, who afterwards became a part of the Philistines. Knobel conjectures that they trace their origin to Caria, basing his supposition on the fact that, at the time of their invasion of Philistia, Minos the king of Crete had driven the Carians from the islands and from the Asiatic mainland, and they had entered military service under foreign rulers. (Pomp. *Mela,* i. 16 : Caria Habitator incertæ originis. Alii indigenos, sunt qui Pelasgos, quidam Cretas existimant. Genus usque eo quondam armorum pugnæque amans, ut aliena etiam bella mercede ageret.) Although, in his history of the Philistines, Hitzig cites the passage just quoted, and supports the view. that the Carians had an important connection with the people whose national development is his theme, yet, in his comments on Gen. x., he traces a subordinate distinction, to which I have not alluded—namely, that the Carians, or Pelasgic people which afterwards came to Philistia by way of Crete and Egypt, first planted themselves on the west bank of the Nile, and then passed, in conjunction with their neighbours the Casluhim, to Palestine. In this way Hitzig explains the origin of the Pelasgic word Valaxa.

To trace the Philistines proper back to a maritime stock, would seem to conflict, to a certain extent, with Deut. ii. 23, inasmuch as that passage appears to imply that the conquerors of the Avites, the Caphthorim, came directly by ship from their former home, without first settling in the western part of Egypt, and passing thence to Philistia. The biblical account is express, that the Cretans (Cherethites, Caphthorim) were the agents in subduing the Avites; and it is to be supposed, therefore, that the later tribe must have lived side by side with the Philistines, living even in Gerar and in the neighbourhood of Gaza, without coming into hostile conflict with them. They may have even lived on more friendly terms with these people of a common stock than with the Carian Cretans, who were strangers in the land. The connection between the Philistines proper and the Semitic Hyksos, is also a prominent objection to their origin as Pelasgic or Carian.

2. *The Philistines proper.*

The Philistim[1] of Gen. x. were also immigrants into the country which afterwards bore the name Philistia, and which extended from Gaza to Ekron. They found on their entrance that the land was peopled, the city of Gath for example, whose inhabitants put to death the Ephraimites (1 Chron. vii. 21), who wished to settle in that region; unless, with Munk,[2] the people who lived there be not considered the first generation of Philistine immigrants. We read in Gen. x. 19, that the early Canaanites extended from Sidon to Gerar and Gaza: it touched the territory of the Avites, therefore, who were reckoned among the old Canaanitic tribes inhabiting the neighbourhood of Beersheba; and whose territory, although a little way farther back from the sea than Gerar, yet was from the very earliest times a noted locality, for it was traversed by the great highways from the Arabian east and the Syrian west, the Assyrian and Canaanitish north and the Egyptian south. It was a district frequently chosen for the interviews of shepherd princes. With the inhabitants of southern Palestine and the southern Canaanites, who were driven out of their homes by the Israelites, several tribes of the same Semitic stock stood in close alliance, and for a long time contended for their homes. Among these were the Rephaim, the Anakim, the Kenites, Geshurites, Gergesites, and in especial the tribe of the Amalekites, who are spoken of both in Num. xxiv. 20 and in 1 Sam. xxvii. 8 as among the earliest of all existing tribes. Their ancient home was in and around the desert of Shur, whither Hagar fled from Sarah. The Amalekites were descended from Shem and his son Lud (Gen. x. 20), who went farther south than his brothers, Elam, Asshur, Aram, Arphaxad, who settled on the Euphrates and the Tigris. These descendants of Lud afterwards proved themselves unequal to the task of competing with the Assyrians (as we learn incidentally from the account

---

[1] Knobel, *Die Völkertafel*, pp. 201–214, 216–221. See Movers, *Phönizier*, pp. 28–39.
[2] Munk, *Palestine*, p. 83.

of the war of Chedorlaomer against the five allied Assyrian kings[1]), and were driven to the west; and although very much broken up into subordinate tribes, were driven hither and thither over the whole region between Lebanon and Egypt. Conspicuous among these subdivisions were the Amorites in the north, whose five kings are mentioned in Josh. x.; in the south the Amalekites, who belonged to those Ludites or primitive Arabians[2] who formed themselves into small political divisions,—all united, however, by the tie of a common language and the consciousness of a common origin. Hence their uniform traditions, that their primitive home was on the Erythræan Sea, and that they came thence, confirmed as it is by the Sinaitic inscriptions which Tuch[3] ascribes to a Semitic origin, and connects with those Amalekites who are mentioned in Ex. xvii. 8 as going forth boldly to meet Moses at Rephidim, and who are known by later inscriptions to have once had their home in the neighbourhood of Wadi Feiran. But the most ancient north Arabian and pre-Mohammedan authorities make this warlike tribe, "the oldest among the nations," to be in close alliance with the cities of western Canaan, with the ancient race of giants, with the Hyksos, the Philistines, and other valiant tribes of a cognate origin. With them were also connected the primitive inhabitants of Gath, the founders of Askelon and Azotus, and also several of the primitive Canaanite tribes, of whom, in truth, very little of historical authenticity is known. This may be the key to that worship of Baal which they shared with the Philistines, and the common diffusion of all their religious institutions.

While very few historical details[4] have been preserved regarding the immediate descendants of Lud, the primitive Semitic races, from which sprang the Arabians, sons of Joktan, the Abrahamic Hebrews, and other tribes; and while many of the early Canaanitic peoples passed away from the face of the earth, the Philistines, who had been crowded back as far as to

---

[1] Tuch, *Bemerkungen zu Genesis*, ch. xiv., in *Zeitsch. d. deutsch. morgenl. Ges.* Pt. i. pp. 161–165.

[2] Movers, *Die Phönizier*, vol. i. p. 4.

[3] Tuch, *Ein und zwanzig sinaitisch Inschriften, Versuch einer Erklarung*, in *Zeitsch. d. deutsch. morgenl. Ges.* vol. iii. pp. 145–151.

[4] Knobel, *Die Völkertafel*, pp. 168, 178, 214.

the Pelusiac branch of the Nile, began to be in the ascendant, and took a distinguished place in history, till the age of Solomon, when their power was effectually broken. But the older race is mentioned only casually, and with little of that fulness of detail with which the deeds of the Philistines are recounted. The five Amorite kings are only alluded to in connection with the victory gained over them: the more powerful tribe of Amalek, living farther southward, is named by the Old Testament historians only as a stubborn opponent of Israel; and it is to a man of their own race, who wrote in the times of the Mohammedan ascendancy, that the Amalekites are indebted for the chief glory which crowns their primitive history. I refer to Abulfeda, who asserts that the Amalekites once overran Egypt, and maintained their power there up to the time of Moses.

This story is unquestionably that which is connected in our minds with the traditions of the Hyksos, or shepherd kings spoken of by Manetho and Josephus, whose sway over Egypt continued for many years. They seem to have had much to do with the Philistines, but to have been long antecedent to the rise of the Israelitish power ; Salatis, the first of the Hyksos, reigning about 2100 years B.C., while the rule of king Menephthis,[1] under whom the Hebrews withdrew from the land, was as late as 1314. And Ewald[2] has shown that those shepherd kings must have come from no other lineage than from that of Eber, prior to the age of Abraham, and prior to the breaking up of the common Semitic stock, which gave the name of Ebrews or Hebrews to that little branch which reckoned from Abraham, and from which Israel sprang.

Movers[3] has remarked, that the study of the primitive Asiatic theology makes it more and more evident, that the more eminent of the deities recognised by the Semitic nations (and particularly by the Phœnicians, whose worship was much the same with that of the Philistines) repeated themselves in Egypt, and were concealed under the guise of animal forms. He asserts that this is only to be accounted for by a much longer continued influence exercised by Palestine upon Egypt than we have traces

---

[1] Lepsius, *Chronologie*, pp. 338, 358, etc.

[2] Ewald, *Gesch. des Volkes Israel*, i. pp. 327, 444, 450.

[3] Movers, *Die Phönizier*, vol. i. pp. 28, 33, etc.

of within a time less remote than the reign of the shepherd kings, protracted as it was during five hundred years. And it is a matter of historic certainty, that between 2000 and 1600 years B.C., Syrians or Phœnicians, coming from the district afterwards known as Philistia, settled among the Egyptians, but were afterwards driven violently from the land, and forced to take refuge in Numidia, Mauritania, and southern Æthiopia. Some of these refugees went northward, and Diodorus tells us of Danaus and Cadmus, who took their course across the Mediterranean, and established themselves in Greece. But at the time of the Hebrew patriarchs, the relation of the Asiatics to the Egyptians was so much changed, that, when trouble rose among the nomadic tribes of Palestine, they found a secure refuge on the Nile: this the history of Abraham and Jacob abundantly shows (Gen. xii. xlii.). The existence of a mutation in the relations between the people of Canaan and Egypt is clear, however, from the fact that Sarah, the wife of Abraham, held Hagar, an Egyptian woman, in servitude, and shows that there may have been such a development of strength in the nomadic tribes of the mountains, as to enable them to make sudden and successful invasions into Egypt, and carry off whom and what they would. The possession of Egyptian slaves by the Amalekites even down to the time of David, shows the formidable power of these wanderers; and we know that other tribes made the country insecure as far from Arabia Petræa as to the beginning of the Nile marshes.

All these things, and much besides,[1] lead to the conviction that the current of travel and invasion from the north-east towards Egypt in its most flourishing days was much stronger than we are accustomed to suppose, and than the special history of the Israelitish nation would give us reason to believe. The Hebrews were by no means the only people who penetrated to the valley of the Nile, and many Semitic tribes had prepared the way for them before they went thither.

Manetho tells us, that in about the year 2100 B.C., a warlike nomadic race came from Syria to Egypt, subjected the country, burned the cities, slew the men, and took the women and children into captivity. He informs us, moreover, that their king Salatis, whom they placed upon the throne at Memphis,

[1] Lepsius, *Chronologie der Ægypter*, pp. 323, 338.

and who made the whole country pay tribute to him, secured
the eastern frontier against the Assyrians, and against any
warlike races who might follow him over the road which he
had taken, by building the great city of Abaris[1] near Pelusium.
Josephus called this nation which ruled over Egypt for five
centuries Hyksos,—a term of Coptic origin, and meaning
shepherd kings; Josephus translates it as Βασιλεῖς ποιμένες.
Manetho, following Jul. Africanus and Eusebius, called them
Phœnicians. Josephus has made them interchangeable with
the later Jews. Manetho himself said, that they were taken
by many to be Arabians; but they were evidently that people,
of primitive Semitic origin, which Ewald considered as pre-
Abrahamic Hebrews, from whom Abaris (Eberis) received its
name as an Ebrew or Hebrew stronghold. Not only does the
evident Semitic origin of the word throw light upon its Asiatic
derivation; but Egyptian monuments, sculptures, and pictures
representing the expulsion of the shepherd kings by Misphragmuthosis and his followers, show convincingly that western
Asia was the country whence they came.[2]

Tacitus was under a mistake in supposing these invaders to
have been Assyrians, in the later sense of that word; a par-
donable error, since these shepherd conquerors, as well as the
old Semitic tribes driven westward by them, the Ludites and
others, from whom they sprang, belonged to the red-complexioned races, towards whom the Egyptians felt the most intense national hatred. That Manetho called them Phœnicians
involves no real contradiction, remarks Movers, since the country
whence they came, and whither they were driven back, lying
east of the Pelusiac Nile, and at Casiotis, the later Philistia,
was sometimes reckoned by the Romans as belonging to Arabia,
and sometimes to Syria Palestina. This complexity especially
occurred in connection with the district of the ancient Philistim, on the ancient frontier of Egypt between Kadesh and
Shur. These red-complexioned men, the Erythræans, had set
up among the Egyptian idols their red-faced Typhon[3] as their
representative, and who was believed by the Egyptians to be a

---

[1] Tuch, *Bemerkungen zu Genesis*, chap. xiv., in *Zeitsch. d. deutsch. morgenl. Ges.* Pt. i. pp. 161–166.

[2] Rosenmüller, *Bibl. Alterthk.* vol. iii. p. 310.

[3] Lepsius, *Chronol. der Ægypter*, p. 342.

cruel tyrant, who had conquered the holy land of Osiris, and to whom human sacrifices were brought. We are told by Herodotus that this arch-enemy of Egypt was slain on Lake Sirbonis by a thunderbolt; for up to that limit the Hyksos had been driven back. Their great camp of twenty-four thousand armed men, which Salatis had formed at Abaris, or perhaps rather the neighbouring city of Pelusium, became the Typhonium, situated in the Sethroitic Nomos, which received its Egyptian name, in all probability, from Seth or Typhon.

When, at the end of the Hyksos dynasty, after a long contest between the kings of Upper Egypt and these shepherd kings of Lower Egypt, this powerful and hostile race had been driven from the land, the legitimate ruler, Misphragmuthosis,[1] pursued them to the important stronghold of Abaris. This place he was not able to take: he therefore made terms with the enemy, and suffered them to withdraw with all their possessions to Syria.

This triumph, the record of which appears to be portrayed in the great reliefs of the temple of Karnak, is also touched upon, though in a mythical and distorted way, by the great Roman historian Tacitus (*Histor.* v. 2): quidam, regnante Iside [*i.e.* after the re-establishment of the original dynasty] sc. dicunt, exundantem per Ægyptum multitudinem, ducibus Hierosolymo ac Juda, proximas in terras exoneratam . . .; and then again: sunt qui tradant, Assyrios convenas [*i.e.* the Hyksos] indigum agrorum populum parte Ægypti potitos, mox proprias urbes, Hebræasque terras et propriora Syriæ coluisse rura.

On these grounds, Movers[2] formed a decided opinion that these people, who were thus driven back, now no longer a race of shepherd kings, but a nomadic race, were the Philistines, who settled in Palestine, or, if not the whole of that nation, at least a portion of it; for other parts—who, perhaps, had no permanent home in the coast region near by—may have gone farther eastward, as we may conjecture from the account given by Manetho, and the brief allusion by Tacitus.

We thus learn the reason why the Egyptian translators of the Bible always apply the term Allophyloi to the ancient Philis-

---

[1] Lepsius, *Chronol. der Ægypter*, p. 338; Rosenmüller, *Bibl. Alterthk.* iii. p. 310.

[2] Movers, *Die Phönizier*, i. p. 35.

tines. It is unquestionably a traditional word, always current in the language, and testifying to the oppression which their ancestors were supposed to have suffered centuries before at the hands of the ancestors of these Philistines. It is to be supposed that, at the expulsion of the Hyksos, many classes of people chose to accompany them, just as we learn from Ex. xii. 38, and from Num. xi. 4, that a mixed multitude, of which we have no future trace, followed the Israelites on their exit from Egypt.[1]

That in the Lower Egyptian empire established by the Hyksos, the hated builders of the pyramids, whose names even the Egyptians were unwilling to speak, there were traces of the existence then of the Philistines, appears from the mention in Herodotus' narrative of the shepherd Philitis, who pastured his herds close by the pyramids, and after whom those piles were said to be named; and this account chimes with the ancient name given to the Philistines, indicating their wandering, nomadic turn.

Unconnected, fragmentary, and mythical as are the most of the brief data presented above, which have to serve in the place of a coherent and authentic narrative, they are of some value in determining the origin of the Philistim, and in showing their connection with that very ancient colony which came from the east, and established itself in the neighbourhood of Pelusium, Casiotis, and Abaris, whence they are to be traced at a later period, on their return to the east. That the Philistines are to be traced to the people who had formerly been the oppressors of Egypt, and who, after their expulsion, naturally lost the name of shepherd kings and took a new appellation, can hardly be doubted, although data are wanting which allow us to determine the time within five hundred years when they established themselves in the district between Judah and Egypt. It is certain that the Hyksos were expelled from Egypt long before the Israelites left that land; and it is just as certain that the settlement, then fairly effected, of the Philistines in the southern portion of the country afterwards to bear the name of Palestine, contributed not a little to the determination of Moses not to lead the Israelites over the direct road into Canaan, which must have been familiarly known to him and

[1] Ewald, *Gesch. des Volks Israel*, ii. p. 64; Lepsius, *i.a.l.* p. 324.

to his countrymen from the traditions of the times of Abraham
and Jacob,—the road which led by way of Gaza and Gerar,
or Beersheba,—but to take them over a very circuitous route.
For in the district which lay exactly in his path there was a
powerful, warlike, and thoroughly trained nation, which he was
in no condition to meet with his undisciplined forces,—an agricultural people, knowing nothing of the art of war, and needing
just the training which their long encampment in the wilderness gave them. We have the proof of this in Ex. xiii. 17 :
" And it came to pass, when Pharaoh had let the people go,
that God led them not through the way of the land of the
Philistines, although that was near ; for God said, Lest perad-
venture the people repent when they see war, and they return
to Egypt." It is certain, therefore, that at that time, even
if not during the life of Abraham, and the period of his
friendly intercourse with Abimelech (Gen. xx., xxi.), the
Philistines were scattered over the whole territory southward
of Gaza, and lying towards the Egyptian frontier ; otherwise
Moses would not have turned his course southward[1] at Ra-
meses, Succoth, and Etham, on the very edge of the desert.
But whether the Philistines were then masters of the more
northern cities which afterwards came into their possession,
is more doubtful, since, according to Josh. xv. 46, Ekron,
Ashdod, Gaza, and all the country as far as to the river of
Egypt, were reckoned[2] as belonging to Canaan, and were
assigned as a part of the territory of Judah ; which can only
mean that that district was considered as a part of the country
formerly occupied by the Canaanites, before they were driven
out by the Philistine invaders. According to Judg. i. 18,
Gaza, Askelon, and Ekron were actually in subjection to the
tribe of Judah, yet the Bible is not clear as to just how much
is meant by that. The allusion made in the introduction to
the book of Judges can hardly be intended to imply that those
cities were in the complete possession of the Israelites : for in
the old age of Joshua, and just before his death (xiii. 3), there
remained five lords of the Philistines yet unconquered ; and
in the next chapter, giving the account of what immediately
followed his death, we are told that the Hebrews did not know

---

[1] Ewald, *Gesch. des Volks Israel,* ii. p. 54, i. p. 290.
[2] Keil, *Comment. zu Josua,* p. 241.

how to carry on war. And we are told in Judg. iii. 2, that in order that the children of Israel might learn the art of war, there were left five lords of the Philistines and the Sidonians. That, in the account of the conquest of those south-western cities by Judah after the death of Joshua, no special mention is made of the Philistines, affords no sufficient proof that they were not there, where, according to Josh. xi. 21, the sons of Anak, when pursued by Joshua, found a place of refuge. And it is plain, from the direct allusions to the Philistines in the verse quoted above, that they were there at an early period,[1] and could not have come subsequently by sea from Crete. The hypothesis that they did so come, arises from the subsequent arrival within the Philistine territory of the people of Caphthor, and the confounding of these new-comers with the true Philistines. All difficulties which are suggested are solved by the happy conjecture that the nation of the Philistines, as known during the age of the judges and subsequently, was composed of these two originally disunited elements, thoroughly fused,—the primitive continental people, and the subsequent insular addition. The fact that a race of people of kindred origin with the Israelites occupied the country which they were subsequently to conquer, and that this race was filled not with friendship, but with hate, is made evident by Moses' hymn of praise sung after the safe passage of Israel through the Red Sea, and contained in Ex. xv. 14, where, in the allusion made to the inhabitants of Palestina, the Philistines are expressly meant. Ewald, in order to maintain the position which he takes, endeavours to show that this song was thrown into its present form not on the shores of the Red Sea, but in Canaan.

If the Philistim proper formed a part of the great Semitic hordes, the descendants of Lud, who poured from east to west in the age of the Hyksos, and after the expulsion of the latter again drew towards their old eastern home, and took possession of the territory adjacent to that of the southern Canaanite tribes, long centuries[2] must have intervened, and made it not at all improbable that, at the time of Abraham's sojourn in Gerar, the relations between the Hebrews and Philistines were of a wholly friendly character. That this was the case, we

---

[1] Ewald, *Gesch. des Volks Israel*, i. p. 291.
[2] Movers, *Phönizier*, i. pp. 4, 17, ii. p. 258.

learn from several striking passages in Genesis, regarding Abraham's and Isaac's communication with Abimelech at Gerar and Beersheba. The friendly character of those communications have awakened many doubts whether the people over whom Abimelech ruled was the same warlike tribe of Philistines, whose later enmity to the Israelites was the source of so much bitter feeling and such protracted wars.

Ewald, the critical, thorough, and genial student of the old covenant, admits[1] that there are several indirect proofs of great antiquity, that the Philistines were in possession of the southern portion of Canaan as early as the times of the first patriarchs. Still, he adds, the expressions which indicate this are none of them of Philistine origin, and seem to have been recorded after having passed through a long course of oral tradition. In accordance with his theory, he seeks to diminish the force of Gen. xxvi., in which Abimelech is called at the time of Isaac the king of the Philistines, by endeavouring to show that this chapter was so far modified at a subsequent period, as to receive these words in addition to its original contents. His reason for supposing this to have been the case, is that Abimelech is not called in the history of Abraham the king of the Philistines, but the king of Gerar. But Keil,[2] the commentator upon Joshua, remarks in reply, that Ewald overlooks the fact that in chap. xxi. 32, 33—verses which are admitted by all to be unchanged from their original form—the country of Abimelech is called the land of the Philistines, and its king is shown distinctly to have been a ruler of Philistines. Knobel the commentator, upon the list of tribes contained in Genesis, takes the ground that in Gen. xx. 1 there is no allusion[3] to the Philistines, but that the people dwelling then at Gerar were Canaanitic Avites, to whom the name of Philistines was applied at a later period, because the remains of that tribe were afterwards absorbed by the Philistine stock. But if the inhabitants of Gerar and its neighbourhood were genuine Philistines, he adds, they did not then inhabit the country extending from Gaza to Ekron. Dwelling upon this threshold to the subsequent Philistia, they went through that

---

[1] Ewald, *Gesch. des Volks Israel*, i. p. 289.
[2] Keil, *Comment. zu Josua*, Note 3, p. 243.
[3] Knobel, *Die Völkertafel der Genesis*, p. 218.

course of training which lasted for centuries, extending to the
time of Joshua, their princes combining in an alliance for
mutual defence[1] (they were not kings—a term unknown to
the Philistines), and proved themselves brave soldiers, and
occasional victors. Strengthened probably at the time of the
judges by the incorporation of the valiant Cretans (Cherethites)
who had landed upon their shores, they were able at once to
pass to a position of ascendancy over Israel, which they held
until they were overthrown by the combined forces of David,
after which they had to be content with the glory which they
might gain as his body-guard. Although these Philistines, like
the whole group of Semitic tribes with which they were connected, were held, like the Hyksos, in utter abomination by the
Hebrews, the Egyptians, and even the cognate Arabian tribes,
as godless barbarians, and were detested particularly by the
Israelites as heathenish blasphemers, because they did not practise the rite of circumcision (Judg. xiv. 3, xv. 18 ; 1 Sam.
xiv. 6, xvii. 26), yet they were by no means that rude and
savage race which they are generally pictured to have been.

The just and magnanimous character of Abimelech, displayed in his dealings with Abraham, his recognition of the
latter as a man of God (Gen. xxi. 22), and the permission
which he gave to Abraham to dwell in the neighbourhood of
Beersheba, shows that there were kindly sentiments once
cherished by the Philistines towards the Israelites, although
they were subsequently extinguished by the hatred which
divided the two cognate races. This hatred may be seen in its
early stages, in the jealousy with which the Philistine herdsmen
regarded the herdsmen of Isaac, and in the stopping of the wells
which the latter had digged in Gerar (Gen. xxvi. 17–33). In
consequence of the envy which broke out then among the
serving-men, Isaac was compelled to withdraw from Gerar and
encamp near Beersheba. The serious nature of these early
encounters, of which we now know so little, gave intensity
to that deadly hatred which afterwards arose between the
Philistines and the Israelites, and led to wars which lasted for
centuries.

It is plain from the allusion to Phicol, the leader of Abimelech's army, that the Philistines were a warlike people as early

[1] Keil, *Commentar zu Josua*, p. 242.

as the days of Abraham. In the representations which still exist in Thebes of the siege of Abaris, when it was the refuge of the Hyksos, whose armies were probably replenished with Philistine auxiliaries, the latter, as well as the Egyptian besiegers, are represented as being supplied with admirable and skilfully constructed chariots. The shepherd kings, who knew how to use this formidable engine of war, and who were associated with this warlike tribe from Canaan, were the builders of the Egyptian pyramids themselves. The Philistines understood the art of constructing armour at a time when the Israelites were utterly unskilled in it. Deborah tells us in her song (Judg. v. 8), that there were forty thousand men in Israel then without shield and spear. At the time of Samuel, when the Philistines advanced against Michmash in three great bodies (1 Sam. xiii. 19–22), we are told that, " in the day of battle, there was neither sword nor spear found in the hand of any of the people that were with Saul and Jonathan; but with Saul, and with Jonathan his son, was there found. There was no smith found throughout all the land of Israel; for the Philistines said, Lest the Hebrews make them swords or spears : but all the Israelites went down to the Philistines to sharpen every man his share, and his coulter, and his axe, and his mattock."

The combination of the five princes of Philistia, their training in arms, their laws and institutions, ensured the Philistines dominion over the Israelites for forty years. This ended with their defeat at Mizpeh (1 Sam. vii. 13), though for centuries they were able to defend their narrow line of sea-coast from the attacks of the Syrians under Sanherib, of the Egyptians under Necho, of the Israelites under the judges, of the Scythians, and many other powerful nations. When, in the time of Samuel, they pressed victoriously to Gilgal and the Jordan, their forces consisted, according to 1 Sam. xiii. 5, of thirty thousand chariots, six thousand horsemen, and a multitude like the sand of the sea for number.

In their own country, the Philistines practised agriculture, and the culture of the vine and of olives; they kept herds of cattle; and they built walled cities, five of which became eminent as the residences of the leading princes, whose alliance gave such power against the Israelite invaders. In these five most important cities there was no lack of temples, pillars, and sculptured memorials. Here, too, they kept their gods, excepting when they went forth to war, on which occasions they seem to have taken them with them; for we read in 2 Sam. v. 21, that David, after having gained a victory over the Philistines in the valley of Rephaim, and put them to flight, destroyed their idols. Nor was there any greater deficiency in the number of their priests, soothsayers, and magicians, than in the kindred Phœnician worship; and their oracle, Baal-zebub of Ekron, was held in esteem beyond the Philistine frontier (2 Kings i. 2). Although their situation on the Mediterranean was so favourable for commerce, the Philistines seem never to have carried it on; they appear to have left this entirely to their Phœnician neighbours. The situation of all their cities shows that they were built with no reference to the sea; for none of them, Ashkelon excepted, was built on the coast, and even this appears to owe whatever maritime eminence it had to the pre-Philistian period. Whether this want of a commercial character is to be attributed to the want of wood, or to the envy of the Phœnicians, or to the piracy which was so common among the Carians, the Egyptians, and the Phœnicians, or whether it rose from the preference of an agricultural and shepherd life, conjoined with the arts of war as it was, to the fascinations of commerce, cannot now be determined. There was no lack of industry among the Philistines. There has been a suspicion started, but only a suspicion, that their continued enmity to Israel was the effect of rivalry at seeing their business of transferring goods across Canaan taken out of their hands. It must be confessed, however, that the nature of their life and occupations would fit them not ill for the duty of conducting caravans; yet history throws no light upon the matter.

At all events, it is singular that they never seem to have come into hostile collision with the Phœnician settlements in their neighbourhood—Joppa, Dor, and even the places which, though Philistine as we mostly know them, were founded by the Phœnicians—Jabneh, Ashdod, Ashkelon, and Gaza. Notwithstanding that these places afterwards were transferred to new rulers, and the great roads which connected them came under the rule of the Philistines, yet the Phœnicians seem to have always enjoyed free access to the country, and the undisputed right of transit through it. With the exception of a quarrel between Ashkelon and Sidon prior to the founding of Tyre, of which Justinus gives us a brief account, there is no mention of any collision between the Philistines and the Phœnicians; and the Jewish prophets, in their threatened judgments on Tyre and Sidon, always award the Philistines a similar condemnation for complicity with them (Jer. xlvii. 4; Zech. ix. 2-6). ، Perhaps we might gain further light regarding this, however, if we knew more about their religious opinions and observances, as well as about their language, than we are able to glean. Ewald, the most distinguished investigator in this field, thinks that there was a similarity between the Hebrew, the Philistine, and the Canaanitic tongues, since they all sprang from a common stock—the Semitic; and that there were, as is seen in the passage cited by Nehemiah, dialectical differences between the last two and the language current in Jerusalem.[1]

[1] Ewald, *Gesch. des Volks Israel,* i. p. 294.

CHAPTER III.

THE ROUTE FROM THE DESERT OF ET-TIH TO HEBRON AND BETHLEHEM:

BY THE WAY, ON THE EAST, OF WADI ARARA (AROER); AND ON THE WEST, OF WADI EL KHALIL.

E have already had occasion to speak of the two routes which lead from the Sinai Peninsula into the southern part of Palestine. One of these is that which was taken by Seetzen, and which passes by the wells of Bir es Seba, the Beersheba of Abraham: the other lies somewhat farther eastward, and was the route taken by Robinson, von Schubert, Russegger, and others. It leads over the outlying ranges of hills to the outlying mountains, whose height continually advances, and which form the natural southern frontier of the Promised Land. After passing that barrier, we reach a country entirely different from that on the south, with different physical aspects, and with a different population, and we are fairly introduced to Palestine.

It is at the parting of the two roads—the one of which runs westward from the neighbourhood of Arara (Aroer) towards Gaza, and the other of which runs northward to Milh (Malatha, Moladah)—that the first decided change in the character of the scenery occurs in the eastern route, while in the western it may be traced in the tract lying between the well of el-Khuweilifeh and the high village of Dhoheriyeh. Russegger took very careful observations to determine the gradual increase in elevation as we advance from the desert of Edom to the high mountain-land of Judæa. The results of his inquiries, briefly stated,[1] are as follows:

---

[1] Russegger, in Poggendorff's *Annalen*, vol. liii. p. 186.

El-Khulasa (the ancient Elusa),	.	661 feet above the sea.
Jebel Roechy, ...	.	987 ,,
Bir es Saba (Beersheba),	. .	1032 ,,
Jebel Khalil, ...	.	1550 ,,
The village Dhoheriyeh, .	. .	2040 ,,
Hebron, ...	.	2842 ,,

DISCURSION I.

THE ROAD FROM THE DESERT OF ET-TIH TO HEBRON, LEAVING WADI ARARA (AROER), AND PASSING MILH (MOLADAH), GHUWEIN (ANIM), SEMUA (ESHTEMOA), AND YUTTA (JUTTA).

Robinson, on his return from Petra, passed a night in June 1838 among the ruins of Wadi Arara,[1] the site, according to his best judgment, of the ancient city of Aroer, on the southern border of Judah, to whose inhabitants, as well as to those of Jattir and Eshtemoa, David gave a portion of the spoil which he took from the Amalekites at Ziklag (1 Sam. xxx. 26). On the next morning Robinson pursued his course an hour farther on, arriving at the walled well of el-Milh,[2] in which he recognised the long-forgotten Moladah of the Old Testament, and the more recently fortified Roman stronghold of Malatha. Thence he prosecuted his journey in a north-north-east direction towards Hebron, passing Semua and the naked rocky mountain ridge.[3]

On the latter he had reached a new stage in the gradual ascent from the Dead Sea to Hebron. By a careful examination of the list of cities assigned to the tribes of Judah and Simeon recorded in Josh. xv. 48–60, and comparing the groups into which the list is divided, he conjectured that those which had already been identified lay north of the place where he then was; and that those whose location was undetermined lay either behind him or to his left, and southward in that quarter. This conjecture was fully verified by the results of his subsequent investigations.[4] But before commencing the search for ruins and antiquities, he was led to this general thesis, that the ridge which begins not far from Kurmul (Carmel), north-

---

[1] Ritter's *Erdkunde*, xiv. p. 1085.
[2] Wilson, *Lands of the Bible*, i. p. 347.
[3] Robinson, *Bib. Research.* ii. p. 203.
[4] Keil, *Commentar zu Josua*, pp. 290–306.

east of Semua, and runs w.s.w. to Beersheba, is the natural boundary of the high-land region, the mountain district of Judah, while the low land lying south of this ridge, and around Beersheba, contained the cities which lay on the borders of the Edomite territory (Josh. xv. 20-32). In the dry season, when Robinson was there, it is true that this gradually rising district was mostly bare and desolate, and looking towards the west his eye fell upon rocks unpromising indeed to look upon; but, on the other hand, he could not fail to see much good pasturage, and here and there were traces of the habitations of men, and of a former terrace culture. Towards noon of the same day he saw in some fields of oats traces of recent buildings lying between the ruins of el-Ghuwein and those of Attir, a little to the left.

Robinson believes el-Ghuwein to be the Ain which was granted to the Levites as one of their cities (Josh. xxi. 6), and which was first one of the cities of Judah, but was afterwards given with some others to the tribe of Simeon (Josh. xv. 32, xix. 7). But el-Ghuwein lies too far north, and too decidedly in the mountain region, to be rightly reckoned as one of the group of cities which were in the southern part of Judæa, and serious doubts[1] arose regarding the accuracy of Robinson's conjecture. These doubts were confirmed by Wilson, who does not regard el-Ghuwein as Ain,[2] but as the Anim (Josh. xv. 50) whose situation would naturally occur in direct relation with Jattir, now Attir; Socoh, now Shuweikeh; Anab, a little farther north; and Eshtemoa, now Semua. Anim, according to Wilson, is only a contraction for Ainim, *i.e.* the springs, and can pass just as well into the form Ghuwein as Ain. In fact, it is very common for a plural Hebrew word to be reproduced in the Arabic in the singular, as Adoraim, Anathoth, and Mahanaim, for example, which we have in the modern Dura, Anata, Mahaneh.

The ruins of Attir, which Robinson saw on a hill at the west, but which he was unable to visit, correspond fully, so far as we can judge, to the site of Jattir,[3] which was given to the Levites (Josh. xv. 48, xxi. 14). At the time of Jerome (*Onom. s.v. Jether*) it was a large Christian village twenty

---

[1] Keil, *Comment. zu Josua*, p. 294, Note, and pp. 335, 367.

[2] Wilson, *Lands of the Bible*, i. pp. 352-354.

[3] Keil, *Comment. zu Josua*, p. 300.

Roman miles s.s.e. from Eleutheropolis, and near to Molatha (the Old Testament Moladah, and the present el-Milh).

After leaving Ghuwein, Robinson continued his journey northward, and in about forty minutes reached the ruins of a castle with a high tower. The place bears the name of Semua,[1] and was apparently one of the outposts of the crusaders. It lies 2225 feet above the sea. Here Robinson discovered the site of the ancient Eshtemoh or Eshtemoa (Josh. xv. 50). This, too, was originally a city of Judah, afterwards transferred to the Levites (Josh. xxi. 14). At the time of Jerome it was the largest of the villages which belonged to the Jews, and which were comprised within the diocese of Eleutheropolis. At a later period it had lost all that had once distinguished it, and had been completely forgotten, although Seetzen inserted the name Semua in his map.

The identification of the site of Eshtemoa or Eshtemoh with the present ruins of Semua is very important in relation to the special topography of southern Judæa, since it enables us to trace the outlines of the mountain territory occupied by the first group of eleven cities mentioned in Josh. xv. 48-51. It tends powerfully to establish the historical authenticity of the ancient Hebrew records, even in their minutest details, and affords an invaluable key to unlock the history of the Israelitish nation. The help thus afforded is all the more to be prized from its unexpectedness; and the tracing the survival of the Hebrew language in the Arabic words of the present day, must lead to discoveries of undoubted worth in the field already so successfully opened. It is true that, out of the eleven cities mentioned in the group of which we now speak,[2] only five are yet identified; the location of Shamir, Dannah, Goshen, Holon, and Giloh, is entirely unknown; that of Kirjath-sannah, or Debir, is with some probability conjectured to be near el-Burj; while the sites of Jattir, Socoh, Anab, Eshtemoa, and Anim have been handed down in the speech of men for more than three thousand years. The light which comes from what we are able to know in this way, enables us to pick our way where we have no other guidance.

In Semua (Eshtemoa), where Robinson tarried only for an

---

[1] See Roberts, *Views in the Holy Land*, Book viii. No. 45.

[2] Keil, *Comment. zu Josua*, pp. 300, 301.

hour at midday, von Schubert encamped [1] for the night in the month of March. During the evening the men of the village brought into his tent eggs, sour milk, fresh and palatable bread and butter, for all of which they asked but a trifling price. While he ate, they crouched around him and smoked tobacco. One of the men pointed out several good springs at the foot of a neighbouring rock, and told them that within a short distance there were seven others of the same kind; and the gardens full of olive, fig, and pistachio nuts testified to an ample supply of water. An olive grove grew around the whole place; a hill near by was crowned with the remains of a temple-shaped edifice, which Schubert supposed to be of Roman construction; down the wadi, looking southward, he could see the shepherd leading home the sheep for the night; and altogether it was like a glimpse back into the patriarchal times of Abraham.

Robinson, who examined the vicinity very closely from the same height, saw in an E.N.E. direction, Main, the ancient Maon, where the rich Nabal lived. It lies on the border of the desert of Judah, and belongs to the third group of the cities mentioned [2] in Josh. xv. 55, extending as far eastward as to the Dead Sea. Towards the north-east lay Kurmul (Carmel), which he subsequently visited; and still farther north, upon a hill, was Yutta, the ancient Juttah, a city of the Levites (Josh. xv. 55).

Hebron could not be seen from Semua, but Dhoheriyeh could be discerned in the west, a station on the Beersheba road, of which I have elsewhere spoken. Much nearer, Robinson could descry Shuweikeh, the ancient Socoh, one of the group of mountain cities mentioned in Josh. xv. 48.

On setting out on his journey towards Hebron, the American traveller reached in three-quarters of an hour the ruins of Yutta, whose ancient foundation stones probably indicate the home of Zacharias and Elisabeth. It is now a large village on a low hill, surrounded by trees. The inhabitants of the place, who are Mohammedans, [3] have no knowledge of the fact, that their town was hallowed by the birth of John the Baptist, the greatest prophet in the kingdom of God, and who, to employ the words of my dear departed friend Neander, had the high mission

---

[1] Von Schubert, *Reise in das Morgenland*, ii. p. 458.

[2] Robinson, *Bib. Research.* ii. pp. 205, 202, i. p. 494.

[3] *Ibid.* ii. p. 206; von Schubert, *Reise*, ii. p. 460.

of forming the boundary stone between the old and the new covenant, and the bridge to lead from one to the other. Robinson remarks, that at Yutta he had reached a far greater height than that occupied by Carmel, although so near.[1] These observations led him to the discovery of the third group of cities,[2] mentioned in Josh. xv. 55-57. These ten cities lie north of the first group, or that lying on the Judah hills and east of the second group, of which Hebron forms the middle point. Juttah is the centre of the third group. In this one, although the identity of the modern Arabic designations with the primitive Hebrew ones is not always to be traced, there is evidence enough, in the etymology of names yet existing, to prove decisively their Hebrew origin. Of six of the cities mentioned in Joshua—Jezreel, Jokdeam, Sanoah, Cain, Gibeah, and Timnah—nothing is known excepting their names: they evidently have little historic importance. On the other hand, the four most important of those ten cities—Maon, Carmel, Juttah, and Ziph (Tell Ziph)—are fully identified with localities still traceable.[3]

DISCURSION II.

THE ROUTE FROM THE DESERT OF ET-TIH TO HEBRON, BY WAY OF WADI ES SEBA (BEERSHEBA), WADI EL KHALIL, AND THE VILLAGE OF DHOHERIYEH.

The more westerly route from the desert of et-Tih runs by way of Beersheba and Dhoheriyeh to Hebron. It was taken by Robinson, Russegger, and Abeken on their way from Sinai to Jerusalem.

Wilson[4] is the only traveller who has taken the eastern route from Arara (Aroer), and instead of going north by way of el-Milh (Moladah), has taken a north-westerly direction to Wadi el Khulil, and has showed conclusively that two or three hours' distance from Arara the two routes unite in a fine rolling tract of pasture land called Wadi Seba, in which, two

---

[1] Piper, *Evangelischer Kalender*, 1851, p. 66.
[2] Keil, *Comment. zu Josua*, pp. 302, 303.
[3] Comp. Robinson, *Bib. Research.* ii. p. 205 ; and von Schubert, *Reise*, ii. p. 460.
[4] Wilson, *Lands of the Bible*, i. p. 349.

hours' distance southward, Bir es Seba, the ancient Beersheba, lies.

At this place Robinson encamped on the 12th of April 1838, and had the pleasure of pitching his tent, for the first time after traversing the desert, on a bit of what might be called grass land. The place is twelve good hours with the camel from Hebron. Here he saw the ancient wells and ruins, which carried him back to the days of Abraham; and on the next day he advanced on his journey northward.

On the 13th of April[1] he reached the well of Khuweilifeh, lying in a wadi of the same name. Here his eye, long unused to such forms of beauty, was regaled with the sight of flowers of a deep scarlet hue, and of patches of grain. The song of birds gave new delight to the fine spring morning, and the prospect which he was permitted to survey embraced the distant hills of Judah. At seven o'clock he crossed the road running from Gaza to Wadi Musa (Petra and Maon), and two hours later he was at the end of the plain : the hills were near at hand, and he entered the Wadi el Khulil, *i.e.* the Hebron valley. Here he saw the plough used for the first time—a very simply contrived one indeed, but superior to the one which he had seen in Egypt. From that point began a steeper and more rocky road, along which, however, a few trees were found, especially the pistachio and the terebinth of the Old Testament. As he advanced along the road, the barren sides of the wadi displayed some traces of having formerly been terraced and carefully cultivated ; but now the soil was given over to flocks of sheep and goats belonging to the people of Dhoheriyeh. The sight of these was a most grateful one to the traveller, who for thirty days had traversed a continuous desert.[2]

The village of Dhoheriyeh lies high, 2040 feet above the sea, and is seen from almost every direction. It is now a mere cluster of stone huts ; and, in fact, some of the houses are mere cellars, or rude excavations in the earth. Some have squared stones at their entrance, which apparently once belonged to a castle there, of which some collective ruins are still traceable. This was probably one of a series of fortresses whose object was to protect the southern frontier of Judæa, not only in the more

[1] Robinson, *Bib. Research.* i. pp. 207–209.
[2] Comp. Robinson, *Bib. Research.* i. p. 209 ; Russegger, *Reise,* iii. p. 72.

ancient times of Judah, but during the more modern Byzantine epoch ; for it is hardly supposable that a position so important, upon one of the great southern roads, should ever be allowed to remain undefended.

The village included, at the time of Robinson's visit, a hundred men capable of bearing arms, thirty-eight of whom had, at three separate times, been impressed for the Egyptian army. It lay half in ruins, but was rich in herds, and possessed at least a hundred camels. The inhabitants called the place Hüdhr, or Hadhr, *i.e.* " city people," in contradistinction to the Beduins, or rangers of the desert, with whom they are in perpetual contention. The number and the excellence of their flocks and cattle, afforded proof that the excellence of the pasturage in the old patriarchal times still remains. The want of trees, and the prominence of limestone crags, make the soil seem more sterile than it really is ; for in the valleys and low places in the neighbourhood tilled land can be seen.[1]

This place is generally considered to be the site of the ancient Beth Zacharia,[2] the place where the battle of the young king Antiochus Eupator and Judas Maccabæus took place, described in 1 Macc. vi. 31–51. The evidence in favour of this identity is very full and conclusive. The ruins, which are alluded to by many travellers, may be of much earlier construction than the times of the Maccabees, and may date back to the times of Habakkuk ; while the tower, whose remains are still seen, may not go back beyond the Roman and Byzantine epochs.[3]

The road from Dhoheriyeh to Hebron [4] follows the broad top of the ridge known as the Judah mountains, and not very far from the highest peak. This ridge is intersected by several short wadis, which either run eastwardly down into the great Wadi el Khulil, which extends from Hebron in a south-westwardly direction to the open plain where lie the remains of Beersheba, or westwardly to the wadis of Philistia. This Judah

---

[1] Comp. Wilson, *Lands of the Bible*, i. pp. 350–355.

[2] From a MS. of Dr Krafft, 1845. Comp. F. A. Strauss, *Sinai und Golgotha*, p. 197.

[3] Comp. von Raumer, *Pal.* p. 163 ; and the *Chronicon Pascale*, ed. L. Dindorf. vol. i. pp. 151, 282.

[4] Robinson, *Bib. Research.* ii. pp. 212, 213 ; Russegger, *Reise*, iii. p. 74 ; Wilson, *Lands of the Bible*, i. p. 355.

ridge forms the great watershed between the Mediterranean and the Dead Seas, upon whose southern culmination stands Dhoheriyeh, and upon whose northern one is Hebron.

From the height of Dhoheriyeh Robinson descended by a steep path into a deep gorge, and then passed over hills covered with bushes, oaks, and the *arbutus unedo.* After three hours he reached a spring of fine living water, the first since leaving the desert. He then passed some caverns by the side of the road, used during the summer time by the peasants who had left the villages to tend cattle among the hills. Soon after he reached a second spring, whose waters passed into a reservoir of squared stones ; and fifteen minutes later he came to a rippling brook, the first one which he had seen since leaving the shore of the Nile. He soon entered the Wadi el Delbeh, where lay the ruins of the village ed-Daumeh. Five hours more took him over a hill covered with bushes, into a narrow valley where olive trees were growing, and where an enclosed vineyard gave notice of the approach to Hebron, which he soon reached.

All travellers who have taken this route to Hebron speak of the great improvement in the art of agriculture which is observable just before they reach the city, and enter the olive plantations and vineyards which cover all the adjacent slopes.

DISCURSION III.

HEBRON, THE CITY OF THE PATRIARCHS—KIRJATH-ARBA OF THE ANAKIMS— EL-KHALIL OF THE ARABS.

Hebron lies in a deep valley, which, about two and a half miles northward of it, widens [1] out into level country, and which runs from N.N.W. to S.S.E. At the northern part it is broad, and affords room for many vineyards ; but it narrows as it approaches the city, and the mountains grow higher. The houses of Hebron are built either in the valley, or on the lower part of the slopes around. The view of the city, both from the north [2] and from the south, [3] is one of the fairest to be found

---

[1] Robinson, *Bib. Research.* ii. p. 73 et seq.

[2] Bartlett, *Christian in Palestine,* Tab. 69, p.190; Bartlett, *Walks about the City and Environs of Jerusalem,* p. 216 ; Wilson, *Lands of the Bible,* i. p. 359.

[3] Roberts, *Views in the Holy Land,* Book vii. No. 44.

in all Palestine. On both sides of the valley buildings stand, mostly of some external pretension, built of square stones, high, with flat terrace-like roofs, adorned with a great many little domes, thoroughly oriental in appearance, but having this peculiarity not often seen in the East, namely, the existence of open windows in the upper storeys. The most prominent object of all is the fortress-like Haram, once the Christian church, but later, and up to the present time, the chief mosque of the place. It stands on the lower slope east of the valley. As the supposed burial-place of Abraham and other patriarchs, who are held in equal honour by Jews, Moslems, and Christians, this place has for centuries been the goal of devout pilgrimages.

North of this Haram, and on the western slope of the valley, are to be seen the remains, not lofty, but still massive, of a former citadel, whose destruction was commenced by the cannon of Ibrahim Pasha in 1834, and completed by the great earthquake[1] of 1837. In its present state it does not awaken much interest. The knightly D'Arvieux described[2] it in 1660 as a noble castle located on an imposing site; and it is unquestionably the Castellum or Præsidium St Abraham of the crusaders,[3] in which King Baldwin spent several days in the year 1100, before and after his expedition to the Villa Palmarum, south of the Dead Sea. According to the Arabian author of the Mesalek al absar,[4] this citadel was built by the Romans, but when and by whom is not stated. Josephus[5] alludes to the plundering and burning of Hebron by one of Vespasian's generals at the time of the Roman invasion. Whether this old ruin was really the citadel in which David was crowned as king of all Israel, is a question yet open to solution. The investigations of future explorers will unquestionably throw new light upon this subject. The lower part of the city extends directly across the valley from the east to the west side : it consists of

---

,[1] Russegger, *Reise*, iii. p. 77.

[2] D'Arvieux, *Reise*, Ger. trans. Pt. ii. p. 195.

[3] Alberti Aquensis, *Histor. Hierosol.* lib. vii. c. 41, 42, in *Gest. Dei per Francos.* i. fol. 303–306.

[4] Quatremère, Macrizi, *Histoire des Sultans Mamlouks d'Egypte*, T. i. p. 240.

[5] Fl. Josephus, *de Bello, etc.*, iv. 99, ed. Havercamp, fol. 305.

three or four quarters, which, according to Wilson,[1] bear different names. The chief quarter lies around and north of the great mosque, on the eastern slope : here are the bazaars and the principal places of business. This ancient quarter, directly around the cave of Machpelah, is commonly known as Hart el Kadin. North of this, and separated from it by an open space, is a little group of houses, forming a suburb, the Hart el Harbah. This is called the most densely populated quarter, probably in consequence of its narrow streets. On the western slope lies the largest quarter, in which stands the ruined citadel, and into which one first enters coming from Jerusalem. This is the Hart esh Sheikh, or Sheikh's quarter. South of this, and on the same west side, is a little spot covered with houses, the Hart el Kazaz, or the Silk Mercers' quarter, inhabited mostly by Jews.

The legend of the middle ages, which gave the *Civitas quatuor* to Hebron, does not seem to be founded on any reliable basis. In the account given in Josh. xiv. 15 of the giving of this city to Caleb, we are told that it formerly bore the name of Kirjath-arba. The word Arba signifies "four" in Hebrew ; and from this, etymological deductions have been made and brought into currency by Jerome which can hardly be sustained. Monro,[2] who laid some stress on this division into four parts, because he considered it a primitive one, and a proof of the identity of ancient and modern Hebron, fell, like many others, into the error of supposing that the name Kirjath-arba was an older designation of the city than Hebron was. But the latter was the primitive name of the city, which, according to Moses, was built seven years earlier than Zoan in Egypt (Num. xiii. 22). Josephus states that the inhabitants of Hebron not only claimed that their city was older than all others in Canaan, but even asserted that it was more ancient than Memphis, and that in his day it had been built 2300 years. Although in Josh. xiv. 15, in the account of the giving of this city to Caleb, we are told that the name of Hebron was " Kirjath-arba, which Arba was a great man among the Anakims," yet this only relates to the time when the book of Joshua was composed ; for this name, which the city had received from its

---

[1] Wilson, *Lands of the Bible*, i. p. 379.

[2] Monro, Vere, *A Summer Ramble in Syria*, i. p. 233.

warlike possessors, the Anakims, who had plundered the city, but not founded it, and one of whom was called Arba, was, at the time when Caleb took possession of it, forced to give way to the older name of Hebron, which had been current at the time of Abraham, a full half thousand years earlier. For when the patriarch came and dwelt in the plain of Mamre, which is in Hebron, and built there an altar unto the Lord (Gen. xiii. 18), and had to deal with the Hittites, the possessors at that period of southern Canaan, the primitive name had not yet been changed to Kirjath-arba. Under the Hittites Hebron unquestionably enjoyed a greater degree of prosperity than under the subsequent invaders, the Anakim. After these had been driven out by Caleb, the temporary name Kirjath-arba passed into oblivion.[1]

The effort to explain the derivation of the name of the city from a Hebrew word meaning four, we owe to the foolish fancies of the rabbins, who not only asserted that the three patriarchs, Abraham, Isaac, and Jacob, were buried in Hebron ; but, in order to make their theory hold, taught that the arch-patriarch Adam himself was interred here, and made the fourth. They asserted also that his body was made out of a kind of red clay found in Hebron. This fantastical tradition was, with many others, imparted to Jerome by his Hebrew teacher, and through time passed into the belief of the Catholic Church.[2]

Among the records of pilgrimages made during the middle ages, the results which Jerome's idle story wrought among the monks can be easily seen. The pious but not very critical Fabri[3] of Ulm, with his celebrated companion von Breidenbach, not only visited with full faith the red clay field from which Adam was taken, and with hot tears and kisses poured out their long and ardent prayers for the absolution of their sins, but also the many other places and stations which a monkish fancy had connected therewith,—caves, for example, where Adam and Eve lived, and where they bewailed the death of Abel, the spot where Cain slew his brother, and many others of the same sort. The forming of the first man out of that poor material at their feet seems to have confirmed the humility of

---

[1] Keil, *Comment. zu Josua*, p. 278.

[2] *Ibid.* Note 10 ; Robinson, *Bib. Research.* ii. p. 88, Note 4.

[3] Fel. Fabri, *Evagator.* ed. Hassler, ii. pp. 340–353.

the pilgrims : they took some of it home with them, believing it to have medicinal virtues, and so propagated their errors still further.

The certainly not ignorant Fabri and his contemporaries believed that the unbelieving heathen had connected the name *Civitas quatuor* with the four giants, Anak and his three sons, Ahiman, Sesai, and Thalmai; but that true believers, on the contrary, had derived it from the fact that here Abraham, Isaac, and Jacob, and, before the Flood, Adam had dwelt. And according to their easy theory, Hebron, the city of Caleb, had an antiquity coeval with the creation of man.[1]

But whatever account we make of the etymological derivation of the idea of four parts of Hebron, the antiquity of the place is venerable, even if it cannot be traced back to Adam or the Deluge; and the early reverence of the Arabs for it is clearly enough seen in the name which they have given to the city, el-Khalil, *i.e.* the friend of God[2] (see James ii. 23). Edrisi designates it Kabr Ibrahim, or Abraham's Grave; Abulfeda, Beit Hebran, or the House of Hebron, whence the Castrum Abrahami of the crusaders; the oldest of the Arab geographers, Isthakri, calls it Mesjid Ibrahims, or Abraham's Sepulchre.

The city is at present without real walls, although it has some so-called gates. It once was included among the cities of Judah, which king Rehoboam made the most secure of all his strongholds (2 Chron. ii. 10). Since that time it has undergone repeated assaults and partial destruction, one of the most serious being that received at the hands of Simon Maccabæus. The whole neighbourhood of the city von Schubert terms a great, rich olive garden,[3] which he at the time of his visit in March found in its fullest beauty, particularly on the north side towards Jerusalem; and near the brook Eshcol the vineyards were remarkably fine. The grapes produced there retain the size and flavour which gave them their celebrity at the time that the spies sought to ascertain the resources of the land. The pomegranates and figs[4] retain their old reputation (Num.

---

[1] Robinson, *Bib. Research.* ii. p. 78, Note 2.
[2] F. A. Strauss, *Sinai und Golgotha,* p. 362.
[3] Von Schubert, *Reise in das Morgenland,* ii. p. 463.
[4] Isthakri, *Das Buch der Länder,* trans. by Mordtmann, p. 35.

xiii. 24). Isthakri, writing in the tenth century, asserts that in his time dates ripened in the warm valley of Hebron; but he was mistaken. We find no dates there, nor is that fruit mentioned among the articles brought back by the spies. The first condition of fruitfulness, water, is not lacking in the valley of Hebron; for although no brook flows through it, there is a large number of springs in the neighbourhood, which are made very useful to the city and the tilled land adjoining. Before the southern gate there is a great pool, and at the northern extremity of the chief quarter a second and smaller one. The lower pool, according to Robinson,[1] is a hundred and thirty-three feet square, and well constructed of hewn stones: the whole depth is almost twenty-two feet; and the depth of the water when he was there, about fourteen feet. Stairways lead down into the tank, in order to allow people to go and replenish their jugs and skins.[2]

The smaller and upper reservoir[3] is only eighty-five feet long, fifty-five broad, and about nineteen deep. It lies in the middle of the valley. They form together the great means of supply for the city, although they hold only rain-water, and are constantly frequented by servants, who come to carry supplies for the various houses. Robinson discovered a fine spring on the side of the mountain west of Hebron, and another which was used for watering cattle, north of the city. The reservoirs may be of great antiquity, and it is possible that the one within the present town occupies the site of the pool where the murderers of Ishbosheth, Saul's son, were hanged at the command of David (2 Sam. iv. 12). The identity of the two, however, can hardly be determined till we shall know whether the ancient city did not occupy a higher site than the present one.[4]

An equal degree of obscurity rests upon another historical monument, the so-called grave of Abner, Saul's chief general. Pilgrims even now[5] pay their devout reverence to the small

---

[1] Robinson, *Bib. Research.* ii. p. 74.

[2] Comp. Wilson, *Lands of the Bible*, i. p. 368; and Fel. Fabri, *Evagatorium*, vol. ii. p. 351; Della Valle, Pt. i. p. 160.

[3] Bartlett, *The Christian in Palestine*, Plate lxviii. p. 189.

[4] Quatremère, Macrizi, *Hist. des Sultans Mamlouks d'Egypte*, T. i. p. 240.

[5] Von Schubert, *Reise*, ii. p. 477; V. Monro, *Summer Ramble*, i. p. 242; Wilson, *Lands of the Bible*, i. p. 368.

whitewashed dome-crowned building, with its sepulchre twelve feet in length, the whole standing in the court of a Turkish house, and purporting to be the grave of Abner. The story is current, that this great Hebrew general was a giant, greater even than the great Anak himself. However true the tradition may be regarding the place of his sepulture, the story of Abner's death at the hand of Joab, and the sincere sorrow of the magnanimous David, who walked in person behind the bier of his deceased rival, gives a deep interest to Hebron (see 2 Sam. iii. 32, 33). In this city, too, David, whose character exhibits many fine manly traits, resided for seven years and a half, until the capture of Jerusalem allowed him to transfer the royal residence thither. An ancient legend asserts that Jesse, the father of David, was buried on an eminence west of Hebron. These recollections and associations give this ancient city a lustre which makes it specially dear to every Jewish heart; and century after century these old traditions perpetuate themselves, giving an interest and a charm to the present city, which, without them, it would not enjoy.[1]

Von Schubert visited[2] the grave of Jesse, and the wells, a little farther on, which bear the names of Abraham, Isaac, and Jacob. He gives his usually glowing picture of the scenery, and speaks of various plants and fruits which he saw growing by the way, among which were the pistachio nut (*Pistacia vera*), whose fruit Jacob sent to Joseph, the great governor in Egypt; the walnut (*Juglans regia*), which grows wild throughout all Palestine; the fig tree, the apricot, and the grape-vine. The rarer growths of the place, as they were noticed by von Schubert, may be briefly mentioned, to supply our imperfect knowledge of the country. In the last of March he found in full bloom, the Emex spinosus, Crassocephalum flavum, Gnaphalium sanguineum, Linaria chalepensis, Ajuga tridactylites, Lamium tomentosum, Cynoglossum cheirifolium, Anemone coronaria, Ranunculus bullatus, Malcolmia littorea, Pistacia lentiscus and terebinthus, and Trifolium clypeatum; besides several new

---

[1] Von Schubert, *Reise*, pp. 482, 487.

[2] *Ibid.* ii. p. 478; Wilson, *Lands of the Bible*, i. pp. 365, 369. Comp. Jichus ha-Abot, *Tombeaux des Patriarches*, in Carmoly, *Itinéraires de la Terre Sainte.*

varieties of Iris, Gladiolus, Orchis, Arum, Aristolochia, Salvia, Scrophularia, Anchusa, Rubia, and Silene.

The abundant supplies of water, and the elevated position[1] of Hebron—2700 feet according to von Schubert, and 2842 feet according to Russegger, about three hundred feet therefore higher than Jerusalem — giving a cooler temperature than would otherwise be enjoyed, favour a more luxuriant and varied vegetation than can be looked for in the lower, less watered, rocky, and scorched districts in its neighbourhood.

The climate of Hebron[2] seems to be the one in which the grape-vine thrives the best, and which ripens the finest pomegranates and oranges. The first grapes ripen in Hebron as early as July: from this time on to November, Jerusalem is supplied abundantly from the fruitful vines of its ancient neighbour. The general gathering takes place in September; and although the larger portion of the new grapes are sent to Jerusalem, another large portion, converted into raisins (the biggest, Robinson says,[3] that he ever saw), and still another large portion made into a yellow, sweet syrup, and eaten as a general condiment in the place of sugar, yet a part are made into a wine which in fire and flavour is hardly inferior to that of Cyprus or Lebanon. The process of wine-making is attended to only by Jews: for while the Koran forbids the use of wine, the Hebrew Psalmist (Ps. civ. 15) lauded it as a choice gift of God, making glad the heart of man; and in the account of the very earliest personages in the Hebrew lineage (Gen. ix. 20), we are told that there was the skilled laying out of vineyards, doubtless by terraces, the custom from time immemorial in Palestine. According to the Jewish tradition, it was in Hebron that Noah planted the first vines after the Deluge.

The vine and the grape have always been the type among the Hebrews of the rich and profuse blessings of God (Jer. ii. 21; Song of Sol. vii. 9). In the New Testament, too, the vine has received a higher symbolical meaning (see John xv. 1). The vineyards of Hebron are among the most exten-

---

[1] Von Schubert, *Reise*, ii. p. 470; Russegger, *Reise*, iii. p. 77.

[2] Robinson, *Bib. Research.* ii. p. 74. Comp. A. V. Humboldt, *Asie Centrale*, T. iii. pp. 125, 126; *Kosmos*, i. pp. 347–350; v. Schubert, *Reise*, ii. p. 468; Wilson, *Lands, etc.*, i. pp. 358, 379.

[3] Robinson, *Bib. Research.* ii. pp. 83, 211, i. 308.

sive[1] of all Palestine : they extend north-westward as far as to Teffuh, southward as far as Dhoheriyeh, and northward for an hour to Khurbet el Nusarah,[2] on the way to Jerusalem. The little towers which are seen everywhere guarding these vineyards give the whole landscape a romantic appearance; and the annual gathering of the grapes is an occasion of joy, of family gatherings, and of feastings in the East, no less than it is in the West. As far north even as Bethlehem there is a productive yield.

The reputation of the grapes of Hebron is so great throughout all Palestine, that there is no difficulty in believing that the valley of Eshcol was directly north of the city. The Scriptures do not distinctly assert that the place where the spies discovered the grapes which they brought back is there (Num. xiii. 24) ; but the connection of Abraham with Mamre the Amorite, a brother of Eshcol and Aner (Gen. xiv. 13, 24), is sufficient to connect the immediate neighbourhood of Hebron with the place which bore the name of Eshcol.[3]

As the name of Eshcol was applied to a vale, and afterwards lost its primary use as the designation of a man, so the name of his brother Mamre was transferred to the tree ($\dot{\eta}$ $\delta\rho\hat{\nu}\varsigma$ $\dot{\eta}$ $M\acute{a}\mu\beta\rho\eta$ in the Septuagint) or to the grove of Mamre, which was opposite to the cave of Machpelah (Gen. xxiii. 17–19), near to where Abraham dwelt. From the site of his home, he is said to have lived at Mamre—a place associated also with the names of Isaac and Jacob (Gen. xxv. 9, xxxv. 27, l. 13). Yet at the time of the latter patriarch the valley of Hebron is distinctly mentioned, for it was thence that Jacob sent his sons to Shechem to find their brother Joseph (Gen. xxxvii. 14). When Josephus wrote, there was pointed out, six stadia from Hebron, a terebinth[4] tree which was held in great honour, and which was popularly said to have stood there from the beginning of the world. It was called by pilgrims who visited it[5] Abraham's tree, and it was under it that the patriarch was supposed to have pitched his tent when he sat in the door and welcomed

---

[1] Robinson, *Bib. Research.* i. p. 42, ii. pp. 72, 80, 81 ; Bartlett, *Walks,* etc., pp. 216, 221.

[2] Robinson, *Bib. Résearch.* i. p. 211.

[3] Rosenmüller, *Bib. Alterthk.* ii. p. 157.

[4] Reland, *Pal.* p. 712.

[5] Comp. Wilson, *Lands of the Bible,* i. p. 382.

the three visitors who announced to him the destruction of Sodom and Gomorrah (Gen. xviii.).

At the present time, according to Robinson, north-west of Hebron, near the height of the watershed between the valley in which the city lies and the western slope towards the Mediterranean, there stands' by itself a very large and uncommonly fine oak, held by the Arabs in great reverence, as the supposed tree beneath which Abraham pitched his tent. They call the wood Sindian.[1] Just below this tree, in whose neighbourhood there are no remains of buildings, is found as one goes towards Hebron, a succession of vineyards and grain-fields. The position of this Sindian tree does not, indeed, contradict the position of Mamre, as it is merely stated in the book of Genesis to be " over against" Machpelah. But the tree to which Robinson refers is no terebinth, which Josephus asserts that the tree under which Abraham encamped was. It is an oak of the *ilex* variety, and is one of the finest in Palestine, where large and handsome trees are rare. The trunk at the largest places is a little over twenty-two feet in circumference. The' branches run out to a distance of fifty feet on one side, and over eighty on another: the foliage is thick and healthy, and it stands upon a fine clean grass flat, which, taken in conjunction with a neighbouring spring, offers a very attractive place for an encampment, and is much resorted to by parties from Hebron.[2] Robinson discovered that Maundeville visited the same tree in the fourteenth century, Belon in the sixteenth, and Troilo in the seventeenth. This tree could not by any possibility be the one described by Josephus;[3] for although extremely aged, yet the peculiar shape of its leaves, and its whole characteristics, would prevent its being confounded with the oak.

According to the tradition of Jews now living, another locality besides that of the Sindian tree, and farther north of Hebron, is believed to lay the best claim to the honour of being the place where Abraham lived. This view was held, too, by the early Christians ; and it seems to more fully accord with the statements made by Josephus, in consequence of the existence

[1] Robinson, *Bib. Research.* ii. p. 73.   Comp. Rosenmüller, *Bib. Alterthk.* Pt. iv. pp. 229, 233, Pt. ii. p. 299.

[2] Robinson, *Bib. Research.* ii. p. 81.

[3] Comp. Della Valle, Pt. i. p. 168.

at the same place of remains of walls which have been found there. No similar traces occur in the neighbourhood of the oak described by Robinson. The anonymous Jewish author of the Jichus ha-Abot,[1] written in 1537, seems to have taken the ground that this place is correctly supposed to have been the site of Abraham's tent. After describing the sepulchres of Hebron in which the patriarchs were buried, he speaks of the place where Jesse the father of David was interred, outside of the city, and passes to speak of the graves of other Israelites to whom he wishes peace. He then goes on to say, that in the neighbourhood of the city, between the vineyards, are the oaks of Mamre, where Abraham pitched his tent, and the stone on which he sat during the circumcision. This stone, which was regarded as a sacred memorial of the covenant with the Jews (Gen. xvii. 8, 9, 23–27), was visited three hundred years earlier (1210) by the Jewish pilgrim Samuel bar Simson,[2] who tells us that it was held in great reverence by the Arabs, *i.e.* the Ishmaelites. Benjamin of Tudela visited the place in 1160, but his description is very indefinite.

The same tradition was repeated by subsequent pilgrims. Fabri, for example, who came from Bethlehem to Hebron with von Breydenbach in 1483, tells us that the distance between the two places was six leucæ, and that the road was then destitute of cultivation, being overrun with thorns and thistles, but full of relics of ancient vineyards and fruit gardens. Then follows, he says,[3] the lovely vale of Hebron, on both sides of which were wooded hills, vineyards, and orchards. Before they reached Hebron, and while yet the city had not come into sight, the two came to an olive grove where they rested themselves. Here, they were told, stood the primitive city of Hebron, but the name was afterwards transferred to the later collection of houses which sprang up around the cave of Machpelah.

This, although a statement made very cursorily, yet agrees with the account which Benjamin of Tudela gives of the house of Abraham and the well at the north of Hebron ; and his

---

[1] Jichus ha-Abot, in Carmoly, *Itineraires de la Terre Sainte*, pp. 433–435. Comp. Hottinger, *Cippi Hebraici*, pp. 26–88 ; and Wilson, *Lands, etc.*, i. 366.

[2] Samuel bar Simson, in Carmoly, pp. 128, 129, and Note, p. 148.

[3] Fel. Fabri, *Evagatorium*, ed. Hassler, ii. pp. 339, 340.

account also harmonizes with the later Jewish tradition. But Robinson casts a doubt upon the view taken by many who have adopted the opinion of Benjamin of Tudela; and remarks, that at his time no one had visited [1] the place, to see whether ruins of a former city could be traced there. He was aware of the existence of a tradition current among the Jews regarding the place where Abraham lived, and he himself saw and described with his customary exactness all that he could find ; yet it seems to me, that the place to which he refers is not the place [2] meant by Benjamin of Tudela.

I think, however, that at a very ancient period—about 600 —Antoninus Martyr [3] held the view that Hebron once was more elevated than it was in his day, and that it then lay much nearer to Mamre than when he wrote. Speaking of the distance of Hebron from Bethlehem, he states that from the latter, *usque ad radicem Mambræ,* it was twenty-four Roman miles. This *radix Mambræ* must have designated only the mountain north of the city, at whose southern base lay the cave of Machpelah, near the more modern city of Hebron. Bishop Arculfus, [4] too, who lived about 700, found at Mamre the ruins, as he says, of the ancient Hebron ; while in the valley at the foot of its site there were only poor, although numerous huts. And if there were any significance in the rabbinical tradition of the Mishna, [5] that the priests, when they went early every day to the temple in Jerusalem to carry the morning sacrifice, used to be greeted by the cry of the watchman, " It begins to be light as far as to Hebron," it is a plain token that Hebron must have stood in an elevated position, in order to be discerned from the top of the temple ; it could not have been seen if it had been in the valley, as now. This view is confirmed by the fact that all the other cities of refuge, which were early appointed as the place whither persons who had committed accidental manslaughter should flee, were at the tops of high hills. [6] Examples of this may be seen in

---

[1] Robinson, *Bib. Research.* ii. p. 91.   [2] *Ibid.* i. p. 570.

[3] *Beatus Antoninus Martyr, ed. ex Musæo Cl. Menardi Juliomagi Andium,* 1640, p. 22.

[4] Arculfus, *Itin.* in Thom. Wright, *Early Trav. in Palestine,* p. 6.

[5] Winer, *Bib. Realw.* Pt. ii. p. 107.

[6] Wilson, *Lands of the Bible,* i. pp. 367, 369.

Kadesh and Shechem,—the latter unquestionably on Mount Gerizim, where its ruins may be seen, and not in the valley, where the present place is found. The passages Josh. xx. 7 and xxi. 11, leave no doubt on this point regarding the situation of Hebron, and show conclusively that it could have been no city lying in a vale; that the mountain city, so to speak—that which could be seen from a distance—was given to the Levites, while the tilled land and villages around it became the domain of Caleb.

Von Schubert, who was the guest of prominent Jews while in Hebron, was conducted [1] to the most prominent places connected with the Hebrew legends: the place where Abraham's house was, that where Nathan the prophet was buried, and where the palace of king David stood. His account is not very full and definite, in consequence of the haste with which he pressed forward to Jerusalem. " Our way," he says, " which was a little east of the usual highway from Hebron to Jerusalem, led first between the luxuriant vineyards which extend through the valley on the north side of the city. We turned then towards the north-east, away from the road, and passing through green fields of grain, came in about an hour to a wall made of immense pieces of stone, and enclosing a great square space like a court, near one corner of which a finely hewn cistern was seen. It seemed as though the place might be the property of some rich owner of flocks, and that the square court might serve as a good place of safety for them. This partly paved court was overgrown with grass, where a herdsman was pasturing his cows. The tract around the structure, which was called by the guide ' Abraham's house at Mamre,' is among the most fruitful that I have seen in Palestine : the hills with their trees and bushes gave ample indications of the former existence of a forest there. From this point the way ran northward up the slope of the hill, and through a valley full of vineyards, near which stood a little Arab village, with an attractive and almost fortress-like structure, which the guide called the tomb of Nathan the prophet, in which stands a sarcophagus constructed in the ordinary Turkish fashion. Westward of this place runs the regular road from Hebron to Jerusalem, at a place where a stoned well full of fine fresh

[1] Von Schubert, *Reise*, ii. pp. 286, 287.

water offers an excellent resting-place. It took an hour's time to reach this place by a circuitous route, although the direct distance is but a half-hour from Hebron."

At the spot which von Schubert had now reached, there stand the ruins of buildings which even in their present decay and desolation display traces of former splendour. His Jewish companion told him that the place is called Luar, that it is not Hebron proper, but the place where David lived during his seven years' residence in that neighbourhood as king of Judah. A later traveller than Schubert has entered more fully into the description of this interesting historical monument. I refer to Samuel Wolcott, an American missionary, who has examined the whole country between Jerusalem and Hebron with uncommon care, and has brought the subject of the antiquities above referred to before the world in a way which will give great interest to future researches.

But before speaking at any length of the observations of Wolcott[1] regarding the imposing ruins referred to above, let me briefly refer to what Robinson has collected[2] regarding them. After passing out of Hebron, and traversing the vineyards, he turned to the right towards Tekoa, and following a path so little worn as to be scarcely distinguishable, he reached at length the foundation walls of an immense building, which raised his curiosity to the greatest height. It seemed to be the commencement of a structure, laid out on a Titanic scale, but never completed. Two walls were standing, one of them two hundred feet long, the other a hundred and sixty. These had but two layers of hewn stones above the level of the ground, every one of them three feet and four inches high. One of these was fifteen and a half feet long, and over three feet in thickness. In the north-western corner of the ruins there stands an overarched shallow well or cistern. The object of the structure it was hard to conjecture. Was it a church, or the commencement of a fortification? At all events, it could not be older than the first centuries of the Christian era, since the colossal stones do not permit us to conjecture that it was of earlier construction. The name Rameh el Khulil, which is applied to it, is said by the

---

[1] Comp. S. Wolcott, *Excursion in Hebron, Carmel, etc.*, in *Bib. Sacra*, 1843, No. 1, pp. 44-46.

[2] Robinson, *Bib. Research.* i. pp. 215, 216.

Hebrew Jews to signify the "house of Abraham," and to indicate the place where Abraham's tent stood near Mamre. If the structure was erected by Jews in honour of their great patriarchal ancestor, the extensive area[1] enclosed would seem to keep in remembrance that he was the owner of the numerous herds which would be naturally gathered there; and the walls of such a monument would not need to be carried up very high, and may be conceived to have been purposely left in the present state.   Another theory of their origin is, that this was the foundation of the magnificent Basilica,[2] which we are told the Emperor Constantine caused to be erected two Roman miles from Hebron, to commemorate the spot where the first Jewish patriarch lived.   Certainly, in respect to distance, there is a singular agreement between that of Constantine's Basilica from Hebron, and that of this ruin.   The great objection to this view is the one adduced by Robinson, that whereas there are no signs that this structure was ever carried beyond a certain stage of completeness, the edifice constructed by Constantine was finished. The words of the *Itinerary* are : inde terebintho, ubi Abraham habitavit et puteum fodit sub arbore terebintho et cum angelis loquutus est et cibum sumpsit.   Ibi Basilica *facta est* jussu Constantini miræ pulchritudinis.   Inde terebintho Cebron, etc.

Mr Wolcott,[3] and Mr Tipping, a painter who sketched the ruins, and who was very familiar with ancient styles of architecture, tried in vain to solve the problem as to the origin and use of these apparently unfinished walls.   Mr Wolcott came upon them from a different direction from that of Robinson ; but his general estimate of their extent agrees with his, while his language of surprise regarding their extent is even more unqualified than that of Robinson.   The whole amount of ground embraced within the walls he asserts to have been ten acres : he speaks, too, of important foundation stones lying north and east of the great wall, many of them being bevelled. The whole surface of the ground is strewn with mosaic fragments.   From the great walls at this place, a path ascends to the top of the hill, which is covered with pieces of hewn stone,

---

[1] See Bartlett, *The Christian in Palestine,* Tab. lxx. p. 193 ; and *Walks about Jerusalem,* p. 213.

[2] *Itiner. Hierosol.* ed. Parthey et Pinder, p. 282.

[3] Wolcott, *Excursion,* p. 45.

among which may be seen some pieces of columns. From this point the Mediterranean can be seen[1] through a cleft on the north-east. In four different places in this neighbourhood, Wolcott discovered traces of such ruins as those already referred to. He attributes their existence to the great sanctity in which the place has always been held, which led, even before the time of Josephus, to its being the gathering-place of countless multitudes of heathen. These celebrated their Lupercalian orgies, and it was to prevent their celebration that Eusebius had a church erected there. After the Hegira the Mohammedans regarded the place as sacred, and paid pilgrimages to it as the place where the "friend of God" once lived. The united reverence of all these, solves the problem why this place should be now found covered with the ruins of buildings long since built, but now in a state of decay; buildings whose original uses are not entirely understood, but which, it is hoped, will be made the subject of future investigation.

We turn back from the now desolate but universally revered spot which we have every reason to believe was the ancient home of Abraham, in the plain and grove of Mamre the Amorite, to the place of his burial, the cave of Machpelah, on the field of Ephron the Hittite, and in the vale.[2] It is plain that the two places were somewhat apart from each other: the very fact that one was originally possessed by an Amorite, and the other by one of the descendants of Heth, shows it. The former place is now desolate, and marked only by ruins; the latter forms the central object of interest in the present city of Hebron, which, it would seem, has gradually grown up around it, and which owes the most of its fame to its being the burying-place of the ancient Jewish patriarchs.

As one approaches Hebron from the north over the highway alluded to above, after passing the neighbourhood of the ancient Mamre, and attaining the summit of the last hill, the prospect suddenly widens, and takes in the whole deep valley of Hebron, in whose foreground on the left appears the palace and yet fortress-like burial-place of the patriarchs, with its four minarets; and on the right hand, and towards the east, the bulk

[1] Wolcott, *Excursion*, p. 57.
[2] See Bartlett, *Walks about Jerusalem*, p. 216; also Wilson, *Lands of the Bible*, i. p. 354; Robinson, *Bib. Research.* ii. p. 85.

of the city, with the green valley stretching away in a tortuous line into the distance, offering a view of corn-fields, olive groves, gardens, and vineyards, hardly to be surpassed in all Palestine. At the extreme south-east, and beyond Dhaheriyeh, the horizon is formed by the desert sand in the neighbourhood of Beersheba, while westward, the outlook is terminated by the mountains of the Dead Sea and of Moab.

The great Haram, or Holy Place, which has for centuries upon centuries formed the central point around which human interests have clustered, is not only remarkable as the sepulchre of the founders of the Israelitish nation, and therefore a spot hallowed by the most remote of historical scenes; but in a merely architectural point of view, it has always exercised a great influence, and in its blending of simplicity with magnitude it is conspicuous among all the works of man in Palestine.

The twenty-third chapter of Genesis gives not only a vivid hint of the original character of this place of sepulture, but also a most delightful and graphic portrayal of patriarchal life. Its simplicity, its deep religious warmth, and its chivalrous spirit, are more than Homeric in their character; while its historical character is so strictly authentic, as to transport us at once to the scene, and to that remote period. The death of Sarah, whom the grey patriarch mourns and weeps over; the tender feeling which masters him, and prompts him, a stranger, and among a strange people, to provide for himself and for his family a place of burial; the childlike request made to Ephron to grant him the cave of Machpelah;—all this transfers us at once to the field of the " son of Heth," who had recognised in the stranger a prince especially favoured of God, and who gladly and without mention of reward offered him one of the choicest burial-places in the gift of his people. Yet Abraham, mindful of his own dignity, of his situation as a stranger among a foreign people, of the promise made to his seed, to be fulfilled in a distant future, is not content to receive the cave as a free gift, but only consents on condition of paying four hundred shekels of silver for it, and for all the land and the trees standing near it. This is assented to in the presence of witnesses; the bargain is confirmed; and the burying-place passes into the hands of Abraham, who laid there the bones of Sarah.

At the age of a hundred and seventy-five years the aged

patriarch too died, and was buried there by his sons (Gen. xxv. 9). Isaac, too, at the completion of his hundred and eightieth year, was interred in the same spot (xxxv. 29); and still later, the body of Jacob was laid there. Before the death of the latter in Egypt, after blessing his twelve sons, he ordered that he should be buried in the cave of Machpelah (Gen. xlix. 29). This was done under the direction of Joseph, then prime minister in Egypt, who obtained permission of the monarch Pharaoh to go up to Canaan and fulfil his oath to his father. After the Egyptian process of embalming the body had been completed, and the usual mourning of seventy days had ended, the great burial procession began its march. It was followed not only by the sons, but by nearly all the servants, of Jacob and Joseph, and the chief courtiers and officials of the Egyptians. In Gen. l. 9 we are told, at the close of the account of the procession, that " it was a very great company." The route chosen was not the short and direct one, but across the northern part of Arabia Petræa, up the east coast of the Dead Sea, through Moab, and then over the Jordan. The latter part of the way was that taken subsequently by the Hebrews under Moses. They crossed the Jordan at the threshing-floor of Atad, the site of the subsequent Gilgal; and such was the pageantry displayed on the occasion, that the people of Canaan were so filled with surprise, that they said, " This is a grievous mourning to the Egyptians;" and they commemorated the passage of the cortege by changing the name of the place where they lived. After the remains of Jacob had been deposited in Machpelah, Joseph and all the rest went back to Egypt.

The procession which came to Hebron under such interesting circumstances, was certainly one of the most imposing which could ever have visited the place. The impression made by such an event upon the minds of the whole people was so deep, that it must have gone far towards establishing that extraordinary veneration for the patriarchs, which has been carried even to a fanatical extent for three thousand years among all the peoples and sects of the East. The burial of Achilles and Patroclus, says Michaud,[1] the historian of the Crusades, was not more imposing than that which was celebrated by the twelve sons of the old Hebrew patriarch in his honour.

[1] Michaud et Poujoulat, *Correspond. d'Orient*, T. v. p. 225.

Ought it to surprise us to know that, even in its very earliest days, this memorial sepulchre, so peculiar and so massive in its present form, surpassing all others in Palestine in this respect, was a place of no slight pretensions? If we strip away all that time and the bigoted superstitions of man have invested it with, there will remain even in what stands around the ancient cave (for the interior has been guarded from the eyes of Jews and Christians for centuries), traces of that same union of simplicity and massiveness which characterizes the pyramids of Egypt. A statesman like Joseph, standing at the cave-sepulchre which contained the bones of his ancestors, can easily be conceived as thinking of doing honour to their remains, by building over their ashes a monumental pile worthy of them; and the peculiar type of architecture found in the lower walls now standing, answers well to what we should suppose would be the structure built by an Egyptian governor. The colossal and simple forms which lie at the bottom of the structures at Hebron, are in striking contrast to those which have been erected upon them by the zeal of monkish and Moslem fanatics.

The external portion of the sepulchre at Hebron consists of a large, high structure, in the form of a parallelogram, whose longest dimension is in the direction of the valley, *i.e.* from N.N.W. to S.S.E., and whose length is about a hundred and fifteen feet. The height of the wall varies from fifty to sixty feet;[1] and its want of uniformity in this respect is increased yet more to the eye, by the inequality in the surface of the ground. The wall runs up to the eastern declivity of the hill, where the quarries lie whence the stone was taken, and from the top of which a view can be taken of the court surrounded by the wall.[2] This would otherwise be unknown, because for centuries neither Jew nor Christian has been permitted to enter.[3] Schubert measured the broad ring-like wall which encircles the court, containing the former church and present mosque, and found it only eighty to ninety feet in length,[4] and about a hundred

---

[1] Robinson, *Bib. Research.* ii. p. 75.

[2] See Bartlett, *The Christian in Palestine*, Tab. lxix. p. 190 ; Wilson, *Lands, etc.*, i. p. 355 ; Roberts, *The Holy Land*, Book vii. Plate xliv.

[3] Irby and Mangles, *Trav.* pp. 342, 343.

[4] Von Schubert, *Reise*, ii. pp. 470, 471.

and forty in width. It is the four minaret-like towers at the corners that give it its imposing appearance. These four towers, of which two have fallen, were probably intended to serve as means of defence. The mosque, which stands in the court, always conveys the impression of a Christian church when seen from above. In the limestone cliffs east of and above the mosque, there are still seen the remains of ancient burial-places, the interior of many of which has never been disturbed. Here were probably the graves which are referred to in the account of Abraham's transaction with Ephron, from which the Hittites told him to choose one of the best. The Dead Sea cannot be seen from that place. Wilson found several Moslem graves there, which tradition asserted to be relics of a former city once built on the height.[1]

The outer walls referred to above, are built at the foundation of very large quarried stones, all hewn smooth and bevelled. In all respects they are similar to those which are found in the oldest part of the walls of the temple at Jerusalem, which date back to the reign of Solomon.[2] Robinson thought, however, that the line of bevelling is not quite so deep at Hebron as at Jerusalem, and the stones seemed to him of less size; yet he admitted one of the greatest to be eighteen feet in length. Subsequent measurements, so far from proving this to be an exaggeration, have shown that it understated rather than overstated the truth: for the careful Legh, Irby, and Mangles, found stones of twenty-five feet in length; and Wilson measured one which was thirty-eight feet long, and more than three feet high, —truly colossal proportions.[3]

This wall is decorated with square pilasters, of which there are sixteen on each side, and eight on each end. They are without capitals, but connected by a kind of cornice, which runs along the whole wall. The surface of this is unbroken by windows or by any other features besides the pilasters just mentioned. The lower portion of the wall, says Bartlett,[4] a judge of architecture, is characterized by the peculiar type of

[1] Wilson, *Lands of the Bible*, vol. i. p. 367.

[2] Krafft, *Die Topographie Jerusalems*, p. 113.

[3] Irby and Mangles, *Trav.* p. 343; Wilson, *Lands of the Bible*, vol. i. p. 366.

[4] Bartlett, *Walks about the City, etc.*, p. 218.

pilaster used, and has an architectural character wholly unique: nothing in Roman or Greek art is like it; and yet it is so definite a type, that it may be considered the accepted precursor of that which was adopted in the construction of Solomon's temple, as well as in the building of the tower of Hippicus at Jerusalem by Herod. Here at Hebron we find the first structure of its kind.[1] The lowest part of the wall, which, on historical grounds, Robinson concluded to be Jewish workmanship of a period at least prior to the destruction of Jerusalem,[2] does not rise by any means to the upper part of the structure; for upon the older portion a later one has been placed, less massive in character, more ornamental, and decorated with little towers at the corners. All that can be seen is merely a wall which encompasses an open court, leading to the cave, at the opening of which a church has been built in comparatively modern times; this has more recently been changed into a mosque. The statement of Flavius Josephus, who speaks of monuments of the finest marble decorated with rare devices, and placed at the tomb of Abraham by his descendants, leaves us to conclude that, at a very early period, memorial structures were erected there, which gradually changed their form, at length appearing in the Christian church, and last of all in the Mohammedan mosque, the continued closing of which against Christians and Jews leaves us in doubt concerning what it might reveal to us. The Jewish traditions ascribe the building of the oldest parts of the structure to both Abraham and to David;[3] the monkish legends make the Empress Helena the founder; but all are without real foundation.

According to Ali Bey, who entered the building in disguise, the church in the court dates from the Greek time, but the arches appear to be of the period of the Crusades. The entrances[4] at the corners of the wall are unsymmetrically placed; there are two of them in the northern corners. A long, broad, covered, and gently ascending staircase runs along every side of the structure, and leads to a door opening into the court. The one at the north-west corner, with the most

---

[1] Comp. Bartlett, *The Christian in Palestine*, Tab. xliii. p. 145.
[2] Robinson, *Bib. Research.* ii. p. 79.
[3] Jichus ha-Abot, in Carmoly, *Itin.* p. 433.
[4] Irby and Mangles, *Trav.* p. 343; Robinson, *Bib. Research.* ii. p. 76.

convenient entrance, seems to be the most important one of all.

With regard to the building of a Christian church in this place, all accounts fail us. Procopius, although mentioning the various edifices erected by the Emperor Justinian in Bethlehem, on Sinai, and other places, says nothing about Hebron. That this church, however, existed a hundred years later than his time, is evident from the itinerary of Antoninus Martyr,[1] who about the year 600, and while Hebron was still under Byzantine rule, visited the place, and speaks of seeing there a Basilica ædificata per quadrum, with an open Atrio in the middle, and divided by a partition into two parts, one of which was open to Christians, and the other to the Jews, who brought their incense offering. For he says that after Christmas there came to the grave of Jacob and to that of David a great multitude of Jews from all lands, to burn incense and torches there, and to offer gifts. In the *Bourdeaux Itinerary*, written A.D. 333, mention[2] is made, indeed, of a Basilica Constantini standing where Abraham once lived; but at the tomb of Abraham there is allusion only to a Memoria or Sepulcrum, making it plain that then no church had been built. Three hundred years later, Antoninus speaks of the Basilica there, and makes it plain that it could hardly owe its origin to the Empress Helena. A hundred years later still, about A.D. 700, Bishop Arculfus[3] was allowed to see the interior of the burial-place, where the Hebrew patriarchs (among whom he names Adam) rested. He says that their heads, contrary to what he thought ought to be the custom, were towards the north, and their feet towards the south. A low wall surrounded the burial-places, every one of which was covered with a single stone in the form of a church (he probably refers to a cover sloping like a church roof). Robinson thinks the epithet "low" applied to the word wall must have crept in, and be incorrect, for he thinks the wall was always a high one. Arculfus asserts that the spot where Adam lies is some distance from that where the other three great patriarchs were interred : it was less ornately decorated, as were the tombs of

---

[1] *Antonini Mart. Itinerarium*, p. 22.

[2] *Itinerar. Hierosolym.* ed Parthey et Pinder, p. 283.

[3] Adamnanus ex Arculfo, ii. 10 ; comp. Thos. Wright, *Early Travels in Palestine*, p. 7.

the wives of the patriarchs, than were those of Abraham, Isaac, and Jacob. The front court could not at that time have been hidden from view by the upper wall, which during recent centuries has covered the colossal lower one, and must have permitted free access to the door of the sepulchre. In 637, Palestine had been brought under the dominion of the caliphs by Omar, who was by no means so fanatically opposed to the Christians seeing the holy places as his fellow-believers were after the Crusades. This may be seen by his mild treatment[1] of Sophronius at Jerusalem, and his leaving the Christian church there undisturbed. During his sway, entrance to the graves of the patriarchs at Hebron appears not to have been denied. When the Anglo-Saxon Saewulf[2] visited Hebron in 1102, at the beginning of the Crusades, he found the once beautiful city entirely destroyed by the Saracens; but the burial-places of the patriarchs, he says, were surrounded by an uncommonly strong wall; and every one of the three sepulchres, which resembled churches or chapels in appearance, and in each of which were two coffins, was arched over, so that those who stood within the enclosed space could perceive that the air was charged with the odours of spices used in the embalming process. Only a year before Saewulf's visit, Godfrey of Bouillon had made the chivalrous Gerhard of Avesnes[3] master of Hebron. William of Tyre, the historian of the first Crusade, alludes expressly to Hebron, and says that heretofore there had been no bishop stationed there, only a prior. And, notwithstanding the appointment of a suffragan bishop, in 1167, at Hebron as well as at Bethlehem and Lydda, the distance of Hebron from Jerusalem, its exposed position in relation to Egyptian attacks, as well as to those of the wild Arabs, have always rendered it a place of less interest than Bethlehem with its Church of the Nativity.

---

[1] Robinson, *Bib. Research.* i. p. 389.

[2] Saewulfi *Relatio de Peregrinatione ad Terram Sanctam, anno* mcii. *et* mciii., in *Recueil de Voy. et Mem.* publ. par la Soc. de Geogr. Paris, 1839, T. iv. p. 849. Comp. Wilken, *Gesch. d. Kreuz.* Pt. ii. p. 44; Alberti Acquensis *Histor. Hierosol.* vii. c. 15, in *Gesta Dei per Francos* and *Willerm. Tyr. Histor.* lib. x. c. 8, fol. 781.

[3] Michaud et Poujoulat, *Corresp. d'Orient*, T. v. p. 229. Comp. Jacobus de Vitriaco, *Histor. Hierosol.* c. xli. in *Gesta Dei per Francos*, i. fol. 1077.

Benjamin of Tudela[1] in 1165, at the time of King Amalrich and Sultan Saladin, and the Rabbi Petachia eleven years later, had access [2] to the interior of the graves of the patriarchs: no mosque had as yet hindered free entrance. During the time of the Mohammedans, says the former, meaning before the Crusades, the Jews had a synagogue there. At his time the monks had already begun to form idle foolish legends, and to enrich themselves at the expense of credulous pilgrims who came thither : the Christians, he says, had erected six *sepulcra* there, regarding which they asserted that they contain the graves of Abraham and Sarah, Isaac and Rebecca, Jacob and Leah, and demanded money for the exhibition of them. If a Jew came and paid the custodian of the place an extra fee, he opened an ancient iron gate, and with a lighted torch in his hand led the way through an empty cavern into an inner one, and from that into a third, wherein, he said, were the original and authentic places of burial. They all have inscriptions : over Abraham's burial-place are the words, "This is the grave of our father Abraham, with whom be peace." A lamp burns day and night there ; and, says Benjamin of Tudela, himself a Jew, boxes filled with the bones of Israelites, carried thither by their own countrymen, were to be seen at the time of his visit.

The next Jew who made a pilgrimage to Hebron, Samuel bar Simson,[3] in 1210, in company with the distinguished scholar, Rabbi Jonathan Ben-David ha-Cohen de Lunel, of Provence, had more difficulty in gaining access to the sepulchre of the patriarchs ; for it was the time when the power of the Christian King John of Jerusalem [4] had little real influence beyond Ptolemais, and was so weak elsewhere, that the Saracens, who were alike hostile to Jews and to Christians, must have been in the ascendancy at Hebron. It was only from Samuel bar Simson's accidentally meeting the chief Jewish rabbi at Bagdad, who was then making a pilgrimage through Palestine, that he was enabled, under the protection of the powerful firmans enjoyed by the latter, to attain his object. Yet they were not permitted to visit the sepulchre of the patriarchs by day, but

---

[1] Benjamin von Tudela, *Itinerar.* ed Asher, vol. i. pp. 76, 77.
[2] Carmoly, *Itin.* p. 433.
[3] Samuel bar Simson, in Carmoly, *Itin.* pp. 118–128.
[4] Wilken, *Gesch. der Kreuz.* Pt. vi. pp. 53–64.

were permitted to pay a stolen visit at midnight.[1] The custodian
of the place took them· by a staircase so narrow that one cannot
turn in it, and let them see the three shrines which had been
erected six hundred years before, about A.D. 614, shortly before
the Arabian invasion, and shortly after the visit of Antoninus
Martyr, who makes no allusion to them. The *sancta domus*, as it
was called, in which the three shrines stood, was said by the guide
to be close by the cave Machpelah. The pilgrims prostrated
themselves in prayer, confessed their sins, and then returned to
Jerusalem. Not long after this, access became more difficult
still, and Nowairi relates that Sultan Bibars decisively forbade
Jewish and Christian pilgrims access to the grave of Abraham.[2]
Makrizi tells us that the Emir Jaouli built the Hebron mosque
now called the Haram, and that since his day the sultans of
Egypt had made pilgrimages to Hebron. Mejr ed Din, who
died in 1520, alludes in his history to the building[3] of the
mosque by Greeks, by whom he probably means the crusaders.
He describes it as having a large cupola between two smaller
ones, on the east and west ; he also speaks of a pulpit of wood,
the Merhele, or praying-place, marked with the date 484 after
the Hegira, *i.e.* A.D. 1091. It had only been brought hither
by Saladin after the destruction of Askalon in 1187.

John Maundeville mentions, in 1322, that at that time no
Christian is allowed to visit the grave of Abraham without permission of the sultan.[4] He· also explains the use of the term
" double cave," which has generally been applied to it, asserting
that there are two, which lie one over the other ; a statement
which appears to be confirmed by the testimony of several
witnesses.   Ishak Chelo,[5] the rabbi from Aragon, who was there
ten years later, found fellow-believers of his own at Hebron,
engaged day and night in services of the deepest devotion ; for at
that time. the Jews, as L. de Suchem assures us, had permission,
on the payment of money, to go into the inner and holy place,
while Christians were compelled to remain without: yet those who

---

[1] Carmoly, *Itin.* p. 129.

[2] Quatremère in Makrizi, *Hist. de Sult. Mamlouks de l'Egypte*, T. i. 245.

[3] Mejr ed Din, in von Hammer, *Fundgruben des Orients*, ii. p. 375 ; after
Robinson, *Bib. Research.* ii. p. 78.

[4] J. Maundeville, in Wright, *Early Trav.* p. 101.

[5] Ishak Chelo, *Les Chemins de Jerus.* in Carmoly, *Itin.* p. 242.

were in his company managed to smuggle themselves in under false pretences. At a later period the right to enter was again taken away from the Jews; and at the time of Jichus ha-Abot,[1] in A.D. 1537, it was allowed to them to peep through a small window, and see what might be revealed by the light of torches. Fabri, the lector from Ulm, and his distinguished companion von Breidenbach, who visited Hebron in 1483, were equally[2] debarred entrance, notwithstanding their strong letters to the governor; for, on being asked whether they had been allowed to enter the great mosque at Jerusalem, and replying that they had not, he said that the Haram at Hebron was far more sacred. The pilgrims[3] were permitted to go only to the staircase of the mosque, and there to repeat their prayers and kiss the sacred precincts.

The Spaniard Badia, under the assumed name of a Mohammedan, Ali Bey,[4] gained access, as I have elsewhere said, to the interior of the Haram, and has described it, though in a rather vague way. He ascended by a fine broad staircase to a gallery, passed through a little court, then turned to the left through a portico resting on square pillars, to the vestibule of a temple divided into two apartments. In one of these Abraham was said to rest, in the other Sarah. In the nave of the mosque, or former church, which he calls Gothic in its type of architecture, there stands, between two great pillars, and on the right, a little chapel, with the grave of Isaac; on the left a similar one, containing that of Rebecca. Here stands the Merhele, or place where the Friday's prayers are offered. On the other side of the mosque, in a vestibule, were two compartments, containing, according to the tradition of the place, the graves of Jacob and Leah. At the end of a portico, on the right, there runs, he says, a long gallery, serving as a mosque, and opening into another room in which is Joseph's grave, though, according to Josh. xxiv. 32, he was buried at Shechem. The coffins were not to be seen, for they were covered with rich silk cloths, wrought with figures of gold. These were green when covering the

---

[1] Jichus ha-Abot, *Tombeaux des Patriarches*, p. 433.

[2] Fel. Fabri, *Evagatorium*, ed. Hassler, ii. p. 349.

[3] Comp. Fel. Fabri, *Evag.* ii. p. 350; D'Arvieux, *Reise*, Pt. ii. p. 195; Abulfedæ *Tab. Syriæ*, ed. Koehler, p. 87, Note 52.

[4] Ali Bey, *Trav.* ii. pp. 232, 233.

coffins of the patriarchs, and red when over those of their wives. In many cases these were not single thicknesses, but of several; there being nine over the presumed remains of Abraham. The floors in the neighbourhood of the graves were carpeted, and the entrances provided with iron trellis-work, silver-plated, and with doors. Over a hundred persons were employed as servants in this temple : they all demanded baksheesh, and made the visit a costly one.

Vere Monro,[1] on the occasion of his visit to Hebron in 1833, gave a description of the interior of the Haram. He does not claim to have seen it, but he fails to indicate his authorities ; on which account Robinson calls the authenticity of his statements in question. He gives the dimensions of a small mosque, only forty paces long and twenty-five wide, at the side of which stand the places of burial, like little booths, with stone partitions between : only those of the men can be visited, those of the women cannot. These, however, he says, appear to be but imitations of graves : the real coffins of the patriarchs lay in a deep cave, the entrance to which was always lighted, but never entered. According to the statement of the Mohammedan servant of von Schubert,[2] and who had seen the interior of the mosque several times, the cave is strongly guarded by lattice-work.

A single authentic inscription, dating from the fourth or fifth century, written in Greek, and purporting to be over the grave of Abraham, states that at that time the Christians who visited the place held the authenticity of the spot to be indisputable. It was written by one Nilus, a son of one Daniel, and by his companions, all of whom subscribed themselves as sworn to the service of St Abraham. These have been copied and presented to Mr Schultz, Prussian consul in Jerusalem, who in his turn gave a transcript to Captain Newbold.[3] The account of the latter may be found in the sixteenth volume of the *Journal of the Royal Geographical Society of London.*

Outside of the Haram, on a side street, and near the gateway of a khan, there is an inscription with the date 679 of the

---

[1] Vere Monro, *A Summer Ramble in Syria*, vol. i. pp. 243, 245 ; Robinson, *Bib. Research.* ii. p. 709.

[2] Von Schubert, *Reise*, ii. p. 473.

[3] Capt. Newbold, *Mem. on the Site*, in *Jour. of the Roy. Geog. Soc. of London*, vol. xvi. Pt. i. p. 337.

Hegira, *i.e.* A.D. 1280, with the statement that it was placed there by the Egyptian sultan Seif ed Din.[1] With regard to the inhabitants of Hebron we have no full and authentic account, since their fanaticism and their predatory lives have for centuries made the place very inaccessible; and the constant strife between Jerusalem, Bethlehem, and Hebron have added to it. Since, however, the storming of their city in 1834 by Egyptian troops under Ibrahim Pasha, and the destruction of a large portion of the population, a degree of quiet has been attained which was not known before, and strangers have been allowed to pass through the place unmolested. But since that time also there has been a diminution in the importance of the city, its trade and its wealth : its houses have fallen into ruin, and the inhabitants of the city have fallen into deplorable poverty. The Jews, on the other hand, have of late years been increasing in numbers and in wealth : the Egyptian Government has allowed them to carry on trade and different branches of business; whereas in former times they were tolerated there only on condition of paying a large tax, and enduring almost every kind of indignity and suffering.

When Seetzen visited Hebron[2] in 1806, there was only a single Christian resident in the place. In Irby[3] and Mangles' time (1818) no Christian ventured to reside there; in 1838, Robinson found but one within the walls.[4] Although Russegger[5] was the bearer of letters which secured him a polite reception in the house of a Mohammedan, yet he soon learned that the old Moslem hatred to Christians had not died, but was prevented by Ibrahim's iron hand from showing itself. Monro,[6] who visited Hebron in 1833, when there was some police authority, was not protected so securely even by his firman, as to escape being followed by crowds of rough fellows, who assailed him with stones. But since 1835 it has been different; and von Schubert, Robinson, Wolcott, Wilson, Bartlett, Strauss,

---

[1] Wilson, *Lands of the Bible*, i. p. 368.
[2] Seetzen, *Mon. Corresp.* xvii. p. 132.
[3] Irby and Mangles, *Trav.* p. 343.
[4] Robinson, *Bib. Research.* ii. p. 88.
[5] Russegger, *Reise*, iii. p. 77.
[6] Vere Monro, *Summer Ramble*, i. p. 233.

and others, have been treated with politeness, been efficiently protected, and allowed to prosecute those inquiries which it is hoped will in the future lead to more full results than those already attained.

The little place, although shorn of much of its former glory and magnificence, is tolerably well populated. According to Robinson,[1] there are sixteen hundred taxable Mohammedans dwelling there, forty-one taxable Jews, and two hundred Jews under the protection of European consulates. Shortly before Robinson's visit, Ibrahim Pasha had established seven hundred and fifty Moslem soldiers in Hebron, and the entire population was estimated to be not far from 10,000 souls.

Bartlett,[2] the skilful artist, was surprised at the beauty of the inhabitants of Hebron, whose countenances contrasted strongly with the sallow faces and meagre forms which he had become familiar with at Jerusalem. Poujoulat confirms the same fact, and attributes it to the healthful situation, the pure air, and the more abundant, better, and cheaper means of living, which include mutton, fruit, raisins, and other articles with which the bazaar abounds.

At Seetzen's time, while Hebron was enjoying its more prosperous days, there were khans there for the reception of every one who chose to take advantage of them; and besides these, to meet the wants arising from the trade of the people with the wandering Beduins, there were nine rooms within the city where strangers were entertained without cost in the manner so common on the east side of the Jordan, but which is now hardly known on the west side. This custom, whose perfection may still be seen at Kerak and Szalt, has since ceased in Hebron, with the changed condition and circumstances of the place. In former times, says Seetzen, the Mohammedan pilgrims from Jerusalem to Mecca took Hebron in their way; and this gave the ancient city a great advantage, which it has since lost, the caravans taking their way now by way of Jericho, and joining there the companies which come from Damascus.[3]

[1] Robinson, *Bib. Research.* ii. p. 715.
[2] Bartlett, *Walks about the City*, p. 218; comp. *Corresp. d'Orient*, T. v. p. 221.
[3] Comp. Irby and Mangles, *Trav.* p. 344.

Seetzen speaks[1] of the chief articles of manufacture which he noticed at Hebron, as warm woollen goods, skin bottles for the transportation of water, and glass ware. These, in addition to all kinds of agricultural produce, formed the staples of trade. In one glass workshop there were eight kinds of bottles and hollow ware made; in others, in which boys were the chief workmen, bracelets, rings, and corals were made in immense quantity. These were sold at very low prices,—a hundred bracelets for two piastres, and a hundred rings for one piastre. They were of all sizes and colours, blue predominating. For the corals there were eight furnaces in operation, for the rings seven, for the bottles formerly four, but then only one. The manufacture dates back to the time of the Crusades; and Rabbi Ishak Chelo,[2] writing in 1333, tells us that it was introduced from Venice, and prosecuted by the Jews, who carried on an active trade in it, as well as in the woollen goods which they spun and coloured.

Fabri makes mention[3] of the glassmakers of Hebron, whom he found there in 1483. Monro speaks of the quality of the article manufactured as thin, green, and very brittle; von Schubert, who spent the Easter holidays there, found the workmen in constant activity; according to Wilson, all of them are Mohammedans. The little articles made there, particularly the imitations of coral, are carried into the most remote parts of the neighbouring desert, and are purchased by every wild roving tribe; while the more useful articles, the bottles, lamps, etc., find a market in every village between Alexandria and Damascus. Von Schubert saw whole camel trains, laden with this ware on their way to Jerusalem, for the use of the Greek and Armenian pilgrims whose habit was to gather there at Easter. The fuel used in the glass-houses was obtained by tearing up the stumps on the plain of Mamre, although this supply was nearly exhausted, or by cutting down the few fir trees which were springing up to supply the place of the terebinths that once stood there. Towards the east, and on the way to the Dead Sea, forests are still standing, whose natural growth supplies to a large extent the needs

---

[1] Seetzen, MS. Communication.

[2] Ishak Chelo, *Les Chemins de Jerusalem*, in Carmoly, *Itin.* p. 242.

[3] Fel. Fabri, *Evagator.* ii. p. 341 ; Monro, i. p. 245.

of the glass furnaces. A thousand years ago, as is clear from the account of Arculfus, a great pine forest covered the hills in the neighbourhood of Hebron, which are now deserted and bare.

Wilson[1] found the Mohammedan glass-workmen very frank in communicating to him the whole method of manufacture, which seemed to him more simple than the European methods. Yet the glass seemed to him less clear and transparent than that which is found at the north, and which has lately been scattered by Bohemian glass merchants through Damascus, Aleppo, and Beirut, compelling the poorer article to yield to the better.

On the other hand, the Jews have through all Syria enjoyed the monopoly of dyeing granted them in the twelfth century, and have carried it to great perfection; on which account the Jewish pilgrims often sojourned when at Hebron at the houses of people of their own faith, whom they mention as dyers. At a later date, however, after the great persecution of the Jews, we find no more mention of them as dyers, nor of silk weavers, although one quarter still retains the name given it as the place inhabited by the people of this occupation.

Another occupation in which the Jews of the Hebron of the present day actively engage, is the preparation of raisins, syrup, and wine, from which they derive no slight profit. With the first of these an active business is kept up, and the Jews have even come into the possession of vineyards of their own.[2] The men who but a little while ago were hardly tolerated within the walls of Hebron, are now in the possession of little olive plantations and vineyards. The larger vineyards, particularly those in the vale of Eshcol, they do not hire, but receive the grapes when ripe from the Mohammedan owners, and dry them partly for raisins, boil them down partly for the syrup known as dibs, and make the rest into wine. The Hebron grove, remarks Hasselquist,[3] is of the same variety with that produced on the Rhine, and the wine of Hebron has that fiery yet pleasant flavour which the Rhine wine possesses, although richer in sugar, and with a more delightful bouquet. The Swedish naturalist was led from this coincidence to adopt

[1] Wilson, *Lands of the Bible*, i. p. 377.
[2] Von Schubert, *Reise*, ii. pp. 464, 467 ; Wilson, *Lands*, etc., ii. p. 369.
[3] Hasselquist, *Reise*, p. 256.

the theory that the Rhine grape was carried to Europe by the crusaders. In Hebron the native wine is drunk by the Jews, who place it before their guests, in accordance with a custom universal in the convents of Palestine.

Von Schubert, when in Hebron, was the guest[1] of the chief rabbi. The Jewish quarter lies near the southern entrance to the city, and is a perfect labyrinth of houses, and narrow, dark streets. He was there during the Easter or passover holidays, and was surprised to find that at that time a degree of neatness was attained by the Jews which is rarely met in the East. Among them he found nearly sixty families from Poland and Russia, and six hundred souls from Spain. After his long sojourn in the desert, he says that he was surprised to find it possible to supply even the simplest wants of life ; the emerging from the wilderness to civilisation, even in its ruder form, being a change so great that he could scarcely realize it. He found the Jews of Hebron allowed at certain times to look into the sacred Haram through a window covered with lattice-work ;[2] and there he often saw the Jewish women, particularly those from Spain, uttering their lamentations. At the same place they were accustomed to celebrate their religious rites ; and in the sixteenth century, according to Jichus ha-Abot, they distributed their alms[3] of bread and meat in the name of father Abraham, and gave utterance to their joys and their griefs, accompanied with choral music and the beat of a drum.

The celebrated Jewish millionnaire, Sir Moses Montefiore, whose efforts in behalf of the people of his own faith in Syria and Palestine have been so fruitful in good, did not succeed in entering the cave where the bones of his fathers repose, notwithstanding the efforts made by the governor of Hebron. He was taken beyond the wall which surrounds the Haram ; but the terribly vindictive feeling which it raised in the minds of the Mohammedans made him fear that, after his departure from Hebron, their wrath would be fearfully wreaked upon the Jews, and caused him to desist from the effort to explore the interior recesses of the Haram.[4]

---

[1] Von Schubert, *Reise*, ii. p. 464.
[2] *Ibid.* p. 470 ; Robinson, *Bib. Research.* ii. p. 79.
[3] Jichus ha-Abot, in Carmoly, *Itin.* p. 434.
[4] Bartlett, *Walks, etc.*, p. 220.

The most thorough examination into the present condition of the Jews at Hebron has been made by Dr Wilson, who visited the place in 1843, and who, on account of his familiarity with their language and literature, as well as in the fulfilment of his duties as a missionary, was well fitted to discharge such a trust. He was very hospitably received and entertained by the sects of the Sephardim (the Spanish Jews) and the Ashkenasim (the Polish and German Jews), particularly by the superior of the first-named body. He had brought letters of introduction from prominent Jews in Bombay, representing him as a man of influence; and these secured him the favourable reception which was accorded to him.[1]

The Sephardim community in Hebron, according to Wilson, is poor and small, consisting of forty-five families, and two hundred and fifty souls. They had come to this ancient city for the sad purpose of bewailing the condition of their race at the tombs of the patriarchs. They live mainly on the alms which are given them by their fellow-believers who come on brief pilgrimages to the place: they have very little occupation; a little gardening and wine-making is all. Their school in the synagogue consisted of thirty scholars, and the main study pursued seemed to be the reading of the Old Testament and the Talmud in the Hebrew and Spanish languages. Only two or three of them understood Arabic. They lived in very small and narrow houses, very seldom owning them themselves. They were exceedingly oppressed by the Mohammedans, who took every course to extort money from them. They enjoyed freedom in their peculiar religious worship, but it was evident that this was accorded only as a pretext for demanding money. The very protection which they had from the insults which had once been offered them in the streets had all to be liberally paid for: the grasping Mohammedan[2] authorities of Hebron were too greedy to allow the Jews the possession of anything that they could claim and appropriate. In the eyes of these men, cunning was a far greater recommendation than honesty. The governor of the place, who on the occasion of Wilson's visit did what he had never done before, viz. entered the house of a Jew, in order to return Wilson's call, took occasion to praise

---

[1] Wilson, *Lands of the Bible*, i. pp. 369–379.
[2] *Ibid.* pp. 358, 361 ; Strauss, *Sinai und Golgotha*, p. 199.

the cunning of father Abraham in his purchase of the cave of
Machpelah of the Hittites. He said that he purchased as
much as the hide of an ox would cover, but that he was shrewd
enough to cut it into thongs, and demand as much as could be
included within it all.

Wilson says that there are very few of the Ashkenasim
settled in Hebron, and of the Karaim or Karaites almost none.
They listened attentively to his account of his journey through
Sinai and Edom, kissed reverently the stones and other objects
which he brought thence, but seemed to understand very little
regarding the fulfilment of the prophecies concerning Idumæa ;
for though very well read in the Psalms and in the Mosaic
books, they had very little knowledge of the prophets.

The Ashkenasim had two little schools. Their rabbi, who
was very oddly attired, said, with a very consequential air, that
he knew nothing about the Sephardim, and did not trouble
himself about them ; showing that even in this ancient city,
whose interest to the whole Jewish race is a common one, the
hateful spirit of sect is manifest. His community consisted of
fifty or sixty members, mostly Poles and Russians, whose great
hope is to die and be buried near the ashes of their forefathers.
None of them could read Arabic, and only a few of them had
even such a knowledge of it as would enable them to utter the
phrases of conventional intercourse.[1] Such is the sad condition
of this stiff-necked race even in the ancient home of their
fathers: here they live in their blindness, unconscious of the
high meaning even of the words which those fathers uttered
and recorded, whose memories they so deeply revere.

DISCURSION IV.

THE WAY FROM HEBRON TO BETHLEHEM. THE GROUPS OF MOUNTAIN CITIES IN
JUDAH, ACCORDING TO THE LIST IN JOSHUA : HULHUL, JEDUR, BEIT SUR,
BEIT UMMAR, BEIT AINUN, AND TEKUA ; WITH THE SCRIPTURE SITES WHICH
THEY IN PART REPRESENT.

We now leave Hebron, and take the great highway which
leads to Bethlehem and Jerusalem, and which passes the place
once supposed to have been the home of Abraham, and the ruins

[1] Wilson, *Lands of the Bible,* vol. ii. pp. 617–625.

alluded to a few pages back. If we now turn once more to the Hebron of Joshua, we find its name included in the second group of the mountain cities of Judah. It seems to be the central one of the nine whose names are presented together. Of these nine, the location of only two has been determined with any degree of probability,—that of Hebron and that of Beth-Tappuah, the modern village of Teffuh. It is evident, however, that the location of the whole must have been in the immediate vicinity of Hebron. Their names were (Josh. xv. 52-54)—Arab, Dumah, Eshean, Janum, Aphekah, Humtah, and Zior, besides Hebron and Beth-Tappuah, whose locality is known.[1] In the fourth group of six mountain cities, namely those lying north of Hebron (Josh. xv. 58, 59), the sites of three[2]—Haihul, Beth-zur, and Gedor—have been determined by recent investigators ; and those of Maarath, Beth-anoth, and Eltekon ascertained with a considerable degree of probability, the latter being supposed to be the Elthecue or Ecthecue of Jerome. To these four groups of ante-Hebraic cities Joshua adds a fifth, lying west of Jerusalem, and on the northern frontier of the territory of Judah,—a small group, consisting of but two cities, Kirjath-Baal[3] and Rabbah. These all lie within that hilly region which Joshua calls the mountains of Judah and Israel, and to which he alludes in the words (xi. 21), " And at that time came Joshua, and cut off the Anakims from the mountains, from Hebron, from Debir, from Anab, and from all the mountains of Judah, and from all the mountains of Israel : Joshua destroyed them utterly, with their cities." Here the word "mountains" is used in a general sense, and indicates the whole hilly country, extending from Anab and Hebron -westward to the heights near Eglon (Debir). These mountains of Judah constitute the southern, and the mountains of Israel the northern, part of the broad range, which extends from the plain of Esdraelon to the southern border of Palestine, and which, in its general character, may be compared to an arched plateau, its elevation above the sea being considerable. The natural boundary, so far as one exists, although none is mentioned in the Testament, appeared to Robinson[4] to be the great Wadi Beit Hanina. The name " mountains of Israel" is not

[1] Keil, *Comment. zu Josua*, ch. xv. 52, 54, p. 301.   [2] *Ibid.* p. 303.
[3] Comp. Robinson, *Bib. Research.* ii. p. 225.   [4] *Ibid.* ii. p. 9.

mentioned for the first time in connection with the division which followed the death of Solomon.[1] Even as early as when Judah was in possession of its territory at the south, and while the other tribes were in Gilgal; still later, when Ephraim and Manasseh had taken possession of their portion, and all the rest excepting Judah were encamped in Shiloh; this method of designating the different parts of southern Palestine must have been in use. It rested rather upon convenience than upon striking physical characteristics. And so, in like manner, the expression " mountains of Ephraim" (Josh. xix. 50, xx. 7, xxiv. 30) must be understood as referring rather to special territory readily designated by that term, than to a district whose geographical peculiarities were particularly marked. In Moses' narrative (Deut. i. 7, 19) the mountains of Judah were called the mountains of the Amorites. In the review given by Joshua (x. 1–42) of his conquest of southern Palestine, extending from Kadesh-Barnea over Gaza, Goshen, Gibeon, and as far as Gilgal; and in the review of the northern campaign (xi. 1–15), we read (ver. 16), " So Joshua took all that land, the hills, and all the south country, and all the land of Goshen, and the valley, and the plain, and the mountain of Israel, and the valley of the same."[2]

These words are a happy classification of the five different districts which constituted the region conquered by Joshua.

The first, " the hills," embraces the territory known specifically as Judah, and comprehending the five groups of mountain cities to which reference has already been made.

The second division, " all the south country," is southern Canaan, extending from the border of Edom on the east to Philistia on the west, and from the desert on the south to the mountains of Judah on the north. This district was, at the first apportionment of land, given to the tribe of Judah : its cities are mentioned in Josh. xv. 21–32. At the second apportionment many of these cities fell to the tribe of Simeon (xix. 1–9), although they were at a later period absorbed again in Judah (1 Sam. xxvii. 10, xxx. 14 ; 2 Sam. xxiv. 7).

The third division, " the land of Goshen," indicates the long coast plain extending from Gaza to Carmel (Josh. ix. 1).

The fourth division, which in the English version is speci-

[1] Keil, *Comment. zu Josua*, p. 217. [2] *Ibid.* p. 201.

fied as the valley and the plain, but which Luther renders as
the bottoms and fields, designates the hill region lying between
the coast plain and the mountain district proper, and also
embracing the lower basins of the brooks which drain the
higher country of the interior.

The fifth, finally, refers to the mountains of Israel at the
north.

Having taken this preliminary view of the territory held by
the tribe of Judah at the time of Joshua, we are the better
prepared to advance on the way from Hebron to Jerusalem,
and speak intelligently of the ruins and localities on the road.
North of Khurbet el Nusarah, and in the neighbourhood of
Neby Junas (Prophet Jonah), already mentioned, there are the
shattered vestiges of an old town on the right side of the highway. No traveller has yet explored it, but it is called by the
Arabs Hulhul,[1] in which name Robinson thinks that he recog-
nises the Halhul of the fourth group of Joshua's mountain
cities. Jerome speaks of it as Elul, and locates it in the
neighbourhood of Hebron. As the place has never been visited,
Robinson's conjecture has had no opportunity of being verified.
He mentions, however, that Ebn Batuta speaks of the grave
of Jonah, and that Niebuhr alludes to the burial-place of the
prophet Nathan, without mentioning the name Hulhul. Ishak
Chelo, the Aragonese pilgrim, visited Halhul[2] in 1333, and
speaks of seeing there several Jews, who showed him the tomb
of the prophet Gad, who counselled David, when a refugee in
Moab, to leave that land and enter Judah (1 Sam. xxii. 5).
Wilson[3] confirms the locality of Hulhul; he saw other ruins
not laid down on Robinson's map, but could not ascertain their
names.

A large village, an hour distant N.N.W. from Hulhul, is
entered on Robinson's map by the name Beit Ummar. He
did not learn any particulars regarding it, however. Wilson[4]
speaks of it as a large village on a hill on the left of the road
to Bethlehem. Just behind it was Jeddur or Jedur, a name
which is often confounded[5] with others that sound like it, such

---

[1] Ishak Chelo, in Carmoly, *Itin.* p. 242.
[2] Robinson, *Bib. Research.* i. p. 216.
[3] Wilson, *Lands of the Bible*, i. p. 383.   [4] *Ibid.* p. 386.
[5] Keil, *Comment. zu Josua*, pp. 296, 297.

as Gedera, Gaedue, etc. It stands on the western border of
the high mountain region, although it cannot be seen[1] from
the highway on the east; looked at from the west, it was in
sight for days together.

It seems to correspond to the Hebrew Gedor mentioned in
the fourth group of mountain cities (Josh. xv. 56) : a visit to
it would probably well repay the trouble. On the other side of
the road Wilson discovered a place called Beit Ainun,[2] which
he conjectured might be the Beth-anoth of the fourth group,
mentioned in immediate connection with Maarath and Eltekon,
and directly after Gedor.

Wolcott had the good fortune[3] to visit this important ruin,
which up to his time had never been examined by any traveller. On the way from Jerusalem to Ramel el Khulil he had
seen the ruins from afar; they seemed to him to be the largest
in the entire neighbourhood. He left Ramel, proceeded north-
easterly, and in a half-hour reached the place. He followed an
ancient paved road, and afterwards came to one like it in
general appearance, though unpaved, leading from Ramel to
Hulhul. Within the ruins of Beit Ainun he saw two small
prostrate columns with capitals, and near them a fountain with
reservoirs. The ruins extend a half English mile in length
and breadth ; many of the stones are bevelled in the ancient
manner. The principal ruin is eighty-three feet long and
seventy-two broad ; but fragments of columns set in masonry
attest its comparatively modern construction. Many ruins are
scattered around, showing that a city was once there; and
indeed many of the street lines are still visible. The largest
quarried stones are six feet in length, three in breadth, and are
bevelled. In the upper part of the ruins there are four
cisterns. The immediate connection of Beth-anoth in Joshua
with Halhul and Beth-zur, whose names are now seen to exist
in modern Arabic words, led Wolcott to believe that Beit Ainun
and Beth-anoth are identical.

Only a quarter of an hour farther north, on the road to
Tekoa, lies Sai, with a little heap of ruins, called Abuduweir.
The places known as Ras Tureh and Ras el Adeiseh were

[1] Robinson, *Bib. Research.* ii. pp. 14, 16, 70, 71.
[2] Wilson, *Lands of the Bible*, i. p. 384.
[3] Wolcott, *Excursion to Hebron, etc.*, in *Bib. Sacra*, 1843, pp. 58, 59.

mentioned as being in the neighbourhood, although he was unable to see any ruins of them. But on the south-west of Beit Ainun there was a rocky place called Zeiteh, with ruins overgrown with bushes. An hour farther south-west Wolcott found the fruitful Wadi Beni Salim, with a spring of the same name. On the roads thither, which, though now so deserted of men, show abundant traces of a dense population there at a former day, Robinson[1] found marks of human skill indeed, but none that the use of carriages had ever been known there. This puzzled him, for he had not failed· to notice that it is expressly stated in the account of Joseph's sending for his relatives, that wheeled vehicles went up to Egypt to bring them (Gen. xlv. 19-21, 27); and in the conveying of the body of Jacob to Hebron, carriages must have been used (Gen. l. 9, 14). Wilson[2] has, however, been able to detect the marks of wheels in many places; and Dr Krafft[3] has traced ruts on the main highway to Bethlehem above Deir el Banat, above Urtash, the ancient Etham, along the pools of Solomon and the ancient aqueduct.

A short half-hour after Robinson left Neby Yunas, and had passed Hulhul, he saw on his left a fallen tower, which he considered to be a relic of the time of the Crusades. Five minutes later he came to a spring with a stone receptacle, round which lay ruins like those of a fortification. The stones were very large; the rocks near so much cut away as to form a perpendicular wall. This place, which lies two hours north of Hebron, was called ed-Dirweh;[4] and Robinson suspected, after failing to find traces of the celebrated fortress Beth-sur farther to the west, where the legend of the monks placed it, that he had found its site here. His conjecture was fully confirmed by the result of Wolcott's inquiries, who learned from the intelligent sheikh who accompanied him, and who had not the faintest suspicion that he was seeking a name which should sound like the scriptural Beth-zur, that the Arabic name of the place is Beit Sur. Wilson[5] was led to believe that this place

---

[1] Robinson, *Bib. Research.* ii. p. 357.

[2] Wilson, *Lands of the Bible*, i. p. 382.

[3] Dr Krafft's Manuscript Communication, July 1848.

[4] Robinson, *Bib. Research.* i. p. 459, ii. pp. 65, 221.

[5] Wilson, *Lands of the Bible*, i. p. 384.

was the one which in the fourth century was universally
believed to be the place where the eunuch was baptized by
Philip, although it does not lie on the most direct route from
Jerusalem to Gaza[1] (Acts viii. 26, 28). Dr Krafft,[2] who visited
the spot in 1845, examined it with more care than any of his
predecessors. At ed-Dirweh, he says, there is a very fine
spring close by the road, in whose immediate neighbourhood
there stand the ruins of a little but very ancient Basilica. He
ascended the hill lying opposite, whence he beheld the remains
of a large tower. Beside these there were the foundations of
an old town, which was surrounded by a thick wall in the
manner of a fortress. This place the camel-driver called Bet
Zur, a name which suggested to Dr Krafft the probability that
it was the Beth-zur of the book of Joshua. The view from it
took in all the mountains of southern Judah ; Hulhul, with
its tower, was at the south-east, Beth Ummar north-east,—the
latter a prominent locality, probably the ancient Maarath,
mentioned in the Scripture in connection with Gedor, Beth-
zur, and Beth-anoth. The place was also an admirable position from which to judge the nature of the mountain-land of
Judah, a rolling country, with frequent hills, whose tops are
broad and flat, and whose sides are terraced so as to afford good
vineyards.

A closer examination of these ruins shows that the lower
portion of them dates from a period of great antiquity, and that
the immense square stones which are so old serve to sustain a
structure of much more recent origin. At the south-west are
to be seen sepulchres hollowed from the rock ; among them,
one with a great gate and two small side-gates. The ancient
Basilica near the spring has a vestibule ; three covered doors
lead to the nave. The walls are immensely thick, and display
windows which are like port-holes in appearance. The waters
of the spring flow into a long and handsome stone basin, connected with which is one for drinking. In the vestibule of the
Basilica there is a circular basin cut in stone, and resembling a
baptismal font. It is here that the traditions of the fourth
century located the baptism of the eunuch by Philip. And, in
truth, there was a highway from Jerusalem to Gaza running

---

[1] Comp. *Itiner. Antonini Aug. et Hierosolym.* ed. Parthey, p. 282.
[2] Dr W. Krafft, MS. Communication, 1848.

by this place, and even now the marks of wheels may be seen. It was built in the manner of the Roman *via militaris*, and was the ancient mountain road. Another and more direct route led westward from Jerusalem to Ramlah, passing through a district of valleys. No traces of wheels are to be seen in the line of this road. The language of the passage in Acts is so definite regarding the vehicle in which the eunuch rode, and the convenience of this water basin for the purpose of baptism so evident, that it is probable[1] that the tradition of the *Itin. Burdig.* and of Jerome is more correct than that which has generally prevailed since the time of the Crusades, and which has been inculcated by Cotovicus, Maundrell, Pococke, and others, who have supposed the place of baptism to have been farther westward, and have overlooked the claims of Beth-zur.

On the side of the spring the rocky wall is entirely hollowed out into graves, which in modern times have been used as the lodging-places of pilgrims and hermits. The road running by ed-Dirweh is still paved with large stones. The fountain runs across the way, passing into three successive basins. Only a few steps northward is to be seen a Roman inscription, mostly illegible, yet remaining in a sufficiently perfect state to show that it was the twentieth milestone from Jerusalem. This Jerome states to have been close by the place where the eunuch was baptized. The name Beth-zur (*domus petræa*) also indicates the site of a strong fortress, such as we know that it was at the time of the Maccabees, when it was besieged by Antiochus Eupator. Josephus also alludes to the great strength of this position. It may therefore be regarded as certain, that the ancient Beth-zur is now located and identified with the ruins above mentioned, whose evident importance is coincident with that of the city whose memory they illustrate.[2]

The discovery of this place gave a certain degree of completeness to the investigation into the fourth group of mountain cities mentioned by Joshua; and the five cities mentioned as in the desert of Judah,[3] between the mountains and the Dead

---

[1] Robinson, *Bib. Research.* ii. p. 65 ; Keil, *Comment. zu Josua*, p. 304 ; v. Raumer, *Pal.* p. 164, Note 162.

[2] Reland, *Pal.* pp. 658–660 ; von Raumer, *Pal.* pp. 163, 164 ; Keil, *Comment. zu Josua*, pp. 303–305.

[3] Keil, *Comment. zu Josua*, p. 306.

Sea (Josh. xv. 61, 62), including Beth-arabah and the City of Salt at the northern and southern extremities of that body of water, will probably be identified in the course of future investigations, although the location of Middin, Secacah, and Nibshan is at present unknown. Enough has been determined already to set in a clear light the great excellence of the book of Joshua, as one of the most remarkable documents which still exist relating to the geography of the very earliest time. In view of the great completeness of that record, it must seem very singular that no mention is made of Bethlehem, which lay so near to the cities already referred to, and to which allusion is made in the book of Genesis (xxxv. 19): " So Rachel died, and was buried in the way to Ephrath, which is Bethlehem." In the Septuagint, however, the name is crowded into a list of eleven cities between the fifty-ninth and sixtieth verses of Josh. xv. The opinions of scholars have varied regarding the genuineness of this passage; but the recent very thorough inquiries of Keil have convinced him that the passage regarding Bethlehem in the Septuagint is genuine, and that it has been accidentally omitted from our Hebrew text.[1]

The whole of the route from Hebron to Bethlehem, which to most travellers is a dreary desert, with almost no redeeming features, was to the susceptible English artist Bartlett[2] one of great interest and beauty. Although he traversed it under a blinding light and scorching heat, he was thrown into constant admiration at the ruins, wells, springs, gardens, hills and bottom lands, the herds, droves of camels and donkeys, and the mothers surrounded by their playing children. The whole scene carried him back to patriarchal days.

[1] Note 16 in Keil, *Comment. zu Buch Josua*, pp. 304, 305 ; compare v. Raumer, *Pal.* p. 278, Note 107.

[2] Bartlett, *Walks about the City,* etc., p. 213.

DISCURSION V.

WAY FROM THE RUINS OF THE ANCIENT BETH-ZUR, PASSING THE THREE POOLS
OF SOLOMON AND THE WADI URTAS, THE FORMER ETHAM, OR SOLOMON'S
GARDENS, TO BETHLEHEM. THE SITUATION OF BETHLEHEM; ITS BASILICA
AND CONVENT; THE CONDITION OF THE BETHLEHEMITES.

From the ruin of Beth-zur, on the great road from Hebron
to Bethlehem, there is a road two hours in length leading
through the open country. Yet, before Bethlehem is reached,
lying as it does a quarter of an hour's distance, and upon a low
double hill, the traveller descends the gentle slope leading to
Wadi Urtas, which derives its name from a small ruin similarly
designated. The road runs from the celebrated pools of Solomon
eastward, by the cavern of Khureitun, and by the southern base
of the Frank Mountain to the Dead Sea. Wadi Urtas slopes
away eastward from the main line of watershed on which lies
the little village el-Khude, now distinguished by a mosque,
formerly the Convent of St George,[1] and to be seen north-west
from the pools. This village of el-Khude was formerly very
much visited, but is now almost entirely deserted. As one
passes south-eastward from that village, half an hour brings
him to the upper part of Wadi Urtas, with the three pools of
Solomon, which no traveller passes without seeing, and which
are called by the Arabs el-Burak. The aqueduct, which led
eastward through the site of the ruined Urtas, we have had
occasion to speak of in another place; but the basins themselves, and their northern outlet towards Jerusalem, we must
treat of before we come to Bethlehem. The best accounts of
this complicated system of water-works are unquestionably those
of Maundrell, written in 1697, and of Robinson in our own
day. These observers have studied their structure with a fidelity
which leaves nothing undone, that is attainable without the aid
of that thorough mathematical survey which it is hoped will be
undertaken by some future traveller.[2]

Robinson passed south-westward from Bethlehem, down a

[1] Robinson, *Bib. Research.* i. p. 218, ii. p. 3.
[2] Fel. Fabri, *Evagatorium,* iii. p. 187. Comp. H. Maundrell, *Journey
from Aleppo to Jerusalem,* pp. 88, 89; Robinson, *Bib. Research.* ii. pp.
473–477.

steep path leading to the Wadi Taamirah, adorned with gardens, vineyards, and fine olive trees, in the expectation of coming to springs. Instead of these, he found two openings leading into an aqueduct, running through a kind of low arch. A number of women were there, getting water in their skin bottles to carry to Bethlehem. They assured him that there is no spring of fresh water either in or near the city. Passing on for an hour, and leaving Urtas on the west, he reached the famous pools of Solomon. They lie a hundred and fifty paces in the rear of a ruined Saracen or Turkish khan or castle, in which a number of families are accustomed to live, keeping their cattle in the neighbourhood. Here are three immense artificial cisterns, built of square quarried stones, and dating back to the remotest antiquity. Lying in this deserted and mysterious valley, they are not arranged in a straight line, but nevertheless are so placed that the bottom of the second lies higher than that of the first, and that of the third higher than that of the second. The upper one[1] was not full when Robinson saw it; and in the lower two water stood only in the most sunken portion, for the bottoms were not level, but sloping. The inner walls are covered with stucco, and the lowest one had been shortly before repaired. Maundrell says, that although these cisterns are of different lengths, they are generally square. Robinson, however, who measured them more accurately, says they are neither square nor perfectly regular in shape. The cubical contents of the lowest one are the greatest; of the highest one, the least. The length of the upper cistern was three hundred and eighty feet, the breadth about two hundred and thirty, the depth twenty-five. There were fifteen feet of water in it at the time of Robinson's visit. The middle cistern was four hundred and twenty-three feet long, from one hundred and sixty to two hundred and fifty feet broad (it being irregular in shape), and thirty-nine feet deep at its eastern end. There were fourteen feet of water in it. The lower cistern is five hundred and eighty-two feet long, from one hundred and forty-eight to two hundred and seven broad, and fifty feet deep. There is not much water in it now. They are all built of regularly hewn stones, and are carefully terraced. The great road from Hebron to Jerusalem passes just

[1] Bartlett, *Christian in Palestine*, Tab. lxi. p. 170. See also a sketch in Cassas, *Voy. Pittoresque de la Syrie;* Bartlett, *Walks, etc.*, p. 212.

westward of them. Wilson tells us that the great tanks[1] in India are much larger and much finer than these colossal cisterns in Syria; but whether the Indian ones are of as remote origin is uncertain: those in Ceylon date back to the Roman period. The purpose for which those in India were constructed was different from that held in view in Palestine: it was merely to collect water for purposes of irrigation, but not, as here, to supply the needs of a distant capital.

The chief source whence these cisterns draw their supply, appears to be a sunken spring lying in the open and gradually ascending fields, two hundred paces back of the castle Burak, and at the western end of the tanks themselves. At these cisterns there can be seen the opening of a narrow fountain, which was formerly closed with a great and immoveable stone. Of this entrance Maundrell has given us the best description. He says that this passage, which is twelve feet in length, leads into an arched room fifteen paces long and eight broad. This opens directly into a similar one, although somewhat smaller. The arches which support the roof are handsomely constructed, and are possibly the work of Solomon himself. In four places here water springs from the earth. It is conducted by a subterranean channel down to the successive cisterns. This description of a hidden sunken spring[2] is very valuable, for the light that it throws upon the manner in which king Hezekiah was able to cut off a supply of water from the Assyrian army while they were beleaguering Jerusalem. (See 2 Kings xx. 20; 2 Chron. xxxii. 3, 30.)

This subterranean passage, which in the monkish legends is considered to be the sealed fountain of Solomon's Song (iv. 12), ends at the uppermost corner of the north-west cistern, but not in the cistern itself. One arm, twenty-four feet long and five broad, enters the tank; but another runs along its northern side, and divides in like manner at the middle cistern, and finally enters the lower.

Besides this main tributary to the cisterns, traces of other fountains have been discovered. The aqueduct which leads from the neighbourhood of Bethlehem, northward to Jerusalem, is fed by two main channels. One flows from the cisterns

---

[1] Wilson, *Lands of the Bible*, i. p. 387.

[2] W. Krafft, *Die Topographie Jerusalems*, p. 121.

and their tributary spring; another comes down the Taamirah valley, south of Bethlehem. "The whole immense work," remarks Robinson, "must have been of incalculable value, both to Bethlehem and Jerusalem, at the time when it was in perfect condition, and doubtless contained ample supplies of water for the needs of both cities." How much the aqueduct, as we see it at the present day, owes to the repairs of Pontius Pilate,[1] is uncertain; but both the Talmudists and Josephus coincide in giving him credit for valuable improvements. Yet the work which he began appears to have been broken off suddenly, and to have been finished by other hands.

Even at the present day, these cisterns send water to that great mosque in Jerusalem which is built on the site of Solomon's temple. Robinson could not gain a view of the entrance of this water into the central area; but from his study of the course of the aqueduct, he had no doubt where it terminated.[2] Bartlett was subsequently led to coincide with Robinson in these views; and Tobler[3] followed the aqueduct in 1847 from Etham to the Suk Bab es Sinesleh, in the neighbourhood of Mekhemeh, the house of the kadi. Near Bethlehem, Robinson saw water flowing at the bottom of the pipe. South of the city it lies twenty feet below the surface; and there is an opening, to which reference was made above, where women let down their water-skins to obtain supplies for Bethlehem. As a general thing, the pipe lies close to the surface, and has the appearance of great antiquity. In some places it is made of earthen tiles, but generally it is of stone laid in mortar; the channel is a foot broad and a foot deep. Lying so near the surface as it does, it could of course easily be cut off in time of war; but when the city was in a state of siege, it is probable that supplies of water were gained elsewhere.

"The size and nature of the cisterns make it probable," says Robinson, "that the aqueduct which supplied Jerusalem with water was of very ancient origin, and that it once served the purpose of furnishing the gardens around the city with the moisture which they needed, although no mention is made of

---

[1] Krafft, *Topog.* pp. 134, 189.

[2] Robinson, *Bib. Research.* i. pp. 347, 348; Bartlett, *Walks about the City*, etc., pp. 58, 212.

[3] Tobler, in *Ausland*, 1848, No. 19, p. 73.

it in the Old Testament." Later Jewish statements in the
Talmud speak of the water which was supplied to the temple
from the spring of Etham. In 2 Chron. xi. 6, Bethlehem,
Etham, and Tekoa are mentioned in immediate connection, as
cities which Rehoboam converted into fortresses; and, according to Josephus (*Antiq.* viii. 7, 3), Solomon adorned Etham,
which lay not far from Jerusalem, with gardens and streams
of water. The passage in the Talmud probably relates, according to Robinson, to this watercourse, which in ancient as well
as in more recent times connected the neighbourhood of Bethlehem with the temple at Jerusalem. It seems, therefore, all
the more strange, that no one of the earlier pilgrims—no
writer, in fact, before the Crusades—has made any mention of
such a connection. Of other aqueducts constructed by the
Jewish kings we have repeated mention; but no account seems
to relate specifically to the one now under discussion. One
passage in Josephus seems, however, to be an exception to this,
although it appears to contain a mistake which Schultz[1] has
set in its apparently true light. Of Pontius Pilate, Josephus
says that he constructed [probably restored] an aqueduct which
led to Jerusalem, defraying the expense from the surplus funds
of the temple, which exasperated the Jews against him. This
he brought from a distance of four hundred stadia (τετρακοσίων
σταδίων). As this is absurd, Schultz conjectures that we ought
to read forty instead of four hundred; and this would exactly
apply to Etham and its cisterns. The work begun by Pilate
appears to have been left uncompleted, and to have fallen into
neglect, since at the end of the thirteenth century, Mahmud
ibn Kelaoun, who ruled over Syria and Egypt, caused the
work of restoration to be renewed, as may still be seen by the
inscription (the date is obliterated), where the aqueduct is conducted by means of arches across the valley of Hinnom and
below the pool of Gihon.[2]

The pilgrims subsequent to the Crusades—William of Bal-
densel and L. de Suchem, 1336–1350—are the first who speak
of the cisterns of Jerusalem as if they were filled with water,
which was conducted beneath the earth from Hebron, allowing
the aqueduct, however, to be seen along the way. The Jewish

---

[1] Schultz, *Jerusalem*, p. 94.
[2] Krafft, *Topograph. Jerus.* pp. 112, 189.

pilgrim Ishak Chelo,[1] who visited Etham in 1333, found a few of his fellow-believers there, worshipping in a synagogue, one of the seven which were to be found in all Palestine. They said that the place was called en-Etham, *i.e.* the spring of Etham, on account of the water which was conducted through pipes to Jerusalem. Cotowyk, who visited the place a hundred years later (1598), is the first who described the cisterns with any degree of detail. Since his time they have been repeatedly touched upon in the accounts of travellers, but never fully described till Maundrell gave his complete sketch. Fabri,[2] who was there in 1483, alluded briefly but distinctly to the Piscinæ Salomonis Regis in his *Evagatorium*, describing them as three immense tanks of clear water, lying on successive terraces, and flowing into each other, then watering the gardens of Solomon, and sending through a pipe laid for the purpose a supply for the use of the temple at Jerusalem, where, he says, it may be seen emerging.

At the time of Fabri's visit, the extensive repairs which the reigning Sultan of Egypt was carrying on in connection with the Jerusalem aqueduct, were such as to lead to a general belief that he was purposing to remove his residence thither. And when the learned lector of Ulm went out to Etham, he was very much surprised to find a camp there of six hundred workmen, who were engaged in the work of restoration. Of the further execution of this work, nothing more is known than what we learn from this glimpse of Fabri's; but even this indicates sufficiently clearly, that the works must have undergone repairs from time to time, and that they must always have been regarded as a great boon to the land.

The blessing which the system of irrigation carries to every part of the East, has been felt and seen in this little valley of Etham, which, narrow and small as it is, has been converted into a perfect paradise. This Wadi Urtas is, in all probability, the scene of Solomon's gardens; and it is of them, without much doubt, that the words recorded in Eccl. ii. 5, 6, were written: " I made me gardens and orchards, and I planted trees in them of all kinds of fruits: I made me pools of water, to water therewith the wood that bringeth forth trees; " as

---

[1] Ishak Chelo, *Les Chemins de Jerus.*, in Carmoly, p. 241.

[2] F. Fabri, *Evagatorium*, iii. pp. 183-187.

well as those in the Song of Solomon, iv. 16: "Awake, O
north wind; and come, thou south: blow upon my garden, that
the spices thereof may flow out." Josephus, in his description of the buildings erected by Solomon, and of his pomp and
splendour, relates that the king, who was a lover of horses and
chariots, then great rarities in a Jewish palace, used to ride out
in the early morning, surrounded by his body-guard, and with
his hair powdered with gold, as far as to Etham, and then,
having inspected his gardens there, returned to the capital.

Robinson was delighted to find a murmuring brook flowing
through the place. Wilson was so struck with the loveliness
of the place, that he supposed that it must be a favourite resort
of the people of Jerusalem, who desired to exchange the city
for so pleasant and attractive a retreat. Von Schubert, who
encountered spring in 1837 in Egypt in the month of January,
found it renewed at Sinai in February in all its freshness, and
met it yet again at the Wadi Urtas in March. Here, on the
twenty-eighth of that month, he found cherries and apricots[1]
in full bloom, and heard the notes of the turtle-dove. Wilson,
who was there in March 1843, was struck with the fresh spring
beauty of the place, and with the faithful manner in which it
mirrored the description of spring given in the Song of Solomon[2]
(ii. 11–13): "For, lo, the winter is past, the rain is over and gone;
the flowers appear on the earth; the time of the singing of
birds is come, and the voice of the turtle-dove is heard in the
land. The fig-tree putteth forth her green figs, and the vines
with the tender grape give a good smell. Arise, my love, my
fair one, and come away." It is true, the beauty of Wadi
Urtas has been exaggerated by pilgrims, for the place only
needs such simple language as the above to set it in the right
light.[3]

Ephrata, Bethlehem, the Beit-Lahm of the Arabs.

No one has ever doubted, remarks Robinson,[4] that the
present Beit-Lahm, *i.e.* house of flesh, is identical[5] with the

---

[1] Von Schubert, *Reise*, ii. p. 489.
[2] Wilson, *Lands of the Bible*, i. 358 ; Strauss, *Sinai und Golgotha*, 300.
[3] Fabri, *Evag.* iii. 183 ; Bartlett, *Christian in Palest.* p. 168, Tab. lix.
[4] Robinson, *Bib. Researches*, i. pp. 470–477.
[5] Reland, *Pal.* pp. 643-648.

ancient Hebrew Bethlehem, *i.e.* house of bread: the distance from Jerusalem—six Roman miles—exactly coincides with the space to be traversed to-day, a two hours' walk. Its history runs back, like that of Hebron, to the age of the patriarch Jacob; and in Gen. xlviii. 7 we are told that Rachel died a little way from Ephrath, and was buried in the way of Ephrath, or Bethlehem. The place of her burial is even now pointed out by the wayside, and the road still bears the name Ephrata. Bethlehem was the home of Boaz, who married Ruth, and whose son was Obed, and whose grandson was Jesse, the father of David. Here the latter tended his father's sheep, and here he was anointed by Samuel as king of Israel and Judah (1 Sam. xvi. 11-13). From this circumstance Bethlehem is often called in the New Testament the city of David; as, for example, in Luke ii. 4, 11, "The city of David, which is called Bethlehem;" and, "For unto you is born this day, in the city of David, a Saviour, which is Christ the Lord;" unquestionably, as von Schubert[1] says, the most beautiful and the most important of all birth-places in the world, in whose green fields the shepherds watched their flocks by night, and received the announcement of the great joy which had come over the world that night. From this place went up the triumphal song of praise, "Glory to God in the highest, and on earth peace, good-will toward men." And as the wise men from the east sought the star which came and stood over that little hamlet, so, during the many centuries which have followed, thousands have gone thither from the West, to find the same star there, and it has become the guiding light of their lives. Bethlehem has thus become a sacred name and a sacred place, although it is so small, and poor, and mean, and unimportant; but unfortunately, to many who visit it, its higher significance is lost: they kiss the wood of the manger, but it is mere dry wood to them; they miss the living spirit which once began that earthly career there which had been prepared for it from the foundation of the world. This place,[2] which has been consecrated in the affections of so many generations of men, hardly deserves mention on its own account, having scarcely a single marked characteristic excepting the green carpet which remains

[1] Von Schubert, *Reise*, ii. p. 491, iii. p. 12.
[2] Dr Strauss, *Sinai und Golgotha*, pp. 355-357.

unchanged from the time when the shepherds wandered over it, and the clear blue sky which echoed back their songs of joy and praise.

The city of Bethlehem lies two short hours' distance south of Jerusalem, east of the road leading to Hebron, upon two moderately-sized hills, one at the east and the other at the west. These hills are separated by a narrow pass. The northward and eastward declivities are those where the houses of the place are chiefly found. On the south, Bethlehem is bounded by the Wadi et Taamirah,[1] which runs north-eastward at first, bounding the northern base of the Frank Mountain, and receives the valley of the Mar Elias Convent, lying north of Bethlehem. The two, when united in one, run to the Dead Sea. The western of the two hills on which Bethlehem stands is called Kilkel; it is crossed on its north side by the road which leads to the Mar Elias, and sinks away north-westward to Wadi Ahmed: farther north, and upon the slope of the same hill, is "David's Well,"[2] with its deep shaft and its clear cool water. The eastern slope of the Kilkel from the pass onward sinks towards the Wadi el Chambeh, past the Beit el Chambeh, the "Village of Shepherds,"[3] and then dividing into several wadis, stretches on as far as to the Saba Convent[4] in the Kedron valley. In the pass between the two hills the larger part of the village lies. East of this, on the slope, and moreover on the top of a prominent and bold mass of Jura limestone, stands the Church of the Nativity, picturesquely, and in the manner of a fortress, surrounded by the three convents—the Latin and Greek ones on the north, and the Armenian one on the west. The Latin Convent, von Schubert, who made his sojourn there, found to be 2409 feet above the sea, though Russegger[5] determined it to be 2538 feet, which is about sixty feet higher than Jerusalem. Below the picturesque height, cultivated gardens and tilled fields can be seen. Westward, there is a succession of hills and valleys as far as to Rachel's grave. The terrace-shaped

[1] Dr Tobler, *Bethlehem in Palästina*, p. 2 : see the map of Bethlehem.

[2] F. Fabri, *Evagator*. ii. p. 437.

[3] Wilson, *Lands of the Bible*, i. p. 395.

[4] Bartlett, *Christian in Palestine*, p. 165, Tab. lvi. ; Roberts, *The Holy Land*, Book v. Plate xxxii.

[5] Russegger, *Reise*, iii. p. 79.

jurassic hills of Bethlehem give the place a picturesque appearance, and cause it to resemble an amphitheatre. Only on the southern side does the western hill have a steep descent: the north-east side of the knoll which sustains the convent has also a precipitous face, looking into a side wadi. The whole length of the two hills from west to east is scarcely a quarter of an hour's walk; neither of the hills is high. The village is of small circumference, and is but about eight hundred paces long and six hundred broad. The pass between the hills divides it into two parts; from which cause we have the many and so widely different views of Bethlehem.

From the flat roof of the Latin Convent a part of the Dead Sea can be seen, and the Arabian mountains beyond; farther north, Mar Elias; but Jerusalem cannot be descried. Only from the roof of the Armenian Convent[1] can Tekoa be discerned, and the cone-shaped Frank Mountain.

The climate of Bethlehem, according to Tobler, is similar to that of Jerusalem, but milder: at Christmas-time he found pasturage still green and fresh, and the weather delightful; in the summer the region was dry, but in comparison with other parts of Palestine, very favourably situated in regard to the supplies of water. The aqueduct was repaired in 1845, in order to furnish the city with an abundance, since before that time there was no supply but that which was collected in cisterns; and the three which stood in front of the great church were only suitable for the necessities of cattle. The one which bears the name of David's Fountain (2 Sam. xxiii. 15) is finely built, is from seventeen to twenty-one feet deep, and is situated in the neighbourhood of the house which is shown to pilgrims as that of Jesse. The soil in the immediate neighbourhood of the town is very well adapted to the growth of olives, pomegranates, almonds, figs, and grapes; but the attention paid to their culture is very small, compared with that given in former times. The wine[2] which is made here is excellent, but does not keep long, and produces slightly intoxicating effects. This city has not the splendour[3] which it had at the time of the Byzantine supremacy, when the Emperor Justinian built the

---

[1] Tobler, *i.a.l.* p. 5.   [2] *Ibid.* p. 15.
[3] Procopius, *De Ædificiis Justiniani*, v. 9, fol. 328, ed. Dindorf. *Opp.* iii.

wall and completed the Abbey of St John, which Antoninus Martyr called a *locus splendidissimus:* the town suffered much at the time of the great earthquake of 1837,[1] and since that time the houses which were thrown down have been permitted to stand filled with rubbish just as when they had freshly fallen. In the general rising throughout Syria, in opposition to the encroaching power of the Egyptian ruler, the fiery Christian population took part with the Egyptians at the time when they seemed discouraged; for the hatred which the Christians felt towards their Turkish oppressors was their master passion, and they were ready to welcome any change. The success of Ibrahim Pasha was followed by a ruthless persecution of the Mohammedans in Bethlehem, and the Christians supposed that they should be compensated for all their losses. They were not, however; and the general order that the people of the land should be disarmed did not exempt them: they, too, were treated as if they had been enemies. The hate which the Christians had formerly cherished against the Turks was now turned against the Egyptians. Since that time, however (1834), Bethlehem has been inhabited almost exclusively by Christians. The Jews, who were forbidden, even as early as the Emperor Hadrian's time, from living in the city, are now utterly lacking there.[2] The convent quarter is the place where all pilgrims tarry; while all artisans, who are mostly members of the Greek Church, live in one of the other seven quarters of the town. The Armenians have still another. The few Moslems who are there are crowded into one of the upper and highest groups of houses. The Roman Catholics' houses are scattered through the whole city; they may often be distinguished by the cross and shield of their patron St George over the doorways. It is not uncommon to find fragments of the ancient architecture built into the modern buildings.

The inhabitants of Bethlehem surprised Russegger,[3] who spent a whole day there, with the fine faces of the women and girls, among whom he saw true Madonnas, with very delicate features and pale complexions, with black eyes, rather swimming than fiery, and with fine, long black hair. They were

[1] *B. Antonin. Martyr. Itin.* p. 22.
[2] *Benjamin v. Tudela*, ed. Asher, i. p. 75.
[3] Russegger, *Reise*, iii. p. 81.

generally arrayed in white, the main garment being a mantle so folded as to envelope the whole body. The boys were remarkable for the excellent voices which they displayed in singing the music of the Latin service. This observation of Russegger is not a solitary one. The artist Bartlett[1] also observes, that when he rode out of the city to the aqueduct and to the gardens, there was a great deal of curiosity to see him as well as his companions: he was surprised, too, at the beauty of the women, who were carrying children in their arms, or water urns upon their heads, and who formed the most charmingly picturesque groups. The youth were full of life and fire; everything which he saw made upon him the impression that the people were full of energy, of a restless temperament, and of much intelligence. The Bethlehemites have always been difficult to hold in check : they have been prone to break out into acts of violence against those whom they imagined their oppressors ; and reminded Bartlett of his Scotch countrymen in this respect. Their warlike contests with their neighbours were celebrated all through the middle ages, and their internal dissensions have lasted up to the present day. The birth of the Saviour in their town seems to have had no further influence upon the people, than to lead to the establishment of the ceremonies which are celebrated in the religious institutions in which the town abounds. And it is only by the establishment of a better administered government, Bartlett thinks, that the Bethlehemites will be able to advance beyond the stage where they now stand. At the time of his visit, the American missionary Whiting had just established a school in Bethlehem, the first mission school in the place.

Tobler[2] took great pains to gain information regarding the inhabitants of Bethlehem. In early times these were 7000 in number ; but the recent rising was the occasion of the loss and banishment of many; and the plague, which is often experienced there, has swept many others away also. Of Latins he found sixteen hundred ; of Greeks, twelve hundred; of Armenians, two hundred ; of Moslems, three hundred : Jews were utterly wanting, and even those who casually passed through the place were regarded with no favourable eye. But

[1] Bartlett, *Christian in Palestine*, p. 211.
[2] Tobler, *Bethlehem*, pp. 43-76 ; Russegger, *Reise*, iii. p. 81.

the numbers of these different sects seem to be constantly changing. The prevailing complexion varies from a dark yellow to a brown, and even to one perfectly clear; and great as are the physical differences in the character of the population, that of the various forms of religion is just as great. The strifes which grow out of the last are the principal cause of the changes in the condition of the population. In the eleventh century only Christians lived in Bethlehem: at the time of the Crusades there were Jews there also. At first the Christians were Greek and Syrian, but at the middle of the seventeenth century, Roman Catholics also began to settle there; and after the opening of the eighteenth, some Armenians found their way thither. The Moslems, who were entirely driven out by Ibrahim Pasha, began under the Turkish rulers to creep back again, coming in mainly from the neighbourhood of Hebron, where the most of them appear to have found a refuge. Such scenes carry us back to the time of David, when the people were driven out to Moab, Ziklag, and to the wilderness of Engeddi.

One prominent class of the population of Bethlehem are the descendants of the crusaders. These people call themselves Venetians, and mainly speak Italian : they are chiefly interpreters by occupation, and prefer to serve as guides to pilgrims, rather than to undertake any regular trade. The Frank language appears to have come down traditionally from the time of the Crusades to the present day; and it would apparently be worth the time and pains, were some traveller to pay particular attention to the remnant of the old European stock, whose mission was fulfilled in the Crusades. The principal regular employments carried on in Bethlehem are, in addition to agriculture, cattle-raising and wine-making, just as at Hebron. Bees, too, are largely owned : the demand for wax candles for the use of pilgrims may make this profitable. In addition to this, the manufactures consist of the well-known rosaries, which are here made in immense numbers; and all kinds of so-called[1] "convent-fabrics," mainly plaster casts of the sacred objects of Bethlehem, some of them neatly done, but most of them rough and coarse. Crosses are made out of mother-of-pearl, and selenite, and asphaltum from the Dead Sea; drinking cups are made from the black fig tree wood; a few articles are made

[1] Russegger, *Reise,* iii. p. 81 ; Robinson, *Bib. Research.* i. p. 472.

from black coral, which is rare and expensive in Bethlehem. The fruit of the cathedral palm, the kernels of the small brown date, and in some rare cases ivory, serve to make rosaries from: the grains of some cereals, and the seeds of some kinds of wood, are also used for the same purpose, and are sent in their first stage of preparation from Phik, on Lake Tiberias, and Szalt, in Belkah, to Bethlehem. The thick hide of the rhinoceros is also used for making crosses, and other articles ; and these, when hallowed by the priests, are sold in the bazaar and by pedlars to the pilgrims of all zones. Besides the people engaged in the manufacture of all these articles, there may be met an occasional gunsmith, carpenter, potter, and cotton-spinner. The hand-mills for grinding meal are in use in every house, just as in the most ancient times. Many of the people are guides and couriers. The dyers are not found here, as in the twelfth century; nor are the tattooers, who gained a good living by marking the bodies of pilgrims in the seventeenth and eighteenth centuries.

In spite of the industry of the Bethlehemites, however, they are, as a general rule, poor ; made so by the strong and oppressive arm of Turkish taxation. Formerly the place had a Christian sheikh, and was able to send a hundred armed men into the field; but it has now been placed under the control of a Moslem sheikh.

The central point of attraction to the myriads of pilgrims who flock to Bethlehem is the great Church of St Mary, containing the supposed birth-place of Jesus. The silver star, surrounded by its lamps, shows the entrance to the grotto where the Saviour is said to have first seen the light. The manger itself is exhibited, and a countless number of stations, each of which is hallowed by some monkish legend ; the events of many, very many, saints from David down to Christ, and of the shepherds, the wise men, of Elisabeth, John, Joseph, and Mary, and of the good men of the first centuries of the Christian era down to the time of Jerome, are localized here; and even the most credulous of pilgrims may well have been surprised to learn that almost all the great events of which they heard, transpired in this little spot, and mainly in caves and grottos.[1]

[1] Fel. Fabri, vol. ii. p. 334 ; Russegger, *Reise,* Pt. iii. p. 87.

Maundrell called attention[1] to the unnaturalness of the pretended fact that so many important events had transpired in subterranean places in and around Bethlehem, and to the evident contradiction which it offers to the language of Scripture.[2] For example, in Matt. ii. 11, we read of the wise men who came from the east: "And when they were come into the house, they saw the young child with Mary His mother, and fell down and worshipped Him." This does not seem as if it referred to a cave, although von Schubert[3] has endeavoured to put that interpretation upon it. In Luke ii. 7, we are told that Mary "brought forth her first-born son, and wrapt Him in swaddling clothes, and laid Him in a manger; because there was no room for them in the inn." This manger refers evidently to the stables ordinarily used to keep cattle in, and cannot refer to a cave, of which the earlier writers—Eusebius, Origen, Socrates, Cyprian, and Nicephorus—say nothing whatever; not to mention the fact, that the passage down is by means of a narrow staircase, over which it would be impossible to drive any kind of cattle.[4] Still less probability is there that there is any authentic connection between the humble place where the child Jesus saw the light, and the countless stations on which the imagination of the monks has exhausted itself in devising fanciful legends, and which are tricked out with all the finery of gold, and silver, and tapestry, and marble, lighted with lamps which never go out, and affording a place of almost regal splendour for pilgrims to repeat their prayers and perform mass. Nothing but the misguided fancy which led such men as Jerome to a life of seclusion, could have so perverted the judgment, as to make men suppose that grottos and caves were the places which would be naturally selected for the scene of our Saviour's nativity. The delusion has doubtless been strengthened by the fact, that during the dark days of trial and persecution those caves were the places to which men fled for safety; and in them, it may be, the humble followers of Jesus have cherished their faith. And we must not speak slightingly of that undoubted ardour

[1] Maundrell, *Journey, etc.*, p. 114.
[2] Comp. Wilson, *Lands of the Bible*, i. p. 392; Robinson, *Bib. Research.* i. pp. 414, 417.
[3] Von Schubert, *Reise*, iii. p. 17.
[4] Bartlett, *Walks about the City*, p. 210.

and sincerity which could prompt such a man and such a scholar as Jerome was, to seek his home in the immediate neighbourhood of the place of Jesus' nativity, and even to excavate with his own hands a grotto where he might live, and even die, and which led the Empress Helena to build costly churches, and to establish religious institutions directly over the spot where the Saviour first saw light. It was the same lofty impulse which drew Paula and Eustachium thither, and caused them to leave chapels and churches as the testimonial of their love and adoration. Of all this let us speak reverently ; but we have no occasion so to speak of the lying legends which have perverted the simple verities of the place, and made them minister to falsehood and idolatry. They ought, on the contrary, to be spoken of in condemnation, and driven, if possible, out of sight. But it is impossible in this work to enter into any discussion of what may be called pilgrim literature : I must content myself with referring to the exhaustive work of Tobler,[1] in which he has discussed the entire subject of the traditions of Bethlehem with praiseworthy thoroughness and candour. But I cannot suppress a word of regret, that that distempered zeal of many Christians who minister at Bethlehem, has placed the great barrier which it has done in the way of the humble pilgrims who go thither with hearts yearning after the truth, and that it has caused so much scandal in connection with the name of Christian throughout the East, and also serious damage to the church. The variety of opinions which clash in Bethlehem has led to bitter words, and even to blows, before the altar of the Church of the Nativity, making the Mohammedans wonder and doubt very naturally whether the truth is with those who display such hatred in a place whose associations are so sacred. The very purpose of the gospel, which is to unite all men, and to make them brethren, here seems to lose all its hallowed intent, and to be turned into a wild and brutal mockery.

The great church of Bethlehem, the Church of Mary, surrounded by its three spacious convents, and the immense fortress-like wall shored up by pillars below, is one of the most splendid[2]

---

[1] Tobler, *Bethlehem*, pp. 77–266.

[2] Bartlett, *Walks about the City*, etc., pp. 206–210. See *Christian in Palestine*, p. 166, Plate lviii. ; Russegger, *Reise*, iii. p. 382.

in Palestine, and is unquestionably the one which was built on a grand scale by Helena, the mother of Constantine. A Basilica in the nave, exhibiting forty-eight columns, finely worked out of a light, brownish-yellow marble, and supporting a richly wrought cedar ridge pole, is a hundred and seventy feet in length and eighty in breadth.[1] Although allowed to fall into neglect and decay, it is by no means in a state of ruin; but owing to the constant strifes of the religious bodies which meet there, it is rapidly advancing to such a condition. The jealousy of each one of the confessions prevents either of the others from beginning the work of restoration; and the case is made worse by the greed of the Turks, which prompts them to take off masses of the lead from the roof, only sparing just so much as may not defeat their own plans and leave the place a ruin. This five-naved Basilica is the more worthy of a visit on this account, that it is known to have been constructed almost exactly similar to the Basilica of St Peter built in Rome by Constantine, and to the slightly more modern one of St Paul,[2] just outside of Rome.

It has undergone very slight changes since it was built, with the exception of a wall which has been thrown across, directly in front of the high altar, and which has a most unfavourable effect in comparison with the impression which the view of the whole at once would make. Yet Bartlett,[3] the English artist, was not much troubled by this: for the *genius loci* moved him so powerfully, that as he walked through the place he felt the influence of its great antiquity with its full force, notwithstanding that the church had been robbed of so much of its former beauty. The broken marble pavement, which had re-echoed to the tread of so many generations of pilgrims; the iron clamps in the walls, formerly employed to hold the marble tablets in their places, now all removed to decorate other buildings; the weather-stained walls and mosaics of saints and martyrs, dating back to the Byzantine period; the patches of glittering gold which still may here and there be seen,—all show what the ancient splendour of the place must have been.

---

[1] Tobler, *i.a.l.* p. 83.

[2] Kugler, *Handbuch der Kunstgeschichte*, p. 361.

[3] Bartlett, *Walks about the City, etc.*, p. 209; Wilson, *Lands of the Bible,* i. p. 392.

To these may be added the long nave and the few silver lamps, the offerings of earlier ages, whose combined effect made upon the sensitive mind of the artist an impression which could not be forgotten.

The scene is quite different which is presented on entering the side wings of the church, which have been appropriated by the three different confessions. In one of them the Armenians have their altars and their service; in another the Roman Catholics theirs; and in another the Greeks celebrate with great pomp and ceremony their mass. Into these three buildings the throng of pilgrims presses, crowding around the stations and shrines overladen with ornament, and hallowed in the minds of the credulous believers by the burden of legends which is heaped upon them. From them they pass down into the grotto or cave where the Saviour is said to have been born, and into which the same jealous rivalry has been carried, the three different confessions having divided it among themselves, in despite of the sentence over the entrance: Hic de virgine Maria, Jesus Christus natus est. The lesson of brotherhood which this sentence ought to teach has been entirely disregarded.

The jealousy which the three confessions feel towards each other continues unabated, and leads not to bad feeling alone, but to continual acts of violence. The Armenians, says Russegger,[1] are the most discreet of the three : they are far more thoughtful of consequences than their hot-blooded and riotous western brethren : they say but little, have much business to attend to, and possess considerable property. The Roman Catholics are mainly represented by Spanish and Italian monks, but are without income : they are unable, therefore, to bribe the Turkish officials, as the other two confessions can do. The schismatic Greeks, to whom large amounts of money flow from Russia, have almost all the sacred places under their control; and it is only by their tolerance that the others are allowed to have altars, and to burn their sacred lamps. They have the entrance of the grotto, too, in their sole possession. The tattered tapestry which was once an ornament to that place, the Catholics wished to restore; but the Greeks refused them the privilege, lest it should lead to a demand for some share in the possession of that portion of the place. One can now un-

[1] Russegger, *Reise*, iii. p. 85.

derstand the reason of the complaints which the three confessions heap upon each other, the depreciation of each other, and the threat of calling in their common enemy the Turks, as their auxiliaries against their schismatic fellow-believers. It is a sad state of things for the interests of the Christian church in the East; and it is equally so in Jerusalem, where the same controversies are in progress. On the flat roof[1] of thé high range of convent buildings surrounding the central church, there is a broad panoramic view over the Holy Land; and the soul which has been vexed and disquieted by the contentions and angry passions below, here settles back into repose on witnessing the undisturbed face of nature.

The history of the convents seems to have been an uneventful one, and yields very little to reward the toil of the antiquarian, else Tobler[2] would have been able to gain more than the scanty facts which he has collected. The place seems to have been a mere lodge for pilgrims. As the seat of the Bethlehem episcopate, it never had much renown. The crusaders[3] took possession of the city at the request of the Christian inhabitants of Bethlehem; and in the year 1110, King Baldwin I. raised the place to the dignity of an episcopal see. Pope Pascal II. confirmed this act, and for a time it continued to bear this title in the Romish Church; yet it seems to have had no long continuance as an episcopate. The termination of that honourable distinction may perhaps have been in some way connected with the invasion of the Genghiskhanides from the Euphrates valley, who were called in as auxiliaries by the Egyptian Sultan Ejub, to aid him in his efforts to subdue Palestine. The desolation which was spread over the country at that time may have cost Bethlehem the honour which it had attained as a Christian centre.[4]

---

[1] Bartlett, p. 206; Wilson, *Lands of the Bible*, i. p. 391.
[2] Tobler, *Bethlehem*, pp. 241–247.
[3] Robinson, *Bib. Research.* i. p. 472.
[4] Wilken, *Gesch. der Kreuz.* Pt. vi. pp. 630-645.

APPENDIX I.

———◆———

ESSAY ON THE FORMATION OF THE BASIN OF THE DEAD SEA, AND THE CHANGES WHICH HAVE TAKEN PLACE IN THE LEVEL OF THE LAKE.[1]

COMMUNICATED TO THE "SOCIETÉ GEOLOGIQUE DE FRANCE," AT THE MEETING OF MAY 1, 1865, BY MONS. LOUIS LARTET, ETC. ETC.

TRANSLATED BY GEORGE GROVE, ESQ., HONORARY SECRETARY TO THE PALESTINE EXPLORATION FUND.

———

I. ON THE ORIGIN OF SALT LAKES IN GENERAL.

OF all the problems which the study of the physical geography of continents is continually bringing before the notice of geologists, there are few which more eminently merit their attention than that of the origin of salt lakes or inland seas.

The question has occupied physical philosophers from the earliest times, and the explanations proposed have been usually based upon the probability of an ancient communication between these isolated basins and the main ocean.

The theories of Xanthus, Strato, and Eratosthenes, which were accepted by most of the ancient philosophers, have been consecrated by the great authority of Buffon and Pallas, so far as concerns the salt lakes of Western Asia.

The question of the Asiatic lakes was entirely re-examined by Humboldt, who applied to it all the information which his erudition and his profound knowledge of Asia enabled him to

[1] Extracted from the *Bulletin de la Societé Geologique de France*, 2d series, vol. xxii. p. 420.

give. He also made use of the then recent researches of the Russian *savans* on the subject of the depression in the level of the Caspian, as well as of his own discoveries on the physical constitution of Central Asia.

These investigations led him to the conclusion, that before the so-called historic era, and at an epoch not far distant from the latest changes in the surface of the earth, the salt steppes of Turan were covered by an inland sea, which comprised both the Aral and the Caspian. This sea (to which the Asiatic traditions of the existence of a primeval bitter sea would seem to refer) possibly communicated on one side with the Euxine, and on the other, by larger or smaller channels, with the Frozen Sea, and the lakes of Telegoul, Tagis, and Balgache. The existence of a vast sheet of brackish water occupying, at a time anterior to the human period, large districts around the Caspian, and maintaining, like the Caspian, a *fauna* of a character intermediate between those of ordinary lakes and our present seas, may be taken as proved by the researches of the geologists who have explored the countries in question since Humboldt's time. It was therefore not unnatural to refer to this primitive sea the origin of those salt lakes which exist in such large numbers about the Caspian; and this theory, on the other hand, necessarily exercised a great influence on the proposed explanations of the formation of other salt lakes existing below the level of the ocean. Thus M. Angelot, in endeavouring to make a general application of this theory, was led to consider the Dead Sea, and the other depressed salt lakes in the neighbourhood of the Mediterranean, as so many remnants of a great Asiatic Ocean, which he believed to have originally occupied the centre of the continent, and to have divided it into three distinct districts.[1]

This theory has been discussed by M. D'Archiac,[2] who has demonstrated that it was impossible, even in the Tertiary era, for any communication to have existed between the Dead Sea and the Aralo-Caspian basin; and, in fact, that it was

---

[1] *Recherches sur l'origine du haut degré de salure de divers lacs placés dans le fond de grandes dépressions du sol des continents et en particulier de la Mer Morte, suivies des considérations sur l'origine du sel gemme en couche* (*Bull. Soc. Geologique de France*, Ser. i. xiv. 356).

[2] *Histoire des progrès de la Géologie*, i. 300.

impossible to believe that these two basins had ever formed part of a single sea. And, on the other hand, it may be asked whether, in order to explain the saltness of the water in these lakes of depression, it is absolute^l, necessary to attribute to them a marine origin, and whether it is not equally natural in most cases to seek for the source of their saltness in the districts which surround them.

Many of the salt lakes in Western Asia have, in fact, considerable masses of rock-salt in their immediate neighbourhood, or are surrounded by districts very rich in saliferous deposits.[1] The same thing is true of a large number of the lakes of Southern Russia[2] and of Asia Minor.[3] Similar deposits have been observed in the neighbourhood of the Chotts and Sebkahs of Western Africa,[4] as well as of the Great Salt Lake of the Rocky Mountains of America.[5]

The fact that large masses of rock-salt on the edge of the Dead Sea have existed from time immemorial, and are mentioned in the chronicles of the Crusades, as well as in the works of modern travellers, was familiar to M. Angelot; and he has endeavoured to explain it in harmony with his theory, by supposing the lake to have deposited these masses of salt at a time when its waters stood higher than at present. But upon this M. D'Archiac remarks with justice, that if there ever was a moment when the saturation of the water of the Dead Sea was sufficient for the formation of the existing masses of salt, it is difficult to see why, at the present day, when the level is lower, the saturation of the water should be

---

[1] See these indicated in the geological map of Western Asia which accompanies the second vol. of Ermann's *Archives* (1842).

[2] M. de Verneuil has pointed out that the Lake Elton and the other salt lakes of Orenburg are situated in the *Zechstein*, a formation frequently containing much rock-salt.

[3] See Dubois de Montpereux (*Voyage autour du Caucase*); Abich (*Mem. Acad. S. Petersburgh*, 1859) ; and Hamilton (*Trans. Geol. Society*, 2d Series, v. 589).

[4] See Fournel, Renou, and particularly Dubocq (*Ann. des Mines*, 1853, p. 249).

[5] See Fremont (*Report, etc.*, Washington, 150–158). The name of one of the affluents of the Great Salt Lake is *Rio Salado*. On the salt lakes of Central America, see D'Orbigny, and (in opposition to him) Darwin (*Geolog. Observ. in S. America*, 1846).

less than when it was higher, since the conditions which keep down the saltness of the Lake of Tiberias do not exist in the Dead Sea.[1]

Further, without intending to dispute that certain lakes (such as the closed basins at the mouths of the Rhone, or those along the sea-coast of Lower Egypt) may have had an oceanic origin, it is surely not necessary to have recourse to the hypothesis of M. Angelot to explain the saltness of a large number of these continental basins, and in particular of the Dead Sea. Is it necessary to conclude, with the learned geologist in question, that because these continental depressions contain a greater or less extent of salt or salt water, they are therefore in every case the isolated bottoms of ancient sea lakes, in which an accumulation of salt has taken place through the evaporation of their water? May it not be that the exceptional position of such basins has been favourable to the progressive accumulation within them of saline materials constantly collected from the neighbouring districts, and brought in by surface drainage, or even by subterranean springs?

When the districts round a lake contain beds very rich in salts, it is easy to understand that the concentration of its waters will be thereby powerfully assisted. A lake which is fed by water containing large quantities of salt, and is at the same time subjected to an active evaporation, will in course of time attain a degree of saltness quite abnormal.

It is in the Dead Sea that this double action is seen most clearly, and has produced the greatest effects. The importance of the study of the basin of that lake for the solution of the questions relating to the origin of salt lakes of depression did not escape M. Angelot, as is shown by the very title of his work, and by the following reservation which accompanies his conclusions : " A complete investigation of the Dead Sea may throw light upon this question, and possibly negative part of my hypothesis ; but all that we know at present of the districts which form the basin of that lake, seems rather to support than to contradict me."[2]

At the time M. Angelot wrote these words, but little was positively known of the geology of the basin of the Dead Sea.

---

[1] *Histoire des progrès, etc.*, i. 301.
[2] Angelot, p. 389.

A few years later, the Austrian geologist Russegger was called to Egypt by Mehemet Ali. In the course of numerous journeys he visited Syria and the northern portion of the basin of the Dead Sea; and in his work[1] on the geology of that region, he has combined his own personal observations on the western side of the lake with information obtained from the Arabs, and with occasional notes on those portions of the basin which he did not himself visit, extracted from the travels of Seetzen, Burckhardt, Robinson, Schubert, etc. Although often mistaken as to the age and distribution of the rocks which form the basin of the lake, Russegger nevertheless recognised with remarkable sagacity the primitive isolation of the basin. Amongst other things, he suggested that the saltness of the water might be caused by the constitution of the surrounding rocks.

Some ten years later, Dr Anderson, who was attached as geologist to the American expedition of Lieutenant Lynch, made a more complete and detailed investigation of the north of the basin, and of a portion of the shore of the lake;[2] but his work, though conscientious and carefully done, as far as description goes, is very vague, and even contradictory, on the subject of the origin and mode of formation of the lake and its basin. He appears to admit the return of the ocean after the first immersion of the basin, and the excavation of the principal wadis which form the hydrographic system of the region. Nevertheless, it is easy to see that he inclined to the belief that a large portion of the salts in solution in the water may have been furnished by the surrounding rocks. And this, no doubt, induced him to make researches on the solubility of some of these salts in water charged with carbonic acid.

During last year I enjoyed the rare opportunity of exploring, under the direction of the Duc de Luynes, the entire circumference of the Dead Sea and its basin from end to end. Our examination was necessarily rapid, but I was able in different parts of the basin (especially its eastern and southern portions, hitherto so little known) to observe many facts which appeared partially to confirm the predictions of

---

[1] *Reisen in Europa, Asien, und Afrika,* iii. Pt. ii. 196.

[2] *Official Report of the United States Expedition to the Dead Sea and River Jordan,* by Lieut. Lynch: Baltimore, 1852, p. 79.

Russegger; and I have come to the conclusion, that this lake
—the most characteristic type of a salt lake of depression—
has never been in communication with the neighbouring oceans,
although its waters formerly stood at a much higher level than
they now do.

My conclusions are based upon a number of observations
relating to the principal points of the question, and which it is
now my object to state in detail.

II. GENERAL VIEW OF THE PHYSICAL GEOGRAPHY OF THE BASIN OF THE DEAD. SEA, IN RELATION TO THE GEOLOGY OF THE COUNTRY GENERALLY.

Few countries are so simple in their orographical and hydrographical features as Syria. Its Mediterranean coast is for the
most part bordered by a chain of mountains parallel to the shore-
line. Beyond these mountains, and running nearly due north
and south, is an enormous *trench*, consisting of valleys, often of
great depth, the centre portion of which was happily named by
the ancients *Cœle-Syria*, or " Hollow Syria."

The trench in question, or rather the series of successive
valleys which compose it, forms a natural and sharply-defined
limit between the districts which border on the Mediterranean,
and are under Turkish dominion, and the high plateaux to the
east, which are incessantly traversed by the free wandering
tribes of Beduin.

The changes in level in the bottom of the trench divide it
into several basins, which are drained by three principal rivers,
the Nahr el-Asy (Orontes), the Nahr Kasimieh (Leontes), and
the Sheriat el-Kebir (Jordan). The first of these runs northward, the other two southward. The Nahr el-Asy and the
Nahr Kasimieh both take their rise in the highest portion of
the trench—the plain of the Bekaa, and from that common
point of departure proceed in different directions, both emptying
themselves into the- Mediterranean—the first to the north near
Antioch, the second to the south near Tyre—each abandoning
its original course through the valley at a point not far from its
mouth, and by a sudden turn forcing a passage across the chain
of hills which separates it from the sea.

The other stream, the Jordan, so renowned for the part it

has played in both Jewish and Christian history, rises at the foot of Anti-Lebanon, in the neighbourhood of Hasbeya, and not far from the bend of the Nahr Kasimieh. In its first portion it bears the name of Nahr Hasbany; but after having received large accessions of water from the springs at Banias and Tell el-Kadi (usually considered as the real sources of the Jordan), it assumes its ancient and venerable name. It then passes, in its course, from north to south, through the Bahr el-Huleh (Samachonitis) and the Bahr Tubarieh (Lake of Tiberias or Gennesareth); on leaving which it receives the waters of a considerable affluent, the Wadi Jarmuk. Farther down it is joined by several other torrents and streams, and, under the Arab name of Sheriat el-Kebir, at length throws itself into the Dead Sea, the final receptacle of the waters of this basin.

The valley of the Jordan runs in the general direction of north and south, but the valley of the Bekaa is forced out of that direction by the parallel chains of Lebanon and Anti-Lebanon, between which it lies. The valley of the Jordan is of great depth, and stretches in a straight line from Anti-Lebanon to the Dead Sea. On its left side it is bounded by the cliffs and abrupt slopes which lead to the irregular plateaux of Jaulan, Adjlun, and the Belka; on its right, the valley is separated from the Mediterranean by the highlands of Judah and the hill country of Galilee, which connects those highlands with Lebanon, and which, to use the expression of Mr Sherwood,[1] form the backbone of Palestine.

The Dead Sea itself is hemmed in between the mountainous country of Judah and the mountains of Abarim, the buttresses of the high and undulating plateaux of Ammon and Moab. Beneath its dense and bitter waters lies concealed the most depressed portion of that vast trench of which its basin forms a part, and which stretches still farther south into Arabia Petræa.[2]

In fact, the Arabah, which like an enormous ditch separates

[1] *American Journal of Science,* 1845, p. 1; and *Bibl. Univ. de Genève,* 1845.

[2] I am only able here to give the main features of the physical geography of this region. For further detail I must refer my readers to the excellent description in Dr W. Smith's *Dictionary of the Bible,* under the head of *The Salt Sea.* Mr Grove has there succeeded in bringing together in a few pages all the most interesting and exact information on the Dead Sea and its basin.

the mountains of Idumæa from the Peninsula of Sinai, follows so nearly the general direction of the Jordan valley, that both it and the Gulf of Akabah, which succeeds it on the south, may fairly be considered as a prolongation of the longitudinal trench we have so often mentioned.

III. ON THE HYPOTHESIS OF AN ANCIENT PROLONGATION OF THE JORDAN TO THE RED SEA.

The northern portion of the Great Valley of the Arabah, discovered in 1812 by Burckhardt, forms a natural part of the basin of the Dead Sea. At about two-thirds of its length south of the lake, the floor of the valley rises imperceptibly; and the alluvial beds by which up to that point it is covered, give place at that point to hills of cretaceous formation, which hills thence continue for some distance to form a connection between the secondary deposits on the two sides of the valley, at the same time acting (not very efficiently) as a natural barrier to the incessant progress of the sand, which is accumulated by the south-west wind in the southern portion of the Arabah.[1] These cretaceous deposits divide the Arabah into two very distinct districts, and form the summit of a double anticlinal line, separating the two basins of the Dead Sea and the Red Sea.

The discovery of this immense valley, extending from the lake to the Red Sea, naturally suggested to those travellers and geographers who first became aware of it, that it was an ancient channel by which the water of the Jordan had formerly flowed into the Gulf of Akabah. In 1828, M. de Laborde, on the faith of a series of topographical observations made by him from Akabah to Petra, as well as on his interpretation of the Bible narrative, further announced his opinion, that the interruption in the course of the Jordan had taken place at the time of the destruction of the cities of the plain, and that the formation of the Dead Sea was due to that interruption. M.

---

[1] It has been remarked by several travellers, that the Arabs give to the southern portion of the Arabah the name of Wady Akabah—from the little village at its southern end, on the shore of the eastern arm of the Red Sea, to which also it gives its name—while they reserve that of Wady Arabah for the northern portion, next to the Dead Sea. I shall adopt these distinctions, and shall designate the whole region by the general term Arabah.

Letronne,[1] however, interpreted the passages differently, and was the first to express a doubt on the reality of the supposed ancient communication. He grounded his conclusion mainly on hydrographical arguments drawn from Laborde's own map. He recalled the fact that Seetzen had remarked the existence of powerful streams running from the southern portion of the Ghor into the Dead Sea; and from the different direction of the lateral valleys in the northern and southern portions of the Arabah, he inferred the existence of a watershed in the middle of the assumed canal, and thence deduced the complete independence of the basins of the Dead Sea and the Red Sea.

The conclusions of Letronne, however, were the result of pure speculation, based on a limited number of observations by travellers whose opinion was directly opposed to his own; and they were therefore insufficient to combat the seductive idea that the course of the Jordan had been interrupted at the time of the destruction of Sodom and Gomorrah. Letronne was therefore stoutly opposed, especially by the Abbé Caneto, who upheld the theory of Laborde with much learning and ability. There the question would probably have rested, but that in 1837 the hypsometric measurements of Messrs Moore and Beek, and the barometrical observations of Schubert, revealed to the scientific world the fact that the waters of the Dead Sea, which both Seetzen and Burckhardt had believed to stand higher than the ocean, were in reality enormously depressed below it.[2]

In 1837, M. de Bertou[3] explored the district, and fixed the amount of the depression at 419 metres (1374·7 feet). This figure was challenged by Captain Caillier, who erroneously endeavoured to reduce it to 200 metres; but notwithstanding this, the observations of De Bertou, as well as the measurements of Captain Lynch, and the second measurement of Lieutenant Symonds (Royal Engineers), have been corroborated by those

---

Journal des Savants, 1835, p. 596.

[2] Had these travellers but climbed the central hills of the country, as at Bethel, where the lake and the Mediterranean can be seen at once, they could not possibly have overlooked the difference in the respective levels of the two, which is very obvious from thence.

[3] *Description de la Vallée du Jourdain, etc.* (*Bull. de la Soc. de Geographie*, sec. 2, xii. 161).

of Lieutenant Vignes, of the French Navy, who accompanied the Duc de Luynes' expedition, and made a series of continuous horary observations with two of Fortin's barometers.[1]

The fact of the depression of the lake had already furnished a powerful argument to those who opposed the idea that the Jordan had formerly emptied itself into the Red Sea; and M. de Bertou, when he first traversed the whole length of the Arabah, confirmed in a remarkable manner the predictions of Letronne, by proving the existence of a watershed in the middle of the Arabah, the summit of which he indicated upon his map at about the latitude of Petra, and which, according to the approximate calculations of this conscientious and able traveller, reached an elevation of about 160 metres (525 feet) above the ocean.

From that moment the problem appeared to be solved as far as physical geography was concerned. In the face of so immense a depression as that of the Dead Sea, separated from the Red Sea by a watershed of 160 metres,[2] and receiving the waters of the Wadi Arabah, it was all but impossible to believe in any ancient connection between the Jordan and the Gulf of Akabah. It was certainly possible to imagine that an immense subsidence of the district had taken place; but such a subsidence could not have happened without enormous derangement of the strata forming the floor of the valley, and is absolutely negatived by the examination of those strata. If, however, it were necessary to add geological argument to the proofs already given of

---

[1] *Note sur quelque determinations de coordonnées géographiques: Connaissance des temps,* for 1866.—The depression was discovered almost simultaneously by Moore and Beek and by Schubert, but the latter alone named a figure (93 toises—637 feet). De Bertou afterwards met Moore in the Lebanon, learned his discovery from him, and shortly afterwards estimated the depression at 419 metres (1374·7 feet). This was increased by Russegger to 435 metres. In 1841, Lieutenant Symonds, R.E., after two sets of trigonometrical observations, made it 1312·2 feet. Lieutenant Lynch's result was 1316·7 feet. The careful observations of M. Vignes give 392 metres (1286·15 feet); and lastly, Lieutenant Wilson, Royal Engineers, in 1865, at the head of a party of sappers, by running a double set of levels from the lake to Jerusalem, and thence to Jaffa, would seem to have fixed the depression at 1292 feet.

[2] The level of this watershed was taken by M. Vignes with the barometer by gradual and most careful operations, giving a result of 240 metres (787·44 feet).

the non-interruption of the Jordan, I might say that an attentive study of the ground in the neighbourhood of the watershed of the Arabah leads me to the conclusion that the summit is a cretaceous barrier, separating in the most complete manner the two slopes of the district.

At that altitude the cretaceous strata are covered with their own *débris* alone, and show no trace of any ancient watercourse in the direction of the Red Sea. It is also observable, that in the ancient alluvial beds of the Wadi Arabah the pebbles increase in size as the watershed is approached (in travelling to the south); and further, that in the same ancient alluvium at the south-eastern end of the lake, flints are found belonging to certain varieties of felspathic and quartziferous porphyries, the existing beds of which are only found still farther south.

IV. ON THE HYPOTHESIS OF AN ANCIENT MARINE COMMUNICATION BETWEEN THE DEAD SEA AND THE SURROUNDING OCEANS, ESPECIALLY THE RED SEA.

The discovery of the depression of the basin of the Dead Sea, while it destroyed the possibility of the Jordan having formerly run into the Red Sea, gave some support to the more novel idea, which we have already mentioned, of an ancient marine communication between the lake and the ocean. But this latter hypothesis, attractive though it be, was not consistent with the fact of the flow of the waters from the two sides of the watershed of the Arabah, and especially with the height of that watershed above the Red Sea. To overcome this difficulty, it was necessary to assume that the watershed was the result of an elevation of the soil, probably occasioned by the protrusion of eruptive rocks, the existence of which had in fact been noticed in the neighbourhood of the watershed. Supposing such an elevation of the ground to have separated the Gulf of Akabah from the arm of the sea formerly occupying the depression which now receives the waters of the Jordan; and supposing the internal salt lake thus formed to have been submitted to an active evaporation, its level would naturally have fallen foot by foot, until an equilibrium was established between the supply and the solar evaporation, from which conditions would obviously result both the extreme saltness and the enormous depression of the waters of the lake.

In order to combat this hypothesis, it is not necessary to refer to the hydrography of the country, so happily made use of by M. Letronne; we will rather proceed by examining the age and nature of the eruptive rocks just spoken of, in the neighbourhood of the watershed. We shall thus be able to estimate the influence their protrusion has exercised on the elevation of the strata which form this transverse barrier. The result of my researches on the relation of these eruptive rocks to the stratified beds in their neighbourhood, leads me to think that the epoch at which they protruded was by no means near to our own. Their rise would seem to me to have been anterior not only to the deposit of the calcareous rocks which form the watershed, but even to that of the more ancient sandstones and greywackes which form the eastern side both of the Wadi Arabah and of the Dead Sea, and from which the monuments of Petra are excavated. They are for the most part felspathic and quartziferous porphyries, offering strong points of resemblance to those of France—in particular those of the Esterel—and, like them, exhibiting the most varied colours.

At several points in the Wadi Arabah, especially at the Wadi Mafrah (between Petra and the watershed), felspathic porphyries are met with, not quartziferous, deeper in colour than those just alluded to, and containing felspar of the sixth system. This latter porphyry is rarer than the former, and only occasionally found, as for example in the Wadi Safieh, surrounded with very fine *breccia*, and with complicated conglomerates, the materials of which are mostly derived from the granite or from the porphyry itself. These porphyries range nearly north and south from the Dead Sea to Mount Hor. They reappear on the western side of the Arabah; and after encircling the granite masses of Sinai, join the porphyritic beds of Upper Egypt and Nubia. In these latter spots they were observed by Russegger and Le Fevre in the midst of the same sandstone and cretaceous greywackes which accompany them at Mount Hor—sandstone which I designate by the name of Nubian sandstone, given to it by Russegger.[1] In fact, the country

---

[1] Russegger himself admits that there are sandstones of different ages in Nubia; and it might therefore have been better to substitute for the vague designation adopted in the text some such name as " Petra sandstone." But I have thought it better to waive the advantage of such a name, partly

which we are now examining corresponds in many points with the Isthmus of Sinai, Nubia, and the north of Africa in general.

There is reason to believe that in the African districts just mentioned, as in Syria and Arabia Petræa, the Nubian sandstones, whether felspathic or not, have borrowed a large portion of their constituents from the granite and porphyries. To the same source they probably owe the oxides which colour them; since their colours appear to vary according to their proximity to eruptive rocks containing the same oxides.

At various points—as, for instance, around Mount Hor—it is possible to obtain even more certain evidence that the eruption of the porphyries took place before the deposit of the Nubian sandstone. At the base of that sandstone at Mount Hor a pudding-stone is found, composed of pebbles which, where not decomposed (as they mostly are), still exhibit the elements of felspathic porphyries: it may therefore be concluded that the latter rock was protruded before the deposit of the sandstone. At the same time, the protrusion can have had no effect on the cretaceous beds at the watershed of the Arabah, since those beds are deposits of a still later date than the Nubian sandstone. The porphyries probably played at best a purely passive part; their great compactness causing them to act as enormous wedges or levers on the softer rocks surrounding them. Everything leads me to the belief that these eruptive rocks themselves were lifted at the time of the general elevation of the ground. The action which raised the watershed of the Arabah, with the whole of the region, to its present altitude, must have taken place after the cretaceous and eocene beds, which form the skeleton of the region, had been raised out of the Tertiary ocean; in any case, must have taken place before the formation of the Wadi Arabah, the oldest alluviums of which show no trace of any derangement since their deposit.[1]

out of respect to Russegger, and partly to facilitate the comparison of his observations with my own.

[1] The general rise of the region having taken place after the appearance of the porphyries, and long before that of the volcanic rocks, one is tempted to inquire if it was not accompanied by the eruption of some new plutonic rock. In the neighbourhood of Mount Hor, in the midst of the quartziferous porphyries, a granite is met with of a totally different look from the

In addition to this ancient dislocation, it is probable that slight movements may have taken place in a portion of the upper crust of the district, which is still often acted on by earthquakes. To movements of this description is due the existence of raised beaches at various points on the Mediterranean coast (for example, at Jaffa), covered with species of marine shells still living in the Mediterranean. None of these beaches have been raised more than very small distances, and it is impossible to believe that the action which raised them was powerful enough to have elevated the cretaceous limestones of the watershed of the Arabah in any sensible degree.

Thus there is no reason to believe that the rise of the felspathic porphyries can have had anything to do with the formation of the summit by which the Arabah is divided into its two anticlinal slopes. Nor, on the other hand, can we suppose that the more recent actions which have left their undeniable traces on the coast of the Mediterranean were sufficiently powerful to make the changes in question on the surface of the country. It is more probable that the action which imprinted on the region its present orographic physiognomy, and distributed the waters of the Arabah between the two basins of the Dead Sea and the Red Sea, occurred at an intermediate period—viz. during the rise of the cretaceous and eocene deposits, before the formation of the existing valleys, and the deposit of their most ancient alluvial beds.

To the arguments already adduced may be added certain important negative evidence of the complete and original independence of the two basins, and of the non-existence of any marine communication between the two seas. These are—the

common Egyptian rose granite of the East, and containing white felspar and black mica in smaller quantities. According to Russegger, a similar granite is found at Sinai, associated with syenite and porphyry. And he remarks, that while porphyry often traverses white fine-grained granite, granite does not traverse porphyry,—a fact of great significance if it could be well established, since it would throw back the eruption of the granite beyond that of the porphyry. On the other hand, I believe that at Mount Hor I noticed that in the neighbourhood of the granite in question the cretaceous beds exhibited some unusual undulations. But such derangements can only be of very small importance; and, indeed, my investigation was too rapid to allow of my insisting on the point. I only desire, therefore, to call the attention of geologists travelling in the country to it.

fact of the complete absence, at any level, along the shores of the Dead Sea, as well as throughout the whole of the region which separates it from the Red Sea, of any deposits of a marine character,[1] and the want of any marine organic remains such as would testify to the existence of an arm of the sea subsequent to the rise of the cretaceous and eocene beds.

If, therefore, we take into consideration—

1. The absence of any remains of marine organizations in the most ancient strata of the basin ;

2. The fluviatile character of the post-eocene deposits of the Arabah ;

3. The existing traces of the direction of the streams towards the Dead Sea ; and

Lastly, the non-existence of any material elevation of the ground in the middle of the Arabah since the formation of the present valleys ;—

If we take these things into account, it will be seen that the observations of geologists are quite in harmony with the deductions from the physical geography of the country. These two classes of observations, and the important results derived from them, lead me to reject the hypothesis of a marine communication between the Dead Sea and the Red Sea, as well as that of an ancient prolongation of the Jordan to the Gulf of Akabah.[2]

---

[1] It is difficult not to believe that the discovery of the specimen of *porites elongata* brought home by the Marquis de l'Escalopier, after a short visit to the Dead Sea, and presented by him to the Museum of Natural History at Paris, is the result of one of those tricks which the appetite for *bakshish* so often causes. Without doubt, it came from the Gulf of Akabah, where the species in question is very frequent, and whence it may have been brought by the Arabs or by some dragoman. It is much to be regretted that Humboldt should have attached so much importance to this isolated discovery, which during thirty years has received no confirmation whatever.

[2] I say nothing here of the evidence to be drawn from the differences in the constituents of the water of the Dead Sea and of the ocean. The differences—as M. Elie de Beaumont remarked in presenting the present memoir to the Academy of Sciences—are well known, owing to the numerous analyses that have been made of the water of the lake. The extraordinary quantity of bromine, potash, and magnesia it contains, and the absence of iodine, will be strikingly manifested when M. Terreil has completed his examination of the specimens of water obtained by our expedition at different spots and different depths, and which our employment of a modification of Aimé's apparatus enabled us to procure with great pre-

V. VARIOUS THEORIES ON THE ORIGIN OF THE DEAD SEA.

If I have seemed to prolong the examination of the two hypotheses on the origin of the Dead Sea, it is because they have been the object of much warm discussion, and also because they have an intimate relation to the object of my present investigation. It is not necessary to examine with the same care all the theories which have been put forth on this subject; in particular, those founded upon the idea of an ancient subterranean communication between the lake and the ocean. Russegger has happily characterized that idea as a physical absurdity, since it is simply impossible for such a communication to exist, when the difference of level between the two bodies of water is so immense. Neither is it necessary to linger over theories based upon a subsidence of the ground, produced by the combustion of the inflammable substances which are generally believed to exist in great abundance on the shores of the lake. It is only necessary on this point to remark that the bituminous limestones probably only became so by the rise of bitumen from below, and that they are no more than isolated accidents, confined to the middle of the cretaceous beds in the neighbourhood of the lake. The accidental specimen of bituminous impregnation of limestone at Nebi Musa, on the pilgrims' route to the Jordan, is not sufficient to establish this hypothesis; and, indeed, in a scientific point of view, it has no standing ground.[1]

The fragments of sulphur found on the shore of the lake (the quantity of which has been much exaggerated) are almost always found closely associated with gypsum, or in the neigh-

---

cision (see Appendix II.). M. Malagutti, of Rennes, informs me that he has analyzed a considerable quantity of salt obtained by the natural evaporation of $7\frac{1}{2}$ kilogrammes of the water of the lake, and has not succeeded in discovering any trace of silver therein, which exists in both the Atlantic and Pacific, and which ought to have been very appreciable in the Dead Sea water if it contains as much as that of the ocean.

[1] It must be borne in mind that M. Gaillardot, who, amongst others, sought to explain the depression of the basin of the lake by the combustion of bituminous limestone, made his observations under very unfavourable circumstances. His visit to the north end of the lake was made during the heat of the war between Egypt and the Porte, and he was compelled to divide his attention between the care of the wounded and scientific research. He appears now disposed to abandon his theory.

bourhood of gypsum beds. There is no doubt that this sulphur is formed by the reduction of the gypsum, according to a well-known action often observed elsewhere.[1]

In America, in 1850, on the strength of information fur-nished by the American missionaries, Hitchcock suggested the existence of a fissure extending from Akabah to the Jordan valley. Captain Lynch also, in a letter to Dr Anderson, specially called the attention of the latter to the influence which such an action might have exercised on the formation of the valley. More recently still this was the favourite idea of an eminent philosopher, whose loss both his friends and the scientific world at large are still deploring : I allude to the late Dr Hugh Falconer, who formed that impression during a hurried visit to the Jordan valley.

VI. THE OPINION OF RUSSEGGER.

Russegger admits the existence of an opening in the strata, but exaggerates unduly the influence of volcanic action in forming the basin of the Dead Sea, which, with the Lake of Tiberias, he regarded as crater-like depressions along the length of the fracture.

It is impossible to deny the importance of volcanic action in this region, and the alteration which it may have caused in the surface of the ground on the east of the lake. From my own observation, I can confirm the existence of several large *coulées* terminating in the lake, chiefly at three points on its eastern side.[2] They often cover a considerable extent of ground, and

---

[1] It is chiefly in the neighbourhood of Jebel Usdum that important beds of gypsum are met with above the rock-salt ; and hence the frequent occurrence of sulphur at that spot. At the Lisan I frequently found frag-ments of sulphur associated with the pieces of gypsum so thickly spread through the marl which forms the peninsula.

[2] The first and most northerly of these reaches the lake at the mouth of Wadi Ghuweir. It can be seen for a long distance issuing from a conical eminence, which Gablan, the sheikh of the Nemr-Adouans, called Mergab es-Suweimch. The second appears to issue from el-Hummar, near Jebel Attarus, where conglomerates are found composed of cinders and basaltic scoriæ. This *coulée* occupies the bed of the Zerka Main, and offers some remarkable examples of prismatic contraction. It then stretches along the margin of the lake from the mouth of the Zerka to the plain of

must have been discharged at a geological epoch not very remote from our own, since they often follow (as in the Zerka Main and in the Wadi Mojeb) the actual beds of the torrents, and therefore must date, at least in part, from after the formation of the valleys. There is reason to believe that they issued from existing gaps in the strata, and were not accompanied by convulsions powerful enough to have modified the basin of the lake in any important manner.

Russegger also examined the probability of the existence of a slope from the lake to the Red Sea, by which, before the formation of the basin of the former, the waters of the Jordan might have flowed away. This idea, however, he negatives, and with it that of an interruption in the course of the river. He appears to suppose, that since the formation of the basin the accumulated waters of the Jordan have been reduced by evaporation below the highest point of the barrier separating the lake from the Red Sea; and that, after many oscillations, the waters of the lake were gradually reduced till they reached their present depressed level. Russegger simply makes these statements without any support of evidence; and it is surprising that, in the absence of positive documents and geological observations on the southern portion of the basin, by which alone the problem can be solved, he should have possessed penetration enough to suggest an explanation so similar to that which the careful study of the region necessitates.

VII. THE DOUBLE HYPOTHESIS OF DR ANDERSON.

Dr Anderson has put forth two hypotheses on the subject of the formation of the basin of the lake, which correspond in some degree to those of Russegger, and between which he carefully refrains from deciding. The first of these is, that the Jordan valley and the depression of the Dead Sea owe their origin to a fissure or a series of fissures. The actual

---

Zarah, crowning the variegated sandstones and greywackes which form the cliffs. The third seems to take its rise at a sharp conical hill, which Gablan called Mountar ez-Zarah. It appears to be very short, and lies on the south of the little plain of Zarah, which is thus bounded by volcanic *coulées* on both north and south, as well as being furrowed out in all directions by hot springs, which have covered it with deposits of considerable thickness.

face of the country is due, under this hypothesis, to the action of erosion by atmospheric agents. It is, in other words, the hypothesis of Hitchcock, already mentioned. The rectilineal direction of the Ghor,[1] and the difference between the strata on the two sides of the valley, are both evidence in favour of this idea ; but, unfortunately, Dr Anderson, while acknowledging these facts, has not used them as he might in support of his theory.[2]

His second hypothesis he has developed with much more care and predilection. In this case he assumes the existence of a vast fissure sloping with an easy and uniform gradient to the Gulf of Akabah, and originally forming the bed of a stream. Certain geological actions, the nature of which, however, he does not specify, have at a later date interrupted the uniformity of this fissure, and produced the elevations and settlements which formed and isolated the two lakes. Dr Anderson candidly admits that his theory is beset with difficulties, to meet which he is obliged to assume that the whole Syrian continent, after having first emerged at the end of the Secondary period, was again immersed in the ocean. During this second immersion the erosive action of the sea reduced the eminences of the country, and destroyed all trace of the watercourse which had originally discharged itself into the Red Sea. The region, after having re-emerged in its modified form, has acquired its

---

[1] Since the time of Ibn Haukal (the Arabic writer of the tenth century) the name *Ghor* has been usually applied to that portion of the great trench which lies between the Lake of Tiberias and Akabah. Some travellers have confined the name to smaller portions of the district in the neighbourhood of the Dead Sea ; but, like Russegger and Anderson, I take it in its more general sense to designate the great trench in question—the most characteristic feature of the physical geography of the country, a feature perfectly appreciated by the Arabs, who are so quick in observing the characteristics of the ground.

[2] Dr Anderson objects to this hypothesis, that it fails to explain the origin of sinuous valleys, so much more numerous than straight ones. If by this he means the wadis which intersect the heights along the middle portion of the Ghor, it does not seem necessary to insist on so close a connection between the origin of the principal valley and that of the lateral ones. The latter may, in fact, have commenced by shallow and irregular fractures, the natural result of those movements of the ground which contorted the strata. The secular erosion of the rocks by atmospheric agents is quite sufficient to have done the rest.

present distinctive features through the action of the ordinary atmospheric agents.

The weak points of this theory are patent on the surface. If it was the Tertiary ocean which lowered the eminences, and destroyed every trace of the ancient valley, what new action can be invented to explain the total absence or the complete disappearance of marine deposits, or organic *débris*, belonging to the second period of immersion? for during so long a period the ocean must inevitably have left traces of its presence. Indeed, Dr Anderson himself is so little satisfied with his theories, as to preface them by an express declaration of his want of confidence in them. One point, however, appears to him indisputable, whether the origin of the Ghor was a fissure, or whether it was the result of excavation by a stream discharging itself into the Red Sea, and interrupted at a later date. In either case he is convinced that the Ghor, and some of its tributary valleys, were in existence long before the Tertiary epoch.[1]

VIII. THEORETICAL RESULTS OF THE OBSERVATIONS OF M. LARTET HIMSELF ON THE FORMATION OF THE BASIN OF THE DEAD SEA.

The uncertainty of Dr Anderson, and the variety and number of the theories successively proposed, do not give me much encouragement to state any opinion of my own; nevertheless, as my exploration was perhaps made more at leisure, and therefore ought to be more complete than those of my predecessors, and as I had the opportunity of collecting a larger number of facts and positive observations than they had, I should be wanting in my duty, and in my sense of the honour conferred upon me, if I did not state my conclusions. This is hardly the place to enter into a detailed geological description of the district containing the basin of the Dead Sea; for, to be of use, such a description must be accompanied by geological maps and sections, and by plates of the numerous and interest-

---

[1] I may remark here, that the existence of the eocene rocks, by proving that the district was covered by the ocean at the commencement of the Tertiary era, brings down the date of the formation of the valley far below the limit assigned to it by Anderson.

ing fossils collected. But I have every prospect of being enabled, by the liberality of the Duc de Luynes, to offer such a description to the Society on a future occasion. To make what follows intelligible, it will be only necessary here to take a rapid view of the nature and succession of the formations of the district.

The skeleton of Palestine in general, and of the mountains immediately surrounding the basin of the lake, is formed of cretaceous and eocene beds, closely allied both in character and in the perfect conformity of their stratification. It is vain to seek for more ancient stratified rocks, or for the jurassic formation of which Russegger and Anderson have made so much, and of which they report the existence of beds probably extending still further back in the scale of secondary formation.[1] There is no appearance, in the neighbourhood of the lake, of the lower cretaceous beds, viz. the neocomian limestones of Lebanon and Anti-Lebanon, which in those districts cover the ferruginous sandstones from which lignites have been obtained. In the basin of the lake these ferruginous (sometimes also felspathic) sandstones, always bare of fossils, and of a considerable thickness, form the foundation of the most ancient cretaceous rocks that are visible. They appear on the eastern side of the basin only, at the foot of the mountains, where they form a series nearly continuous and rectilineal, running north and south from the middle of the Jordan valley to Mount Hor, near the watershed of the Arabah. These sandstones, which we designate as Nubian, are covered by cretaceous beds, very rich in *echini* and *exogyres*, and with the same general fossils as in Egypt and Algeria.[2] The latter beds are, in their turn, covered

[1] It is true that at the northern end of the basin, at the foot of Jebel es-Sheykh (Hermon), and on the steep ascent leading up to the Castle of Banias, I collected some *echini*. Notwithstanding their very bad preservation, M. Cotteau, whose authority is indisputable, has recognised them as *collyrites*. They approach most nearly to *coll. bicordata* (Desm.), which in France characterizes the base of the coral formations. But it must be remembered that the genus *collyrites*, which was hitherto believed to be confined to the jurassic beds, has been recently discovered by M. Coquand, in the neocomian strata of Constantine (Algeria).

[2] It is to these beds that we must refer the dolomites and cidariferous limestones (*calcaires à cidaris*) which Russegger considers to be jurassic. By the latter name he wished to indicate the frequent occurrence in the

by the upper chalk and the eocene limestones, and these again
pass insensibly into other cretaceous beds, containing at certain
points—as, for example, at Sebastieh and Mount Gerizim—
large quantities of nummulites.[1] In the upper portion of the
cretaceous beds on the borders of the lake, saliferous and bitu-
miniferous gypsum is encountered, the most important deposits
of which are at Jebel Usdum and Zuweirah-el-foka.[2] At the
same level, from the Dead Sea to Anti-Lebanon, often in the
middle of bituminous rocks, strata are found rich in remains of
fish, which are probably the continuation of the pisciferous
marls so well known in the Lebanon.

Considered generally, the disposition of the formations on
both sides of the basin is very simple. From the Mediterranean

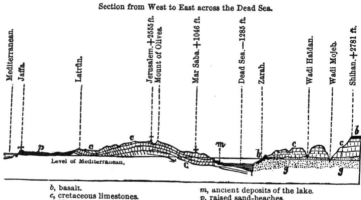

Section from West to East across the Dead Sea.

b, basalt.
c, cretaceous limestones.
g, Nubian sandstone.

m, ancient deposits of the lake.
p, raised sand-beaches.

they rise gradually to the highland ridge of Judæa, which is
connected with Lebanon by the hills of Galilee. They then

cretaceous strata of *echini*, such as the *hetero diadema lybicum*, *holectypus
serialis*, and (more often) *hemiaster*, which I myself collected at the very
spots referred to by Russegger.

[1] I discovered beds still richer in nummulites than those named in the
text at Wadi Ghurundel, south of the water-bed of the Arabah. M. Gaillardot discovered them on the coast of Phœnicia, near Sidon (*Bull. de la
Soc. Geol.* Ser. 2, xiii. 538), and some years before Anderson found them at
Arbey. M. Conrad gives a figure of these, and calls them *numm. arbyensis*.

[2] Almost exactly at this level are found the banks of salt and gypsum,
in Algeria ; which, from their great thickness, are called by the natives (as
at the Dead Sea) "salt mountains." The similar formations in Armenia
and Persia stood apparently at the same general level.

dip more suddenly, sometimes abruptly, in the opposite direction, towards the sea, on the farther side of which appear the Nubian sandstone and other cretaceous beds of greater age than those on the western side. The arrangement of the beds is shown in the annexed section, taken from Jaffa to Shihan across the highlands of Judah, the Dead Sea, and the plateau of Moab. Except a few local and unimportant undulations, the cretaceous and eocene beds which form the platform on the eastern side dip but very slightly from the horizontal; but in the immediate neighbourhood of the Ghor and the Dead Sea, they suddenly take a considerable inclination towards the depression. This is very visible at the Wadi ed-Drah, where the beds are actually broken at the point at which the dip commences.

The position of these beds on both sides of the Jordan valley, and the striking rectilineal character of the valley itself, would seem to favour the idea of the existence of a vast line of fracture through the middle of the country; but, in fact, instead of corresponding, the western and eastern sides of the valley are not on the same geological level: nay more, there is every reason to believe that if the beds on the eastern side could be seen below the waters of the lake, it would be found that at that depth the difference in throw would be still greater.[1] I have already said that the highlands which form the mountains of Judah dip towards the Dead Sea. Lynch's soundings[2] show that on the west side of the lake the slope of the shore is moderate, and in correspondence with the dip of the strata. On the eastern side, however, the shore is almost vertical, and a transverse section through the central part of the lake presents nearly the form of a right-angled triangle. The cretaceous beds below the water form nearly the hypothenuse of the triangle, until they meet the older beds on the eastern side, which are almost vertical, and form the short side of the right angle. This state of things is analogous to that which is observed in the case of fissures, and Hitchcock's hypothesis is therefore the one which most satisfactorily accounts for the facts.

[1] If this assumption is tenable, the real throw of the beds at the bottom of the lake must exceed the apparent throw of the cliffs by at least 300 metres.

[2] These soundings were carefully verified by M. Vignes, who has satisfied himself of their accuracy.

The axis of the Dead Sea is not, it is true, an exact continuation of that of the Valley of the Jordan, but nevertheless the form of the bed of the lake supports Hitchcock's theory. If we lay down the various sections of the lake from Lynch's soundings, we shall arrive at last at an extremely elongated ellipse, comprised between the Wadis Zerka Main and Mojeb, and representing the greatest depth of the basin. Now it is very remarkable that the main axis of this ellipse is an exact prolongation of that of the Valley of the Jordan. In the same way, we find that the direction of the sandstone cliffs in the southern part of the basin is not quite coincident with that of the Wadi Arabah, which bends slightly towards the west. South-east of the lake from Mount Hor to the Ghor es-Safieh the line of sandstones is interrupted by bands of felspathic porphyries, following the same general direction from north to south. A large number of the earthquakes which have so long affected Syria follow the same line, as do also the hot and mineral springs and the sources of bitumen.

It follows, then, that if these conditions cannot be actually identified with those of ordinary geological faults, they are enough to imply that at some very distant epoch a fracture took place in the soil of this district in the general direction of north and south. Further, it would appear that before the deposit of the cretaceous rocks the fracture had begun to show itself in the southern portion of the basin. The porphyries (which, as we have just seen, are older than the cretaceous beds) no doubt made their appearance at this epoch; at any rate, this may be inferred from their disposition and direction. At a later date, the movements which caused the rise of the ocean bed corresponding to Syria and Arabia Petræa may have extended the fracture towards the north, and at the same time formed the mountain chains which accompany it.

Owing to the unequal strength of the different portions of the earth's crust, the general movement may have produced great inequalities of level in the cretaceous beds, corresponding to the two sides of the line of fracture. The eastern side of the highlands of Judah must have undergone a considerable downward movement all along the line of dislocation, and thus originated the depressed trench which separates Palestine proper from the highlands on the other side of the Jordan.

This theory is justified by the sudden dip of the eastern side of the highlands of Judah, by the form of the bottom of the Dead Sea, and by the want of correspondence of the beds on the two sides of the depression; and it appears to me to explain the facts better than any other.

IX. THE FORMATION OF THE LAKE, AND THE SUCCESSIVE VARIATIONS IN ITS LEVEL.

Having thus endeavoured to discover the manner in which the basin of the Dead Sea was formed, it remains to examine the extent of the depression in the level of the water of the lake in reference to the ocean. This question is, as Dr Anderson has justly remarked, entirely independent of that of the depression of the bottom of the basin. From what has gone before, it appears that the cretaceous and eocene rocks, which did not rise from the ocean until after the commencement of the Tertiary period, form the limit of the basin. They are the last marine beds to be found there; and, since their appearance, the basin has been subjected to the influence of atmospheric agents alone. The present wadis have been no doubt entirely the work of the rains, which conveyed through them to the bottom of the depression the materials washed from the neighbouring rocks,—an action which they have continued until they have fixed on the country the principal features of its present physiognomy. It is in the immediate neighbourhood of the lake that the beds of the eastern slope of the mountains of Judah dip most suddenly. It was at this spot, therefore, that the first *accumulation* of water must have taken place, and thus a lake was formed which, at the beginning, was probably fresh, but which must quickly have become salt, owing to the neighbourhood of the saliferous deposits mentioned above.

This Tertiary lake was the sole receptacle of the waters of the basin : its size must have been regulated by the evaporation; and even at that remote period, since its waters were continually being thrown off, and leaving in the basin their constituent salts, the lake may have acquired a degree of saltness quite exceptional.[1]

[1] Dr Anderson appears to think that the amount of magnesia contained in the dolomites and basalts may have had a powerful effect on the concen-

Assuming that the lake was thus formed, and that its extent is dependent solely on the equilibrium between the evaporation and the natural supply, it is a legitimate subject for inquiry, whether its size has ever been greater than at present; whether it formerly occupied a much larger area; or whether, on the contrary, it did not exist at first in a rudimentary form, of which traces are preserved in the salt mountain of Jebel Usdum.[1]

I need not insist on the importance of this question, a solution of which would reveal the nature of the ancient climate of the district, as well as the changes it has since undergone. If I have proved my position, that the Dead Sea was always a closed basin cut off from the ocean, it is clear that the level of its water must always have been an index to the proportion between the atmospheric supply and the evaporation, and must have varied as one or the other predominated, just as is the case at the present day. The level of the lake must therefore have varied with the condition of the atmosphere, and must have left traces of those variations,—traces which are invaluable, if we wish to investigate the state of the climate of the basin at times very remote from our own.

Such isolated lakes as the Dead Sea may, in fact, be considered as instruments provided by nature for the use of those who inquire into the secrets of the past, with the view of accounting for ancient phenomena beyond the reach of actual

tration of the waters of the lake. I will not dispute such a possibility with regard to the dolomites; but as to the basalt I will only remark, that before its eruption the water of the lake must, to judge by its ancient deposits, have already contained much magnesia. It is the gypsum and the saliferous beds which must have exercised the most influence on the saltness of the lake, as well as the hot mineral springs, of which a great number are now only represented by their ancient encrustations. There is every reason to believe that these springs were formerly more numerous and more copious than at present. That at Emmaus [? near Tiberias], if we may trust the analysis of Dr Anderson, still contains bromine; and it is probable that in this manner we may account for the enormous proportion of that base that is present in the waters of the lake.

[1] Before dismissing the latter supposition, I beg to refer to what M. D'Archiac has said on the subject, merely adding that the salt of Jebel Usdum is deposited in beds which occur at the upper limit of the cretaceous rocks, the latter having been deposited at the bottom of the ocean long before Palestine emerged therefrom.

observation. These reservoirs may be looked on as vast rain-gauges, constructed to register the relation between the quantity of water which has fallen and the quantity which has been evaporated. It is true that they do not register *minima*, but they record indelibly the *maxima* of those remote periods. They record them in the successive deposits left by the lake as its waters rise; and they have this advantage over our meteorological instruments, that they give us not only the level, but the constitution of the water, at the time of its attaining each successive elevation.

X. THE ANCIENT DEPOSITS OF THE LAKE.

Traces of the nature last mentioned may be observed round the lake far to both north and south of its present limits. They consist of marly and sandy deposits, similar to those which appear to constitute the bulk of the peninsula of the Lisan. I shall therefore often mention them as "Lisan beds," since it is there they have attained their maximum. They present in general the form of innumerable layers of marl of a clear grey colour, alternating with extremely thin beds of a different colour, and sometimes a different nature, and often composed of saline substances, as, for instance, lenticular gypsum or saliferous clays. The whole mass is usually made up of beds not more than one or two decimetres (4 to 8 inches) in thickness, and presenting, from their difference in colour, a riband appearance, by which they may be easily recognised. Occasionally, as on the western side of the Lisan, the gypsum beds are thicker, and composed of large hemitropal crystals, displaying in their cleavage the spear-head form so often met with in the lacustrine gypsiferous marls of the Parisian Eocene. The deposits of the Lisan contain almost exact duplicates of the laminated marls found in the upper portion of the Parisian beds. Owing to their want of coherence, they have been extremely cut up by the rains, and present occasionally the oddest and most picturesque forms, which have been compared by travellers to ruined cities or dismantled fortresses, or even actual camps.

The subjoined section across the shore, between the Wadi Seyal and the lake, where the deposits have been very much cut up, will give an idea of their forms, and the succession of the beds composing them.

Section of the ancient deposits of the Dead Sea, taken across the beach from the mouth of the
Wadi Seyal to the Lake opposite the Lisan.

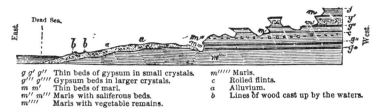

g g' g''   Thin beds of gypsum in small crystals.   m''''' Marls.
g''' g'''' Gypsum beds in larger crystals.   c   Rolled flints.
m m'   Thin beds of marl.   a   Alluvium.
m'' m'''   Marls with saliferous beds.   b   Lines of wood cast up by the waters.
m''''   Marls with vegetable remains.

If we consider how thick these deposits are in some places,
and, at the same time, how extremely numerous are the thin
beds composing them, it is impossible to resist the conclusion
that their complete deposit must have extended over an enormous period.

In the neighbourhood of the synclinal axis of the basin the
strata are remarkably uniform, both in appearance and composition; but as the edges of the basin are approached, they become intermixed with beds of flint and gravel, which have for
the most part come from the cretaceous rocks, and especially

View of the arenaceous deposits lying upon the calcareous limestones, and forming the transition
between the deposits of the Lisan and the alluviums of the Wadis, and upon which are seated
the ruins of Zuweirah et-Tahta.

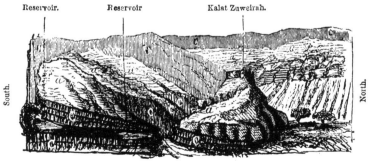

Reservoir.   Reservoir   Kalat Zuweirah.

a, Ancient alluviums (arenaceous marls and mud).   c, Cretaceous limestones.

from the numerous bands of flint superposed on them. They
would even seem to have some connection with the ancient
alluviums[1] of the wadis, which contain more sand and flint, and

[1] These ancient alluviums are now planted against the side-walls of the
wadis, and consist of immense accumulations of gravel, sand, and mud, not
unlike in appearance the Quaternary deposits of the European valleys.

less salt and gypsum, as they approach the mouths of the wadis.

The Lisan deposits are found throughout the whole of the western shore of the lake, reposing against the cliffs—as, for example, at Ain Feshkah, at Wadi Marabba, at Ain Jidy, and, above all, on the beach which stretches from the Wadi Seyal to the south side of Sebbeh (Masada). They are also found about the Wadi Zuweirah and Jebel Usdum. South of the lake they form, for the most part, that bent line of ancient cliffs which closes in the marshy plain of the Sabkah, and from thence extend still farther south into the Wadi Arabah. The deep ravines through which the Wadi el-Jeib and its other southern affluents flow into the Dead Sea, exhibit most interesting sections of these deposits, showing at the base beds of gravel, often consisting of the *débris* of felspathic porphyry, with marls and gypsiferous alluviums above them.

East of the lake the amount of these deposits is but small, which is probably due to the abruptness of the slope of the cliffs on that side : a few traces only are to be found embedded here and there in the hollows of the soil. In the peninsula of the Lisan alone do they show any important development on that side of the water. North of the lake they cover a great space in the valley on each side of the Jordan, which, like the Wadi el-Jeib, has excavated its bed, and deposited its alluviums, in the middle of these strata.[1]

If we follow these deposits far to the north, we shall find that they preserve their external characteristics throughout in a remarkable manner. I observed them near the Jordan, opposite the mouth of the Wadi Zerka (Jabbok), at which point

[1] Neither the Jordan nor any other of the streams which run into the lake are now in contact with the saliferous and gypsiferous deposits above mentioned. They run through a yellowish mud, which produces the most luxuriant vegetation, while the white deposits of the Lisan can support nothing beyond a thorny bush or two, or at best a few saliferous plants. The mud of the Jordan is brought down from the higher districts drained by its tributaries. It lines the hollow of their primitive beds, and ensures the purity of their waters by preserving them from contact with gypsiferous and saliferous marls. To this fact, and the dryness of the valley, it is due that the Jordan receives but the minutest quantity of the salts contained in the ancient deposits in question, and thus arrives at the Dead Sea almost as pure as when it first left its sources.

they reached the height of at least 100 metres above the level of the lake. Their thickness at that spot gives reason to believe that they exist still farther north.

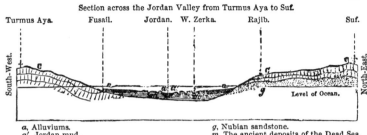

Section across the Jordan Valley from Turmus Aya to Suf.

a, Alluviums.
a', Jordan mud.
c, Cretaceous limestones containing Hemiaster Fourneli.

g, Nubian sandstone.
m, The ancient deposits of the Dead Sea.

Not having examined the portion of the Jordan valley between this point and the Lake of Tiberias, I am unable to say if these deposits exist in the neighbourhood of that lake. At its southern end, grey marls occur in very thin beds, and closely resembling in appearance the deposits in question; but, on the other hand, they are only five or six metres in thickness, and do not appear to contain either gypsum or salt.[1] As at that point they are more than 200 metres above the level of the Dead Sea, it is necessary to establish their connection with the sedimentary beds of the Dead Sea beyond doubt, before we can admit that the waters which deposited *the beds of Lisan* ever extended as far as the Lake of Tiberias. Notwithstanding many very minute investigations, I have failed to discover in *the deposits of the Lisan* any vestige of organized life, with the single exception of some impressions of plants at the entrance of the Wadi Seyal, in a thin bed of marl, three inches in thickness, between two layers of gypsum.[2]

[1] The latter fact might be explained, even if we take these beds to be a continuation of the deposits of the Lisan, by supposing that they had been deposited near the mouth of a stream coming from the north, and emptying itself into the northern end of the original lake. In any case, the marls above mentioned must be ancient, since we do not find any trace in them of those basaltic *débris* with which the bottom of the Lake of Tiberias and the ground around it are covered.

[2] It is not unfrequent to meet with melanopsides and melanies, often discoloured, and having all the appearance of fossils, in the top beds of these deposits, but never in the unexposed beds; and careful examination

These beds are very regularly stratified, and are remarkable for the thinness of the layers of which they are composed, as well as for the large proportion of salt and gypsum they contain; and in this respect they are very analogous to what is now going on at the bottom of the lake, if one may judge from the specimens brought up by the lead, and from the soil of the Sabkah. The bottom seems to consist in general of marls and clays containing crystals of salt and gypsum in small lenticular forms, very like those which are found *in the deposits of the Lisan.*[1]

To explain the formation of the deposits of the Lisan, it thus becomes necessary to assume that, at a remote epoch, the level of the lake was much higher than at present,—that its water was then extremely salt, and probably even then incompatible with the existence of animal life, as appears to be shown by the absence of organic remains in the deposits. Such water was capable of throwing down the gypsiferous and saliferous sediments which so strongly resemble the contemporary deposits of the Dead Sea.

The absence of all trace of basaltic rocks[2] and bituminous[3]

will generally discover the remains of a stream bed or basin, or ancient spring, formerly the abode of these shells.

[1] In the soundings made by M. Vignes between Ain Ghuweir and Wadi Zerka Main, some crystals of gypsum were brought up in a greyish-blue clay, containing numerous cubical crystals of salt. It may be said that these crystals of gypsum proceed merely from the washing down of the Lisan itself; but the manner in which they exist in the clay, and the sharpness of their angles, leads to the belief that they are really of a contemporary formation.

[2] Notwithstanding every endeavour, I did not succeed in finding any basaltic *débris* in the deposits of the Lisan. Fragments of scoriæ are met with on the beach of the lake, even on the western side, where no volcanic eruptions have taken place; but these scoriæ are light enough to have floated across. It is necessary to be on one's guard against hasty inductions from the presence of basaltic scoriæ. Basalt has always been employed in these countries for millstones, which are still made in the neighbourhood of the Lake of Tiberias, and in the Hauran, and exported thence.

[3] It is true that in the Wadi Mahawat (first explored by the Rev. Mr Tristram) the bitumen has impregnated the ancient alluviums which are at least coeval with these deposits; but this arises from the bitumen having leaked out of the underlying cretaceous rocks, from the crevices of which it is constantly escaping, and forming stalactites. The phenomena at the

beds in these deposits, goes to show that they were formed before the occurrence of those volcanic eruptions, the traces of which are so abundant in the Jordan valley; and on the same ground, it is safe to believe that they were deposited before the appearance of the bitumen, which we know from the ancient historians to have been produced in such large quantities in the lake itself.

Since the deposit of these beds a very considerable time has elapsed, during which the level of the water fell, and the streams gradually excavated their beds in the valley in the middle of the new deposits. During this long interval, the volcanic forces appeared, and attained that important development which we find in the plains of the Hauran and of Jaulan, and then burnt themselves out, probably before the arrival in the country of any of those nations who have furnished our most ancient traditions. These volcanic eruptions, like those in our own districts of Vivarais and Catalogne, appear not to have produced any changes in the face of the country, beyond occasional accumulations of lava, due in part to eruptions probably not far distant from our own era.[1]

XI. THE PROBABLE CAUSES OF THE PRESENT DEPRESSED LEVEL OF THE WATER OF THE DEAD SEA.

The sinking of the water of the Dead Sea is the most remarkable change which has taken place in the country since the deposit of the marls of the Lisan, and it appears to imply a serious modification in the climate of the region. It indicates, in fact, clearly, either that the lake formerly received more water than it does now, or that the evaporation was less. The relative importance of these two conditions can only be ascer-

---

spot in question are probably very modern; and it would seem that when the alluviums of the Wadi Mahawat were formed, the bitumen had not appeared in such quantities as it has subsequently,—perhaps had not begun to appear; since, if it had, the deposits of the Lisan must have retained traces of it.

[1] In Syria, as in Auvergne, and in the district of Asia Minor known as the Katakekaumene, there have probably been several successive ages of these eruptions; at any rate, it is only natural to consider the black compact basalt of Moab and Ammon as older than the doleritic lavas, which are often found following the beds of the existing streams.

tained by an investigation of the wadis, in their relation as feeders to the lake. The greater number of them are at present dry during most of the year; others are only supplied after the rains by springs; and all display in the present quantity of their water a striking disproportion to the great depth and size of the valleys through which they flow. To account for the formation of these valleys, as well as the great accumulations of ancient alluviums which they contain, one is driven to believe that for long ages they contained copious and permanent streams; and taking into account the quantity of water which, when full, they would discharge into the lake, it is easy to understand that its level was once much higher than at present. Further, if, since the date of which we are speaking, the atmospheric conditions have become less favourable to that rise of level (which is evident from the present state of the streams), such a change would naturally betray itself by a fall in the level of the lake.

Such a diminution of the rainfall, and the consequent condition of the streams of Syria, is quite in agreement with what takes place in the European valleys, and with the information which we possess of the state of the climate of this hemisphere at the end of the Tertiary and beginning of the Quaternary epochs. At the time at which it is now generally allowed that the mountains of Europe were covered with glaciers, and when the Mediterranean contained animals of an arctic character, the temperature must have been lower than it is at present; and there is no reason to doubt that at the same epoch the climate of Syria was also cooler. The recent observations of that distinguished *savant*, Dr Hooker of Kew, have revealed in the Lebanon obvious traces of an important ancient series of glaciers, the moraines of which he traced to no less than 1200 metres below the highest summits—which summits themselves are not now perpetually covered with snow.[1] The cedars—the

[1] *Natural History Review*, Jan. 1862. The moraines which Dr Hooker discovered in the Lebanon, and which Sir Charles Lyell does not hesitate to class among the erratic deposits of the earliest glacial period, would seem to correspond to the calcareous pudding-stones originally described by Botta. Russegger mentions the existence in the Orontes valley of ranges of pudding-stone formation, united by a brittle calcareous cement, the abnormal arrangement of which struck him much, and which he considered as diluvium. It is also met with at the foot of Anti-Libanus, and on the eastern

last representatives of the ancient flora of a colder climate—still persist in their long growth in the middle of the moraines of the ancient glaciers, near which their ancestors, no doubt, existed in larger numbers and at less elevation.

If, then, the Lebanon was at one time covered with perpetual snow, it follows that the climate of Palestine must have been favourable to the flow of the streams, at the same time that it diminished the evaporation of the lake to a point far below what it is at present. These two conditions, acting together, must have been sufficient to produce in time a considerable rise in the surface of the lake; and when they disappeared, a corresponding fall must have followed. It is easy to imagine the possibility of the same effects being assisted by agents of another description. For instance, the large basaltic currents which have forced themselves as far as the Jordan valley, at the north part of the basin, may have diverted some of the northern affluents of the lake.[1] In the neighbourhood of the lakes of Huleh and Tiberias they have actually produced barriers analogous to those which interrupted the course of the streams, and produced lakes, in the Auvergne and Katakekaumene.[2]

Similar effects might certainly be produced by torrents of lava like those at Banias, or like those which have so seriously

shore of the Lake of Tiberias. In every case these pudding-stones are remarkable for the absence of basaltic pebbles even in those districts where basalt is most frequent,—a fact which establishes their antiquity. I have never observed any scratched stones, or other traces of glacial action in these deposits. I shall content myself, while on this subject, with calling the attention of future explorers to the brittle pudding-stone which occurs on the crests and scarped flanks of the mountains surrounding Mount Hor. The total thickness of the deposits cannot be less than 100 metres. Their general position is in a line from north to south.

[1] The water of Banias, which is considered, wrongly or rightly, as the source of the Jordan, gushes out, like that at Tell el Kady, from beneath a mass of basalt which has proceeded from the plateau of Jaulan and forced itself into the plain. Near the sudden bend which is made by the Litany when it leaves its original and natural course towards the Jordan for the Mediterranean (a change of direction the causes of which should be carefully studied) there are many basaltic eruptions in the Wadi Hasbany, nearly up to the source of the Hasbeya.

[2] The lakes of Aïdat and Chambon in Auvergne, and the lake Marsh, near Koola in the Katakekaumene.

narrowed the Valley of the Jordan between the Lakes Huleh and Tiberias; and in this way the eruptions of basalt may, in a small degree, have assisted in depressing the water of the Dead Sea. Nevertheless, the present level of the surface must be due chiefly to a diminution of the streams, consequent on a change of climate; and it is tempting, as I have already said, to compare the ancient condition of those streams with the analogous changes produced on the European rivers by atmospheric phenomena, which appear to have been at their height at the commencement of the Quaternary epoch. Dr Hooker's observations go to confirm this analogy, which is also strongly supported by the investigation of the ground, and by a due consideration of the probable duration of the geological phenomena which preceded and followed that great climacteric crisis, which may be taken as the dividing limit of the Tertiary and Quaternary epochs.

Once ascribe the ancient lowering of the lake to so general a cause as this, and it follows that the effect of such a great atmospheric change cannot have been confined to so small an area as that of the Dead Sea basin. The same change may offer an explanation of the ancient extent of the lakes in Asia, Africa, and America,[1] an extent evident enough from the nature of the ground round them.

If we wish to penetrate to the causes which actually operated in lowering the level of the water, we are stopped by our want of knowledge of those great changes in the relative distribution of land and sea which took place at the end of the Tertiary period. It would be difficult to decide whether the general diminution of the water-supply of the district in question were the effect of a rise in temperature, or of a modification in the hygrometric condition of the winds, which, in the regular course of nature, supplied the rainfall. This latter question deserves the attention of geologists. The most direct and powerful effect on the water in the Dead Sea and the zone of Asiatic lakes, of which it forms a part, would follow from the drying up of the winds which formerly supplied them. And this may have been brought about either by the substitution of land for sea over a part of their course; or by the rise of a chain of mountains in the path of these winds, the snowy summits of which,

[1] *Silliman's Journal*, 1847, pp. 19, 20, and 93.

by lowering their dew-point, would necessarily retain a great part of the vapour which had previously supplied the rainfall of the lakes.

In the former case it is easy to find in the track of the winds which may have supplied the Asiatic lakes, such districts as the Sahara,—a sandy desert in the middle of which sea-shells are found, identical with those which actually exist in the ocean, and which appears to have been protruded after the Tertiary period.

In the second case there is a little more difficulty; but nevertheless it is to this cause that Captain Maury, the learned director of the Observatory at Washington, and author of *The Physical Geography of the Sea,* would attribute the drying up of the district containing the Asiatic lakes, as well as the reduction in the level of the Dead Sea, and which he proves by the fact of the extreme saltness of the latter. Captain Maury believes that the drying up of these lakes is due to the south-east trade winds of Africa and America returning to our hemisphere as currents from the south-west. It is upon the track of these winds that we must look for a chain of mountains, the elevation of which has robbed them of their original humidity; and this Captain Maury finds in the Andes, the geological date of which appears, in fact, to be not very remote.[1] However this may be, it is to the influence of three main causes that the depression of the water in the Dead Sea since the deposit of the gypsiferous marls is probably due :—

1. An elevation of the mean annual temperature, or at least that of the winters, manifesting itself in a great increase in evaporation.

2. The rise of a vast sea-bottom in the track of the winds which pass over the Dead Sea, which have been thereby dried up, owing to the substitution of burning sands for the water from which they formerly derived their humidity; or,

3. The formation in the track of the same winds of a chain of mountains sufficiently high to cause a condensation of their vapours, and thus to retain their humidity.

[1] It is possible that in the north of Africa mountains may yet be discovered of a date contemporary with the Quaternary period, which, owing to their comparative proximity to Asia, would have exercised a more direct effect on the drying up of these lakes than the Andes can have had.

Such are the phenomena among which it seems to me natural to seek for the causes of the depression in the level of the water of the lake. Nevertheless, it must not be denied that it is probably impossible to apportion exactly to each of these causes its part in the operation; but it may be possible, from our notions on the epochs at which these causes acted, to gather such indications as may throw light on their relative importance.

XII. RESUMÉ AND CONCLUSIONS.

In reviewing my geological study of the basin of the Dead Sea, I am led to think—

1. That at the end of the Eocene period, and in consequence of an upward movement (the date of the commencement of which cannot be determined), an ocean bed was protruded corresponding to the continent of Syria and Arabia Petræa.

2. Before this protrusion (even before the deposit of the cretaceous rocks), disturbances had taken place in the submarine beds, and a fissure was opened from north to south through which the felspathic porphyries made their way, which now mark the line of the fissure between Petra and the Dead Sea.

3. This fissure may have been prolonged towards the north by subsequent movements which determined the formation of the highlands of Palestine; while the fall of the eastern side of those highlands all along the line of dislocation may have caused that narrow and lengthened depression which separates Palestine from Arabia.

4. The basin of the Dead Sea has thus been formed without any influence from or communication with the ocean; whence it follows that the lake which occupies the bottom of the basin has never been anything but a reservoir for the rainfall, the saltness of which originally proceeded from the constitution of the environs of the lake, and has greatly increased under the influence of incessant evaporation.

5. Towards the end of the Tertiary period, or the commencement of the Quaternary period, the water of the lake stood at more than 100 metres above its present level, and then deposited marls rich in salt and gypsum beds.

6. At a later period volcanic eruptions have taken place to

the north-east of the basin, which produced important *coulées* of basalt, some of them extending as far as the Jordan valley itself. Other eruptions of less importance took place directly east of the lake, of which three reached its eastern shore near the Wadis Ghuweir and Zerka Main, and the south end of the little plain of Zarah.

7. Hot and mineral springs, bituminous eruptions similar to those which accompany and follow volcanic action, and earthquakes, which are still frequent in the district, were the last important phenomena by which the basin of the Dead Sea was affected.

APPENDIX II.

———◆———

ON THE COMPOSITION OF THE WATER OF THE DEAD SEA, OF
THE SPRINGS IN THE NEIGHBOURHOOD OF THAT LAKE,
AND OF THE JORDAN.

By M. A. Terreil.[1]

THE water of the Dead Sea has been the subject of numerous analyses, the principal of which were made by Lavoisier, Masquer, Marcel, Klaproth, Gay-Lussac, Gmelin, Marchand, Boutron and Henry, Boussingault, etc.[2] Those which I have now the honour to submit to the Academy may perhaps throw light on some points which escaped the decision of the eminent chemists just named. The specimens analyzed were collected at the end of March and beginning of April 1864, by M. Louis Lartet, during the scientific expedition of the Duc de Luynes. The water was obtained at various spots, at the surface, and at depths extending to 300 metres, and each specimen was enclosed in a glass tube of 130 to 180 centimetres wide, hermetically sealed on the spot.

On breaking the end of the tubes, a disagreeable smell was perceived, resembling sulphuretted hydrogen and bitumen. The smell was most observable in the specimens taken from the middle of the lake, opposite Ras Mersed.

The water had an oily appearance, and wetted the sides of the glass with reluctance; each tube contained a slight ochreous sediment composed of oxide of iron, alumina, silex, and some

[1] Translated by Mr Grove.
[2] To whom M. Terreil might have added Apjohn, Herapath, and Gregory on this side the Channel, and Booth in America.

other organic substance, the nature of which could not be
determined owing to the small quantity of deposit. Some of
the specimen tubes contained a little mercury, derived from the
apparatus by which the water was obtained from a depth.

The tubes containing water from the springs round the
lake emitted neither gas nor smell on being opened, and the
sides of the tubes were mostly covered with small rhomboidal
crystals of carbonate of lime and carbonate of magnesia.

Out of the numerous specimens submitted to me, I made
exact analysis only of a few taken at very various depths, and
in different parts of the lake. The quantity of each specimen
was so small, that in the case of certain constituents I was
unable to measure the exact quantity, and contented myself
with merely indicating their presence. With the rest I took
the density of the water, measured the salts it deposited, and
the quantities of bromine and potash it contained.

With the specimens of water from streams and springs I
took their density and the quantity of salts deposited, and then
confined myself to a quantitative analysis of the salts held in
solution.

The result of my analyses is given in the following tables:

I.

	In the lake near to Ras Dale.	Lagoon north of Usdum.	Near the island at the N.W. extremity of the lake.	In the lake five miles east of Wadi M'rabba.	In the lake near Ras Mersed.	In the lake five miles east of Ras Feshkah.	In the lake five miles east of Ras Feshkah.	In the lake five miles east of Wadi M'rabba.
Depth in metres) (3·28 ft.).	Surface	Surface	Surface	20	42	120	200	300
Density at 59° Fahr.	1·0216	1·0375	1·1647	1·1877	1·2151	1·2225	1·2300	1·2563
Deposit of salts (dry)	27·078	47·683	205·789	204·311	260·994	262·648	271·606	278·135
Water . .	972·922	952·317	794·211	795·689	739·006	737·352	728·394	721·865
Chlorine . .	17·628	29·826	126·521	145·543	165·443	166·340	170·423	174·985
Bromine . .	0·167	0·835	4·568	3·204	4·834	4·870	4·385	7·093
Sulphuric acid .	0·202	0·676	0·494	0·362	0·447	0·451	0·459	0·523
Carbonic acid .	Traces	Traces	Traces	Traces	Traces	Traces	Traces	Traces
Hydrosulphuric acid	Traces	Traces	Traces	Traces	Traces	Traces	Traces	Traces
Magnesium . .	4·197	3·470	25·529	29·881	41·004	41·306	42·006	41·428
Calcium . .	2·150	4·481	9·094	11·472	3·693	3·704	4·218	17·269
Sodium . . .	0·885	7·845	22·400	13·113	24·786	25·071	25·107	14·300
Potassium . .	0·474	0·779	3·547	3·520	2·421	3·990	4·503	4·386
Ammonia . .	Traces	Traces	Traces	Traces	Traces	Traces	Traces	Traces
Alumina and iron .	Traces	Traces	Traces	Traces	Traces	Traces	Traces	Traces
Silex . . .	0·006	Traces	Traces	Traces	Traces	Traces	Traces	Traces
Organic matters .	Traces	Traces	Traces	Traces	Traces	Traces	Traces	Traces
	25·709	47·912	192·153	207·095	242·628	245·732	251·101	259·984

II.

Spots at which the specimens were collected. (From the surface only.)	Density at 59° Fahr.	Deposit of salts (dry).	Bromine.	Anhydrous potash.
In the lake at the entrance of the Jordan .	1·0185	24·182	0·486	5·070
Do. at the entrance of Wady Mojeb	1·1150	146·336	3·590	3·875
In the passage between Ras Senin and the southern end of the Lisan peninsula .	1·1700	210·366	2·662	...
In the lake near Jebel Usdum . . .	1·1740	209·154	2·633	4·332
Two miles east of Ain Ghuweir . . .	1·2280	256·010	4·463	...
Five miles east of Wadi M'rabba . .	1·2310	273·572	4·754	5·250
Two miles east of Ain Ghuweir . .	1·2320	276·989	4·456	5·984
Five miles east of Wadi M'rabba . .	1·2340	274·643	4·411	5·943

III.

Springs and Streams.	Density at 59° Fahr.	Deposit of Salt.
Water of Ain Jidy	1·000032	0·394
Do. Ain Zarah	1·000820	0·716
Do. Jordan	1·001000	0·873
Do. Wadi Zerka Main	1·001660	1·569
Do. Ain Suweimeh	1·002300	2·162
Do. Ain Terabeh	1·002400	3·032

IV. THE WATER OF THE JORDAN, COLLECTED BY M. LOUIS LARTET AT THE "FORD OF THE GHAWARINEHS," TWELVE KILOMETRES ABOVE ITS ENTRANCE INTO THE LAKE.

Dry residuum	0·873	Brought forward .	0·688
Water	999·127	Lime	0·060
		Magnesia	0·065
Chlorine	0·425	Potash	Traces
Sulphuric acid	0·034	Silica, alumine, and iron .	Traces
Carbonic acid	Traces	Organic matter . . .	Traces
Soda	0·229	Substances not weighed .	0·060
Carry forward . .	0·688		0·873

From these analyses the following conclusions may be drawn :—

1. The density of the Dead Sea water increases with its depth below the surface.

2. The composition of the water differs at different parts of the lake at the same time, even avoiding those parts which are near the entrance of streams or springs. Thus, five miles east of Wadi M'rabba, it contains four times as much calcium as it does five miles east of Ras Feshkah, while the latter exhibits twice as much sodium as the former.

3. The concentration of the water also varies extremely at different points (excluding, as before, the neighbourhood of streams). Thus, at a depth of sixty metres east of Wadi M'rabba it contains more salts in solution than at a depth of two hundred metres off Ras Feshkah.

4. The water collected in the lagoon to the north of Usdum contains more chloride of sodium than chloride of magnesium, which is not ordinarily the case elsewhere in the lake, and which explains the presence of small living fish at that spot.

5. The constituent salts remain in the same proportion, whether the specimen is taken from the surface or from a depth—excepting the bromides, which are much concentrated at a depth of 300 metres.

6. The water contains no iodine, and, to all appearance, no phosphoric acid.

7. The salts deposited by the water exhibit under the spectroscope neither lithium, cœsium, nor rubidium. They contain little sulphuric acid, and consist almost exclusively of chlorides of magnesium, sodium, calcium, and potassium, with a certain quantity of bromides of the same bases. The proportions of bromine and potash contained by this water are large enough to attract the attention of manufacturers. There can be no doubt that the Dead Sea will one day become an abundant source of these two substances, the latter of which in particular is so valuable in chemical manufactures.

8. The salts deposited by the waters of the springs and streams in the immediate neighbourhood of the lake are composed of chlorides, sulphates, and carbonates of lime, magnesia, soda, and potash, and contain no bromine—at least not in any quantity sufficient to affect the analyses.

APPENDIX III.

———◆———

REMARKS ON THE VARIATIONS IN THE SALTNESS OF THE
DEAD SEA WATER AT DIFFERENT PLACES ON ITS SUR-
FACE, AND AT DIFFERENT DEPTHS; AND ALSO ON THE
PROBABLE ORIGIN OF THE SALTS WHICH ENTER INTO
ITS COMPOSITION.

BY M. LOUIS LARTET.[1]

THE specimens of the Dead Sea water, of which M.
Terreil has presented his analysis to the Academy,
were procured by means of an apparatus which,
ensured a high degree of precision. The principle
of this apparatus was the invention of M. Aimé, but ours had
modifications which made its use at once easier and more
certain. The specimens were brought to France in glass tubes
of convenient size, which were closed with the blow-pipe
directly after being filled; the whole being under the direction
of the Duc de Luynes, with the assistance of Lieut. Vignes
of the Navy, and Dr Combes, who, like myself, were attached
to the expedition. The examination of such new materials
cannot fail to throw a fresh light on the question of the saltness of the Dead Sea; for hitherto the analyses, though numerous enough, and by chemists of the highest ability, were all
made on specimens taken from the surface only, and from the
north-east shore,—a place which, though the only one accessible
to travellers, was most unfavourable for the purpose; the specimens being always collected either too near the place where
the fresh water of the Jordan enters, or else in the lateral eddy,
where the more concentrated water flowed northwards from
the centre of the lake. Hence the great discrepancy in the

[1] Translated by Mr Grove.

results. It became necessary, therefore, if these researches were to have a greater value than their predecessors, that they should be based on a number of observations, taken at widely different points on the surface of the lake, and at different depths; and this I have been permitted to do, thanks to the rare advantage of a prolonged stay on the lake, and of the apparatus already mentioned for procuring the water.

It is well known that the density of the Dead Sea water is such that the human body will not sink in it; and that its saltness is also so great as to extinguish all animal life. Of the latter fact I myself made proof, by transporting into the lake some small fish, of the genus *Cryprinodon*, from a very salt pool close by, which died directly they were immersed. The density of the water increases rapidly with the depth, up to 150 or 200 metres, but below that point re-diminishes sensibly. As the bulk of the fresh water affluents enter the lake from the north, the density increases slightly towards the south end.

In a memoir which I submitted last year to the Academy, I endeavoured to show that the basin of the Dead Sea was originally independent of the ocean, and I was led by that conviction to attribute the saltness of the lake to local causes. The favourable opinion then expressed by M. Elie de Beaumont proved a most valuable support to my hypothesis, which was further corroborated by the announcement of M. Malaguti, that he had been unable to discover any silver in the residuum left from the Dead Sea water after spontaneous evaporation, although the salts deposited by the same volume of ocean water had yielded very appreciable quantities of that metal.

The researches of M. Terreil disclose neither cœsium, rubidium, lethium, nor iodine; all which agrees satisfactorily with the indications from the geological and orographical examinations of the district. Nevertheless it must be acknowledged that the saltness of the Dead Sea approaches sufficiently near to that of the mother liquor of the ocean; but it may be said that, at the close of a similar series of successive separations, bodies of water which differed considerably in their initial saltness would end by retaining those constituents only which were able to resist such eliminations, and by approaching those extreme degrees of concentration of which the Dead Sea and the Lake Elton are such remarkable instances.

The abundance of bromine contained in the water appears (as M. G. Bischoff [1] has observed) to be an evidence of a very prolonged evaporation. The quantity increases in regular ratio with the depth, and at 300 metres below the surface attains the enormous amount of 7·093 grammes per kilogramme of water. At the surface the proportion of bromine does not vary with the density, for it is found in smaller quantities at the south than at the north of the lake. This fact, together with the purity of the rock salt of Jebel Usdum, prevents my agreeing with Volney and De Bertou in attributing the complicated saltness of the Dead Sea solely to those masses of salt which occur at the upper portion of the cretaceous bed near its southern end.

The Jordan furnishes a large amount of salts to the lake; but in so doing, it is, in fact, only restoring what it took up during its lengthened passage over the sediments originally deposited by the lake at the time of its greatest extension. And this must be true also for most of the other feeders of the lake, and for many of the springs on its edge. The larger hot springs of the basin, however, being connected with the line of dislocation, which is the most characteristic trait of the district, issue at a high temperature directly from the cretaceous rocks, and in the neighbourhood of volcanic agency. Such are especially the springs at Zarah and Callirhöe, on the eastern side of the lake, which contain (with the exception of bromine, which, even if present, would hardly have shown itself in the limited quantity of water submitted) all the elements of the saltness of the lake; and, again, that of Hammam, near Tiberias, in which Dr Anderson succeeded (in addition to the other constituents just mentioned) in discovering traces of bromine, which has not been found in any other spring in the basin.

I do not imagine, as Professor Hitchcock does, that the hot springs of Tiberias are the origin of the saltness of the Dead Sea; but I believe that the existence of those substances there is more or less connected with the axis of dislocation of the basin, and is chiefly due to the ancient existence of more numerous and more active springs throughout the lake and its shore. True, the hot springs have one by one disappeared in

[1] *Lehrbuch, etc.*, 1864, ii. seq.

the wake of volcanic phenomena, with which they appear closely connected, and are now only represented by deposits, which still tell the tale of their ancient importance, and by a few hot springs which serve to convey its constituent salts to the lake. In addition to these, there are submarine springs which only betray themselves by the difference in the saltness of the water near their sources; such, for instance, as that which appears from comparing the water collected five miles east of Wadi M'rabba with that collected off the Ras Feshkah, a little farther north; and such also as that near Ras Mersed, at the spot where the smell of sulphuretted hydrogen is so powerful, and where the water is exceptionally rich in bromides and chlorides. It is very natural that hot springs at great depths should be both more numerous and more copious than on the shore, since the synclinal line at the bottom of the lake should coincide with the axis of dislocation with which such springs are closely connected. Thus the same conditions may be found realized in the case of the water of the Dead Sea that seem to have ruled at the formation of the salt beds of Stassfurt-Anhalt, in which the position of the boracite shows the spot at which hot springs anciently issued from the bottom of the basin where the salts themselves were produced.

In any case, it is to the existence of hot springs in connection with the axis of dislocation of the basin of the Dead Sea, that I find it most natural to attribute the main origin of the ingredients of the lake, much more so than to the rock salt and gypsum of the cretaceous beds, the effect of which has been of secondary importance in the concentration of the water.

The presence of bitumen in the middle of the lake appears to me to belong to an order of analogous phenomena; as I hope to show in another memoir which I shall have the honour to submit to the Academy at a future day.